BLACK SEA

Diyarbakir
Deir ul-Zaferan • Mar Gabriel
Urfa
Nusaybin
Hassake

Antakya
Aleppo
Serjilla
SYRIA
LEBANON
Bcharre
BEIRUT Baalbek
Beit-ed-Din • Seidnaya
Kefr Birim DAMASCUS
ISRAEL
WEST BANK
Jericho
JERUSALEM
Mar Saba
Mar Theodosius
JORDAN

From the Holy Mountain

By the same author

IN XANADU: A QUEST
CITY OF DJINNS: A YEAR IN DELHI

FROM THE HOLY MOUNTAIN

FROM THE HOLY MOUNTAIN

A Journey Among

the Christians of the Middle East

WILLIAM DALRYMPLE

Henry Holt and Company / New York

Henry Holt and Company, Inc.
Publishers since 1866
115 West 18th Street
New York, New York 10011

Henry Holt® is a registered trademark
of Henry Holt and Company, Inc.

Originally published in 1997 in Great Britain
by HarperCollins*Publishers*

Library of Congress Cataloging-in-Publication Data
Dalrymple, William.
From the holy mountain : a journey among the Christians of the
Middle East / William Dalrymple.
p.   cm.
Includes bibliographical references and index.
ISBN 0-8050-5873-7 (hb : alk. paper)
1. Middle East—Description and travel.   2. Christians—Middle East.
3. Middle East—Ethnic relations.   4. Church history—Primitive and
early church, ca. 30–600.   I. Title.
DS49.7.D24   1998   97–42800
915.604'53—dc21

Henry Holt books are available for special promotions
and premiums. For details contact: Director, Special Markets.

First American Edition 1998

Printed in the United States of America
All first editions are printed on acid-free paper∞

10   9   8   7   6   5   4   3   2

For my parents,
with love and gratitude

ACKNOWLEDGEMENTS

The journey recorded in this book took place over a single summer and autumn, but incorporates a few episodes from two visits, to Israel and Egypt, made earlier in the year. The identity of a great many people has been disguised, particularly in those sections dealing with Turkey, the Israeli-occupied West Bank and Egypt. I sincerely hope that no one comes to any harm through what I have written.

A great many people have helped me during the four years this book took to write. I would particularly like to thank the following, without whom it could not have come into being: Abbas, Mohammed Sid Ahmed, Canon Naim Ateek, Abdullah and Noah Awad, Leila Badr, David Barchard, Andrew Berton, Robert Betts, Gaby Bostros, Dr Sebastian Brock, Derek and Eileen Brown, Yvonne Lady Cochrane, Con Coughlin, Alkis Courcolas, Hew Dalrymple, Fr. Jock Dalrymple, His Beatitude Diodoros I Patriarch of Jerusalem, Abouna Dioscuros of the Monastery of St Antony, Alistair Duncan, Eustathios Matta Rouhm Metropolitan of the Jazira and Euphrates, Mike Fishwick, Robert Fisk, Kadreya Foda, Robert Franjieh, Archie Fraser, Jenny Fraser, John Freely, Patrick French, Dr Nicholas Gendle, Sami Geraisi, David Gilmour, Charlie Glass, Philip Glazebrook, Giles Gordon, Juan Carlos Gumucio, Malfono Isa Gulten, Harry Hagopian, Roy Hange, Milad Hanna, Richard Harper, Bernard Haykel, Sarah Helm, Dr Isabel Henderson, George Hintlian, Jill Hughes, Mar Gregorios Yohanna Ibrahim Metropolitan of Aleppo, His Holiness Mar Ignatius Zaki Iwas Patriarch of Antioch, Fr. Jeremias of the Monastery of Iviron, Walid Jumblatt, Mansour Khaddosh, Nora Kort, Robert Lacey, Fr. Emmanuel Lanne, Dominic Lawson, Tony Mango, Dr Philip Mansel, Peter Mansfield, Philip Marsden, Sally Mazloumian, Dr Otto Meinardus, Sam Miller, Bishop Mesrob Mutafian,

Mark Nicholson, Maggie Noach, John Julius Norwich, Anthony O'Mahony, Dr Andrew Palmer, Dr Philip Pattendon, Fr. Michele Piccirillo, Hugh Pope, Rebecca Porteous, Tom Porteous, Annie Robertson, Max Rodenbek, Sir Steven Runciman, Dr Bernard Sabella, Assem Salam, Dalia Salam, Archbishop Georges Saliba, Professor Kamal Salibi, Victor Samaika, Anthony Sattin, Neville Shack, His Holiness Pope Shenoudah III, Antoun Sidhom, Fania Stoney, Jane Taylor, Fr. Theophanes of the Monastery of Mar Saba, Timotheos Metropolitan of Lydda, Tony Touma, Christopher J. Walker, Bishop Kallistos Ware, John Warrack, Zhogbi Zhogbi.

I would particularly like to thank Alan and Brigid Waddams, who not only looked after me in Damascus but also lent their house in Somerset, where much of this book was written and edited.

I am also very grateful to Cistercian Publications (Kalamazoo, Michigan and Spencer, Massachusetts) for kind permission to quote from *John Moschos: The Spiritual Meadow*, translated by John Wortley, © Cistercian Publications, 1992.

My greatest thanks are, however, reserved for Olivia, friend, lover, adviser, illustrator, editor-in-chief, occasional travelling companion and beloved wife.

Finally, I would like to acknowledge the unique contribution of my daughter Ibby, born soon after the return from this journey, who provided a many-splendoured distraction throughout its writing, but for which this book would certainly have seen the light of day at least six months earlier.

WILLIAM DALRYMPLE
Provis, Somerset, November 1996

I

THE MONASTERY OF IVIRON, MOUNT ATHOS, GREECE
29 JUNE 1994. THE FEAST OF SS. PETER AND PAUL

My cell is bare and austere. It has white walls and a flagstone floor. Only two pieces of furniture break the severity of its emptiness: in one corner stands an olive-wood writing desk, in the other an iron bedstead. The latter is covered with a single white sheet, starched as stiff as a nun's wimple.

Through the open window I can see a line of black habits: the monks at work in the vegetable garden, a monastic chain-gang hoeing the cabbage patch before the sun sets and the wooden *simandron* calls them in for compline. Beyond the garden is a vineyard, silhouetted against the bleak black pyramid of the Holy Mountain.

All is quiet now but for the distant breaking of surf on the jetty and the faint echo and clatter of metal plates in the monastery kitchens. The silence and solemnity of the place is hardly designed to raise the spirits, but you could hardly find a better place to order your mind. There are no distractions, and the monastic silence imposes its own brittle clarity.

It's now nine o'clock. The time has finally come to concentrate my thoughts: to write down, as simply as I can, what has brought me here, what I have seen, and what I hope to achieve in the next few months.

3

My reference books are laid out in a line on the floor; the pads containing my library notes are open. Files full of photocopied articles lie piled up below the window; my pencils are sharpened and upended in a glass. A matchbox lies ready beside the paraffin storm lantern: the monastery generator is turned off after compline, and if am to write tonight I will have to do so by the light of its yellow flame.

Open on the desk is my paperback translation of *The Spiritual Meadow of John Moschos*, the unlikely little book which first brought me to this monastery, and the original manuscript of which I saw for the first time less than one hour ago. God willing, John Moschos will lead me on, eastwards to Constantinople and Anatolia, then southwards to the Nile and thence, if it is still possible, to the Great Kharga Oasis, once the southern frontier of Byzantium.

This morning, six days after leaving the damp of a dreich Scottish June, I caught ship from Ouranopolis, the Gate of Heaven, down the peninsula to the Holy Mountain.

We passed a monastic fishing boat surrounded by a halo of seagulls. Opposite me, three large monks in ballooning cassocks sat sipping cappuccinos under an icon of the Virgin; over their grey moustaches there rested a light foam of frothed milk. Behind them, through the porthole, you could see the first of the great Athonite monasteries rising up from sandy bays to crown the foothills of the mountain. They are huge complexes of buildings, great ash-coloured fortresses the size of small Italian hill-towns, with timber-laced balconies hanging below domed cupolas and massive, unwieldy medieval buttresses.

The first monastic foundation on Athos was established in the ninth century by St Euthymius of Salonica who, having renounced the world at the age of eighteen, took to moving around on all fours and eating grass; he later became a stylite, and took to berating his brethren from atop a pillar. Some two hundred years later – by which time St Euthymius's fame had led to many other monasteries and *sketes* springing up around the saint's original foundation – it came to the ears of the Byzantine Emperor that the monks were in the habit of debauching the daughters of the shepherds who came to the mountain to sell milk and wool. Thereafter it was decreed that nothing female – no woman, no cow, no mare, no bitch – could step within its limits.

Today this rule is relaxed only for cats, and in the Middle Ages even a pair of Byzantine Empresses were said to have been turned away from the Holy Mountain by the Mother of God herself. But 140 years ago, in 1857, the Virgin was sufficiently flexible to allow one of my Victorian great-aunts, Virginia Somers, to spend two months in a tent on Mount Athos, along with her husband and the louche Pre-Raphaelite artist Coutts Lindsay. A letter Virginia wrote on her visit still survives, in which she describes how the monks had taken her over the monastery gardens and insisted on giving her fruit from every tree as they passed; she said she tasted pomegranate, citron and peach. It is the only recorded instance of a woman being allowed onto the mountain in the millennium-long history of Athos, and is certainly the only record of what appears to have been a most unholy Athonite *ménage-à-trois*.

This unique lapse apart, the Holy Mountain is still a self-governing monastic republic dedicated to prayer, chastity and pure, untarnished Orthodoxy. At the Council of Florence in 1439 it was Athonite monks who refused to let the Catholic and Orthodox Churches unite in return for Western military help against the Turk; as a result Constantinople fell to the Ottomans within two decades, but Orthodoxy survived doctrinally intact. That deep pride in Orthodoxy combined with a profound suspicion of all other creeds remains the defining ideology of Athos today.

I disembarked at Daphne, caught the old bus to the monastic capital at Karyes, then walked slowly down the ancient foot-polished cobbles, through knee-high sage and clouds of yellow butterflies, to the *lavra** of Iviron.

The monks had just finished vespers. As it was a lovely balmy

---

* Explanations of all ecclesiastical and technical terms can be found in the glossary.

evening, many were standing around the courtyard enjoying the shade of the cypresses next to the *katholikon*. Fr. Yacovos, the guestmaster, was sitting on the steps of the domed Ottoman fountain, listening to the water dripping from the spout into the bowl. He stood up when he saw me enter the courtyard.

'Welcome,' he said. 'We've been expecting you.'

Yacovos was a garrulous, thick-set, low-slung monk, bearded like a brigand. On his head, tilted at a jaunty angle, sat a knitted black bonnet. He took my bags and led me to the guest room, where he poured a glass of ouzo and offered me a bowl full of rose-scented *loukoumi*. As he did so, he chattered happily about his life in the merchant navy. He had visited Aberdeen on a Cypriot ship in the winter of 1959, he said, and had never forgotten the fog and the bitter cold. I asked where I could find the librarian, Fr. Christophoros. It had been Fr. Christophoros's letter – surmounted by the great Imperial crest, the double-headed eagle of Byzantium – that had originally lured me to Athos. The manuscript I was looking for was in Iviron's monastic library, he had said. Yes, it had survived, and he would try to get the Abbot's permission for me to see it.

'Christophoros will be down at the Arsenal at this time,' said Fr. Yacovos, looking at his fob watch, 'feeding his cats.'

I found the old man standing on the jetty, holding a bucket full of fishtails. A pair of enormous black spectacles perched precariously on his nose. Around him swirled two dozen cats.

'Come, Justinian,' called Fr. Christophoros. 'Come now, Chrysostom, *wisswisswisswiss* . . . Come on, my darlings, *ela*, come . . .'

I walked up and introduced myself.

'We thought you were coming last week,' replied the monk, a little gruffly.

'I'm sorry,' I said. 'I had trouble getting a permit in Thessaloniki.'

The cats continued to swirl flirtatiously around Christophoros's ankles, hissing at each other and snatching at the scattered fins.

'Have you managed to have a word with the Abbot about my seeing the manuscript?'

'I'm sorry,' said Christophoros. 'The Abbot's away in Constantinople. He's in council with the Ecumenical Patriarch. But you're welcome to stay here until he returns.'

'When will that be?'

'He should be back by the Feast of the Transfiguration.'

'But that's – what? – over a fortnight away.'

'Patience is a great monastic virtue,' said Christophoros, nodding philosophically at Kallistos, a rather scraggy, bow-legged old tom-cat who had so far failed to catch a single fishtail.

'My permit runs out the day after tomorrow,' I said. 'They only gave me a three-day *diamonitirion*. I have to leave by the morning boat.' I looked at the old monk. 'Please – I've come all the way just to see this book.'

'I'm afraid the Abbot insists that he must first question anyone who . . .'

'Is there nothing you could do?'

The old man pulled tentatively at his beard. 'I shouldn't do this,' he said. 'And anyway, the lights aren't working in the library.'

'There are some lamps in the guest room,' I suggested.

He paused for a second, indecisive. Then he relented: 'Go quickly,' he said. 'Ask Fr. Yacovos: see if he'll lend you the lanterns.'

I thanked Christophoros and started walking briskly back towards the monastery before he could change his mind.

'And don't let Yacovos start telling you his life story,' he called after me, 'or you'll never get to see this manuscript.'

At eight o'clock, I met Fr. Christophoros outside the *katholikon*. It was dusk now; the sun had already set over the Holy Mountain. In my hands I held the storm lantern from my room. We walked across the courtyard to the monastic library, and from his habit Fr. Christophoros produced a ring of keys as huge as those of a medieval jailer. He began to turn the largest of the keys in the topmost of the four locks.

'We have to keep everything well locked these days,' said Christophoros in explanation. 'Three years ago, in the middle of winter, some raiders turned up in motorboats at the Great Lavra. They had Sten guns and were assisted by an ex-novice who had been thrown out by the Abbot. They got into the library and stole many of the most ancient manuscripts; they also took some gold reliquaries that were locked in the sanctuary.'

'Were they caught?'

'The monks managed to raise the alarm and they were arrested the following morning as they tried to get across the Bulgarian frontier. But by then they had done much damage: cut up the reliquaries into small pieces and removed the best illuminations from the manuscripts. Some of the pages have never been recovered.'

Three locks had now opened without problem; and eventually, with a loud creak, the fourth gave way too. The old library doors swung open, and with the lamps held aloft, we stepped inside.

Within, it was pitch dark; a strong odour of old buckram and rotting vellum filled the air. Manuscripts lay open in low cabinets, the gold leaf of illuminated letters and gilt haloes from illustrations of saints' *Lives* shining out in the light of the lantern. In the gloom on the far wall I could just see a framed Ottoman *firman*, the curving gilt of the Sultan's monogram clearly visible above the lines of calligraphy. Next to it, like a discarded suit jacket, hung a magnificent but rather crumpled silk coat. Confronted dragons and phoenixes were emblazoned down the side of either lapel.

'What is that?' I whispered.

'It's John Tzimiskes's coat.'

'The Emperor John Tzimiskes? But he lived in the tenth century.'

Christophoros shrugged his shoulders.

'You can't just leave something like that hanging up there,' I said.

'Well,' said Christophoros irritably, 'where else would you put it?'

In the gloom, we found our way past rank after rank of shelves groaning with leather-bound Byzantine manuscripts, before drawing to a halt in front of a cabinet in the far corner of the room. Christophoros unlocked and opened the glass covering. Codex G.9 was on the bottom shelf, wrapped up in a white canvas satchel.

It was a huge volume, as heavy as a crate of wine, and I staggered over to a reading desk with it, while Christophoros followed with the lamp.

'Forgive me,' he said, as I lowered the volume gently onto the desk, 'but are you Orthodox or heretic?'

I considered for a second before answering. A Catholic friend who had visited Athos a few years previously had warned me above all never to admit to being a Catholic; he had made this mistake, and said that had he admitted to suffering from leprosy or tertiary syphilis he could not have been more resolutely shunned than he had been after that. He told me that in my case it was particularly important not to raise the monks' suspicions, as they have learned to distrust, above all their visitors, those who ask to see their manuscripts. They have long memories on Athos, and if the monks have never forgiven the Papacy for authorising the ransacking of Constantinople during the Fourth Crusade over eight hundred years ago, they have certainly not forgotten the nineteenth-century bibliophiles who decimated the libraries of Athos only a century ago.

The English traveller the Hon. Robert Curzon is still considered one of the worst offenders: after a quick circuit around the monastic libraries of Athos in the late 1840s (in the company, I am ashamed to say, of my great-great-uncle), Curzon left the Holy Mountain with his trunks bulging with illuminated manuscripts and Byzantine *chrysobuls*; in his travel book *Visits to Monasteries in the Levant* he writes of buying the priceless manuscripts from the Abbot by weight, as if they were figs or pomegranates in an Ottoman market. Worse still is the memory of the German bibliophile Herman Tischendorff. Some twenty years after Curzon's trip to Athos, Tischendorff left the Greek Orthodox Monastery of St Catherine's in Sinai with the *Codex Sinaiaticus* – still the earliest existing copy of the New Testament – tucked into his camel bags. Tischendorff later claimed that he found the various leaves of the manuscript in a basket of firewood, and that he had saved it from the monks, who were intent on burning it to keep them warm in winter. The monks, however, maintain to this day that Tischendorff got the librarian drunk and discreetly swapped the priceless manuscript – which, like Curzon's plunder,

9

duly found its way into the British Library – for a bottle of good German schnapps.

Noticing my silence, Christophoros asked again: What was I, Orthodox or heretic?

'I'm a Catholic,' I replied.

'My God,' said the monk. 'I'm so sorry.' He shook his head in solicitude. 'To be honest with you,' he said, 'the Abbot never gives permission for non-Orthodox to look at our holy books. Particularly Catholics. The Abbot thinks the present Pope is the Antichrist and that his mother is the Whore of Babylon. He says that they are now bringing about the Last Days spoken of by St John in the Book of Revelation.'

Christophoros murmured a prayer. 'Please,' he said, 'don't ever tell anyone in the monastery that you're a heretic. If the Abbot ever found out, I'd be made to perform a thousand prostrations.'

'I won't tell a soul.'

Christophoros relaxed slightly, and took off his glasses to polish them on the front of his habit. 'You know, we actually had another Catholic in the monastery earlier this year?' he said.

'Who was that?' I asked.

'He was a choirmaster from Bavaria,' said Christophorus. 'He had a beautiful voice.'

I eased the book up onto a reading stand, and began to unbutton its canvas cover.

'He said our church had wonderful acoustics,' continued Christophoros, arranging the lamps on the desk. 'So he asked Fr. Yacovos if he could sing a *Gloria* inside the *katholikon*, under the dome.'

'What did Fr. Yacovos say?'

'He said that he didn't think he could let a heretic pray *inside* the church. But just this once he said he would let him sing a little *alleluia* in the porch.'

I had now got the protective canvas off, and the beautifully worked leather binding gleamed golden in the light of the lantern.

I opened the cover. Inside, the text was written in purple ink on the finest vellum – strong, supple and waxy, but so thin as to be virtually translucent. The calligraphy was a beautifully clear

10

and cursive form of early medieval Georgian. According to the library's detailed catalogue, the volume had bound together a number of different early Byzantine devotional texts. The first folio I opened was apparently a shrill sermon by St Jerome, denouncing what he considered the thoroughly pagan practice of taking baths: 'He who has bathed in Christ,' fumed the saint, 'does not need a second bath.'

Only towards the end, on folio 287 verso, did I come to the opening lines of the text I had come so far to see. Its author was the great Byzantine traveller-monk John Moschos, and the book had been compiled at the end of his life as he prepared for death in a monastery in Constantinople, 1,300 years ago.

'*In my opinion, the meadows in Spring present a particularly delightful prospect,*' he wrote. '*One part of this meadow blushes with roses; in other places lilies predominate; in another violets blaze out, resembling the Imperial purple. Think of this present work in the same way, Sophronius, my sacred and faithful child. For from among the holy men, monks and hermits of the Empire, I have plucked the finest flowers of the unmown meadow and worked them into a crown which I now offer to you, most faithful child; and through you to the world at large . . .*'

Turning up the lamp, I opened a fresh page.

In the spring of the year 578 A.D., had you been sitting on a bluff of rock overlooking Bethlehem, you might have been able to see two figures setting off, staves in hand, from the gates of the great desert monastery of St Theodosius. The two – an old grey-bearded monk accompanied by an upright, perhaps slightly stern, and certainly much younger companion – would have headed off south-east through the wastes of Judaea, towards the fabulously rich port-metropolis of Alexandria.

It was the start of an extraordinary journey that would take John Moschos and his pupil, Sophronius the Sophist, in an arc across the entire Eastern Byzantine world. Their aim was to collect the wisdom of the desert fathers, the sages and mystics of the Byzantine East, before their fragile world – already clearly in advanced decay – finally shattered and disappeared. The result was the volume in front of me now. If today in the West it is a fairly obscure text, a thousand years ago it was renowned as one of the most popular books in all the great literature of Byzantium.

Byzantine caravanserais were rough places, and the provincial Greek aristocracy did not enjoy entertaining: as the Byzantine writer Cecaumenus put it, 'Houseparties are a mistake, for guests merely criticise your housekeeping and attempt to seduce your wife.' So everywhere they went, the two travellers stayed in monasteries, caves and remote hermitages, dining frugally with the monks and ascetics. In each place, Moschos seems to have jotted down accounts that he had heard of the sayings of the fathers, and other anecdotes and miracle stories.

Moschos was taking to an extreme the old Orthodox tradition of the wandering monk. In the West, at least since St Benedict introduced the vow of stability in the early sixth century, monks have tended to be static, immured in their cells: as the saying went, 'A monk out of his cell is like a fish out of water.' But in the Eastern Churches, as in Hinduism and Buddhism, there has always been a tradition of monks being able to wander from guru to guru, from spiritual father to spiritual father, garnering the wisdom and advice of each, just as the Indian *sadhus* still do. Even today, modern Greek Orthodox monks take no vow of stability. If after a period of time in a monastery they decide they want to sit at the feet of another teacher in a different monastery, possibly in a completely different part of Greece (or indeed in Sinai or the Holy Land), then they are free to do so.

The Spiritual Meadow was a collection of the most memorable sayings, anecdotes and holy stories that Moschos gathered on his travels, and was written as part of a long tradition of such *apophthegmata*, or Sayings of the Fathers. However, Moschos's writings are infinitely more evocative, graphic and humorous than those of any of his rivals or contemporaries, and almost alone of the surviving examples of the genre, they can still be read with genuine pleasure.

For as well as carrying a still potent spiritual message, on another level the book can be enjoyed today simply as a fascinating travel book. Moschos did what the modern travel writer still does: he wandered the world in search of strange stories and remarkable travellers' tales. Indeed his book can legitimately be read as the great masterpiece of Byzantine travel writing. For not only was Moschos a vivid and amusing writer, he also had an extraordinary tale to tell.

Reading between the lines of John Moschos's memoirs, it is clear that he and his friend were travelling in dangerous times. Following the collapse of Justinian's great attempt at reviving the Empire, Byzantium was under assault: from the west by Avars, Slavs, Goths and Lombards; from the east by a crescendo of raids by desert nomads and the legions of Sassanian Persia. The great cities of the East Mediterranean were in fast decay: in Antioch, huts full of refugees were springing up in the middle of the wide Roman avenues which had once buzzed with trade and industry. The great Mediterranean ports – Tyre, Sidon, Beirut, Seleucia – were becoming idle; many were reverting to little more than fishing villages.

As the physical world fell into decay, thousands left their families, intent, like Moschos and Sophronius, on becoming monks and hermits in the desert. Yet even in the great monasteries there was no safety: frequently the two travellers arrived at a destination to find that the abbey where they intended to spend the night had been torched by raiders, and the monks massacred or led off in great stumbling caravans to the slave markets of Arabia. It was not a picture of total holocaust: in those isolated areas of the Empire unaffected by the Persian wars, the monastic scriptoria and workshops were hard at work producing some of the most beautiful Byzantine manuscripts, ivories and icons ever designed. But these oases of monastic calm were exceptions. John Moschos's writings make clear the horrifying, almost apocalyptic, nature of the destruction he witnessed around him.

In 614 A.D. the travellers' own home monastery of St Theodosius was burned to the ground by the marauding Persian army, and all their brethren – hundreds of unarmed monks –

were put to the sword. Shortly afterwards Jerusalem fell and those who survived the massacre – including the city's Patriarch – were led off as slaves to the Sassanian capital of Ctesiphon. From then on John and Sophronius continued on the road as much refugees as travellers. They took shelter in Alexandria, and when the Persians massed outside the city walls, the pair managed to get onto the last galley out of the beleaguered city.

The following year, the two pilgrims finally reached the shelter of the great walls of Constantinople. There, just before exhaustion brought about his death, Moschos completed his travel memoirs. *The Spiritual Meadow* received an ecstatic reception across the Empire. Within a generation or two it had been translated into Latin, Georgian, Armenian, Arabic, and a variety of Slavonic languages; to this day many of its anecdotes are common currency among monks and peasants across the Orthodox world.

Most surviving Byzantine texts from the period have a curiously opaque quality: we read either of the flitting shadows of a hundred upstart emperors, rising suddenly through palace coups and disappearing equally rapidly via the assassin's dagger; or else of saints so saintly as to be virtually beyond comprehension. Nor, for all its often hypnotic beauty, does the surviving corpus of Byzantine art much help in visualising the world that gave it birth. There are the great mosaics at Ravenna with their celebrated portraits of Justinian and Theodora accompanied by their retinues of eunuchs and admirals, generals and bishops, courtiers and sycophants; the same intrigue-ridden court familiar from the written sources. But away from these two isolated Ravenna panels, Byzantine art is strictly non-secular, strictly transcendent. Across the broken apses and shattered naves of a hundred ruined Byzantine churches, the same smooth, cold, neo-classical faces of the saints and apostles stare down like a gallery of deaf mutes; and through this thundering silence the everyday reality of life in the Byzantine provinces remains persistently difficult to visualise. The sacred and aristocratic nature of Byzantine art means that we have very little idea of what the early Byzantine peasant or shopkeeper looked like; we have even less idea of what he thought, what he longed for, what he loved or what he hated.

Yet through the pages of *The Spiritual Meadow* one can come closer to the ordinary Byzantine than is possible through virtually any other single source. Although it often seems a fairly bizarre book – an unlikely fricassee of anecdote, piety and strange miracles – as a historical text it adds up to the most rich and detailed portrait that survives of the Byzantine Levant immediately before the advent of Islam. Through its pages forgotten monasteries rise suddenly from the sand; even a great metropolis such as Byzantine Alexandria – from which not one building, indeed barely one wall, has survived – is brought back to life, peopled by credible characters, villains and eccentrics.

Most intriguing of all are the tales which tell of the more humble folk, the sort who normally slip through the net cast by the historian. One typical story tells of a muleteer from Rome whose donkeys trample and kill a small child at an inn. He takes ship to the Holy Land and flees to the desert, where he is overcome by remorse and tries to kill himself. Only when a lion refuses to savage him does he reconcile himself to the possibility of divine forgiveness. We meet a repentant Alexandrian grave-robber who claims he was seized by a corpse whose shroud he had tried to steal (he was not released until he promised to take up a more respectable profession); a novice who, overcome with desire, pays a visit to the brothel in Jericho (he is quickly struck down by leprosy); a merchant's wife from Ascalon who is forced to prostitute herself after her husband's ship goes down.

Some of the figures are oddly familiar. One story revolves around a Byzantine version of Fr. Christophoros, an animal-loving monk from a suburban monastery outside Alexandria who not only feeds the monastery's dogs, but also gives flour to the ants and puts damp biscuits on the roof for the birds. Other characters are rather more exotic than anything you are likely to find today, such as the monk Adolas who 'confined himself inside a hollow plane tree' in Thessaloniki, cutting 'a little window in the bark through which he could talk with people who came to see him'.

Moschos is an unpredictable narrator. He was a champion of Orthodoxy at a time when it was challenged by a dazzling variety

15

of heterodox currents circulating through the caravan cities of the East, and Monophysites, Jews, Manicheans, Zoroastrians and Gnostics all receive short shrift from a man whose tolerance of the beliefs of others was clearly every bit as limited as that of his modern successors on Mount Athos. Yet there is also a carefree scholar-gypsy feel to *The Spiritual Meadow*, and an endearing lightness of touch and gentle sense of humour evident in its stories. One of my favourite tales concerns a novice from Antinoe in Upper Egypt 'who was very careless with his own soul'. When the novice dies, his teacher is worried that he might have been sent to Hell for his sins, so he prays that it be revealed what has happened to his pupil's soul. Eventually the teacher goes into a trance, and sees a river of fire with the novice submerged in it up to his neck. The teacher is horrified, but the novice turns to him, saying: 'I thank God, oh my teacher, that there is relief for my head. Thanks to your prayers, I am standing on the head of a bishop.'

Of course to the modern eye much of the world described in *The Spiritual Meadow* is not just curious: its beliefs and values are so strange as to be virtually incomprehensible. It was a world where eunuchs led the imperial armies into battle; where groups of monks were known to lynch and murder pagan ladies as they passed in their litters through the fashionable bazaars of Alexandria; where ragged, half-naked stylites raved atop their pillars; and where dendrites took literally Christ's instruction to imitate the birds of the air, living in trees and building little nests for themselves in the upper branches.

But what is perhaps most surprising about the Eastern Mediterranean as it emerges from the pages of Moschos is the fact that it is Christian at all. In the popular imagination, the Levant passes from a classical past to an Islamic present with hardly a break. It is easy to forget that for over three hundred years – from the age of Constantine in the early fourth century to the rise of Islam in the early seventh century – the Eastern Mediterranean world was almost entirely Christian. Indeed, at a time when Christianity had barely taken root in Britain, when Angles and Saxons were still sacrificing to Thor and Woden on the banks of the Thames and in the west the last Christian Britons were fighting a rearguard action under a leader who may have been called Arthur, the Levant was the heartland of Christianity and the centre of Christian civilisation. The monasteries of Byzantium were fortresses whose libraries and scriptoria preserved classical learning, philosophy and medicine against the encroaching hordes of raiders and nomads. Moreover, for all the decay, the Levant was still the richest, most populous and most highly educated part of the Mediterranean world: three quarters of the revenue of the Byzantine exchequer came from the eastern provinces. They contained the main centres of industry and within living memory their ships and caravans had conducted a hugely profitable trade with the Orient; even in the chaos of the late sixth century that trade had still not entirely disappeared. There was nothing in the West to compare with this high Eastern Byzantine culture. In the late sixth century, Byzantium was still the focus of the entire Eurasian land mass.

It was not to remain so for long. John Moschos was an almost exact contemporary of Mohammed. When Moschos died in 619, the Empire was still ruled, however shakily, from the Veneto to Southern Egypt. But a few years later, Moschos's young companion Sophronius saw the eastern half of the Byzantine dominion shatter and fragment. In his old age Sophronius was appointed Patriarch of Jerusalem, and it was left to him to defend the Holy City against the first army of Islam as it swept up from Arabia, conquering all before it.

Fresh from the desert, the Arabs were not very adept at siegecraft: when stalled outside Damascus, the great army of the Prophet had to borrow a ladder from a nearby monastery to get over the walls. But with the Imperial legions already ambushed while crossing the River Yarmuck, there was no prospect of relief for Jerusalem. After a siege lasting twelve months Sophronius prepared to surrender, with only one condition: he would hand Jerusalem over to no general. The Holy City would surrender only to the Caliph himself.

On a February day in the year 638 A.D., the Caliph Omar entered Jerusalem, riding upon a white camel. The Caliph wore the filthy robes in which he had conducted his campaign; but the

Patriarch was magnificently dressed in his robes of Imperial silk. Sophronius handed over the keys of the city and through his tears was heard to murmur: 'Behold the abomination of desolation, spoken of by Daniel the Prophet.'

He died, heartbroken, a few months later. He was buried in the ruins of the Monastery of St Theodosius; in the next niche lay the body of his friend, teacher and travelling companion John Moschos. Sophronius had faithfully honoured his friend's last wish: that his embalmed corpse be carried from Constantinople to be buried in what was left of his own home monastery, at the edge of the deserts of the Holy Land.

I first read about John Moschos in Sir Steven Runciman's great three-volume *History of the Crusades*. Intrigued by a passing reference to *The Spiritual Meadow*, I wrote to Runciman and received – by return of post – a reply in Edwardian copperplate asking me over to the historian's medieval tower house in the Scottish Borders. One cold April day I drove under grey cloudbanks, through the barren sheep tracts of Annandale and Eskdale, to take up the invitation.

Runciman has always been a most undonnish don: he has been besieged by Manchu warlords in the city of Tianjin, but escaped to play a piano duet with the Emperor of China; he has lectured Ataturk on Byzantium and been made a Grand Orator of the Great Church of Constantinople; he has smoked a *hookah* with the *Celebi Effendi* of the Whirling Dervishes and, by reading their tarot cards, correctly predicted the death of King George II of the Hellenes and Fuad, King of Egypt.

He is well into his nineties: a tall, thin, frail old man, still very poised and intellectually alert, but now physically weak. He has heavy-lidded eyes and a slow, gravelly voice, with a hint of an old fashioned Cambridge drawl. During lunch, Runciman talked of the Levant as he knew it in his youth: of Istanbul only a month after the last Ottoman was expelled from the Topkapi, when there were camels in the streets, when there were still hundreds of thousands of Greeks in Anatolia, and the Turks still wore the red tarboosh; of the Lebanon, 'the only place I've seen books bound in human skin'; of the monasteries of Palestine before the Zionists expelled half the Palestinians and began to turn the country into an American suburb; of Egypt when Alexandria was still the most cosmopolitan city east of Milan.

Later, over coffee, I broached the subject of John Moschos and his travels. What had attracted me to *The Spiritual Meadow* in the first place was the idea that Moschos and Sophronius were witnessing the first act in a process whose dénouement was taking place only now: that that first onslaught on the Christian East observed by the two monks was now being completed by Christianity's devastating decline in the land of its birth. The ever-accelerating exodus of the last Christians from the Middle East today meant that *The Spiritual Meadow* could be read less as a dead history book than as the prologue to an unfolding tragedy whose final chapter is still being written.

Islam has traditionally been tolerant of religious minorities: to see this, one has only to contrast the relatively privileged treatment of Christians under Muslim rule with the terrible fate of Christendom's one totally distinct religious minority, the unfortunate European Jews. Nevertheless that Islamic tradition of tolerance is today wearing distinctly thin. After centuries of generally peaceful co-existence with their Muslim neighbours, things are suddenly becoming difficult for the last Christians of the Middle East. Almost everywhere in the Levant, for a variety of reasons – partly because of economic pressure, but more often due to discrimination and in some cases outright persecution – the Christians are leaving. Today they are a small minority of fourteen million struggling to keep afloat amid 180 million non-Christians, with their numbers shrinking annually through emigration. In the last twenty years at least two million have left the Middle East to make new lives for themselves in Europe, Australia and America.

In Istanbul the last descendants of the Byzantines are now leaving what was once the capital city of Christendom. In the east of Turkey, the Syrian Orthodox Church is virtually extinct, its ancient monasteries either empty or in the process of being evacuated. Those who have made it out to the West complain of protection rackets, land seizures and frequent murders. In Lebanon, the Maronites have now effectively lost the long civil war, and their stranglehold on political power has finally been broken. Most Maronites today live abroad, in exile. The same is true of the Palestinian Christians a little to the south: nearly half a century after the creation of the State of Israel, fewer Palestinian Christians now remain in Palestine than live outside it. According to a Palestinian Christian writer I talked to in London, things have got so bad that the remaining Christians in Jerusalem could be flown out in just nine jumbo jets; indeed there are now said to be more Jerusalem-born Christians living in Sydney than in Jerusalem itself. In Egypt, the Copts are also profoundly troubled and apprehensive: already facing a certain amount of discrimination under the current regime, they are well aware that things are likely to get much worse if President Mubarak falls and an Islamic revolution brings the fundamentalists to power.

Everywhere, in short, the living successors of those Christian merchants, monks and bishops visited by John Moschos now find themselves under intense pressure. Yet when I began to research into Moschos's travels, I discovered that despite this great Christian exodus, a surprising number of the monasteries visited by Moschos and Sophronius still – just – survived.

The monasteries on Mount Athos and in Coptic Egypt are apparently relatively healthy. Elsewhere, in south-east Turkey, Lebanon and Palestine, these timeless islands of Byzantium, with their bells and black robes and candle-lit processions, are said to be occupied by an ever-diminishing population of elderly monks whose heavily-whiskered faces mirror those of the frescoed saints on the monastery walls. The monks' vestments remain unchanged since Byzantine times; the same icons are still painted according to the same medieval iconographic rules. Even the superstitions have endured unaltered: relics of the True Cross and the Virgin's Tears are still venerated; demons and devils are still said to lie in wait outside every monastery wall. In the early fifth century Bishop Parthenius of Lampsacus reported that he had been attacked by

Satan in the form of a black dog; on my last visit I was told an almost identical story by an old Greek monk in the Holy Sepulchre. A couple of years ago there was great excitement in a Coptic quarter of Cairo, when the Virgin was clearly seen floating over the towers of the Church of St Damiana.

Driving back home from Runciman, I knew what I wanted to do: to spend six months circling the Levant, following roughly in John Moschos's footsteps. Starting in Athos and working my way through to the Coptic monasteries of Upper Egypt, I wanted to do what no future generation of travellers would be able to do: to see wherever possible what Moschos and Sophronius had seen, to sleep in the same monasteries, to pray under the same frescoes and mosaics, to discover what was left, and to witness what was in effect the last ebbing twilight of Byzantium.

The wooden *simandron* has just begun to call from the church; matins will begin in ten minutes.

Soon it will be dawn. The first glimmer of light has begun to light up the silhouette of the Holy Mountain. The paraffin in my lamp is exhausted, and so am I. The day after tomorrow I must leave Athos; ahead lies four or five days' travel across Thrace to Constantinople, the great Byzantine capital where John Moschos completed his *Spiritual Meadow*.

The *simandron* is being rung for the second time. I must shut this book and go down to the church to join the monks at prayer.

II

PERA PALAS HOTEL, ISTANBUL, TURKEY, 10 JULY 1994

After the penitential piety of Mount Athos, arriving here is like stepping into a sensuous Orientalist fantasy by Delacroix, all mock-Iznik tiles and pseudo-Ottoman marble inlay. A hotel masquerading as a Turkish bath; you almost expect some voluptuous Turkish odalisque to appear and disrobe behind the reception desk.

I ate breakfast in a vast Viennese ballroom with a sprung wooden floor and dadoes dripping with recently reapplied gilt. The lift is a giant baroque birdcage, entered through a rainforest of potted palms. On the wall nearby, newly dusted, is a framed diploma from the 1932 Ideal Homes Exhibition, signed by the Mayor of East Ham.

The Pera Palas was bought by the Turkish government last year, and attempts to renovate the old structure seem to have started manically, then been abruptly given up. In the dining room the gilt is so bright you have to wear sunglasses to look at it; but upstairs the carpets are as bald as the head of an Ottoman eunuch.

The hotel has a policy of naming its bedrooms after distinguished guests, which has unconsciously acted as a graph of its dramatic post-war decline: from before the war you can choose to sleep in Ataturk, Mata Hari or King Zog of Albania; after it there is nothing more exciting on offer than Julio Iglesias.

25

At dawn the Sea of Marmara appears like a sheet of silver, with the stationary ships sitting as if welded to its surface. Now, at night, it becomes invisible but for the lights of passing ships and the distant lamps of Uskudar and Kadi Koy – Byzantine Chalcedon – shining across the Bosphorus.

From the old Byzantine Acropolis to the waters of the Golden Horn, the yellow glow of the sulphurous streetlights silhouettes the city's skyline, with its minarets and rippling domes and cupolas. The perfect reflections of the great Ottoman mosques and palaces that form in the water below are intermittently shattered by skiffs and caiques crossing and recrossing the Hellespont. No other city on earth has so magnificent a position. With its remarkable configuration of hills and water, sitting astride the land and sea routes connecting Europe with Asia, the Black Sea with the Mediterranean, and commanding one of the greatest anchorages in the world, there could be no more perfect position for a great imperial city.

For over a thousand years Constantinople was the capital of Christendom, the richest metropolis in Europe and the most populous city west of the great Chinese Silk Route terminus of Ch'ang-an. To the Barbarian West Byzantium was an almost mythical beacon of higher civilisation, the repository of all that had been salvaged from the wreck of classical antiquity. In their sagas, the Vikings called it merely Micklegarth, the Great City. It had no rival.

From the Great Palace on the shores of the Sea of Marmara Justinian, probably the greatest of the Byzantine emperors, controlled an empire that ran from the walls of Genoa clockwise around the Mediterranean to the Pillars of Hercules at Ceuta, embracing Italy, the Balkans, Turkey, the Middle East and the North African littoral. From Constantinople armies were dispatched to build a line of border fortresses on the Tigris, to repair the walls of Rome and to reconquer North Africa from the Vandals. Architects were ordered to construct basilicas in the marshes of Ravenna, on Mount Zion and in the sands of the Sinai. When the Emperor ordered Anthemius of Tralles and Isidore of Miletus to build the greatest church in the world and dedicate it to Haghia Sophia, the Divine Wisdom of Christ, stone was specially brought from as far afield as Libya, the Lebanon, the Atlantic coast of France, Mons Porphyrites in the distant deserts of Southern Egypt and the green marble quarries of Hellenic Sparta.

Half a century later, when John Moschos arrived in Constantinople, the city probably had a population of around three quarters of a million; it was said that seventy-two different tongues could be heard in its streets. Coptic monks rubbed shoulders with Jewish glassblowers, Persian silk traders and Gepid mercenaries who had walked to the city after padding across the ice of the frozen Danube. In the city's great markets and bazaars, Aramaic-speaking Syrians would haggle with Latin-speaking North Africans, Armenian architects and Herule slave traders who knew only some debased dialect of Old German. Goldsmiths, silversmiths, jewellers, ivory carvers, workers in inlay and enamel, weavers of brocade, sculptors and mosaicists all found ready markets for their wares. Already, by the second quarter of the fifth century, the city boasted five imperial and nine princely palaces, eight public and 153 private bath houses; by the time of Justinian there were over three hundred monasteries within its walls.

Few who were brought up in this most cosmopolitan and sophisticated of cities could bear to leave it for long. 'Oh, land of Byzantium, oh thrice-happy city, eye of the universe, ornament of the world, star shining afar, beacon of this lower world,' wrote a twelfth-century Byzantine author forced to absent himself on a diplomatic mission, 'would that I were within you, enjoying you to the full! Do not part me from your maternal bosom.'

After its fall to the Turks in 1453 the importance of the city was, if anything, increased. For the next two hundred years the Ottoman Empire was the most powerful force in all Eurasia, and Constantinople again became the Mediterranean's greatest port. The sixteenth-century Grand Vizier Mehmed Sokollu Pasha simultaneously planned canals between the Don and the Volga, and the Red Sea and the Mediterranean; one day he might send armaments to Sumatra to thwart the Portuguese, the next choose a new King of Poland to thwart the Russians. He ordered pictures and clocks from Venice, decorated his capital with one of the most beautiful mosques ever built, and commissioned an eleven-arched bridge over the River Drina which was only recently destroyed by Croatian bombs.

The achievements of early Ottoman Constantinople were built on the foundation of religious and ethnic tolerance. The great majority of senior Ottoman officials were not ethnic Turks, but Christian or Jewish converts. At a time when every capital in Europe was ablaze with burning heretics, according to the exiled seventeenth-century Huguenot M. de la Motraye there was 'no country on earth where the exercise of all Religions is more free and less subject to being troubled, than in Turkey'. It was the gradual erosion of that tradition of tolerance under the tidal wave of nineteenth-century nationalism that as much as anything finally brought down the Ottomans.

The end result of that sterile hardening of attitudes is that Istanbul, once home to an inspirational ferment of different ethnicities, is today a culturally barren and financially impoverished mono-ethnic megalopolis, 99 per cent Turkish. The Jews have gone to Israel, the Greeks to Athens, the Armenians to Armenia and the United States. The great European merchant houses have returned home, the embassies and the politicians moved to Ankara. For all its magnificent monuments, for the first time in two millennia, Istanbul now feels almost provincial.

It is ten years since my last visit to this city. Since then much has changed: many of the old wooden houses with their intricately latticed balconies have been swept away and replaced by grey apartment blocks. A smart new tram rattles around Sultanahmet, past new flotillas of Russians squatting on the pavements trying to sell their sad piles of Soviet junk: shapeless jeans, hideous shirts and sub-standard leather jackets. There is a blight of seedy news-stands filled with a surprising profusion of Turkish hard porn (there is even a glossy called *Harem*; one notices these things after a week in the celibate purity of Athos). The most striking change of all, however, is the rise of the Islamic right, which this sort of thing has helped to bring about. On every wall are election posters for the hardline *Refah* party, which recently won the municipal elections both here and in Ankara; there is now serious talk of them sweeping into power nationally at the next election. In the meantime many of the young men have taken to wearing thick, moustacheless Islamic beards, while their womenfolk are increasingly shrouded in veils.

In many ways, Turkey's development since the Second World War seems to have followed exactly the opposite course to that of India. There Gandhi tried to wean the whole country onto *dhotis*, non-violence and spinning wheels; the result was crass materialism and the almost daily burning of brides in 'kitchen accidents' if they fail to deliver the new moped or colour television promised as dowry. In Turkey Ataturk tried the reverse approach: he banned the fez, outlawed the Arabic script and tried to drag the Turks kicking and screaming into Europe. The result: a resurgent Islamic movement, mullahs being cheered in the mosques whenever they announce that the earth is flat, and the sophisticated career women of Istanbul competing with each other to wear the most all-enveloping veil or medieval-looking *burkha*.

ISTANBUL, 17 JULY

This afternoon I walked along the Golden Horn to the Phanar, the oldest surviving institution in the city and the nearest thing the Greek Orthodox have to a Vatican. For in a series of humble buildings surrounded by a modest walled enclosure in Istanbul's backstreets lives the successor of St John Chrysostom, the senior Patriarch to millions of Orthodox Christians around the world.

The Patriarch's secretary, to whom Fr. Christophoros had given me an introduction, was out. So while I waited for him to return

I drank tea in a small, dark *chahane* nearby: sawdust on the floor, the acid stink of cheap Turkish cigarettes stinging the nostrils, the incessant thump of heavy hands on wooden card-tables; unshaven, unemployed men playing game after game of poker. Outside a man in a waistcoat, flat cap and dirty apron pushed a handcart of fruit along the cobbles. It could have been a Bill Brandt photograph of the London East End in the thirties.

I walked back to the Phanar an hour later. The Patriarch's secretary had still not returned, but this time I did manage to speak to a member of his staff. Fr. Dimitrios was initially suspicious and evasive, but after reading Fr. Christophoros's letter he took me up to his office overlooking the Patriarchal church. There we talked about the city's dwindling Greek minority, the last descendants of the Byzantines left in what was once their capital city.

According to Fr. Dimitrios the population of Istanbul was still almost 50 per cent Christian at the end of the nineteenth century. The tumultuous events of the first quarter of the twentieth century – the fall of the Ottoman Empire, the Turkish victory in the 1922 Greco–Turkish War and the expulsion of all the Greeks in Anatolia in exchange for the Turkish population evicted from Northern Greece – did not alter this. By the terms of the 1923 Treaty of Lausanne, the 400,000 Greeks in the city and its suburbs were specifically allowed to remain in their homes with their rights and property intact.

All this changed in 1955 when Istanbul played host to the worst race riot in Europe since *Kristallnacht*. In a single night, with the police looking on, thousands of hired thugs descended on the city's Hellenic ghettos. Almost every Greek shop in the city had its windows broken; cemeteries were desecrated; the Tombs of the Patriarchs were destroyed; seventy-three Orthodox churches were gutted.

'I was still a baby,' said Fr. Dimitrios. 'The rioters came into our house, but my mother had wrapped me up in the Turkish flag so the rioters did not harm me; instead they just broke the windows and the furniture then moved on. Afterwards the government said it was just a few ignorant people, but that's not true: the riots were very well organised, all over Istanbul.'

'I don't understand what the Turks would gain by organising such a pogrom,' I said.

'The Greeks still controlled the commerce of the city,' replied Dimitrios. 'They wanted to drive us out and take over our business. They succeeded. By 1965, when I was ten, the Greek population had sunk to around seventy-five thousand. Today there are only – what? – five thousand Greeks left. All my childhood friends, everyone I grew up with, they've all moved away.'

Dimitrios shrugged his shoulders.

'I love this city, of course: it is my home. But frankly life is impossible here if you are not a Turk. The boys get abused on their military service; they are always sent to the most dangerous postings on the Kurdish front line. Then afterwards, when they come out, they can't get government jobs. If you live here you have to spend your life pretending you are Turkish. Those Greeks who have stayed have started calling themselves Turkish names: if you're called Dimitrios, you change your name to Demir; if your name is Fedon, you ask your friends to call you Feridun.'

Dimitrios said that the war in Bosnia – with Orthodox Serbs committing atrocities against Muslims – and the recent resurgence of Islamic fundamentalism in Turkey, had made everything much worse. The Phanar windows were broken by stones on an almost daily basis, while its perimeter walls were regularly covered with spray-painted threats such as 'Patriarch you will die!' Moreover, there had been a renewed bout of grave desecration at the disused Greek cemetery at Yenikoy; blazing rags soaked in petrol had been thrown over the Phanar walls, starting a small fire; and three small firebombs had gone off a month previously in two nearby Greek girls' schools and the Church of the Panaghia.

But the most serious problem, said Dimitrios, revolved around the Phanar gateway. In 1821 the Greeks sealed the main door of the Phanar after the Sultan had hanged the then Patriarch, Gregorios, from its lintel. The Turks always considered the sealing a snub, and recently the *Refah* party had revived the issue by threatening to break open the gate by force. Then last month, on the eve of the anniversary of the fall of Byzantium to the Ottoman Turks, a huge bomb was found planted next to the gate inside the main courtyard. It was defused in time, but had it gone off not only the gate but the entire Phanar would have been reduced to a large crater.

'They left a note near the bomb,' said Dimitrios. 'I've got a translation somewhere.'

He rummaged around in his drawers and drew out a file. From it he took a single sheet of foolscap. 'Read this,' he said.

FROM THE GENERAL HEADQUARTERS OF THE
FIGHTERS OF LIGHT

Our administration has targeted the Patriarchate and its occupying leader, who behind what he considers insurmountable walls takes pleasure in the shedding of the blood of the Muslim people of the East, and to this end he is working on suspect and fiendish plans. We will fight until the Chief Devil and all the occupiers are chased off; until this place, which for years has contrived Byzantine intrigues against the Muslim peoples of the East, is exterminated. Occupiers disappear! These Lands are ours and will remain ours. We warn you one more time: there is no right to life for those who are occupiers.

Until the Greek Patriarchate and the Devil, the ridiculous Bartholomaios who wears the robes of the Patriarch, disappears from behind the thick walls where he plans his fiendish intrigues, our fight will continue. Patriarch you will perish!

Long live our Islamic Fight! Long live our Islamic Liberation War!

THE CENTRAL HEADQUARTERS OF LIGHT

'After this,' said Dimitrios, 'our young have finally become convinced that there is no future for them here.'

'I can see their point.'

'Now it's just the old who remain. Our priests here are sick and tired of funerals. A single baptism – or rarer still, a marriage – is the event of the year.'

I asked whether the Phanar was getting enough young priests coming up to keep the place going.

'The Turks closed our only seminary in 1971,' replied Dimitrios. 'It's cut the bloodline of our existence. A decade from now, when the older bishops have all died, there will be no clergy left. After 1,500 years, the Ecumenical Patriarch will have to leave Constantinople.' Dimitrios sighed. 'A century ago this was the centre of Greek Istanbul. Today there are no Greeks at all left around here. On a very good Sunday the Patriarch may still get a hundred people in this church. On a bad one he can't even fill the first two rows of pews. Come down and see what it's like at vespers.'

'Who will be there?'

'I fear just you, me and the angels.'

Fr. Dimitrios's apprehensions were justified. The service had already begun. One old bishop was standing at a lectern chanting hymns for the saint of the day. The other officiating priest, a bent-backed octogenarian, clanked a thurible from behind the iconostasis. There was no congregation in this, the senior church of Eastern Christendom, the Orthodox St Peter's; not one person occupied the empty pews. After a few minutes the bishop gave the dismissal and both old men quickly left the church.

'Look at your watch,' said Fr. Dimitrios. 'Exactly 4.15. It never takes a minute longer when it's an empty church. Our priests don't feel inspired. In fact they feel almost embarrassed.'

From the Phanar I walked through the old city to the Armenian Patriarchate in Kum Kapi, overlooking the Sea of Marmara. In London, Armenian friends had told me horror stories about the fate of the sixty thousand Armenians left in Istanbul: that *Refah* party activists had taken to slopping buckets of human urine into Armenian church services, as well as regularly vandalising the graveyards and churches. My friends had told me that the parish councils hushed these things up for fear that they would be accused of 'making anti-Turkish propaganda', but I hoped that the staff of the Patriarchate might at least be able to confirm or deny what I had heard.

The Patriarchate was a lovely wooden Ottoman building with a pediment and slatted louvres. After a short wait I was shown in to a plump Armenian priest, who called for tea and chatted happily about his trip to England twenty years previously. But when I turned the conversation to politics he just raised his palms and shrugged, indicating clearly – if wordlessly – that it would be undiplomatic for him to comment.

As I was leaving, I mentioned that I had just been to the Phanar: 'Watch out, then,' he whispered. 'The Phanar is full of informers. Your phone will be tapped and they've probably followed you here. Don't leave your notebooks – or anything valuable or incriminating – in your hotel room.'

The old Middle Eastern paranoia, one of the strongest legacies of the Ottomans, a shadow which falls uniformly from the Danube to the Nile. I smiled, but – as always happens after such a warning – did find myself looking behind me on my way back, to see if I was being followed.

Of course, there was nobody there.

ISTANBUL, 20 JULY

John Moschos did not like Constantinople, and he makes this dislike quite apparent in *The Spiritual Meadow*. One of his Constantinople stories concerns the astonishing sexual appetites of the Emperor Zeno; another is about a priest in the capital who 'was indulging in murder and dabbling in witchcraft'; a third is an anti-Semitic rant against a Jewish glassblower who tries to burn his eldest son to death after the boy announces that he plans to convert to Christianity. There are several other such tales, all designed to show the Byzantine capital – 'the city where the wicked rulers lived' – in a very dim light.

34

In some ways, Moschos's reaction is a little surprising. After all the monk admired the other two great Byzantine metropolises – Antioch and Alexandria – for their learning, and this was something in which the Imperial capital also excelled. Certainly Constantinople's university could not compare with that of Alexandria, but ever since the Emperor Theodosius II endowed a number of chairs in subjects such as medicine, grammar, rhetoric, law and philosophy, it had grown in size and stature, its reputation augmented by the presence nearby of the city's great public library.

Shortly before John Moschos arrived in the capital, his friend and mentor Stephen the Sophist had been lured to Constantinople from the School of Alexandria, where for many years he had lectured on medicine, philosophy, astronomy, astrology, horoscopy and ecclesiastical computus. Stephen should have been able to introduce Moschos to Constantinople's leading luminaries, men like the great historian Theophylact Simocatta; yet there is no indication in Moschos's writing that he met any particularly inspiring figures during his stay in the city.

There was another attraction which should have recommended Constantinople to Moschos: its extraordinary number of sacred relics. Moschos comments on the existence of such relics in almost every place he writes about; only in Constantinople does he omit to mention the number of holy objects on show in the churches, even though the capital's collection was the finest in Christendom. In one shrine alone, that under the Porphyry Column in the Forum of Constantine, were secreted the holy nails used in the crucifixion, the axe with which Noah built the Ark, and the *Dodekathronon*, the twelve baskets in which had been collected the leftover loaves and fishes from the feeding of the five thousand, which had been miraculously rediscovered by the dowager Empress Helena near the Sea of Galilee. Elsewhere in the city could be found the Crown of Thorns, the head of John the Baptist ('complete with hair and beard', according to one source,) the bodies of most of the innocents murdered by King Herod, and great chunks of the True Cross.

However dubious their pedigrees may seem to our eyes, to the

Byzantines relics were objects of priceless value. To see or to touch them was to come into direct contact with a God who was otherwise almost unimaginably distant and inaccessible. Relics were holes in the curtain wall separating the human from the divine. By contemplating them, and by reaching out and touching them, the Byzantines felt they were reaching through the great barrier which separated the visible from the invisible, the mundane from the transcendent. Gregory of Nyssa, a century before Moschos, described the emotion felt by ordinary Byzantines when they touched a sacred relic: 'Those who behold them embrace them as the living body [of the saint] itself; they bring all their senses into play and shedding tears of passion address to the martyr their prayers of intercession as if he were alive and present.'

Moschos must have had good reason to dislike a city full of such precious and holy objects, and a quick reading of the sources gives a good idea of what it was. For it seems that even by metropolitan Byzantine standards, Constantinople was a deeply degenerate place. When Justinian legislated on the Empire's brothels, the law he published contained a preamble which gives some details about the state of the capital's morality. Agents, it seemed, toured the provinces luring girls – some of them younger than ten years old – into their clutches by offering them fine clothes and shoes; once in the capital they were made to sign contracts and provide guarantees for their attendance at their bordello. Otherwise the unfortunate girls were kept imprisoned inside the whorehouses, shackled to their beds.

Nor was Constantinople's aristocratic elite renowned for its marital fidelity. Asterius of Amasia scolded his congregation: 'You change your wives like your clothes, and build new bride-chambers as casually as stalls at a fair.' St John Chrysostom blamed the city's famously lascivious theatre: 'When you seat yourself in a theatre and feast your eyes on the naked limbs of women, you are pleased for a time, but then, what a violent fever you have generated! Once your head is filled with such sights and the songs that go with them, you think about them even in your dreams. You would not choose to see a naked woman in the marketplace, yet you eagerly attend the theatre. What difference does it make if the stripper is a whore? It would be better to smear our faces with mud than to behold such spectacles.'

St John Damascene was even more shocked by what he heard of the 'city filled with impiety'. Constantinople was the setting of dances and jests, he wrote disapprovingly, as well as of taverns, baths and brothels. Women went about with uncovered heads and moved their limbs in a provocative and deliberately sensuous way. Young men grew effeminate and let their hair grow long. Indeed, complained the monk, some went so far as to decorate their boots. In such a climate even the bishops grew foppish. The *Ecclesiastical History* of Socrates talks of Bishop Sisinnios, who 'was accustomed to indulge himself by wearing smart new garments, and by bathing twice a day in the public baths. When someone asked him why he, a bishop, bathed himself twice a day, he replied: "Because you do not give me time for a third." '

The chief witness for the prosecution must, however, be Procopius, Justinian's official court historian. For most of his adult life, Procopius faithfully produced volume after volume of oily sycophancy, praising Justinian for his skill as a general, his taste as a builder and his wisdom as a ruler. Then quite suddenly, towards the end of his life, it seems he could stand it no more. He cracked, and the result was *The Secret History*, a short volume of the purest vitriol, in which the old historian sought to correct the honeyed lies he had been writing for thirty years. Justinian's reign, he wrote, had been an unmitigated disaster, leading to fiascos on many fronts, but above all to a situation of unparalleled moral anarchy. And he knew who to blame: Justinian's wife, the scheming Empress Theodora. Brought up in a circus family,

> as soon as she was old enough she joined the women on the stage and promptly became a courtesan. For she was not a flautist or a harpist; she was not even qualified to join the corps of dancers; but she merely sold her attractions to anyone who came along, putting her whole body at his disposal . . .
>
> There was not a particle of modesty in the little hussy: she complied with the most outrageous demands with-

out the slightest hesitation. She would throw off her clothes and exhibit naked to all and sundry those regions, both in front and behind, which the rules of decency require to be kept veiled and hidden from masculine eyes ... In the theatre, in full view of all the people, she would spread herself out and lie face upwards on the floor. Servants on whom this task had been imposed would sprinkle barley grains over her private parts, and geese trained for the purpose used to pick them off one by one with their bills and swallow them.

She used to tease her lovers by keeping them waiting, and by constantly playing about with novel methods of intercourse, she could always bring the lascivious to her feet; so far from waiting to be invited by anyone she encountered, by cracking dirty jokes and wiggling her hips suggestively she would invite all who came her way, especially if they were still in their teens. Never was anyone so completely given over to unlimited self-indulgence. Often she would go to a dinner party with ten young men or more, all at the peak of their physical prowess and with fornication as their chief object in life, and would lie with all her fellow diners in turn the whole night long: when she had reduced them all to a state of physical exhaustion she would go to their menials, as many as thirty on occasion, and copulate with every one of them; but not even so could she satisfy her lust.

And so it goes on, for (in the Penguin edition) 194 pages. It seems likely that Procopius had some personal grudge against the Empress, who may have been responsible for blocking his promotion or somehow harming his career. Even so, it is a remarkable testimony. At the end of the book, Procopius tells of Theodora's attempts in her old age to control prostitution. Overcome with guilt for her former sins, she closed the brothels, bought up all the prostitutes, and put them in a former Imperial palace which she converted into a Convent of Repentance.

But, notes Procopius, this was one of Theodora's less popular enterprises. According to him, the girls found this new way of life so dull that most 'flung themselves down from the parapet during the night' rather than be turned into nuns.

In the cool of the evening I walked over to the Hippodrome. In what was once the stalls, where the violent Byzantine circus factions once knifed it out, large Turkish ladies in headscarves now sit quietly gossiping on park benches. Their husbands squat nearby, under the chestnuts, cracking pistachio nuts. The occasional salesman with a glass cupboard on wheels wanders past, hawking paper cones full of chickpeas. Gulls hover silently overhead. It is strange to think that the hippodrome once held 120,000 people – double the present-day capacity of Wembley Stadium.

The obelisk of the Emperor Theodosius still stands in the centre of the old racetrack, rising from the plinth where it was placed in the 430s. A carving on the side shows the cat's-cradle of ropes and pulleys which was used to raise it. On another face is carved a picture of the Emperor in the imperial baldachin overlooking the races; these are illustrated at the base with a series of small relief carvings of what look like horse-drawn bathtubs.

Between the Emperor and the charioteers stand his bodyguard, a remarkably effeminate gaggle of fops with long floppy 1970s fringes, every bit as willowy as St John Damascene's blood-and-fire sermons might have led one to expect. Certainly these gentle cosmopolitans not only look remarkably unthreatening, they appear to be much more interested in the races than in guarding the Emperor. Here could lie part of the explanation for the large number of successful assassination attempts in Byzantine history.

At the end of the Hippodrome, then as now, rises the great dome of Justinian's Haghia Sophia, the supreme masterpiece of Byzantine architecture, and still, in the eyes of many, the most beautiful church ever built. No other Christian building is so successful in transporting one to the threshold of another world, or so dazzlingly intimates the imminence of the transcendent. In the golden haze of its interior, with its extraordinary play of light and space, precious stone and mosaic, under a dome that blazes like the vault of Heaven, even the solid walls seem to cease being barriers and become like passages into a higher reality. When it was first built in the 530s, Procopius, in one of his finest passages, described the overwhelming effect it has on the visitor. 'So bright is the glow of the interior that you might say that it is not illuminated by the sun from the outside but that the radiance is generated within,' he wrote in *The Buildings*. 'Rising above is an enormous spherical dome which seems not to be founded on solid masonry, but to be suspended from heaven by a Golden Chain. Whenever one goes into this church to pray, one understands immediately that this work has been fashioned not by human power and skill, but by the influence of God. And so the visitor's mind is lifted up to God and floats aloft, thinking that He cannot be far away, but must love to dwell in this place which He himself has chosen.'

The power of the building has not been diminished by fourteen hundred years of earthquakes and rebuildings, the destruction of much of its mosaic, the stripping of its altars, nor even a city fire which caused molten lead from the dome to run down the gutters in a flood of boiling metal. As you stand in the narthex you can see even the gossiping tour groups falling silent as they enter the dome chamber; if anyone talks they do so in a hushed whisper. The sacred breaks in on the mundane; and one immediately understands what a Byzantine monk must have felt when he touched a relic or gazed at a sacred icon: for a moment the gates of perception open and one catches a momentary glimpse of the Divine. Here, as nowhere else, one is transported back to the mental world of the Byzantium of John Moschos.

Yet the miraculous preservation of this one building – judged by the Byzantines themselves as their most perfect creation – can easily blind one to the amount that has been lost. Geography apart, John Moschos would not recognise much in this city if he came back today. Of the five hundred churches and monasteries which once decorated the land rising up from the Golden Horn, the remains of less than thirty survive, most of them rebuilt and converted into mosques.

This morning I visited the site of St Polyeuctes, once the greatest church in the whole Christian Empire; Justinian was said to have built Haghia Sophia in an attempt to match it. It would have been a familiar monument to John Moschos; indeed it was probably in a monastery attached to some great church like this that he lodged when he came to the city to finish *The Spiritual Meadow*.

The church fell into disrepair, and after the Turkish conquest of 1453 it collapsed and was forgotten. In 1960 it was accidentally rediscovered. Briefly it became famous again, and art historians and archaeologists triumphantly announced that many of the innovations of Justinian's reign were pre-empted by the work at St Polyeuctes.

Thirty years later the various archaeological reports are gathering dust, and St Polyeuctes seems to be returning to the earth. The ruins are an open latrine, and stink too badly to be examined at any length; only the most desperate Turkish tramps linger in its portals. Meanwhile the famous capitals – supposedly the first of the characteristic Byzantine basketwork impost-capitals that were to reach their fullest glory in Ravenna – are scattered around a nearby playground, where they provide seats for courting Turks. This means that anyone who wishes to study this crucial phase of early Byzantine sculpture is forced to spend an afternoon peering like a pervert beneath the legs of entwined couples.

Secular Byzantine architecture has fared even worse. The great Theodosian land walls, in their day the most sophisticated defensive military architecture the world had ever seen, are still there; there is also the great fourth-century aqueduct of Valens and a pair of superb arcaded cisterns dating from the time of Justinian. Yet not one single house from Byzantine Constantinople still stands. Even the two largest Imperial palace complexes, the Great Palace and the Palace of Blanchernae, have disappeared but for a few arches, a line of windows, some buried foundations and a few splendid floor mosaics.

I spent much of the afternoon in the Mosaic Museum, admiring what has survived. All the work there dates from the late sixth century – just after the reign of Justinian – and is from the Great Palace, which once occupied the slope behind the Blue Mosque. These then are the very floors that the Emperor Heraclius must have paced as he heard of the Persian capture of Jerusalem or the fall of Alexandria.

The initial impression is of the unexpectedly persistent Hellenism. The style of most of the mosaics is pastoral and bucolic, and their warm naturalism seems at first to have more in common with the delicate frescoes of Pompeii than with the stiff, hieratic inhabitants of later Byzantine icons or the unsmiling *Pantocrators* which overwhelm the domes of so many medieval Byzantine churches. It is only after you have been in the museum for some time and look a little closer at the pastoral idylls that you begin to worry about the mental state of the mosaic-makers, or perhaps that of their patrons.

At first sight a horse appears to be giving suck to a lion: the perfect symbol of peace, like the Biblical wolf lying down with lamb. Only when you look closely do you see that what is actually happening is that the lion is ripping the stomach out of the horse and biting off its testicles. Another lion rears up and attacks an elephant, but misjudges his leap and impales himself on a tusk. A wolf tears off the neck of a deer. Two gladiators in leather hauberks and plus-fours await the charge of a pink tiger (the tiger is already badly wounded in the neck, and blood is pouring out of its mouth). Elsewhere a winged gryphon swoops down and rips the back of an antelope; another gobbles up a lizard.

One can only speculate what induced the head mosaicist to make his creations so psychopathically violent: after all, with assassinations and palace coups as frequent as they were, it can hardly have been very calming for the Emperor to have to walk over these scenes of gruesome blood-letting day after day. On the other hand they are certainly a blessed antidote to the gloomy piety of most Byzantine literature: those endless saints' *Lives* with their heroic ascetics resisting the lascivious enticements of demonic temptresses. Indeed, after enduring one of the Patriarch's two-hour sermons on chastity, the Emperor may actually have been relieved to return to these lively scenes of carnage and mayhem.

On the way back I passed through the Gulhane Gardens surrounding the Topkapi Palace. As I passed I was surprised to see that the basilica of Haghia Eirene appeared to be open. This was unexpected because, for some reason best known to the Turkish authorities, this magnificent building, one of the very greatest Byzantine churches surviving in the city, is normally kept resolutely locked. This time, however, the door was open and a couple of sophisticated-looking Turkish women were sitting chatting in the porch.

I thought I would take the opportunity to have a look at the church, but as I wandered past the women one of them called out: 'I'm sorry, you can't go in there. It's closed.'

'It looks open.'

'I'm afraid you need a special pass to go in. For security reasons.'

'What do you mean?'

'There are VIPs inside.'

'Politicians?'

'No. Models.'

'Models!'

'Today they are having a beauty contest.'

'In a church?'

'Why not? All Turkey's top models are there. They are currently changing into Rifat Ozbek bikinis.'

Haghia Eirene is the worst possible place to have a beauty contest: it is dark, gloomy and badly lit. But the Greeks desperately want this church back, and the Turks will go to any length, however absurd, to annoy their hereditary enemies. No doubt, however, the Greeks play similar games with the abandoned mosques of Salonica. They would probably do the same to those in Athens, too, had they not bulldozed the lot in the 1920s, in a sadly characteristic outbreak of virulent nationalism.

By ferry to the island known to the Turks as Buyuk Áda, and to the Greeks as Prinkipo. Hazy, all-enveloping heat. Boys bathing by the Bosphorus. The scent of sea-salt, hot wood, rotting fish. We pull away from the Golden Horn, pass around the wooded ridge of the Topkapi Saray, and head out across the narrow stretch of water that separates Europe from Asia.

The other passengers: beside me, a sad-eyed conscript, perhaps eighteen years old, in ill-fitting fatigues. Small moustache. Cropped hair. Gazes vacantly over the sea. Perhaps he is on his way to do his military service on the Kurdish front.

Opposite, a girl in a lilac headscarf and long Islamic raincoat. She is earnestly studying an English-language pharmacology text-book: 'Chapter Two – Drug Permeation'.

On the bench at the back, an old labourer with toothbrush moustache and no teeth. Unbuttoned flies. Cigarette hangs from the side of his mouth.

Shady-looking character in tight T-shirt. Stubble chin. He clacks worry beads from the palm to the back of his hand, and darts furtive looks around him. Fare dodger?

Shaven-headed sailor in war-movie sailor's suit. Thickset and swarthy. His cap is on his knee. Drags deeply on a cigarette, then loses interest and throws it overboard.

Moving from bench to bench: a blind violinist, led by his son who bangs a small wooden hand-drum. Both wear flat caps.

Various salesmen selling Coke, biros, potato peelers, Rolex watches (fake), Lacoste socks (fake), Ray-Ban sunglasses (also fake) and Bic cigarette lighters (apparently genuine, but of the poorest quality). I buy a Coke and it turns out to be a fake too: tastes of warm deodorant.

Halfway through the voyage another fearsome-looking head-scarf-and-raincoat lady appears at the top of the stairwell and begins to harangue us all. I assume she is telling us to vote *Refah*, or ticking off those few middle-aged women who are not wearing a veil. But I'm quite wrong. Her daughter is in hospital and she needs money for medicine. The passengers give generously, especially the old labourer with the open flies, who extinguishes his cigarette to dig deep in his pockets.

The Byzantines used Prinkipo as a prison, and exiled a succession of crooked chancellors and plotting princes to its monasteries. The Ottomans turned it into summer resort, and so it remains: a thin line of lovely slatted wooden houses, with carved balustrades and lattices, prettily painted in cream and light blue. But the site of one of the old monasteries is still an active shrine, and it was there that I was heading. Fr. Dimitrios had told me about it. The Shrine of St George was an example, he said, of something which was once common, but is now rare: a holy place sacred to both faiths, where Greeks and Turks still pray side by side.

Because of a local by-law cars are banned from the island, so at the jetty I hailed an old horse-drawn phaeton. We trotted along the cobbles, up the hill, with gardens and orchards on either side. Apples and apricots hung heavily on the trees; bougainvillaea and jasmine blossomed over orchard walls.

A century ago Prinkipo was exclusively Greek, and today one or two old Hellenes still cling on to their houses: large, ostentatious wooden buildings with pediments and pillars. Occasionally, as we passed the manicured lawns, we caught glimpses of old Greek women sitting in the shade of magnolia trees with shiny green leaves and thick creamy flowers; some were sewing, others sipping glasses of sherbet.

We drove out of the town and up the mountain; pine forests replaced orchards and thick carpets of pine needles rotted in the wheel-ruts. Other than the clip-clop of the horse and the rattle of other phaetons taking farmers and pilgrims back into town, it was completely silent.

After twenty minutes, the driver dropped me beside a graveyard at the bottom of the dusty path leading up to the shrine. Before climbing the hill, I looked inside. It was the last Greek graveyard in Turkey still in use. I wandered through the unkempt memorials, overgrown and unswept, carpeted now, like the road outside, by a thick muffling of pine needles. Many of the headstones were decorated with photographs. Paradoxically, I found that it was these photographs of dead people from a deserted graveyard which, more than anything else, brought to life the world of the Greek Istanbul which had been ended by the 1955 riots.

Fr. Dimitrios had described those who had left – the Greeks who formed such an influential minority in the Istanbul of the nineteenth century – as cosmopolitan, artistic and well educated; but the photographs, less nostalgic, revealed a prosperous petit-bourgeois society of shopkeepers and spinsters: moustaches and double chins, waistcoats and fob watches, bald spots and pinces-nez; line upon line of plump, suspicious men, grown prematurely old in their confectionery shops, moustaches bristling in late Ottoman indignation; pairs of old ladies shrouded in funereal black, plain and bitter, all widows' weeds and pious scowls.

Walking up the hill, among the ebb and flow of pilgrims, I marvelled at what I took to be thick white hibiscus blossom on the bushes near the summit. Only when I reached the top did I see what it really was: on every bush the pilgrims had tied strips of cloth, primitive fertility charms, to the branches. Some were quite elaborate: small cloth hammocks supporting stones or pebbles or small pinches of pine needles. Others were tangled cat's-cradles of threads wrapped right around the bushes, as if packaged for the post.

Inside the shrine it was just as bizarre. At some stage a fire had half-gutted the building, leaving charred rafters and singed window frames standing in the open air. But the rooms, though half exposed and quite unrestored, were filled by a continuous trickle of supplicants. The two nationalities were praying side by side; but they were not praying together. The Greeks stood in front of the icon of the mounted saint, hands cupped in prayer. The Turks put prayer carpets on the floor and bent forward in the direction of Mecca. One veiled Muslim lady scraped with long nails at a tattered nineteenth-century fresco of the saint, then with her fingertip touched a fragment of the paintwork to her tongue.

'The Muslims also believe in St George,' explained a young Greek student I met waiting by the jetty half an hour later. 'They hear St George is working miracles so they come here and ask him for babies. Maybe they don't know he is Greek.'

'They probably think he is Turkish,' said her friend.

'Probably,' said the first girl. 'They think everything is Turkish. I've heard boys say Haghia Sophia and the Hippodrome were built by the Seljuk Turks.'

'They don't know history,' agreed the second girl. 'One day some boy asked my sister, "Why did you Greeks come here? All you do is make trouble." She said, "We didn't come: you did."'

'They even think Homer was one of them,' sighed the first girl. 'They say he was a Turk and that his real name was Omar.'

ISTANBUL, 1 AUGUST

11 p.m.: I have just returned from supper with Hugh Pope, Turkey correspondent of the *Independent*. We ate in a fish restaurant at Bebek, five miles up the Bosphorus, overlooking Asia. Talk soon turned to the Kurdish war currently raging in the south-east.

'At least fifty people are being killed every day,' he said. 'Unless at least two hundred are gunned down, I don't even bother calling the Foreign Desk.'

Hugh told me that the previous December, when the *Independent* sent him to Diyarbakir, he managed to get through to the largest of the surviving Syrian Orthodox monasteries in the south-east, Mar Gabriel. The day before he arrived, a lorry had hit an anti-tank mine two hundred metres from the monastery's front gate. As he drove up, the charred corpse of the driver was still sitting in the burned-out skeleton of the truck, hands welded to

47

the wheel. The mine had apparently been placed by the PKK, the Revolutionary Kurdistan Workers' Party, and was thought to have been aimed at village guards – in the eyes of the PKK, collaborators with the Turkish government – passing on their way to the neighbouring village of Güngören. Although the mine's target did not seem to have been the monastery, it dramatically brought home to the monks how vulnerable they were to being caught in the crossfire between the PKK and the government.

According to Hugh, the Kurdish guerrillas dislike the Suriani Christians as much as the local government does, accusing them of being informers, just as the authorities accuse them of being PKK sympathisers. Moreover, the Kurds have much to gain by driving the Suriani out: they can then occupy their land and farm it themselves.

Yet the problems faced by the Christians and the Kurds have similar roots. The Ottoman Empire was administered by a system which allowed, and indeed thrived on, diversity. Each *millet* or religious community was internally self-governing, with its own laws and courts. The new Turkey of Ataturk went to the opposite extreme: uniformity was all. The vast majority of Greeks were expelled, and those who remained had to become Turks, at least in name. The same went for the Kurds. Officially they do not exist. Their language and their songs were banned until very recently; in official documents and news broadcasts they are still described as 'Mountain Turks'.

It is this ludicrous – and deeply repressive – fiction that has led to the current guerrilla war. Because of it the rebels of the PKK are now involved in a hopeless struggle to try and gain autonomy for the Turkish Kurds, something Ankara will never allow. More than ten thousand people have been killed in the south-east of Turkey in the last five years, and great tracts of land and around eight hundred villages have been laid waste in an effort to isolate and starve out the guerrillas. At least 150,000 Turkish troops are tied down in the mountains of the south-east, fighting perhaps ten thousand PKK guerrillas. At the moment the government seems to have the upper hand, and it is said the average life expectancy of a guerrilla is now less than six months.

Hugh says that the fighting, though currently intermittent, is expected to reach a new climax in the coming weeks: summer is the fighting season.

I plan to set off to the south-east next week. Antioch – modern Antakya – is on the edge of the trouble. Once there it should be easier to judge how bad things really are: it is virtually impossible to gauge the difficulty of getting to the Syrian Orthodox monasteries from here, and the situation changes from day to day. *Inshallah* it should be possible to get through without taking any unreasonable risks. Hugh has given me the name of a driver in Diyarbakir who last year was willing – for a price – to drive him into the war zone.

He also raised the question of whether I should get a press card. On the one hand, he says, the authorities in the south-east hate all journalists: last year his wife was beaten up by the police in Nusaybin when she produced her card. On the other hand, he says that no one will believe me if I say I'm a tourist – no tourist has gone anywhere near the south-east for three or four years now – and if I have no Turkish ID he tells me that there is a real possibility that I could get arrested for spying.

On my return from supper I asked the advice of Mettin, the hotel receptionist, whose home is in the south-east. He seems to think my plans are hysterically funny. 'Don't worry, you'll only get shot if you run into a PKK roadblock, and only get blown up if you drive over a landmine. Otherwise the south-east is fine. Completely safe. In fact highly recommended.'

Becoming serious, Mettin said that if the police did not arrest me, and if I did not drive over any landmines, there was always the delightful possibility of being kidnapped by the PKK. This happened last year to three British round-the-world cyclists. They were not in the least harmed, but as the guerrillas cannot light fires – that would reveal their whereabouts to the army – the hostages were forced to live for three months on snake tartare and raw hedgehog.

'The tourists should consider themselves lucky,' said Mettin. 'If it had been Turkish soldiers that had fallen into the PKK's hands, they would have had their dicks cut off. *Then* the PKK would kill them. Roasted them over a fire or something. Very slowly. Chargrilled them.'

'And this sort of thing still goes on?'

'These guys are committing mass murder *right now*,' answered Mettin.

'But they only do that to Turkish soldiers, right?'

'You can't be too careful in the east,' said Mettin, twirling his moustache. 'As they say in Ankara: Kurdistan is like a cucumber. Today in your hand; tomorrow up your arse.'

ISTANBUL, 3 AUGUST

My last day in Istanbul; tonight the train.

This morning I went to the Phanar to say goodbye to Fr. Dimitrios, and to collect the letters of introduction he has written to the *hegumenoi* (abbots) of the Greek monasteries in the Holy Land and Sinai.

Running down the stairs from Fr. Dimitrios's office, I knocked into a visiting Greek monk who was crouching in the doorway leading into the courtyard, feeding the sparrows. I apologised and we fell into conversation. He said he had been to England once but did not like it much. 'It was so sad,' he remarked. 'All the churches were closed. In Ipswich I went. Not one church was open. Not one!' He added darkly: 'I read in a magazine that the head of the Satan Cult lives in England.'

He disliked London and was unimpressed by Buckingham Palace. In fact only two places really appealed to him. One was Kew: 'Your Kew Gardens! So beautiful! So lovely! I would feed the squirrels and bring them nuts.' The other was a shop in Lambeth which sold religious trinkets. From his suitcase the monk produced a small plastic hologram of Christ. 'It is so beautiful, no? It is by a Swiss artist and is based on the exact likeness of Jesus. Some of the other monks think it is not pleasing to look at, but I do not understand why. Walk around: look! Now our Lord is smiling! Now he is showing his sobriety! Now he is dead. Now he is risen! Alleluia! It is so beautiful, no? I carry it with me always.'

A night ferry across the black Bosphorus to Hyderpasha, the Anatolian railhead of the old Berlin to Baghdad railway that T. E. Lawrence spent so long trying to blow up. Tomorrow to Ankara to pick up my press card.

On the train the conductor had no record of my reservation. But he asked me my nationality, and when I told him, I thought I saw a brief flicker of terror cross his face; certainly, I was immediately upgraded to first class. Only when I sat eating supper in the station restaurant did I discover the reason for this uncharacteristically flexible behaviour: there was a European Cup soccer match that evening between Manchester United and Galatasaray, and the television news was full of the English visitors' traditional pre-match activities: trashing restaurants, picking fights, beating up innocent Turks and so on. For the first time I felt grateful for English football's international reputation for hooliganism: it seemed that my compatriots from Manchester had unknowingly guaranteed me a first-class berth for the night.

NIGHT BUS BETWEEN ANKARA AND ANTIOCH, 6/7 AUGUST

4.15 a.m.: This is a horrible way to travel. It is nearly dawn, and the first glimmer of light has illuminated an expanse of flat plains covered by a wraith of thin mist. The rutted roads, the bracing crash of the long-defunct suspension, the snoring Anatolian peasants: these one expects and can bear. What is intolerable is the deliberate regime of sleep deprivation imposed on all passengers by this driver and his henchman, the moustachioed Neanderthal of a conductor.

Every other hour we pull in to some seedy kebab restaurant. The lights are put on, we are shaken awake and a Turkish chanteuse is put on the Tannoy so loud that we have no option but to vacate the bus. The driver and his friend disappear behind the scenes to pick up their commission from the restaurant owner, while we are all expected to make merry with plateloads of malignant kebabs or, even more horrible in the middle of the night, bags full of sickly-sweet Turkish delight.

Worse is to follow. On returning to our seats, the Neanderthal marches down the aisles, gaily shaking *eau de cologne* over the outstretched hands of the passengers. This can be quite refreshing at three o'clock on a hot afternoon; but it is irritating beyond belief at three o'clock in the dull chill of the early morning. And so on we trundle, rattling and shaking like a spin dryer, smelling like a tart's boudoir, tempers rising steadily with each stop.

6 a.m.: We pull in to a particularly run-down *kebabji* which, with horrible inevitability, has suddenly materialised from nowhere amid the grey wastes of Anatolia. We stumble out of the bus and obediently line up for our breakfast, smelling like a collection of extras from some spectacular epic of an after-shave advertisement. Too weak to argue, too tired to care, I join the queue and load my plate with some slurry that must once have been an aubergine.

8 a.m.: Issus, site of Alexander's great victory over the Persians. It may be one of the turning points in world history, but it's a miserable-looking place now: a scrappy village with a petrol pump, a derelict electricity station and the statutory seedy restaurant over which hangs a terrible smell of grease and dead animal.

My neighbour in the bus, a garrulous traffic policeman from Istanbul, made the mistake of eating a kebab at the last stop and is now being noisily ill in the street; he has attracted a small circle of onlookers who appear to take the view that this is the most interesting thing to have happened in Issus for several months. Despite the early hour, it is already hot and muggy. We're through the Cilician Gates and heading into the plains. On the far side of the road parties of bedraggled peasants are standing in lines, hoeing the dead ground beside the cotton and tobacco fields – or at least some are: most have put down their implements to watch my friend's streetside evacuations.

The men here are a rough-looking bunch, scowling, ill-kempt and unshaven. But – looking around the motley crew filling the tables around me, and glimpsing my own reflection in the mirror – who are we to talk?

9 a.m.: Antioch: a gridiron of dirty alleyways surrounded on three sides by the crescent cliffs of Mount Silpius. As we leave the bus for the last time and stumble into the glare of the bus station the smirking Neanderthal offers us a last splash of *eau de cologne*. I shake my head, but get the horrible stuff poured all over me anyhow.

BUYUK ANTAKYA OTELI, ANTIOCH, 11 AUGUST

Cleansed, vowing never again to go on a night bus, nor ever again to touch *eau de cologne*, I went to bed for the rest of the morning, lulled to sleep by some of John Moschos's more soporific miracle stories: tales of doughty Byzantine hermits fending off the advances of demonic temptresses and saucy 'Ethiopic boys'

With the exception of the mosaics in the museum and a few fragments of the much-rebuilt town walls, it seems that barely one stone remains from what was once the third greatest metropolis in the Byzantine Empire and briefly, under Julian the Apostate, its capital. Of the city's famous buildings – Constantine's Golden Octagon, the Council Chamber where Libanius declaimed, the great hippodrome that could seat eighty thousand people – nothing now remains. Like Alexandria, its traditional rival, Byzantine Antioch is now just a city of memory, forgotten but for the conjectures of scholars.

There is a reason for this. The city is built in the centre of an earthquake zone and has been levelled again and again, at least once every two hundred years. Today it is a sleepy, provincial place, architecturally undistinguished but for a few fine late-Ottoman villas decorated with carved wooden balustrades and with vines tumbling over the shuttered windows. Other than the occasional archaeologist, no one really bothers to come to Antioch any more: not the Turkish politicians, not the journalists, not the tourists, not even the PKK.

It is odd to think that all Europe, much of the Middle East and the entire length of the North African coast was once ruled from this little market town, today a forgotten backwater even by Turkish standards. Perhaps one day Los Angeles or San Francisco will be like this.

When John Moschos visited Antioch in the 590s, there were already many signs that the city was in serious decline. The School of Antioch, once one of the most sophisticated of all theological schools, was no longer in its prime. The days of John Chrysostom and Theodore of Mopsuestia were long past, even though it was probably at this time that Theodore of Tarsus came to the city to receive his training in the Antioch tradition of Biblical exegesis, a training he later brought with him to Anglo-Saxon England when he was appointed the seventh Archbishop of Canterbury. Antioch's port, Seleucia ad Pieria, was beginning to silt up, and the great trade of the Mediterranean had begun passing the city by. The bazaars were empty but for local agricultural produce, and refugees were setting up shacks where once great caravans of merchants traded in silks and spices from Persia, India and the East.

Moreover, corruption had set in, and the city had the most dubious reputation. When the Emperor framed a troublesome Bishop of Antioch for consorting with a prostitute, no one for a minute doubted the bishop's guilt. The Antioch theatre was famed for its great aquatic spectacles featuring (as one source puts it) 'large numbers of naked girls from the lower classes', and the city's eighteen public baths were as disreputable as any in the Empire. St John Chrysostom, later the scourge of Constantinople, began his career as moral watchdog in Antioch, where he attacked the institution of 'spiritual partnerships' between monks and nuns and for good measure went on to accuse the city's upper-class women of habitually exposing themselves before the eyes of their servants, 'their softly nurtured flesh draped only in heavy jewellery'.

But it was sorcery that was the declining city's greatest vice. In an age when demons were considered to fill the air as thickly as flies in a Turkish market (Gregory the Great always used to recommend making the sign of the cross over a lettuce in case you swallowed a demon that happened to be perched on its leaves), in Antioch things had come to such a pass that demonic activities were rife even among the clergy – or so it was whispered. The Antioch hippodrome was a famous centre of such witchery: not only were all kinds of magic practised there against horses and charioteers, but the galleries were packed with nude classical statues believed to be the haunt of those demons who specialised in exciting the carnal passions. Indeed the Byzantine version of the Faust tale involved a Jewish necromancer leading a presbyter to the hippodrome in the middle of the night. The presbyter has been sacked from his position as *oikonomos* (treasurer) by the new bishop. The necromancer succeeds in conjuring up Satan himself, who promises to help the presbyter regain his former position if he first agrees to become the Servant of Darkness, and kisses his cloven foot in submission. The presbyter does as he is bidden, and sells his soul to the Devil.

Surrounded by similar stories, the worried Antiochians looked for guidance not to their clergy, nor to the Byzantine governor or the *magister militum*. Instead they turned to St Symeon Stylites the Younger, a renowned hermit who had set up his pillar a few miles outside the city. From there he issued a series of dreadful threats and warnings to the faithful, calling on them to repent and mend their ways.

His powers were remarkable. According to his anonymous hagiographer the dust from his clothes was more powerful than roasted crocodile, camel dung or Bithynian cheese mixed with wax – apparently the usual contents of a Byzantine doctor's medicine chest. This dust could cure constipation, cast leprosy on an unbeliever, bring a donkey back to life and restore sour wine to sweetness. It was clearly a particularly handy thing to have on board ship in the event of a storm. A certain Dorotheus, a cleric at Symeon's monastery, sailed during the forbidden period of the year in the midst of winter, trusting to the protection of his stylite master. Far out to sea, however, the vessel ran into a tremendous storm which lashed it with waves so high they rolled over the deck. The Captain was in despair, but Dorotheus took some dust which had been blessed by St Symeon and sprinkled the ship with it; 'a sweet fragrance filled the air, the churning sea was pacified, a fair wind filled the sails and safely brought the ship to its destination.'

Symeon was clearly not a man to be trifled with. An Antiochian brickmaker who privately voiced his view that Symeon's miracles might not be the work of God but instead of the Devil found that his hand promptly turned putrid, and 'it was only after he shed many tears of repentance that he was forgiven and restored to health'. Symeon could have an equally dramatic effect on other parts of the body. Moschos tells a story of a renegade monk who gave up the habit, left his monastery in Egypt and settled in Antioch. One day, on his way back to town from a trip to the coast, the ex-monk decided to visit Symeon's pillar. He had no sooner entered the enclosure than the stylite pointed him out amid the crowd of assembled pilgrims: 'Bring the shears!' cried Symeon, miraculously divining his visitor's monastic past. 'Tonsure that man!'

Packing him off back to his Egyptian monastery, Symeon promised the man a sign that he had been granted divine forgiveness. It duly arrived: one Sunday, back in his cloister, when the monk was celebrating the Eucharist 'one of his eyes suddenly came out'. This, oddly enough, was considered a good thing, at least by Symeon's more ardent admirers. 'By this sign,' comments a breathless Moschos, 'the brethren knew that God had forgiven him his sin, just as the righteous Symeon had foretold.'

After lunch, refreshed, I set about trying to find a driver willing to take me to what remains of the stylite's pillar on the Wonderful Mountain, a few miles south of modern Antakya.

In the main bazaar – a vaulted Ottoman street that still follows the line of the old Byzantine *corso* – I met a pious and thickly bearded driver named Ismail. He owned an ancient and much repainted Dodge truck, currently coloured lemon-yellow. We haggled for long enough for both of us to feel we were being swindled, and after Ismail had attended midday prayers we drove off in the truck, jolting out of Antioch, heading due south.

Olives were everywhere: long regimented lines of trees forming neat chequerboard patterns against the ash-coloured soil of the hills. But for the occasional minaret poking up beyond the groves and the groups of baggy-trousered peasants loading firewood onto carts, it could have been Umbria. In the valley to our left shepherds and their barking dogs were leading herds of long-eared goats and sheep, bells tinkling, through the mulberries and aloes. Within a few minutes the perfect pyramid of Mons Mirabilis rose up through the morning haze.

Bouncing off the main road onto a track, we climbed a dry *wadi* in a cloud of dust. We passed an old couple with mattocks in their hands, hoeing a barren terrace. The track continued to spiral steeply upwards; slowly a great vista opened up around us. Ahead lay the distant metallic glint of the Mediterranean; to the south, Mount Cassius and the olive groves of Syria; to the north, the hot, flat, plains of Cilicia. Immediately below us, through the heat haze, we could see the meandering course of the sluggish Orontes, and on either side lines of dark green cypresses.

When John Moschos came here, all the peaks within view were crowned by stylites, and competition between them was rife: if one was struck by lightning – something that clearly happened with a fair degree of frequency – the electrocuted hermit's rivals would take this as a definitive sign of divine displeasure, probably indicating that the dead stylite was a secret heretic. Judging by what Moschos has to say in *The Spiritual Meadow*, visiting these pillar saints was a popular afternoon's outing for the pious ladies of Antioch's more fashionable suburbs. The most chic stylite of all was undoubtedly Symeon, whose pillar lay a convenient palanquin's ride from the waterfalls of Daphne, the resort where Antony took Cleopatra for their honeymoon.

Today it seems that no one comes to Symeon's shrine. There are only a handful of Christians left in Antioch, and they have better things to worry about than the ruins of a forgotten hermit. The broken pillar is surrounded now by the ruins of the churches, monasteries, pilgrims' hostels and oratories that sprang up around it, a crumbling panorama of collapsed walls and fallen vaults. The only intruders are shepherds looking for somewhere to shelter their flocks during storms. Even the dirt track no longer reaches the pillar. I left Ismail bobbing up and down on his prayer carpet at the end of the path, and climbed up to the summit on my own.

Rising to the crest of a hogsback ridge, I could see above me the lines of honey-coloured masonry that marked the exterior wall of the stylite's complex. But it was only as I got much nearer to the ruin that I began to take in the true scale and splendour of the building: high on that empty hilltop with the wind howling over the summit lay a vast cathedral, constructed with great skill out of prisms of finely dressed stone. It was built with deliberate extravagance and ostentation: the basket capitals of solid Proconessian marble were lace-like and deeply cut; the pilasters and architraves were sculpted with an imperial extravagance. It was strange: a ragged, illiterate hermit being fawned over by the rich and highly educated Greco-Roman aristocracy; yet odder still was the idea of a hermit famed for his ascetic simplicity punishing himself in the finest setting money could buy. It was like holding a hunger strike in the Ritz.

I clambered into the basilica over a pile of fallen pillars and upended capitals; as I did so a thin black snake slithered from a marble impost, through a patch of poppies, down into the unseen dark of an underground cistern. I sat down where it had been lying, and opened up *The Spiritual Meadow* to read Moschos's description of the teeming crowds that once thronged the site to look at Symeon, to hear his pronouncements and, possibly, even to be healed. Once the road between Antioch and the coast was jammed solid with devotees and pilgrims coming from all over the Mediterranean world. Now it was just the snake and me.

The complex was based on that of the original St Symeon Stylites, St Symeon Stylites the Elder, who first ascended his pillar near Aleppo a century earlier in an effort to escape the press of pilgrims around him. His pillar was originally just a refuge from the faithful; only by accident did it become a method of voluntary self-punishment and a symbol in itself. The building around the original St Symeon's pillar was erected by the Emperor after the stylite died, so that his pillar became a relic and the church which enclosed it a huge reliquary. But here on Mons Mirabilis there was a crucial difference: the church was built around a living saint. In one of the most unlikely manifestations of Christian piety ever witnessed, it was a living man – a layman, not even a priest – who was the principal object of reverence in the church.

The stump of the pillar rises still from a plinth in the middle of an octagon, around which are stacked tiers of stone benches. In a normal Byzantine episcopal church such stone benches, reserved for the senior clergy of the church and called the *synthronon*, would be placed around the apse and would look onto the altar. But in this church conventional worship was relegated to the flanking side chapels; here the main nave looked not towards the altar (and thus to God) but towards the saint himself. The stylite had become like the Christian version of the Delphic oracle: raised up on his pillar at the top of the highest mountain, a literal expression of his closeness to the heavens, he spoke what all assumed to be the words of God. The Byzantines were constantly haunted by the spectre of heresy, but no one in Antioch ever seems to have suggested that in behaving in this way the stylites or their followers were doing anything in the least bit uncanonical. Even when the Egyptian monks tried to excommunicate Symeon, the rest of the Byzantine Church assumed – perhaps not inaccurately – that they were just motivated by jealousy: after all, the stylites had rather stolen the desert fathers' thunder.

The sun was lowering in the sky, sinking towards the Mediterranean. In the distance, to the east, lightning played on the horizon. But even though it would soon be dark I lingered in the ruins, pacing through the complex in the dusk and wondering at the oddness of the world John Moschos inhabited: sophisticated enough to build this astonishing classical basilica, yet innocent enough to believe that these strange, ragged men shrieking from their pillars were able to pull aside the heavy curtain of the flesh and gaze directly on God. Standing on their pillars, they were believed to be bright beacons of transcendence, visible from afar; indeed in some cases we hear of disciples claiming to be unable to bear the effulgence of the holy man's face, so bright had it become with the uncreated light of the divine.

The Byzantines looked on these stylites as intermediaries, go-betweens who could transmit their deepest fears and aspirations to the distant court of Heaven, ordinary men from ordinary backgrounds who had, by dint of their heroic asceticism, gained the ear of Christ. For this reason Byzantine holy men and stylites became the focus for the most profound yearnings of half of Christendom. They were men who were thought to have crossed the boundary of reality and gained direct access to the divine. It is easy to dismiss the eccentricities of Byzantine hermits as little more than bizarre circus acts, but to do so is to miss the point that man's deepest hopes and convictions are often quite inexplicable in narrow terms of logic or reason. At the base of a stylite's pillar one is confronted with the awkward truth that what has most moved past generations can today sometimes be only tentatively glimpsed with the eye of faith, while remaining quite inexplicable and absurd when seen under the harsh distorting microscope of sceptical Western rationality.

Back in Antioch, the incipient storm had not yet broken and a stuffy afternoon had turned into a heavy and swelteringly hot night. In the backstreets, many families had settled themselves outside, laying straw mats and old kilims out on the pavements. Grandmothers sat on stools at the back, knitting; women in headscarves brought out steaming pilaffs to their cross-legged husbands. The richer families sat in a semi-circle in front of televisions, often placed on the bonnet of a conveniently parked car. The noise of televised gunshots and the murmur of Turkish soap operas mingled with the whirr of cicadas.

I got Ismail to drop me off, and wandered in the dark through the narrow streets, under the projecting wooden balconies of the old houses and the vine trellising of the bazaars. Down alleys, through arched doorways, you could catch glimpses of the hidden life of the courtyard houses: brief impressions of bent old ladies flitting from kitchen to zenana; old men in flat caps gossiping under palms, sticks in their hands.

After nearly an hour I found a café with a marble Ottoman fountain, and there I washed off the dust of the afternoon and settled down to drink a glass of *raki*. From inside came the acrid smell of Turkish tobacco and the sharp clack of dominoes. Gnarled old men with moustachless Islamic beards pushed barrows of figs and pomegranates along the cobbles. Flights of dark-skinned teenagers kicked balls amid the uncollected rubbish of unlit alleyways; smaller children pulled toys made of old crates, with wheels cannibalised from long-rusted prams or bikes. Through the dark, from another part of town, came the thump of drums from an unseen circumcision ceremony.

Later, walking back to the hotel, I took a wrong turning and stumbled by accident across the Greek Orthodox church. It was a substantial eighteenth-century building, Italianate and flat-fronted, with a small belfry facing onto the courtyard. The whole complex lay hidden by a discreetly narrow arch, and was guarded by an old Turk in a pair of baggy *charwal* trousers.

The priest was away in Istanbul, but from the doorkeeper I learned that the Christian community now numbered only two hundred families. In his lifetime, he said, as many as fifteen thousand Christians had left the town for new lives in Syria, Brazil, Germany and Australia. As with the Istanbul Greeks, it was just the poor and the old who were left. If I wanted to know more, he suggested, I should try to find the Italian Catholic priest who had recently come to live in the town; he didn't know the address, but had heard it was somewhere nearby in the old Jewish quarter.

It was not difficult to find him. Everyone seemed to know about the Italian. Fr. Domenico turned out to be a missionary friar from Modena. He was a tall, thin man with a lined, ascetic face and a distant, rather disconcerting gaze. He lived on his own and was finishing his supper when I interrupted him.

He had been in Turkey for twenty-five years, he said, and now thought of it as home, although each year he still crossed the Mediterranean to spend a fortnight with his elderly parents.

Like the gatekeeper at the Orthodox church, Fr. Domenico was gloomy about the future of Christianity in the city. 'Antioch was one of the first centres of the Early Church,' he said. 'St Peter and Paul both preached here. According to the Acts of the Apostles it was in Antioch that the disciples were first called Christian. But now there are barely two hundred Christian families left.'

'What will happen to them?' I asked.

'They are better off than the Greeks in Istanbul,' said Fr. Domenico. 'They are too few to be a threat. The Turks do not mistreat them. But the community will die out. The young are still emigrating, mainly to Brazil. Christians may have been here since the time of the Apostles, but I doubt whether there will be any here at all in twenty years' time.'

I asked what the Antioch imams thought of his activities in their town.

'When I first arrived they came to see me and asked, "What do you believe in?" So I showed them some books in Turkish. One was a hymn book which contained the words "Jesus Son of God". They were scandalised, and half of them left then and there muttering about blasphemy. But two or three imams stayed on for tea and we discussed theology. They accused me of using the wrong gospels and said that only the Gospel of Barnabas was true.'

'The Gospel of Barnabas?'

'It's an apocryphal late-medieval gospel written by a Christian who converted to Islam. The Muslims like it because it says Jesus is a good man and a prophet but not the son of God. I told them that the Gospel of Barnabas was medieval and that its author obviously knew nothing, because he describes Jesus going up to Jerusalem by boat. We argued all day. Since then I've had no real trouble.'

I asked whether he had converted anyone in all the time he had been in the country. He shook his head. 'Not one,' he said, smiling. 'There are only ten Catholic families here, all Maronites who came from Lebanon in the last century. But in the mountains there are many Armenians who have pretended to be Muslims ever since the massacres of 1915. Sometimes they come and get baptised by me, even though I am a Catholic. On their papers they say they are Muslim, but they know – and I know – the real situation.'

As I was leaving I asked Fr. Domenico whether he was lonely living on his own in a foreign country, a representative of what was now thought of as a foreign faith. He shrugged: 'What is loneliness?' he said.

The Buyuk Antakya Oteli is a remarkable example of the provincial Turkish talent for spending large sums of money building a very good hotel, then, in a matter of months, letting it decay into a morass of broken gadgets, leaking geysers and fraying electrics. There are no bulbs in the light sockets, no ballcocks in the lavatories, no water in the taps, no handles on many of the doors.

On returning from Fr. Domenico's, I found a trail of red ants leading into my room, and a small rivulet of water from the flooded cistern snaking out of it in the opposite direction. The red plastic telephone was dead but the cockroach in the defunct shower unit was not. Worst of all, the air conditioner was bellowing hot muggy air into the room with a noise like a marching band. I went back down to Reception to try to get it fixed, and while standing around waiting for help I noticed an envelope in my pigeonhole.

It was from the manager, and contained two bits of bad news. The first was a brief note answering my query about the different ways of getting to the next stop on the way to the Tur Abdin: Urfa, the ancient Edessa. It appeared there was no train and only one bus service: inevitably it left late in the evening and arrived in the early hours of the morning – another night-bus journey. The second item was more ominous. It was a cutting from the English-language *Turkish Daily News* and concerned a PKK raid on a village near Midyat, the principal town of the Tur Abdin. There had been a firefight; two village guards had been killed and five others taken hostage by the Kurdish guerrillas and spirited away to the mountains.

I got out my map and searched for the village. It lay only a couple of miles from the monastery of Mar Gabriel, where I hope to spend much of next week.

HOTEL TURBAN, URFA, 12 AUGUST

The night bus dropped me off at a roundabout on the outskirts of Urfa at 3.00 a.m., and drove off into the night. Disorientated with sleep, it took a few minutes for it to sink in that I was alone, standing in the dark, at a considerable distance from the centre of town. Cursing the weight of the books in my baggage, I wandered through the deserted and dimly lit streets searching for a hotel.

Forty minutes later I arrived outside the Hotel Turban, and rattled like a madman on the door. After a while the owner appeared in his pyjamas. He seemed understandably surprised to see me standing there at four in the morning, hammering on his front door and howling to be admitted. For several minutes he peered warily through the glass, before his curiosity finally got the better of him and he let me in. I filled in a flutter of registration forms, and was admitted to a dingy room lit by a single, naked lightbulb. The room was filthy and contained only a plastic chair and a metal bedstead. But I was long past caring and immediately fell asleep on the bed, fully clothed.

I was woken by the light from the open window six hours later. It was not yet mid-morning, but already it was very hot. Outside, I could hear the tap-tapping of copper engravers at work in the bazaar outside. I shaved in a grimy basin at the top of the stairs, then went out into the glare.

Urfa was a proper Silk Route bazaar-town, straight out of the *Arabian Nights*: a warren of covered alleys loud with a Babel of different tongues – Arabic, Persian, Kurdish, Turoyo, Turkish. Everywhere the air was heavy with thick clouds of kebab-smoke and the smell of grilling meat. Through the shadows, lit intermittently by shafts of sunlight breaking through the skylights, passed a surging crowd of wild, tribal-looking men: lean, hawk-eyed, hard-mouthed Kurdish refugees from Iraq in their baggy pantaloons and cummerbunds; sallow Persian pilgrims from Isfahan in flapping black robes; weatherbeaten *Yuruk* nomads from the mountains above Urfa; stocky Syrian Arabs in full *jelluba* and *keffiyeh*. Herds of fat-tailed sheep wobbled through the medieval arcades. Outside a tea house a party of nomad women, all dressed in different shades of purple calico, were sitting around a silver tray covered with white saucers full of oily vegetable delicacies. Their heads were shrouded under swathes of elaborate turban wraps, but their faces were uncovered and their cheeks were tattooed with crosses and swastika designs. Behind them a cauldron of pilaff steamed on a fire.

Urfa has always been a frontier town, filled with an explosive mix of different nationalities. At the time of John Moschos it lay on the most sensitive frontier in the world, separating the two great powers of late antiquity: Persia and Byzantium. As one of

65

only two legal crossing points from East to West, Edessa – and especially the members of its large merchant class – grew plump on the trade which passed between the pair of hostile empires. From Byzantium the Persians bought gold and manuscript vellum; from Persia the Byzantines purchased Indian spices, Chinese silk and, above all, dark-skinned Asian slave girls. The Imperial treasury became rich from the customs duties – 12.5 per cent – levied on this merchandise, and checks at the border were rigorous. When Apollonius of Tyana, a pagan sage and wonder-worker, returned from a missionary journey to India and the East, he was asked by the Imperial customs officer what he had to declare, and replied: 'Temperance, virtue, justice, chastity, fortitude and industry.' The customs officer had heard all this before. 'Where have you hidden the girls?' he demanded.

Merchants were not the only people to cross the divide. Edessa was one of the great Byzantine university towns, and the scholars it attracted from Persia and beyond led to a rich cross-fertilisation of ideas in its lecture halls. There was a marked influence of Persian and Indian ideas on Edessa's theology, and its theological school became notorious for the dangerous heterodoxy of its teachings. In this cosmopolitan environment the city's most notorious heretic, Bardaisan of Edessa, was able to write an accurate account of the dietary regimes of Hindu priests and Buddhist monks, while Indian stories and legends came to be written down in unexpected new Christian incarnations: it may have been through Edessa that the *Life of the Buddha* passed into Byzantine (and ultimately Western) monastic libraries.

It was not a one-way traffic. There was a School of the Persians in Edessa, and in the sixth century no fewer than three Patriarchs of the Persian-based Nestorian Church were recorded as having spent much of their youth in Edessa studying Greek medicine and philosophy. Built as it was on the philosophical faultline that ran between the Eastern and Western worlds, Edessa became a great crucible fizzing with strange heresies and exotic Gnostic doctrines. One sect, the Elchasiates, believed that two gigantic angels had appeared to their founder, Elchasaios, and told him that Christ was reincarnated century after century, and that each time he was born of a virgin. The angels also instructed Elchasaios that his followers should venerate water as the source of life, and passed on a mystic formula to be used whenever members of the cult were bitten by a mad dog or a snake. To add to the richness of the mix, the Elchasiates observed the ancient Jewish Mosaic laws, circumcising their male children and scrupulously keeping the Sabbath, as well as holding out against new-fangled innovations to the New Testament such as the Letters of St Paul.

More unorthodox still were the Marcionites, who took a rather different attitude to Judaism: they believed that the stern Jehovah of the Old Testament was different from – and indeed was the enemy of – the true, kind, creator-God of the New Testament. If this was so, then, logically, the heroes of the Old Testament were actually villains: all over Edessa Marcionite churches rang with praise of Cain, the Sodomites, Nebuchadnezzar and, above all, the Serpent of the Garden of Eden.

In contrast, the Messalians, bitter enemies of the Marcionites, looked on the Cross as the object of their loathing, and refused to revere Mary as the mother of God. They strongly believed that it was possible to exorcise demons through prayer: if you prayed hard enough, they maintained, the demon would exit from the nose as mucus, or from the mouth as saliva. Once this had happened and the believer had achieved union with the Holy Spirit, he could henceforth do whatever he liked: no amount of sin and debauchery could harm his soul, as it was already part of God. A breakaway group from the Marcionites, the Carpocratians, took this view to an extreme: they maintained that to achieve true freedom the believer must scrupulously ignore the distinction between what is good and what is evil.

Straitlaced clerical visitors to Edessa were horrified to discover that Orthodoxy – true Christianity as understood elsewhere in the Christian world – was regarded by many in Edessa as only one among a considerable number of options available to the inquiring believer, and that the teachings of all these different sects tended to be regarded as equally valid. As in the very early Church of the first century, doctrine was still in a state of continual flux, and no one interpretation of the Christian message and no single set of gospels had yet achieved dominance over any others. Indeed in Edessa in the sixth century the Orthodox were known merely as Palutians, after a beleaguered former bishop of the town. Visitors were appalled: if it were possible to understand Christianity in so many radically different ways in one town, what would happen if these heretical tendencies were to spread across the Empire?

Strange things certainly went on in Edessa. In 578, the year in which John Moschos set off on his travels, a group of prominent Edessans – including the provincial governor – were caught red-handed performing a sacrifice to Zeus. Even worse, many Edessans openly professed themselves Manicheans, members of a cult so weird and inventive – even by local standards – that it was unclear whether Manicheans were heretical Christians, heretical Zoroastrians, Pagan survivals or a completely new religion altogether.

In Edessa it seems that any belief or combination of beliefs was possible – as long as it was inventive, unorthodox, deeply weird and extremely complicated. But what such a flourishing proliferation of different faiths highlights is the fact that it was only by a series of historical accidents – or, if you like, the action of the Holy Spirit – that the broad outlines of our own understanding of Christianity came to be seen as accepted and established, and that Manichean, Marcionite and Gnostic ideas came to be deemed heretical. After all, a theologian as intelligent as St Augustine of Hippo could spend several years as a champion of Manicheism before being won over to what we now regard as more acceptable beliefs. In the uncertain world of early Christianity it does not seem impossible that the Manichees or the Gnostics could have won the day, so that on Sundays we would now read the Gospel of Philip (which emphasises Jesus's lustily red-blooded attachment to Mary Magdalene) and applaud the Serpent of the Garden of Eden. Churches would be dedicated not to 'heretics' like St John Chrysostom but rather to Manichean godlings such as the Great Nous and the Primal Man; reincarnation would be accepted without a second thought, and Messalian mucus-exorcisms would take place every Sunday after evensong.

For months before I set off on this journey, while waiting for my wife to recover from a burst appendix and the succession of operations which followed it, I sat by her hospital bed reading about the bizarre percolation of heresies that once flourished in the Edessan bazaars. But it was only this afternoon, coming out of the bazaar and stumbling by accident across the old Edessa museum, that I was actually able to picture the *milieu* in which this whirligig of strange theologies could flourish. For there in the garden of the museum lay the finely-carved stone images of late antique Edessans who may once have subscribed to some of the heresies that circulated so promiscuously in the city between the first and seventh centuries A.D.

On the left as you entered the sculpture garden stood a figure dressed like a Roman senator, complete but for his missing head. It was an Imperial Roman sculpture the double of which you might expect to see in any archaeological museum from Newcastle to Tunis, from Pergamum to Cologne. Classical superciliousness was expressed in every inch of the man's bearing: one arm hung loose, the other was hitched up to his breast by the fold of his toga; one leg was pushed slightly forward, the shoulders were pulled slightly back. The robes fell easily over a slight but firm physique. The head may have been missing, but the figure's bearing still managed to give the impression of effortless Imperial superiority, the same pose that was adopted by the late Victorians to portray their empire-builders (and whose statues, sometimes similarly headless, now lie tucked into similar corners of museums across India). Who was this toga-wearing plutocrat? A governor posted to the East from his home in Alexandria, Antioch or Byzantium? Some Imperial functionary's ambitious nephew or promising younger son, sent briefly to the Persian frontier before being promoted to a senior position at the Imperial court?

Three feet to the right of the Roman, but representing a world many thousands of miles to the East, stood another male figure, this time in the dress of a Parthian noble: the long flowing shirt and baggy pantaloons, drawn in tight at the ankle, that are still worn with little alteration as the *salvar kemise* of modern Pakistan. Unlike the Roman, this Edessan nobleman was thickly bearded and his hair piled high over his head in a topknot. A sword lay buckled at his waist and he wore a pair of Central Asian ankle boots. The same figure could be seen in a hundred Kushan sculptures across northern India, Afghanistan and Iran; he stood here between the Tigris and the Euphrates, but he would have been equally at home beside the Oxus, or even further to the east, the Yamuna.

Near this Parthian warrior stood a third figure, who represents the typically Edessan synthesis of both the other sculptures. He was also wearing Parthian dress, but his face and hairstyle were Roman: cropped short, with a tightly clipped beard; moreover he did not wear Parthian boots but a pair of Roman sandals. He appeared lost in thought, and held not a sword but a book. He looked bourgeois, educated and highly literate, cross-cultural and probably multilingual. Here then was exactly the sort of character who could have fitted happily into one of those hybrid Edessan cults, their Christian skeleton fleshed out with Indian- or Persian-inspired mystical speculation.

Throughout the rest of the sculpture garden there was a vivid impression of the different cultures that converged at this Imperial crossroads: busts of grand Palmyrene ladies, perhaps courtiers of Zenobia, mysterious and semi-veiled, their identities hidden behind defaced Aramaic inscriptions; Hittite stelae – long lines of bearded men in peaked witches' caps; semi-pagan Seljuk friezes of the Lord of the Beasts; Arabic tombstones; Byzantine hunting mosaics; Roman *putti*; early Christian fonts covered in tangles of lapid vine scrolls.

But perhaps most intriguing of all were those pieces which could have come from any of the great cultures that converged at this point. One sculpture in dark black Hauran basalt showed a magnificently winged female figure, her robes swirling like a Romanesque Christ, as if caught in some divine slipstream. Her navel was visible through her diaphanous robes; one breast was loose, the other covered; there was a terrific impression of forward movement. But her head was missing, and now no one will ever know whether she was a Roman Victory, a Parthian goddess, a Manichean messenger of Darkness or simply a Gnostic archangel.

I slammed the logbook shut.

Night had fallen. I was still sitting in a tea house near the museum; it was hot and muggy, and mosquitoes were whining around the sulphurous yellow lights of the streetlamps. In the background there was the incessant burr of cicadas. Tucking my notes under my arm, I set off back towards the hotel.

On the way I stopped in at the Ulu Jami, which at the time of John Moschos, before its conversion into a mosque, was the cathedral of the Orthodox. Now all that remains of the Byzantine period is an arch, a few fragments of the east wall and the base of the octagonal minaret, once the cathedral tower.

As I was trying to see where the Byzantine masonry ended and the Turkish masonry began, the old blind muezzin came tap-tapping along the path from the prayer hall. Unaware that I was in his way, he brushed past me and, arriving at the door at the base of the minaret, fumbled as he tried to get the right key into the keyhole. Eventually there was a click, and soon I heard the tap-tapping as he wound his way up the stairs.

When he got to the top, the muezzin switched on the microphone a little before he was ready to sing the call to prayer. The sound of his breathless wheezes echoed out over the rooftops of Urfa. Down in the courtyard, under the fir trees, the faithful gathered, several of the old men seating themselves on the upended Byzantine capitals to exchange gossip before going in to pray.

Then the *azan* began: a deep, nasal, forceful sound, echoing out into the blackness of the night: *Allaaaaaaaaah-hu-Akbar!* The words came faster and faster, deeper, louder, more and more resonant, and from all over Urfa people began to stream into the mosque. The call went on for ten minutes, until the prayer hall was full and the courtyard deserted again. The blind muezzin stopped. There was a moment of silence, filled only by the whirring cicadas.

Then the muezzin let out a great heartfelt wheeze of a sigh.

Back at the hotel, I put a call through to the Monastery of Mar Gabriel. By good fortune it was Afrem Budak who answered. Afrem was a layman who had lived in the monastery for many years and assisted the monks. We had corresponded, had friends in common, and most important of all, Afrem spoke fluent English.

I told him I hoped to be with him in three days' time, on Thursday night, the eighteenth. He said the road was open, but warned me to be careful. Apparently since the PKK raid I had read about in the *Turkish Daily News*, the army had been out in force. There should be no problem, he said, as long as I was off the roads by 4 p.m., when the Peshmerga guerrilla units begin coming down from the mountains for the night. Afrem also advised that I take the longer route to the monastery, via Midyat: apparently the short cut via Nisibis is unsafe, being often and easily ambushed.

Unsettled by all this, I went and had a Turkish bath in a subterranean vault next to the hotel. For forty minutes I sat in the steam being pummelled black and blue by a half-naked Turk in a loincloth: my legs were twisted in their sockets, my knuckles cracked and my neck half-dislocated from my torso. It was extremely uncomfortable, but I suppose it did at least succeed in taking my mind off the coming day's journey.

A perfect morning. A storm during the night cleared the air, and it has dawned fresh and cool and clear: a blue sky, a gentle breeze and the whole town looking renewed and refreshed; a faint scent of almond blossom after the rain.

In the early-morning cool I walked through the slowly waking town. At the end of the bazaar, above the eggbox semi-domes of the baths, rose the walls of the ancient citadel, and nestling below these crags, surrounded by a rich thicket of willows, mulberries and cypresses, lay the Fishponds of Abraham, Urfa's most extraordinary survival.

Few of the heresies which flourished in late antique Edessa outlasted the early centuries of the Christian era. Suppressed by the fiercely Orthodox Byzantine Emperors of the late sixth century, then extinguished by the arrival of Islam, a few last embers of Gnostic thought crossed the Mediterranean to reach the southern shores of France in the eleventh century, where they inspired the Cathars – until the Cathars were in turn massacred by the 'crusade' of Simon de Montfort.

Yet some vague memories of these strange cults do linger on in some of the more inaccessible corners of Mesopotamia. In the mountains around the upper Orontes, it is said that the heretical Nusairi Muslims still profess doctrines that derive from the neo-Platonic paganism of late antiquity. Similarly, on the lower Tigris near Baghdad, a secretive sect called the Mandeans claim to be the last followers of John the Baptist, and still practise a religion that represents a dim survival of some early Gnostic sect. There is nothing like that left in Edessa, which is now solidly Sunni Muslim; nevertheless the fishponds do represent a last living link with the city's heterodox past.

The principal pond is a long, brown, rectangular pool fed by its own superabundant spring. Up and down its edge walk tribesmen taking the air with their womenfolk – great walking tents who stagger along in the midday heat, a few steps to the rear of their husbands, smothered under huge flaps of muslin.

On one side of the pool lies an elegant honey-coloured Ottoman mosque from which springs an arcade of delicate arches; on the other is a shady tea garden, surrounded by a screen of tamarisks and lulled by the coo of rock doves and the rhythmic clatter of backgammon pieces. I took a seat and ordered a cup of Turkish coffee; it arrived on a round steel tray accompanied by a saucer of melon seeds and a plate of sweet green grapes. I nibbled the seeds and waited to see what would happen at the ponds.

Every so often one of the tea drinkers would walk up to a boy sitting outside the mosque, buy a packet of herbs from him, and throw a pellet into the pool. Immediately there would be an almost primeval churning of the waters – a horrible convulsion of fin and tail and hungry yellow eyes – as the carp jumped for their food, jaws open, tails flailing.

Close-up, the fish looked like miniature sharks, with slippery brown-gilt scales, great thick bodies and cavernous mouths. They streaked greedily through the water, tails slashing as they leapt to grab the pellet – terrifying the smaller fish, who did their best to swim as far away as they could for fear they might themselves become targets of their larger cousins' appetites. Some of the slower movers were blotchy with bites and the white fungus infections that had taken root in the gashes. Cannibalism is apparently the only danger these fish face, for they are held to be sacred, and believed to be the descendants of fish once loved by Abraham; it is said that anyone who eats them will immediately go blind.

An old imam from the mosque was drinking a glass of tea at a table beside mine. One of his eyes was clouded with a trachoma, and when he smiled he revealed a wide horizon of gum. He invited me to sit, and I asked him about the legend of the creation of the pool.

Father Abraham, said the imam, was born in a cave on the citadel mount, where he lay hidden from its castellan, Nimrod the Hunter. Nimrod nevertheless tracked down Abraham's cradle, and using the two pagan pillars on the acropolis as a catapult, he propelled the baby into a furnace at the bottom of the hill. Luckily the Almighty, realising that his divine plan for mankind was in danger, intervened at this point and promptly turned the furnace into a pool full of carp. The carp, obedient to divine promptings, came together to form a sort of lifeboat. They caught the baby and carried him to the poolside. In his gratitude, Abraham promised that anyone who ate the carp would go blind.

I heard several other versions of the story while in Urfa, most of which tended to contradict each other in the details, but which all agreed on the broad outlines of the tale, one way or another linking Abraham, the citadel, the pond and the carp, with a walk-on part for Nimrod the Hunter. While the Book of Genesis does quite specifically mention Abraham's visit to Haran, only twenty miles from here, quite why Nimrod should turn up in Urfa is a mystery. His brief appearance in the Bible after the Flood in no way links him either to Abraham or to Urfa, yet the imam firmly insisted that it was Nimrod who founded the town, and raised its walls and palace: a bizarre dogleg from both Biblical and Koranic tradition.

But the true history of the fishponds as disentangled by historians is no less bizarre than the versions I heard by the pool. Apparently the ponds may well go back to the era of Abraham, and even the taboo on the consumption of the fish seems to be a remarkable survival from ancient Mesopotamia. For historians are unanimous that the origins of the fishponds are not linked to Islam, nor even to early Christian or Jewish legend. Instead it seems almost certain that they are a relic of one of the most ancient cults in the Middle East, that of the Syrian fertility goddess Attargatis.

The second-century writer Lucian of Samosata, the only reliable ancient source for the goddess's cult, describes the worship of Attargatis as being centred on the adoration of water – naturally enough for a fertility cult that grew up in a desert. In the goddess's temples, statues of mermaids stood on the edge of ponds in which – then as now – swam fish of immense size. The fish were never eaten and were so tame, claimed Lucian, that they came when summoned by name. Attargatis's altar lay in the middle of the lake, in which devotees used to swim and perform erotic ceremonies in honour of the Goddess of Love and Fertility.

When Edessa was converted to Christianity, the new religion

took on much of the colouring of pre-existing pagan cults in the town. The priests of Attargatis used to emasculate themselves; as late as the fifth century A.D. the Christian Bishop of Edessa was still frantically trying to stop his priests from taking knives to their own genitalia. In the same way, astonishingly, the fishponds seem to have succeeded in making the transition from being sacred to an orgiastic pagan fertility cult to being holy to Christianity instead.

In 384 Egeria, the abbess of a Spanish nunnery, arrived in Edessa on her epic pilgrimage to Jerusalem and was invited for a poolside picnic by the bishop. Had she read Lucian's description of the fertility ceremonies performed by the fishponds she might have suspected the bishop's intentions. As it was, clearly ignorant of the ponds' pagan origins, she recounts that they were miraculously created by God and were 'full of fish such as I had never seen before, that is fish of such great size, of such great lustre'.

After the Arab conquest the fishponds continued to attract reverence, but under a new Islamic guise; Islam thus became the third faith to which these fish have been sacred. The name of the religion and the sex of the deity has altered with the centuries, but the fish have remained sacred age after age, culture after culture. It is a quite extraordinary example of continuity despite surface change: as remarkable as finding Egyptians still building pyramids, or a sect of modern Greeks still worshipping at the shrine of Zeus.

In my reading I have found only one reference to these sacred fish ever being eaten. This occurs in the imperious dispatches of the Rev. George Percy Badger, an Anglican missionary who passed through Edessa in 1824 while attempting to persuade the local Christians that what they really wanted to do was to abandon two thousand years of tradition and join the Anglican communion. He was not impressed by Edessa. The Ottoman troops there were 'a cowardly set of poltroons on horseback'; the women 'were excessively ignorant, untidy and not over clean in their persons or habits'; and as elsewhere in the Levant there was a 'severe lack of English clergy ... I had ample opportunity to explain the doctrines and discipline of our church, of which they were profoundly ignorant ... and they seemed pleased when I promised to send them a stock of books on our ritual.' There was not even any rhubarb to be had in the Edessa bazaars, the one thing which recommended Diyarbakir to Badger, for there at least 'Mrs Badger could not resist her home associations' and had made a 'good rhubarb pudding'.

In Edessa Badger visited the fishponds. Dismissing Muslim superstition he commented that: 'the Christians often partake of the forbidden dainty, the fish being easily secured in the streams which flow from the pond through the gardens. They generally cook them with a wine sauce,' notes Badger approvingly, 'and declare them excellent.'

I climbed to the citadel and looked down over Urfa. On every side the hills were brown and parched. It was nearly noon, and beyond the town's limits nothing moved except the shimmering heatwaves and, in the distance, a single spiral of wheeling vultures. But the town itself was a riot of greens, reds and oranges: trees and gardens backing onto flat-topped Turkish houses, with the whole vista broken by the vertical punctuation of a hundred minarets. Some of these were the conventional Turkish pencil-shape, others were more unusual: the Ulu Jami retained its Byzantine octagon, while a square campanile rising above the fishponds with four double-arched horseshoe openings may once also have been the bell tower of an early medieval church.

But there are no functioning churches in Edessa any more. Although legend has it that Edessa was the first town outside Palestine to accept Christianity – according to Eusebius, its King Abgar heard about Jesus from the Edessan Jews and corresponded with Him, accepting the new religion a year before Christ's Passion – there has been no Christian community here since the First World War. For in 1915 the governor began 'deporting' the Armenians: rounding them up in groups, marching them out of town with a 'bodyguard' of Ottoman irregulars, then murdering them in the discreet emptiness of the desert. Fearing this treatment would be extended to the rest of the Christian community, the two thousand remaining Christian families in the town barricaded themselves into their quarter and successfully defended themselves for several weeks. But eventually the Ottoman troops broke through the makeshift defences. Some Christians escaped; a few were spared. More were massacred.

On my way back to the hotel I passed the old Armenian cathedral. Between 1915 and last year it was a fire station; now, as I discovered, it is being converted into a mosque. The altar has been dismantled, leaving the apse empty. A *mihrab* has been punched into the south wall. A new carpet covers the floor; outside lies a pile of old ecclesiastical woodwork destined for firewood. Two labourers in baggy pantaloons were at work on the façade, balanced on a rickety lattice of scaffolding, plastering the decorative stonework over the principal arch. I wondered if they knew the history of the building, so I asked them if it was an old mosque.

'No,' one of the workmen shouted down. 'It's a church.'

'Greek?'

'No,' he said. 'Armenian.'

'Are there any Armenians left in Urfa?'

'No,' he said, smiling broadly and laughing. His friend made a throat-cutting gesture with his trowel.

'They've all gone,' said the first man, smiling.

'Where to?'

The two looked at each other: 'Israel,' said the first man, after a pause. He was grinning from ear to ear.

'I thought Israel was for Jews,' I said.

'Jews, Armenians,' he replied, shrugging his shoulders. 'Same thing.'

The two men went back to work, cackling with laughter as they did so.

A bleak journey: mile after mile of blinding white heat and arid, barren grasslands, blasted flat and colourless by the incessant sun. Occasionally a small stone village clustered on top of a tell. Otherwise the plains were completely uninhabited.

Diyarbakir, a once-famous Silk Route city on the banks of the River Tigris, was announced by nothing more exotic than a ring of belching smokestacks. The old town lies to one side, on a steep hill above the Tigris. It is still ringed by the original Byzantine fortifications built by Julian the Apostate in the austere local black basalt, and their sombre, somehow unnatural darkness gives them a grim and almost diabolic air.

The Byzantines knew Diyarbakir as 'the Black', and it has a history worthy of its sinister fortifications. Between the fourth and seventh centuries it passed back and forth between Byzantine, Persian and Arab armies. Each time it changed hands its inhabitants were massacred or deported. In 502 A.D. it fell to the Persians after the Zoroastrian troops found a group of monks drunk at their posts on the walls; after the subsequent massacre, no fewer than eight thousand dead bodies had to be carried out of the gates.

Today the city retains its bloody reputation. It is now the centre of the Turkish government's ruthless attempt to crush the current Kurdish insurgency, and indeed anyone who speaks out, however moderately, for Kurdish rights. In Istanbul journalists had told me that Diyarbakir crawled with Turkish secret police; apparently in the last four years there have been more than five hundred unsolved murders and 'disappearances' in the town. One correspondent said that shortly after his last visit, the editor of a Diyarbakir newspaper who had given him a slightly outspoken interview had an 'accident', tumbling to his death from the top floor of his newspaper offices; after this the political atmosphere became so tense that local newspapers could only be bought from police stations. No one, said the journalist, dared to speak to him, other than one shopkeeper who whispered the old Turkish proverb: 'May the snake that does not bite me live for a thousand years.'

As we drove, I wondered if my taxi driver would prove equally tongue-tied, so I asked him if things were still as bad as they had been. 'There is no problem,' he replied automatically. 'In Turkey everything is very peaceful.'

As we passed along the black city walls, I noticed a crowd gathering on the other side of the crash-barrier. Armed policemen in flak jackets and sunglasses were jumping out of jeeps and patrol cars and running towards the crowd. I asked the driver what was happening. He pulled in and asked a passer-by, an old Kurd in a dusty pinstripe jacket. The two exchanged anxious words in Kurdish, then he drove on.

'What did he say?'

'Don't worry,' said the driver. 'It's nothing.'

'Something must have happened.'

We pulled up in front of a huge green armoured car that was parked immediately in front of my hotel; from the top of its glossy metallic carapace protruded the proboscis of a heavy machine gun.

'It's nothing,' repeated the driver. 'The police have just shot somebody. Everyone is calm. There is no problem.'

That evening I found my way through back alleys to Diyarbakir's last remaining Armenian church.

In the mid-nineteenth century the town had had one of the largest Armenian communities in Anatolia. Like the Jews of Eastern Europe, the Armenians ran the businesses, stocked the shops and lent the money. Like the East European Jews, their prominence led to resentment and, eventually, to a horrific backlash.

In 1895, during the first round of massacres, 2,500 Armenians were clubbed to death, shut up in their quarter like rabbits in a sealed burrow. When the English clergyman the Rev. W. A. Wigram visited the town in 1913 he reported seeing 'the doors still splintered and patched in the houses which were stormed by the rioters ... and the ghastly bald patch in the midst of the city where the Armenian quarter was razed to the ground and has never been re-erected to this day'. He warned that further massacres were an ever-present danger; and his prophecy was proved horribly accurate only two years later. During the First World War the sadistic Ottoman Governor of Diyarbakir, Dr Reşid Bey, was responsible for some of the very worst atrocities against Christians – both Armenian and Syrian Orthodox – to take place anywhere in the entire Ottoman Empire: men had horse-shoes nailed to their feet; women were gang-raped. One Arab source close to those who carried out the 1915 massacres in Diyarbakir Province estimated the number of murdered Christians across the governorate as 570,000: a high, but not entirely unbelievable, estimate.

Yet despite all this, a handful of Armenians were said still to cling on in the city, and my architectural gazetteer, written in 1987, said that one Armenian church was still functioning. I found the compound easily enough, and was astonished by the size and magnificence of the church: it was inlaid with fine sculptural panels and looked large enough to contain maybe a thousand people. It was only when I looked through the grilles on the window that I realised the church was now a ruin. Holy pictures still decorated the walls; a gilt iconostasis still separated nave from sanctuary; a book stand still rested on the high altar. All that was missing was the roof.

I found a family of Kurdish refugees huddled in the lee of the west porch, cooking a cauldron of soup on an open fire. I asked if they knew what had happened, but they shook their heads and explained that they had only been sheltering there for a few days. They directed me to the door of a house at the back of the compound.

Inside lived two Kurdish brothers, Fesih and Rehman, and in a little annexe to one side, a very old lady called Lucine. Lucine was an Armenian. One of the brothers went to get tea, and I tried to ask the old lady what had happened to the church. She didn't reply. I asked again. It was Fesih who answered.

'It fell in last winter,' he said. 'There was no one left to look after it. A heavy fall of snow brought the roof down.'

'Does she not like to talk about this?' I asked.

'She can't speak,' said Fesih. 'She hasn't said a word for years. Since her husband was killed.'

Lucine smiled absent-mindedly and fingered a cross around her neck. She rearranged her headscarf. Then she walked off.

'Her mind is dead,' said Fesih.

'We look after her now,' said his brother, returning with three glasses of tea. 'We give her food and whatever else she needs.'

'What about her family?'

'They are all dead.'

'And other Armenians?'

'There are none,' said Fesih. 'There used to be thousands of them. Even when I was small there were very many. I remember them streaming out of here every Sunday, led by their priest. But not now. She is the last.'

We talked for twenty minutes, but Fesih would not let me stay to finish my tea.

'You must go now,' he said firmly. 'It is not good to be on the streets of Diyarbakir after nightfall. It's getting dark. You must hurry. Go now.'

Seeing what had happened in the last few months to the Armenian churches of Edessa and Diyarbakir – one in the process of being converted into a mosque, the other collapsing into a state of roofless ruination – reminded me of my first encounter with the increasingly rapid disappearance of Turkey's Armenian heritage.

In the summer of 1987, a year after following Marco Polo's route from Jerusalem to Xanadu, I returned to eastern Turkey to fill out my notes on the region, before setting about writing a book on the journey. The previous year I had spent a happy afternoon in Sivas, admiring the old Seljuk colleges there, and had noticed that in front of the Shifaye Medresse there lay a most unusual graveyard where tombstones inscribed in Ottoman Turkish, Armenian and Greek were all jostled together side by side.

On reflection I decided it must actually have been a lapidarium, or sculpture garden, rather than an ecumenical graveyard, for at no period have Muslims and Christians ever been buried side by side. But whatever it was, when I returned the following year the Armenian stones had all disappeared. The removal of perhaps fifteen heavy slabs and memorials would have been a considerable operation, and it had clearly taken place very recently, for the grass was still depressed and discoloured where they had rested; but when I asked the custodian where they had gone, he resolutely denied that any such stones had ever existed. I could probably have persuaded myself that I was mistaken and that the stones were my own invention, had I not actually written quite full descriptions of them in my notebooks the previous year. It was all very strange.

A week later I left Sivas and went to see a cousin who was working as an agricultural engineer in Erzerum, attempting to reintroduce silk farming to the region. Over dinner one night I happened to mention what I had seen, whereupon my cousin said that he had had a similar experience himself only the previous month. He told me that for four years he had been in the habit of taking an annual fishing holiday in the village of Maydanlar in the hills to the north of Tortum. On previous occasions he had admired a magnificent collection of early medieval Armenian cross-stones (known as *khatchkars*) which lay piled up near the village well; but this year the stones had all vanished. When he asked the villagers what had happened to them they became visibly nervous and would not tell him; it was only when he was alone with one old man that he learned what he believed to be the real story. Government officials from Erzerum had come through the village the previous month; they had asked the villagers for the whereabouts of any Armenian antiquities, and then proceeded to smash the stones up. Afterwards they had carefully removed the rubble.

I had heard other similar stories of the mysterious disappearance of Armenian remains, and the following year, working as a journalist on the *Independent*, I was able to investigate the subject in some detail. The trail led from the Armenian community in Paris, through Anatolia, to the library of the Armenian community in

Jerusalem. By the end I had amassed a body of evidence which showed the alarming speed at which the beautiful, ancient and architecturally important Armenian churches of Anatolia were simply vanishing from the face of the earth.

An incomplete inventory of actively used Armenian churches compiled by the Armenian Patriarchate of Constantinople in 1914, immediately before the genocide, recorded 210 Armenian monasteries, seven hundred monastic churches and 1,639 parish churches, a total of 2,549 ecclesiastical buildings. A 1974 survey of the 913 buildings whose locations were still known found that 464 had completely disappeared, 252 were in ruins and only 197 remained in any sort of sound condition. Since then there had been several new discoveries, but the condition of most of the others had continued to deteriorate dramatically. Many still standing in 1974 had begun to crumble, while some extremely beautiful buildings had collapsed and completely disappeared.

There was nothing very sinister in the cause of the condition of many of the buildings. Some had been damaged by earthquakes; and the explosion of Turkey's population had caused a demand for building materials which the churches readily supplied; others had been fatally undermined by Turkish peasants digging for 'Armenian gold', the legendary El Dorado of riches supposedly buried by the Armenians before they were 'deported' in 1915.

Nevertheless it was clear that the Turkish antiquity authorities had not exactly gone out of their way to stop the Armenian monuments from falling into decay. During the 1980s numerous Seljuk and Ottoman mosques and caravanserais had been restored and consolidated, but this treatment had not been extended to one single Armenian church. The Armenian monastery on the island of Aghtamar in Lake Van, arguably the most famous monument in eastern Anatolia, had belatedly been given a guardian, but this had not stopped the building's decay: five of the main sculptures – including the famous image of Adam and Eve – had been defaced since the guardian's appointment, and there had been no attempt to consolidate the building in any way. One British architectural historian I talked to maintained that there was a 'systematic bias' in what the Turks restored or preserved.

Moreover it was clear that academics – both Turkish and foreign – were strongly discouraged from working on Armenian archaeological sites or writing Armenian history. A British archaeologist (who, like almost everyone I talked to on this subject, begged to remain nameless) told me, 'It is simply not possible to work on the Armenians. Officially they do not exist and have never done so. If you try to get permission to dig an Armenian site it will be withheld, and if you go ahead without permission you will be prosecuted.' The truth of this was graphically illustrated in 1975 when the distinguished French art historian J.M. Thierry was arrested while making a plan of an Armenian church near Van. He was taken to police headquarters where he was fiercely interrogated for three days and three nights. He was released on bail and managed to escape the country. In his absence he was sentenced to three months' hard labour.

Fear of this sort of thing severely restricts the investigation of Armenian remains and leads to a kind of selective blindness in those scholars whose professional careers demand that they continue to work in Turkey. In 1965 plans were announced for the building of a huge hydro-electric scheme centred on the Keban dam, near Elazig in the south-east of the country. The artificial lake this created threatened a number of important monuments, and a team of international scholars co-operated in the rescue operation.

Five buildings were of particular importance: a pair of fine Ottoman mosques, a small Syrian Orthodox church, and two Armenian churches, one of which contained exceptional tenth-century frescoes. The rescue operation is recorded in the *Middle East Technical University (Ankara) Keban Project Proceedings*. The report describes how the two mosques were moved stone by stone to a new site. The Syrian Orthodox church was surveyed and excavated. The two Armenian churches were completely ignored. Although the most ancient and perhaps the most interesting of the threatened monuments, they did not even receive a mention in the report. They now lie for ever submerged beneath the waters of the lake.

Those who flout the unspoken rules on Armenian history still find themselves facing almost ludicrously severe penalties. In early December 1986 Hilda Hulya Potuoglu was arrested by the Turkish security police and charged with 'making propaganda with intent to destroy or weaken national feelings'. The prosecutor of the Istanbul State Security deemed that her offence merited severe punishment, and asked for between a seven-and-a-half- and fifteen-year jail sentence. Her crime was to edit the Turkish edition of the *Encyclopaedia Britannica,* in which was included a footnote reading: 'During the Crusades the mountainous regions of Cilicia were under the hegemony of the Armenian Cilician Kingdom.' It would be impossible to find a respectable academic anywhere in the world who could possibly take issue with the historical accuracy of this statement, but in the view of the prosecutor, Potuoglu was guilty of distorting the facts on a politically sensitive issue: the *Britannica* quickly joined the index of forbidden books, along with such other politically dubious publications as *The Times Atlas of World History* and *The National Geographic Atlas of the World.*

During the 1970s and early 1980s it was clear that the censorship of publications dealing with the Armenians had been dramatically stepped up. The reason for this was the rise of ASALA – the Armenian Secret Army for the Liberation of Armenia – which in the early eighties began attracting international attention with a series of terrorist attacks, directed mainly at Turkish diplomats. The resulting publicity succeeded in bringing the issue of the Armenian genocide back onto the political agenda. This culminated in 1987 in the passing of a resolution in the European Parliament which recognised that the refusal of Turkey to acknowledge the Armenian genocide was an 'insurmountable obstacle' to the consideration of its bid to join the European Community.

The Turkish government argued that although some Armenians may have been killed in disturbances or deportations during the First World War, so were many Turks. Moreover, the Turks insisted, there were never very many Armenians in Anatolia in the first place, and the numbers supposedly massacred – around one and a half million – actually exceeded the total Armenian population of the Ottoman Empire. In 1989 the previously classi-

Above The oldest surviving manuscript of
The Spiritual Meadow, Monastery of
Iviron, Mount Athos

Right Byzantine fops watching chariot
racing, Obelisk of Theodosius, the
Hippodrome, Istanbul.

Above The domes and semi-domes of Haghia Sophia, Istanbul.

Right Turkish workmen converting the Armenian cathedral into a mosque, Urfa (Edessa).

Above Fesih, Rehman and Lucine. The last Armenian in Diyarbakir, with her two Kurdish guardians.

Left A monk of the Monastery of Deir el-Zaferan, Tur Abdin, Turkey.

Below The last two monks at the Monastery of Salah, Tur Abdin.

Suriani woman at the fortress church of Ein Wardo.

The Mausoleum, Cyrrhus, Syria, looking out over the olive groves of the Kurd Dagh.

fied Ottoman archives relating to the period were opened up to a select group of Turkish scholars and combed for material to prove the Turkish case. The Turkish Foreign Minister claimed that when the process of declassification is complete, 'allegations of an Armenian massacre will be no more than a matter of political abuse'.

None of this, of course, created a particularly favourable environment for the conservation of the principal legacy left by the Armenians in Turkey, the hundreds of Armenian churches and gravestones which still littered eastern Anatolia. It is probably no coincidence that it was at exactly this time that reports of deliberate Turkish government destruction of Armenian remains began to multiply. The stories were always difficult to corroborate, for what witnesses there were in these remote regions tended to be illiterate Turkish peasants, and after the destruction of a building it is extremely difficult to distinguish what is alleged to be dynamiting from what could well be earthquake damage.

There are however a small number of intriguing incidents which are difficult to explain away. At Osk Vank, for example, the village *kaymakan* (headman) told J. M. Thierry that a government official from Erzerum had come to the village in 1985. The official asked for help in destroying the church, but the *kaymakan* refused, saying it was far too useful: his people used it as a garage, granary, stable and football pitch.

Another case concerns the once magnificent group of churches sitting astride a deep canyon near Khitzkonk, south-east of Kars. In photographs taken at the beginning of the century, five superb churches can be seen. After the massacres the area was closed off to visitors, and was not reopened until the 1960s. When scholars returned, only one church, the eleventh-century rotunda of St Sergius, was still standing; the other four were no more than one or two courses high. Two had been completely levelled and the stones removed. The peasants told of border guards arriving with high explosives. More reliable witness to what had happened was contained in the remaining building: the cupola was untouched, but the side walls had been blown outwards in four places where small charges appeared to have been laid.

Certainly Armenian scholars are convinced that a deliberate campaign is under way to destroy all evidence of the Armenians' long presence in eastern Anatolia. As my friend George Hintlian, curator of the Armenian Museum in Jerusalem, put it: 'You can attribute disappearing churches to earthquakes, robbers, Kurds, Islamic fundamentalists, men from outer space or anything else you care to blame. The end result is exactly the same. Every passing year another Armenian church disappears and for this the Turkish authorities can only be pleased. They have already changed all the Armenian village names in eastern Anatolia; the churches are all we have left. Soon there will be virtually no evidence that the Armenians were ever in Turkey. We will have become a historical myth.'

THE MONASTERY OF MAR GABRIEL, TUR ABDIN, 18 AUGUST

Mas'ud, the driver I had been recommended, turned up at the hotel at seven in the morning.

We left Diyarbakir by the Mardin Gate and drove down into the brilliant green of the river valley. The Tigris, at its lowest in midsummer, was no wider than the Tweed at Berwick. Its banks were marshy with reeds and lined by poplars and cedars; beyond stretched fields of ripe corn. A fisherman on a flat skiff was spearing fish, like the gold figure of Tutankhamen in the Cairo museum; nearby children were wading in the shallows.

A little downstream, a black basalt bridge several hundred yards wide spanned the river. The central piers – built of great blocks of stones each the size of a coffin – were early Byzantine; the outer ones were more delicate, the work of Diyarbakir's Arab conquerors: the fine kufic inscriptions they carved to record their work still decorated the upper registers. I had just got out my camera to take a picture of the bridge, with the grim black bastions of Diyarbakir crowning the hill in the background, when Mas'ud hissed at me to stop: 'The men in the white car are plainclothes security police,' he said.

I looked where he was indicating. A little behind us a white Turkish-made Fiat had pulled in opposite the fishing skiff. The passenger door was open and a burly Turk was standing looking at us. 'They followed us down from the hotel. If you photograph the bridge they may arrest you.'

I was unsure whether Mas'ud was imagining things, but still put the camera away and got back in the car. We drove on; the white car stayed where it was.

The road followed the slowly meandering banks of the Tigris; soon the walls of Diyarbakir slipped out of view behind a curve in the river. We passed a ford where a shepherd was leading a string of long-haired Angora goats over the rushing water; nearby a party of peasants were dressing a vineyard full of young vines. On either bank the land was rich and fertile; above the sky was bright blue, and a light breeze cooled the already intense heat of the sun. It was difficult to imagine that this peaceful, plentiful countryside held any threat to anyone.

Then, turning a corner, we saw a barricade blocking the road in front of us. A group of men in ragged khaki uniforms, some topped with chequered *keffiyehs*, stood behind a line of petrol cans. Some held pistols, others snub-nosed sub-machine guns; a few held assault rifles.

'Police?' I asked.

'*Inshallah*, village guards,' said Mas'ud, slowing down. 'Just hope it's not PKK. You can't tell at this distance. Either way, hide that notebook.'

We slowed down. The men walked towards us, guns levelled. They were village guards. The leader exchanged a few words with Mas'ud and waved us through without checking our documents. But at a second checkpoint a few miles later we were not so lucky. The commando at the barricade indicated that we should pull in. We did as we were instructed and parked beside a large single-storeyed building.

The building had once been a police station but had now been taken over by the army. Troops were milling around in full camou-flage. To one side, in front of a fortified sandbag emplacement, stood a six-wheeled Russian armoured personnel carrier; on the other were two light tanks and four or five Land-Rovers with their canvas back-covers removed and heavy machine guns mounted over the cabins.

The commando took our documents – Mas'ud's ID and my passport – and left us waiting in a corridor, saying he had to get permission from his superior before we could proceed. After half an hour a telephone rang, and shortly afterwards a group of maybe twenty soldiers jumped into the Land-Rovers and set off at speed. We continued to stand in the corridor.

Eventually we were admitted to a room where an officer was sitting behind a desk. He spoke a little English, told us to sit down, and offered us tea. Then he asked me what I was doing and where I was going. I told him my destination, but following the advice of the journalists in Istanbul, I did not produce my press card, which I kept in my pocket. The officer scribbled down a few details, repeated the advice that we should be off the road by four at the latest, and handed back our documents.

'Be careful,' he said.

We saw what he meant a few miles later. By the side of the road lay the fire-blackened hulk of a car. It had been burned the previous week, said Mas'ud, at a PKK night-time roadblock.

Soon after we passed the skeleton of the car, the road left the Tigris and the landscape began to dry out. The vines disappeared and were replaced by fields of sunflowers; a few coppices filled the valley bottoms. Then they too vanished and we entered a plain of rocky, barren scrub. A convoy of six APCs passed us from the opposite direction. We drove on, passing a succession of road-blocks and more armoured convoys.

Shortly before lunchtime we drove through Mardin, then turned off the main road onto a track; over a hillock, surrounded by silver-grey slopes of olive groves, rose the unmistakable silhouette of the melon-ribbed cupolas of Deir el-Zaferan, the Saffron Mon-astery.

Until the First World War, Deir el-Zaferan was the headquarters of the Syrian Orthodox Church, the ancient Church of Antioch. The Syrian Orthodox split off from the Byzantine mainstream because they refused to accept the theological decisions of the Council of Chalcedon in 451 A.D. The divorce took place, however, along an already established linguistic fault-line, separating the Greek-speaking Byzantines of western Anatolia from those to the east who still spoke Aramaic, the language of Christ. Severely persecuted as heretical Monophysites by the Byzantine Emperors, the Syrian Orthodox Church hierarchy retreated into the inaccessible shelter of the barren hills of the Tur Abdin. There, far from the centres of power, three hundred Syrian Orthodox monasteries successfully maintained the ancient Antiochene liturgies in the original Aramaic. But remoteness led to marginalisation, and the Church steadily dwindled both in numbers and in importance. By the end of the nineteenth century only 200,000 Suriani were left in the Middle East, most of them concentrated around the Patriarchal seat at Deir el-Zaferan.

The twentieth century proved as cataclysmic for the Suriani as it had been for the Armenians. During the First World War death throes of the Ottoman Empire, starvation, deportation and massacre decimated the already dwindling Suriani population. Then, in 1924, Ataturk decapitated the remnants of the community by expelling the Syrian Orthodox Patriarch; he took with him the ancient library of Deir el-Zaferan, and eventually settled with it in Damascus. Finally, in 1978, the Turkish authorities sealed the community's fate by summarily closing the monastery's Aramaic school.

From 200,000 in the last century, the size of the community fell to around seventy thousand by 1920. By 1990 there were barely four thousand Suriani left in the whole region; now there are around nine hundred, plus about a dozen monks and nuns, spread over the five extant monasteries. One village with an astonishing seventeen churches now only has one inhabitant, its elderly priest. In Deir el-Zaferan two monks rattle around in the echoing expanse of sixth-century buildings, more caretakers of a religious relic than fragments of a living monastic community.

Nineteenth-century travellers who visited Deir el-Zaferan often thought it looked more like a fortress than a monastery, and they had a point. Standing under the great ochre battlements, I hammered on the thick, heavily reinforced beaten-metal gate while Mas'ud locked the car. After a few minutes a young monk's bearded face peered suspiciously at us through an arrow-slit. Soon afterwards there was a rattling of bolts and chains and the gate swung open. Abouna Symeon stared at us with amazement.

'You had no trouble getting here?' he said in English.

I described our journey.

'Things are very bad at the moment,' he said. 'We have not had any visitors for many months. No one will come. There is no security in these mountains.'

Abouna Symeon led us up a dark gallery which opened into a wide and shady cloister. In the bright light of the cloister-garth a flat-capped (but barefoot) gardener was watering pots full of geraniums and anemones. To his side rose an astonishing arcaded portico, supported on two deeply cut pilasters rising to a pair of elaborate Corinthian capitals. It was late Roman, yet, astonishingly, it was still employed for its original purpose, and was inhabited by the direct spiritual descendants of the original builders. Here bands of classical acanthus decoration, of a quality equal to the finest Byzantine sculpture surviving in Istanbul, covered sanctuaries in which the Aramaic liturgy was still chanted, unchanged from the day they were built. It was odd to think that these barren and remote hills, now terrorised by troops and guerrillas, and home only to poor and illiterate peasant farmers, were once places of considerable sophistication.

'It is beautiful,' said Abouna Symeon, coming up behind me. 'But for how much longer? Maybe the next time you come sheep will be grazing here.'

'Is that likely?'

'All our people are leaving. One by one our monasteries and our Christian villages are emptying. In the last five years – what? – twenty villages around here have been deserted. Perhaps nine are left; maybe ten. None has more than twenty houses. If the door were open – if the rest of our people could get visas for the West – they would all go tomorrow. No one wants to bring up their children in this atmosphere. They want to go to Holland, Sweden, Belgium, France. Not many years are left for us here.'

We walked through the cloister. At one end sat another monk, a much older man, wearing the characteristic Syrian Orthodox black hood embroidered with thirteen white crosses representing Jesus and his apostles. He was bent over a desk, peering short-sightedly at the page in front of him, and in his hand he held a pen. As we drew near I saw that he was writing in Aramaic with a thick, broad-nibbed pen. I was just about to introduce myself when he looked up.

'You are Mr William?'

'Yes . . .'

'And this is Mr Mas'ud?'

'Yes. How . . . ?'

'The police telephoned from Mardin five minutes ago to see if you had arrived. They said we should phone them when you got here.'

'They followed us from the first checkpoint as far as Mardin,' said Mas'ud. 'Another white car.'

'We were being followed again? Why didn't you tell me?'

Mas'ud shrugged: 'Always they do this.'

As we were speaking the telephone rang again. Symeon went to answer it. Mas'ud and I looked at each other.

'That was the police again,' said Symeon on his return. 'They told us to find out where you are going and to tell them when you leave.'

'You must see the monastery and leave quickly,' said the old monk. 'We don't want the police in here.'

'Anyway, you haven't got much time if you are to get to Mar Gabriel by nightfall,' said Symeon. 'For your own sake you must hurry.'

We left the old monk at his writing desk and Symeon took us down some stairs into the darkness of a vaulted undercroft. It was built of huge quoins with a stone roof, and constructed without mortar. Inside it was hot and damp. We stood in silence, waiting for our eyes to adjust to the semi-darkness.

'This was built about 1,000 B.C.,' said Symeon. 'There was a pagan sun temple here before the monastery. Then when Christianity...' He broke off suddenly. 'Listen,' he said. 'That banging. Can you hear?'

In the dark of the crypt we listened to a distant clash of metal against metal.

'It's the front gate again,' said Symeon. 'But who can it be?'

We climbed the stairs and Symeon sent the gardener off to see who had come. We were now standing next to a great Roman doorway, above which was sculpted an equal-armed Byzantine cross, set in a classical laurel wreath which in turn rested on a pair of confronted dolphins.

'What's this?' I asked.

'In the sixth century it used to be the medical school. It was famous even in Constantinople. Later it became a mortuary. We call it the House of Saints.'

He took us inside. In the middle of the room, a ribbed dome rose from a rectangle of squinches. The walls were lined with an arcade of blind arches, each niche forming a separate burial chamber.

'All the Patriarchs and all our fathers are buried in here,' said Symeon. 'It is said the monastery contains the bones of seventeen thousand saints.'

He led us through a rectangular Roman doorway into the small, square monastery church. Every architectural element was decorated with an almost baroque richness of late antique sculpture: over the omega-shaped sanctuary arch, friezes of animals tumbled amid bucolic vine scrolls and palmettes; feathery volutes of wind-blown acanthus wound their way from the capitals to the voussoirs of the arches, and thence down exuberant and richly carved pilaster strips. The church was sixth-century, yet the architectural tradition from which it grew was far older: the same decorative vocabulary could be seen on Roman monuments two hundred years earlier at Ba'albek and Leptis Magna. At the time of its construction, this sculpture must have appeared not just astonishingly rich; it must also have seemed deliberately conservative, even nostalgic, a deliberate attempt at recalling the grand old Imperial traditions during a time of corruption and decline.

At this point the barefoot gardener reappeared with the new visitors. They were three men, all Turks, dressed in casual holiday clothes: T-shirts, slacks and trainers. They ignored us and began looking around the cloister, making a great show of examining the pot plants and the architecture. It was only when the back pockets of all three men simultaneously burst into crackles of static from hidden walkie-talkies that what was already obvious to Mas'ud and Abouna Symeon became clear to me: the men were plainclothes security police.

A few minutes later, I was still looking at the extraordinary sculpture in the church when the old monk, Abouna Abraham, appeared at the door. He seemed anxious and began nervously turning off the lights, indicating as politely as he could that my visit should be drawing to a close. Abouna Symeon, however, was determined not to be intimidated by this latest batch of uninvited visitors, and asked me upstairs to see the rooms of the old Patriarchs. I followed him up the steps onto the roof terrace.

'Look!' said Symeon. 'On the top of the ridge. Do you see: the ruins of five more monasteries.'

I looked up to where he was pointing. On the rim of the crags high above Deir el-Zaferan rose the jagged silhouette of several lines of ruins.

'On the left, do you see that cave? That's the Monastery of St Mary of the Waterfall. And those ruins? That's the monastery of St Jacob. Next to it, that's St Azozoyel. Then those cells: that's St Joseph, and the last one – another St Jacob's.'

'So many monasteries . . .'

'Two hundred years ago there were seven hundred monks on this mountain. The community has survived so long – survived the Byzantines, the Persians, the Arabs, Tamurlane, the Ottomans. Now there are just the two of us left.'

'Do you think you'll be the last?'

'God alone knows,' said Symeon, leading me over to the other side of the terrace. 'But I certainly hope I'll outlive Fr. Abraham.'

From the battlements we looked south, over the olive-covered hillsides, past the monastic vineyard and on down to the flat plains of Mesopotamia. We stood in silence.

'It's very lovely, isn't it?' said Symeon. 'When I went abroad to do my studies it was this view I always remembered when I thought of home: these vineyards stretching away into the distance.'

'Does the monastery make its own wine?'

'The fundamentalists don't like us doing it. In Dereici village ten miles from here they shot a Christian winemaker. After that most of the village vintners abandoned their vines. But that's not why we stopped. The old monk who used to superintend the vintage died six years ago. Now the grapes are too small and bitter for wine. They're a lot of work and there are simply not enough Christians left in the villages to help us harvest and dress the vines properly. Even the man who is looking after them now is off to Germany next month. His relatives are all there already, and his visa has finally come through.'

'Is the exodus speeding up?' I asked.

'Certainly,' he said. 'It's partly economic. Life is hard here at the best of times, and the stories of the wages and social welfare payments they get in Sweden and Germany have got around by now. But our people also have political problems. I can't ever remember things being as bad as they are at present. Our people are caught in the crossfire between the government and the PKK. And now there is the Hezbollah too.'

'Here? I thought the Hezbollah were in Lebanon.'

'They've just set up here. The authorities seem to tolerate them as a counterweight to the PKK. They help the government in many ways, but of course they hate the Christians. Three or four months ago they kidnapped a monk in Idil district. He was on his way to officiate at a wedding when two gunmen in a car stopped the minibus he was on and ordered him out. They buried him up to his neck, and later hung him upside down in chains. They kept him for two weeks, until a ransom was paid.

'Sometimes the Hezbollah kidnap Christian girls from remote farms and villages and force them to marry Muslims. They say they are saving their souls; it happened to four girls last year. Another Hezbollah unit has taken over Mar Bobo, a Christian village near here: about ten or fifteen gunmen live there now. They've seized the roof of the church as their strongpoint, and they make the Christian women wear veils. They say we should go back to Europe where Christians come from, as if we were all French or German, as if our ancestors weren't here for centuries before the first Muslim settled here. Now our people live in fear. Anything can happen to them.'

'Can't you tell the police?'

'If anyone did the Hezbollah would kill the family . . . Wait: look!'

Fr. Symeon pointed to a dust cloud now rising on the track from Mardin.

'More visitors.'

'It's the army,' said Symeon. 'Two Land-Rovers.'

Below us, Mas'ud had also spotted them and was rushing over to his car.

'What's he doing?' I asked.

'I think he's turning his tape machine off. It was playing a Kurdish nationalist song. The soldiers might have arrested him if they heard it.'

The Land-Rovers pulled to a halt by the monastery walls, and armed soldiers began to pour out, some carrying heavy machine guns.

'My God,' said Symeon. 'Is it war?'

But the soldiers did not enter the monastery. Instead they fanned out into the olive groves, jumping over the fence. One soldier kicked down a gate as he passed; another began to throw stones at a pomegranate tree, attempting to dislodge the ripe fruit. Symeon shouted down at them to stop: 'Use the gate! Don't break the fence.'

He turned to me: 'Look at them! Breaking the tree to get at the fruit. Smashing our fencing. This is too much.'

'Is this all because of my visit?'

'I fear so,' said Symeon.

'I'm sorry,' I said. 'I'd better go.'

'You must go anyway. The sun is beginning to go down. You won't get to Mar Gabriel unless you leave now.'

We walked down through the cloister to the car.

'I'm very sorry for all this,' I said.

'Just make sure you tell the outside world what is happening here,' said Symeon. 'Go quickly now. God be with you.'

Mas'ud pulled away. When I looked behind me I could see the short black-robed figure of Symeon gesticulating at an officer, as the soldiers closed in around him.

The shadows were lengthening into a deep blue slur, spreading softly over the ridges and gullies of the Izlo Mountains. In the narrow river valleys shepherds were leading their flocks through rich groves of fig, walnut and pistachio trees. Women were fetching cooking water from roadside pumps; donkeys with bulging pack-saddles were ambling along the road. It was so easy to forget the troubles: only the continuous gauntlet of checkpoints and the occasional shell of an incinerated vehicle lying abandoned by the roadside reminded one of the dangers that the imminent twilight would bring.

We were making good time. It had just passed 4.30 and we were nearing Midyat, the nearest town to Mar Gabriel. In the distance on the left we could see the church towers of the Christian half of the town, flanked on the right by the minarets of the new Muslim quarter. On the edge of Midyat a large checkpoint had been erected, with a strip of sharpened nails laid out across the road like a fakir's bed in a cartoon; behind it stood a slalom of oil cans. A line of bored soldiers were sitting in the shade, watching the cars zigzag through the obstacles. We were three quarters of the way through before one of the men – an officious looking conscript with a shaven head – decided to pull us in.

The man asked for our documents. He looked through my passport, pausing suspiciously at one of my Indian visas as if he had just uncovered conclusive evidence of my Kurdish sympathies. He examined Mas'ud's ID, turning it over with a growing sneer on his face. Then he asked Mas'ud for the documents concerning the car. Mas'ud fumbled around in the glove compartment looking for them. It was clear we were in for trouble.

The conscript chose to take exception to something written on Mas'ud's driving licence, and spent the next forty-five minutes cross-questioning him. I began to look nervously at the sinking sun and the minute hand on my watch. Eventually Mas'ud passed over a large banknote, folded up in his ID card. The man looked at it, and for an awful five seconds I thought he was about to expose Mas'ud's attempt to bribe him. But he slipped it into his pocket without his colleagues seeing, and after complaining about the state of Mas'ud's tyres, let us go. Mas'ud drove away muttering violent Kurdish curses under his breath.

It was now after 5.30. The sun was sinking behind the hills as we headed into the desolate country on the far side of Midyat. The road was now little better than a track; it contained no other traffic and was surrounded by no signs of habitation. There was no noise, no birdsong. It was completely silent; unnervingly so.

It was only when I began to look carefully at the shadowy country through which we were passing that I realised what it was that was so unsettling about it. It was not just barren: it had been deliberately laid waste. The olive groves on the upper slopes were not naturally so twisted and gnarled: someone had actually burned them, so that their skeletons formed a charred and jagged silhouette on the skyline. It was like a Paul Nash picture of Arras or Ypres in 1916. We were passing through scorched earth.

'The soldiers have done this,' said Mas'ud.

'Why?'

'If they think the PKK are using trees or buildings for cover, the army burns them. It's partly to hurt the guerrillas, partly to punish the local people for allowing the PKK to use their land. Further east, around Hakkari, whole districts have been laid waste. Many villages have been destroyed.'

Eventually we rose over the crest of a low hill. There was just enough light to distinguish ahead of us the crenellated ghost of Mar Gabriel's monastery. The huddled buildings stood alone and exposed on a bare and stony hillside, surrounded by a high wall; as we drew near the rising moon silhouetted the cupolas and spires of the churches, and illuminated a tall tower to one side.

A moonwashed gateway rose out of the gloom; and from beyond

came the faint but comforting sound of monastic chant. A porter opened the narrow wicket, and as we unloaded our baggage from the car, the monks and nuns began to stream out of vespers. In the lead was the Archbishop; and a little behind him, dressed in a blazer, was a layman. He came up and introduced himself. It was Afrem Budak, to whom I had talked on the telephone. He was welcoming, but clearly also a little angry.

'You should have been here at least an hour ago,' he said quietly, shaking his head. He took my rucksack. 'The risks you take yourself are your business. But you could have got us all into trouble if something had happened to you.'

THE MONASTERY OF MAR GABRIEL, 23 AUGUST

I am sitting outside my cell, under a vine trellis. For the first time I am sleeping in a monastery which John Moschos could have stayed in, hearing the same fifth-century chant sung under the same mosaics. Facing me is the south wall of what is probably the oldest functioning church in Anatolia. It was built by the Emperor Anastasius in 512: before Haghia Sophia, before Ravenna, before Mount Sinai; it was already eighty years old by the time St Augustine landed at Thanet to bring Christianity to Anglo-Saxon England. Yet some parts of the monastery date back even earlier, to the abbey's original foundation in 397 A.D.

There is only a handful of churches anywhere in the world this old. It is incredible that it has survived at all, but that it has survived intact and still practising when Persians, Arabs, Mongol and Timurid hordes have all come and gone, Constantinople has fallen to the Turks and Asia Minor has been completely cleared of Greeks – this is little short of a miracle.

One of the monks, Brother Yacoub, has just dropped by, and handed me a bunch of grapes freshly picked from the trellis. He is now standing behind me, watching me write. After years of visiting ruined churches across the length of Anatolia, finding these monks wearing almost identical robes to those John Moschos may himself have worn, still inhabiting a building of this antiquity, feels almost as odd as stumbling across a long-lost party of Roman legionaries guarding some remote watchtower on Hadrian's Wall.

I had had my first unforgettable glimpse of the interior of the churches and buildings of Mar Gabriel on the night of my arrival. After our baggage was brought in, the monastery gate was locked and bolted behind us. I ate supper with the monks in their ancient refectory and afterwards drank Turkish coffee in the cool of a raised roof terrace near the Archbishop's rooms. By nine o'clock the monks were beginning to return to their cells, and Yacoub, a gentle novice of my own age, offered to show me around before I retired for the night.

Yacoub led the way, holding a storm lantern aloft like a figure in a Pre-Raphaelite painting. The electricity supply had failed some time before, a common occurrence, explained my guide, due sometimes to 'load shedding' by the electricity company, and sometimes to the PKK's irritating habit of blowing up the region's generating stations. I followed Yacoub down a wide flight of stairs, along a vaulted corridor and into the thick, inky blackness of the crypt. In the flickering light of the lantern, shadows danced along an arcade of arches.

'This is the Cemetery of the Martyrs,' said Yacoub. 'During the Gulf War this was our bomb shelter. On the floor there: see that capping stone? That's where Mar Gabriel's arm is buried.'

'What happened to the rest of him?' I asked.

'I'm not entirely sure,' said Yacoub. 'In the fifth and sixth centuries our monastery used to fight many battles with the local villagers for the remains of our more saintly fathers. Sometimes monks were killed trying to defend our stock of relics.'

'And you think maybe the villagers got the rest of Mar Gabriel?'

'Maybe. Or perhaps one of the monks hid the rest of the body and took the secret of its resting place with him to the grave.'

'Do the villagers still take an interest in your relics?' I asked.

'Certainly,' said Yacoub. 'And not just the Christians: we get Muslims and even Yezidis [Devil-propitiators] coming here to pray to our saints. Many of the Muslims in this region are descended from Suriani Christians who converted to Islam centuries ago. They go to the mosque, and listen to the imams – but if ever they are in real trouble they still come here.'

Yacoub bent down with the lantern and pointed to a small aperture below the capping stone of the grave. 'You see here? This is where the villagers come and take the dust of the saint.'

'What do they do with it?'

'It has many uses,' said Yacoub. 'They keep it in their houses to get rid of demons, they give it to their animals and their children to keep them healthy during epidemics . . .'

'They actually eat the dust?'

'Of course. It is pure and full of blessings.'

'What sort of blessings?'

'If ever they dig a new well, for example, they place some of the dust of the saint in it so that the water will remain pure for ever.'

I told Yacoub that in Istanbul I had seen barren women come to a shrine of St George if they wanted children. Did the same happen here?

'Mar Gabriel is good for sickness and demons only,' replied Yacoub. 'If they want children they go upstairs.'

'Upstairs?'

'To the Shrine of St John the Arab. Come, I'll show you.'

Yacoub led the way out of the crypt. At the top of the stairs, in a niche covered by a close-fitting arch of dark basalt, stood a small plinth, similar to the one downstairs.

'This is his tomb,' said Yacoub. 'Or rather it is the tomb of his torso.'

'The villagers have been at your bones again?'

'No. The nuns this time.'

'The nuns?'

102

'Yes,' said Yacoub. 'They are in charge of the tomb, and they keep St John's skull in their quarters.'

'What on earth do they do with it?'

'When the local women come, the nuns fill a bowl of water and place it for an hour on the tomb. Then they take St John's skull and, saying the appropriate prayers, they fill the skull with water, then pour it onto the woman's head. This makes the lady have a baby.'

'And people believe all this?'

'Why not?' said Yacoub. 'The nuns think it never fails.'

Yacoub led me out of the shrine into the starlight outside. 'At the moment, because of the troubles, not so many are coming,' he said. 'But before, in the days of peace, there would be long queues every Sunday: people would come from as far as Diyarbakir, especially after they were married. Now of course it is dangerous to travel. Also the Hezbollah are telling the Muslims that they must not come to a Christian shrine.'

We walked over to the main church and Yacoub opened the great door. Amid the herringbone patterns of the brick vaults, the light of the storm lantern picked out the glittering mosaics with an almost magical brilliance. As we drew nearer, the shapes of crosses, vine scrolls and double-handled amphorae glinted in the dancing flame. With Yacoub still holding his lamp aloft, we passed through the sanctuary and into a small side-chapel. In the back wall were two openings, one near the ceiling, the other at shin height.

'At the end of his life Mar Gabriel walled himself up behind here,' said Yacoub. 'His food was put through that hole at the bottom. If he wanted to take communion he would stick his hand through there at the top.' Yacoub pointed to the upper hole. 'Mar Gabriel was a great ascetic,' he said. 'Behind that wall he punished his flesh in order to liberate his soul. Come and see what I mean.'

Before I had time to demur, Yacoub had pushed the lamp through the small lower aperture and wriggled in after it. Left in total darkness, I had no option but to follow. Lying flat on my back and pulling in my stomach, I found I could just fit through the hole. Yacoub extended a hand and helped me to my feet.

'Look here,' he said, pointing to a narrow slit in the wall.

'Sometimes our Holy Father Mar Gabriel felt he was not being hard enough on himself, that he was sinking into luxury. So he would squeeze into this slit and spend a month standing up.'

'Why?'

'He used to say no slave should sit or lie down in the presence of his master, and that as he was always in the presence of his Lord he should always stand up. At other times, to remind himself of his mortality, he would bury himself in that hole in the corner.'

'That's a bit extreme, isn't it?'

Yacoub was already on the floor, about to wriggle his way back to the church.

'I don't understand what you mean,' he said, before disappearing into the blackness. 'Mar Gabriel was a very great saint. We should all try to follow his example.'

The day at Mar Gabriel starts at 5.15 with the tolling of the monastery bells, announcing the service of matins. After four days enjoying the monks' hospitality but sleeping late, I thought I had better make an appearance. So this morning when the bells began to peal, rather than covering my head with the nearest pillow, I rolled out of bed, dressed by the light of a lantern, then picked my way through the empty courtyard towards the echo of monastic chant.

It was still dark, with only a faint glimmer of dawn on the horizon. In the church the lamps were all lit, casting a dim and flickering light over the early Byzantine mosaics of the choir. I kicked off my shoes by the door and stood at the back of the church. To my right four nuns dressed in black skirts and bodices were prostrating themselves on a reed mat. Ahead of me a file of little boys stood in line, listening to an old monk. He had a long patriarchal beard and stood chanting from a huge hand-written codex laid on a stone lectern to the north of the sanctuary. Each phrase rose to a climax, then sank to a low, almost inaudible conclusion.

Slowly the church began to fill up; soon the line of boys stretched right across the length of the nave. Another monk, Abouna Kyriacos, appeared and walked up to the sanctuary. He started chanting at another lectern, parallel but a little to the south of the other, echoing the old monk's chant: a phrase would be sung by the first monk, then passed over to Kyriacos who would repeat it and send it back again. The chant passed from lectern to lectern, quick-paced syllables of Aramaic slurring into a single elision of sacred song.

By now some of the older boys had also begun to go up to the lecterns and were standing behind the monks, joining in with them. The chant rolled on, as deep and resonant as Gregorian plainsong, but with a more Oriental feel, the strangely elusive monodic modulations reverberating under the rolling Byzantine vaults.

Before long an unseen hand was pulling back the curtains from the sanctuary; a boy holding a smoking thurible rattled its chains. The entire congregation began a long series of prostrations: from their standing position, the worshippers fell to their knees, and lowered their heads to the ground so that all that could be seen from the rear of the church was a line of upturned bottoms. All that distinguished the worship from that which might have taken place in a mosque was that the worshippers crossed and recrossed themselves as they performed their prostrations. This was the way the early Christians prayed, and is exactly the form of worship described by Moschos in *The Spiritual Meadow*. In the sixth century, the Muslims appear to have derived their techniques of worship from existing Christian practice. Islam and the Eastern Christians have retained the original early Christian convention; it is the Western Christians who have broken with sacred tradition.

The white light of dawn was filtering in through the great splayed Byzantine windows in the south wall. Inside the church, the tempo of the chant was now sinking. The curtains closed; silence fell. A last eddy of prostration passed through the congregation. The Archbishop appeared and the boys queued to kiss his cross.

Slowly the church emptied; from outside you could hear the birds stirring in the vine trellising.

However alien and eccentric Eastern asceticism sometimes seems, it had an extraordinary influence on the medieval West; indeed the European monks of the early Middle Ages were merely provincial imitators of the Eastern desert fathers. The monastic ideal came out of Egypt, that of the stylite from Syria. Both forms travelled westwards, stylitism, amazingly enough, getting as far as Trier before being abandoned as impossible in a northern climate, with the aspiring German stylite eventually yielding to pressure from his bishop to come down before he froze to his pillar. It was as clear and unstoppable a one-way traffic, east to west, as the reverse cultural invasion of fast food and satellite television is today.

What has always fascinated me is the extent to which the austere desert fathers were the models and heroes of the Celtic monks on whose exploits I was brought up in Scotland. Like their Byzantine exemplars, the Celtic Culdees deliberately sought out the most wild and deserted places – the isolation of lonely bogs and forests, the bare crags and islands of the Atlantic coast – where they could find the solitude that they believed would lead them to God.

Moreover, despite the difficulties of travel, the links between the monastic world of the Levant and that which grew up in imitation of it in the north of Europe were unexpectedly close. Seventh-century Rome had four resident communities of Oriental monks and many Eastern church fathers travelled 'beyond the Pillars of Hercules' to the extreme west. Theodore, the seventh Archbishop of Canterbury, was a Byzantine from Tarsus who had studied at Antioch and visited Edessa; his surviving Biblical commentaries, written in England, show the extent to which he brought the teaching of the School of Antioch and an awareness of Syriac literature to the far shores of Anglo-Saxon Kent.

Many other more anonymous figures seem to have followed in his footsteps. The 'seven monks of Egypt [who lived] in Disert Uilaig' in the west of Ireland were proudly remembered in manuscripts of the Irish Litany of Saints, along with coracle-fulls of other nameless 'Romani' (i.e. Byzantines) and 'the Cerrui from Armenia'. All these diverse figures seem to have found their way to the most extreme ends of the Celtic fringe, where they were revered for centuries to come: indeed so holy was the reputation of these travelling Byzantines that according to the Irish Litany of Saints even to read their names over a sick man was believed to prevent 'boils, and jaundice and the plague and every other pestilence'.

If an intermittent flow of living monks from east to west was possible, then the flow of inanimate books was greater still. Up to the eighth century, *The Life of St Antony of Egypt* by Athanasius of Alexandria was probably the most read and imitated book in Europe after the Bible, and what was true of manuscripts in general was particularly true of manuscript illumination: that early Irish and Northumbrian gospel books took as their principal model work from the Byzantine east Mediterranean is now beyond question.

At Cambridge I spent my final year specialising in the study of Hiberno-Saxon art, and what above all pushed me on to try and get through to the Tur Abdin was the knowledge of the extent to which the early medieval art of Britain was indebted to the artists of the scriptoria of the monasteries there. For though these monasteries now lie forgotten and half-deserted in an obscure corner of a predominantly Muslim country, some scholars believe that work produced in the Tur Abdin may well once have provided the inspiration for the very first figurative Christian art in Britain.

As I lay on my hard monastic bed, unable to sleep, I turned over in my mind an art historical controversy I had once studied in some detail. The debate revolved around a most intriguing tale.

In the mid-sixteenth century Stephanos, the Catholicos of Armenia, prepared to make a journey which he hoped would change the history of the east Mediterranean. Finding his Patriarchal seat of Echmiadzin surrounded on the east by the resurgent Persian Empire, and on the west by the new Ottoman dynasty, he saw his people facing the same fate as had befallen the Byzantines a century earlier: conquest followed by a bitter subjection under the dusty sandal of Islam. Like the Byzantine Emperor Manuel II

Palaeologus, the Patriarch saw only one hope for his people: that he should travel to Europe, somehow forge an alliance with the West, and so surround the Turkish armies in a Christian pincer movement.

Manuel had travelled to the West in vain: though he had acquiesced to many of the doctrinal demands of the Catholic Church at the Council of Florence, and had even been received with honour by King Henry IV of England at a grand banquet at Eltham on Christmas Day 1400, he came back to Constantinople empty-handed, without securing the dispatch of a single Western knight to defend the eastern frontiers of Christendom. Fifty years later, in 1453, his successor Constantine XI Paleologus died fighting on the walls of Byzantium as the Turks finally burst into what had once been the capital of the Christian world.

Catholicos Stephanos thought he could do better; and he hung his hopes on the support of the Pope, Paul III Farnese. Stephanos's spies had told him that Pope Paul had made it his special pontifical objective to liberate the oppressed churches of the Orient. They also told him that the Pope had a special interest in the study of scripture, and that he had called a council of scholars to establish once and for all the authentic text of the Bible. Stephanos knew that if he was to succeed in his mission he would have to establish a personal rapport with the Pope, and for this reason he cast around for a suitable present for the Roman Pontiff. Eventually his advisers hit upon a brilliant idea.

Someone in Echmiadzin had heard that in the libraries of the monasteries of the Tur Abdin there lay an astonishing collection of early Christian gospel manuscripts. One of these was a copy of the *Diatessaron*, a very early and very unusual gospel harmony – the four canonical gospels united into a single life of Christ – originally composed by the priest Tatian in the early second century A.D. For a century or so the *Diatessaron* had been the standard New Testament text in use in the Church of Antioch, but as copies of the original gospels became more widely available, it slipped out of common use and eventually came to be seen as a heretical text. At some stage it seems to have been ordered that manuscripts of Tatian's work were to be destroyed, and only in the obscure recesses of a few remote monastic libraries did copies of the *Diatessaron* survive.

Stephanos sent an envoy hundreds of miles south from the Caucasus to Mesopotamia to locate one of these last *Diatessaron* manuscripts. When eventually one was found, it was agreed that a local scribe, a Syrian Orthodox priest, should copy out the text. It was this copy that was taken to Rome by Stephanos. According to a colophon in the manuscript, the scribe was a native of Hasank-eif, a town on the Tigris, a few miles south of Diyarbakir near Deir el-Zaferan. The overwhelming likelihood is that the original manuscript from which the papal copy was made came from the monastic library of Deir el-Zaferan.

In the event the Catholicos's embassy to the West was a fiasco. Stephanos never saw the Pope, and within a century his people, like the Byzantines before them, had been conquered and their land divided between the Persians and the Turks. The copy of Tatian's *Diatessaron* was never presented to the Holy Father, only getting as far as the office of his secretary. Later it found its way from the Vatican to the Bibliotheca Medicea Laurentiana in Florence.

Four hundred years later, in the winter of 1967, the Danish art historian Carl Nordenfalk was at work in the Laurentian Library when he came across the manuscript and began to browse through its pages. Suddenly he found himself staring at a set of illustrations that made him stop dead in his tracks. Nordenfalk was a specialist in Celtic manuscripts, and he saw immediately that these illustrations in the *Diatessaron* were iconographically identical to those in the first of the great illuminated Celtic gospel books, the Book of Durrow. The *Diatessaron* pictures also had a close relationship with a slightly later Celtic manuscript, the Gospels of St Willibrord.

In the Book of Durrow each gospel is preceded by a whole-page illustration showing the sacred symbol of the Evangelist who wrote the book (in this early case, a man to represent St Matthew, an eagle for St Mark, a bull for St Luke and a lion for St John). Most scholars would accept that these paintings in the Book of Durrow, probably executed in the last years of the sixth century A.D., are the first figurative paintings in British art.

Although the style of the *Diatessaron* and the two Celtic Gospel Books are very different — as you would expect from two manuscripts drawn centuries apart — the poses of the symbols, the angles at which they were drawn and the attitudes they strike are identical with each other, and totally different to anything else in Christian iconography. Moreover, both sets of manuscripts open with nearly identical full-page illuminations showing a double-armed cross embedded in a weave of intricate interlace. The same pattern also found its way onto a Pictish cross-slab, the Rosemarkie Stone, which still lies on the Beauly Firth, a few miles north-east of Inverness.

It took several months of intense study before Nordenfalk felt confident that he had worked out how an obscure mid-sixteenth-century copy of a manuscript from eastern Turkey could have such a close relationship with a pair of Celtic gospel books which were probably illustrated on the isle of Iona, off the distant west coast of Scotland, some eight centuries earlier.

Nordenfalk's thesis was that the illustrations of the Book of Durrow were based on an earlier copy of the *Diatessaron* which had somehow reached Iona from the Levant in the early Middle Ages. He even had a suspect for the carrier of the manuscript from east to west.

In his *History*, the Venerable Bede records that one winter night at the very end of the seventh century, a Frankish galley on its way back from the Holy Land was wrecked off the coast of Iona; a storm had blown the ship around the north coast of Scotland until it came to rest, as fate would have it, on the shores below the island's abbey church. Bede records that on board the vessel was a Gaulish nobleman named Arculph, who dictated a description of the holy places of the Levant to Adamnan, Iona's Abbot. (A copy of the manuscript of Arculph's descriptions, entitled *De Locis Sanctis*, later reached Bede's own scriptorium in Jarrow and became a source of much future Anglo-Saxon comment — both factual and legendary — on the eastern coast of the Mediterranean from Constantinople to Alexandria.) 'It is extremely tempting to assume,' wrote Nordenfalk, 'that [a copy of] the illustrated *Diatessaron* was among the books in Arculph's baggage.'

The realistic portraits in such an Eastern manuscript would have come as a revelation to Celtic monks familiar only with the geometric whorls and trumpet spirals of pagan Celtic art. Nordenfalk proposed, not unreasonably, that the arrival of the *Diatessaron* was the spark which ignited the almost miraculous blaze of Celtic book illumination during the seventh and eighth centuries, a process which culminated in such masterpieces as the Lindisfarne Gospels and the Book of Kells.

In his excitement Nordenfalk went on to make several other, much wilder claims for the Florence *Diatessaron* which were later questioned by rival academics. But the core of his thesis has never been successfully challenged. There can be no doubt that the miniatures and interlace patterns of the Florence *Diatessaron*, a manuscript originally illuminated in a monastic scriptorium somewhere in the Tur Abdin, comes from the same family of manuscripts as those contained within the Book of Durrow and the Gospels of St Willibrord.

Somehow, perhaps in the baggage of a shipwrecked Frankish nobleman, a set of pictures probably originally drawn in a monastery in eastern Turkey came to form the seed from which sprung the first Christian figurative paintings ever drawn in the British Isles. It is a considerable cultural debt, and one that is little known, and certainly unrepaid.

This evening, an hour before vespers, the monks, the novices and the schoolchildren got out the ladders and began the harvest of Mar Gabriel's pistachio trees.

The orchards stood on a ripple of narrow terraces sloping down from the front gate of the monastery. On the lower terraces the grapes were growing black with sweetness and the sheaths of the almonds were near to bursting; but the pistachio trees were so ripe that they would clearly rot if they were not picked that week. So the boys swarmed around the pistachio trees, trying to clamber up into the boughs without using step-ladders, pulling themselves up and swinging over to the ends of the branches. There hung the clusters of green buds which enclosed the soft white nuts. The boys plucked at the trees and threw down the buds to the novices who stood below, holding tin buckets.

As they scrabbled around, the harvesters were chatting to each other in Turoyo, the modern dialect of Aramaic still spoken as the first language of the Suriani. It had a completely different sound to Turkish or Kurdish or any other Anatolian tongue I had ever heard, sounding instead far closer to the guttural elisions of Hebrew or Arabic. Jesus must have sounded much like this when, as a boy, he spoke Aramaic in the carpenter's shop at home or chatted to his friends beside the Sea of Galilee.

After half an hour plucking at the buds, I took a rest and looked on from the edge of the terrace. Afrem came over to join me. He pointed out the burned earth of the slopes of the Izlo Mountains ahead of us, dramatically lit up now in the last light of the sun. 'You see over there?' he said. 'Those were all olive groves. Now they have been burned. It will be years before any trees that are replanted will be ready to harvest.'

'You think there will be a chance to replant them?'

'We have to hope,' he said. 'Without hope we cannot live.'

Yacoub came up and joined us. He put down his bucketful of pistachio buds and sat with his legs dangling over the edge of the terrace.

'We should be thankful,' he said. 'Here they've only burned the trees. Further east, towards Hakkari, they've been clearing all the villages too: seven or eight this year alone. Since the trouble with the PKK began ten years ago they have cleared many Muslim villages, and nearly twenty-five Christian ones.'

Afrem said that a refugee from one of the destroyed Christian villages, a priest, Fr. Tomas Bektaş, was being sheltered by the monastery until he found somewhere to live. He said I should talk to him, and promised to introduce me after dinner.

Afrem kept his promise. After we had all eaten in the monastic refectory – the normal bracing Suriani dinner, a haunch of boiled goat with salty porridge and sticky rice, followed by *pekmez*, a thick slurry of pressed grapes considered the greatest of delicacies in polite Suriani society – the monks withdrew as usual to take coffee on the roof terrace. Fr. Tomas was sitting a little to the side. He was an unremarkable-looking man with a small toothbrush moustache and a nervous tick which made him wink his right eye every few seconds. Afrem had warned me that the clearance of his village had led to Fr. Tomas having a major nervous breakdown from which he had yet to fully recover, and that the priest might not want to talk about what had happened to his village: 'He will get nightmares again,' said Afrem.

In the event, however, Fr. Tomas poured out his heart without hesitation. I sat back on my stool, and the priest talked. 'It was the middle of winter,' he said. 'One day an army officer in a Land-Rover dug his way through the snowdrifts. We gave him tea and then he simply told us that we had twenty days to leave. At first we did not understand what he meant. He said we had all been helping the PKK, that we had been supporting them with food and giving them guns. It was all nonsense, of course: what business do we have with the Kurds?

'The next day I went to the sub-governor in Silopi and pleaded for Hassana, but he would not receive me. His assistant said, "He does not want to speak." So I had to return to my village and tell my people that we had to leave, that there was no choice.

'We all left on the last day, all two hundred of us: thirty-two families in all. My family was the last. I was the priest: I had to make sure they all left safely.

'They came in the evening: five Land-Rovers packed with troops. They did not apologise or give compensation: they simply burned the empty houses and destroyed the gardens. There were no better gardens in Turkey. We had springs and water and earth and flowers and vegetables. The gardens were the livelihood of the village. Now they are barren and destroyed.

'Afterwards some Muslim village guards detained seven Suriani shepherds. They accused them of being Armenian sympathisers of the PKK and tortured them, using molten plastic to brand crosses on their faces.

'I was shocked and became very ill, mourning for my village. My family took me to hospital in Istanbul and I was there for four months. For thirty years I was a priest in that village. How can I start again? With a new congregation somewhere else? I couldn't do it. I cannot forget Hassana.

'Even now I don't feel well about it. My village burned, every house gone, my people dispersed. Some are sheltering here, four more families are at Deir ul-Zaferan; the others have gone to Istanbul. All want to emigrate now. They think there is nothing for them here. They are just waiting for their visas. Not since Ein Wardo has the situation been so desperate for us here.'

I had had my head down, taking notes as Fr. Tomas talked. It was only when I looked up that I saw his shoulders were heaving slightly and tears were streaming down his face. I put my hand gently on his shoulder.

The old priest was crying like an abandoned child.

Later, I asked Afrem what Fr. Tomas had meant when he referred to Ein Wardo.

According to Afrem, at the beginning of the First World War the Suriani saw the Armenians being led away by the Ottoman troops and heard the rumours of what was happening to them. They feared that they would be next, so they made preparations. They bought guns and stored wheat. They chose the most inaccessible of their mountain villages, Ein Wardo, and began to fortify it. They strengthened the walls of the church and secretly prepared barricades to fill the gaps between the houses.

When the Ottomans, backed by Kurd irregulars, began their attacks on the Suriani villages, the then Patriarch gave orders for all the villagers to retreat with their food and weapons to Ein Wardo. For three years the Suriani defended themselves there. Anyone outside the barricades was killed. Nearly every Suriani alive in eastern Turkey today is there because his parents or grandparents took shelter within those walls.

Afrem said that the village still stands, and that one of the defenders is still alive: a priest, ninety-four years old, who had been a child during the siege. He now lives with his son near Midyat. Tomorrow I hope to talk to him.

The Monastery of Mar Gabriel, 24 August

A bad start this morning.

Mas'ud, who has spent the last two days with his cousins in a village near Midyat, was due to return to the monastery early this morning. He did not show up until well after noon. When he did so, he looked white and shaken.

I asked what was wrong. He said that he had been stopped by the security police on his way through Midyat earlier that morning, and subjected to a lengthy interrogation, all on my behalf.

'The police asked me: "Where have you taken the English? Who has he talked to?" They said they had followed you from Ankara to Antakya, then on from Urfa to Diyarbakir, and that they were still watching now. Was that your route? Did you come from Ankara to Antakya to Urfa? You did not tell me that. I said you were just a tourist looking at old buildings, but they said they knew I was lying and that they knew you were a journalist.'

'It's OK,' I said, trying to reassure him. 'I have a press card. The Foreign Ministry must have got in touch with the police here and told them my itinerary. There's no problem.'

'Yes, there is a problem,' said Mas'ud.

'What do you mean?'

'I don't think you understand the situation here,' he said, barely suppressing his anger. 'Last spring I got a call at home. The man on the phone did not say who he was. He just warned me not to take journalists around. Soon after that I lent my car to another driver who wanted to take a foreign correspondent to Hakkari. He left the journalist there. On the way back someone shot the driver and stole my car.'

'The security police?'

Mas'ud shrugged and raised his open palms.

'I'm sorry,' I said lamely, feeling at once guilty and alarmingly out of my depth. 'I should have told you I had a press card. I had no idea you were in that position.'

'I always thought you were a journalist,' said Mas'ud.

'What can I say? I didn't realise your situation. I'm very sorry.'

'Don't be sorry. It's my job. But know you are playing a dangerous game,' he said. 'You don't understand the police here. You think they are like the English policemen we see on the television, the fat man with the blue hat, the little stick in his hand and the old bicycle. They are not like that, not at all like that. If you took my advice you would leave as soon as you can. It's too late to try and cross into Syria today. But tomorrow you must leave. Then I can go back home to my family in Diyarbakir.'

Before I left the Tur Abdin I still wanted to try to interview the old priest from Ein Wardo. An hour later, after Mas'ud had recovered his usual poise, we drove in to Midyat with Brother Yacoub, who had agreed to come and interpret.

We drove in silence through the burned-out landscape, the security I had felt inside the high walls of Mar Gabriel now thoroughly breached by what Mas'ud had said.

'The Archbishop used to make this journey every day,' said Yacoub at one point. 'His office was at the Bishop's House in Midyat. But since the troubles he stays in Mar Gabriel. Now the only people to make this journey are the children. By Turkish law they are obliged to come into the government school during term-time. Of course you know what happened to the truck on the road to Güngören? With the landmine?'

We neared the outskirts of the town and slowly crossed through the checkpoints, then past the sinister plainclothes police manning the crossroads at its centre. They all wore the same regulation dark sunglasses, with M-16 carbines strapped over their shoulders. Following Yacoub's instructions, we drove into the heart of the Midyat bazaar, and finally drew to a halt outside a shabby jeweller's shop.

'This business belongs to the old monk's family,' explained

Yacoub. 'They can tell us whether it would be possible to talk to him.'

Yacoub and I went into the shop; Mas'ud chose to stay outside and guard his car. The owner offered us seats and sent off his two grandsons, one to find out the whereabouts of the old monk, the other for bottles of Pepsi. Then he returned to serving his customers, a pair of elderly ladies upholstered, despite the heat, in velvet dresses with thick white scarves over their heads.

'Can you tell on sight who is Muslim and who is Christian?' I asked Yacoub.

'Only with the old people,' he replied. 'The old Christian ladies wear smaller headscarves which they tie in a particular way. Also they never wear green, the Muslim colour.'

One of the boys came back with the drinks. When Yacoub had taken a gulp, he continued: 'Years ago they say you used to be able to tell what religion someone was just by looking at what they wore: the Christians always had new clothes, while the Kurds had old broken ones.'

'Why was that?'

'In the villages the Christians had the best land; now the Kurdish *agahs* – the tribal chieftains – have just walked in and taken it from them, to distribute among their own people. They steal the crops of the Suriani from under their noses. There is nothing we can do. The government needs the support of the *agahs* if they are to win their fight with the PKK, so they never interfere.'

Yacoub finished his Pepsi and handed the can back to the boy. 'In the towns,' he continued, 'the Christians used to have all the jewellery shops; they were the tailors, shoemakers, leatherworkers. In the old days no Christian craftsman would employ a Muslim. But in the eighties, when most of the young Christians had already emigrated, the shop owners were forced to take on Muslim apprentices. Now those apprentices have opened their own shops. When I was at school fifteen years ago, perhaps 80 per cent of the shops were owned by the Suriani. Now it's less than 20 per cent. We still dominate the jewellery trade, but we are certainly not richer than the Kurds any more. If anything it's the reverse.'

117

Before long the door of the shop opened, and the second grand-son walked in leading a doddering old man in baggy pantaloons. Yacoub greeted him and asked him some questions in Turoyo.

'Is this the old priest?' I asked.

'No,' replied Yacoub. 'This is Bedros, his son.'

'The old man must be pretty ancient.'

'He is. Bedros says his father is very deaf, and quite blind too, but we can certainly try to talk to him.'

We levered the old man into Mas'ud's car and drove through the labyrinth of Midyat's narrow bazaar alleys. Once we were out onto a rubble track in the outskirts, Bedros pointed out the silhouette of a monastery on the skyline, atop a hill overlooking the town.

'He says that this is where he lives,' translated Yacoub. 'It used to be the Monastery of Mar Obil and Mar Abrohom, but now that there are no monks his family looks after the buildings and tries to stop them falling down.'

We drove into the old monastery cloister. Chickens and ducks pecked about the yard; piled up in front of the sculpted doorway leading into one of the two churches was a great mountain of straw. A family of long-haired Angora goats drank water from a disused fountain lying against the nave wall. The monastery had become a farmyard.

Bedros led the way into the house he had built amid what had once been the monastery kitchens. At the back of the living room, fast asleep under a gaudy poster of the Last Supper sat an ancient figure in a black cassock. He was slumped in a wooden chair, his head tilted forward, and over his face was lowered a wide-brimmed Homburg hat. As we walked in, the old man stirred and opened first one eye, then the other. The second eye was clouded blue.

Bedros walked up to the old priest, cupped his hands and bellowed into his father's ear. The old man bellowed back.

'What's he saying?' I asked Yacoub.

Yacoub smiled: 'Abouna Shabo says, "If they are not Christian I will not talk to them." '

Bedros reassured him, and explained what we had come for. An extremely loud Turoyo conversation ensued. Father and son were joined by Bedros's wife, who appeared from the kitchen and joined in the shouting match. At one point the old man lifted his shoe and pointed out to me a hole in its bottom, apparently to indicate that his daughter-in-law was not looking after him to his full satisfaction. But eventually he began to talk of the siege, and as he did so, Yacoub translated.

'It was Mar Hadbashabo who saved us!' shouted the old priest. 'The saint was wearing white clothes and attacking at the front of the Christians, throwing the Muslims back from the barricades of Ein Wardo. At evening time he stood on the church tower. We all saw him, even the Muslims, those sons of unmarried mothers! At first they tried to shoot him, thinking he was a priest, but the bullets went straight through him. Then they thought he was a *djinn*. Only towards the end of the siege, only after three years, did they realise he was a saint.'

'Let's go back to the beginning,' I said. 'What were relations with the Muslims like before the war?'

'They were not good,' said the old man. 'But before the war nobody was ever killed. In those days the Kurds were in the hills and the Christians were near the towns. We lived separately. But we were always fearful of what might happen, so as the war approached we began to sell our animals and buy guns. We had more than three thousand. They were old-fashioned matchlocks, ones that you had to light with a fuse, but they did the job. We melted down all our copper pots to make shot; the monks melted down their plate. We collected together a good stock of wheat. When the war broke out, and the Turks told the Kurds to go and massacre all the Christians, we were ready. By night all the Christian villagers came to Ein Wardo. They came from Midyat, Kefr Salah, Arnas, Bote, Kefr Zeh, Zaz Mzizah, Basa Brin. In the village there were about 160 houses. By the time everyone had gathered there were at least twenty families in every house.'

The old man broke off, turned to his son and began to berate him again.

'What's he saying now?' I asked.

'He's crying "Grapes, grapes," ' said Yacoub, grinning. 'He wants his son to bring him some fruit.'

Bedros's wife was sent off, scowling, to the kitchen. She returned with a huge bunch of ripe grapes. The old man lowered it into his toothless mouth and tore off the bottom three or four. He munched them noisily, and a broad smile spread across his face. When he had finished I asked about the siege.

'We built walls between the houses so that the village looked like a fort,' he continued. 'Then we dug tunnels so that we could go from house to house without getting shot by the Muslims. The strongpoint was the church, and on the roof we had a cannon that we had captured from the Turks in Midyat.

'They came after fourteen days: around twelve thousand Ottoman troops and perhaps thirteen thousand Kurds – irregulars who just wanted to join in the plunder. Any Christian left outside Ein Wardo was killed. Many were too slow and did not make it. In Arnas the Kurds captured thirty-five pretty girls. They locked them into the church, hoping to take them out and rape them one by one. But there was a deep well in the courtyard. All the girls chose to jump in rather than lose their virginity to the Muslims.'

'Did your supplies last for the whole siege?'

'The first summer we were not hungry. But by the middle of the winter things began to be difficult. We ran out of salt and people became ill for the lack of it. One group of about a hundred people tried to escape at night to get some salt from Midyat and Enhil. They were ambushed. Most of them got back, but fifteen people, including one of my brothers, never came back. That winter I lost my sister too. She went outside the barricades to fetch wood. The Muslims were hiding behind rocks. They captured her and cut her throat. That night I found her. Her head was separated from her body. I was twelve years old then.'

The old man's head dropped, and I thought for a minute that he, like Fr. Tomas the previous evening, was going to burst into tears. But after a minute's silence he recovered himself, and I asked if he had fought in the defence of Ein Wardo himself.

'They thought I was too young to hold a gun, but they let me collect stones to drop down the mountain slopes. I did my bit. There was plenty of opportunity. The first year the attack was very strong. Once I remember it was so strong that people ran away from the walls and began to retreat to the church, which was built with four very strong towers that could be held if everything else fell. But the monks, our leaders, threatened to shoot anyone who ran away, and in the end the defences held.

'That winter was very hard. One loaf of bread would go to each family per day, which meant that there was only one piece for each person. Many were wounded, but there was only one doctor; he did what he could, but most of the wounded had to rely on the old men who knew about roots and herbal remedies. But we never gave up. We had heard that the British had landed in Iraq, and we all believed they would come to rescue us. Of course nothing happened, but the hope of relief kept us from despair.'

'The Christians of the West have never done anything for us,' said Bedros, rolling a cigarette with his right hand, and spitting out the spare tobacco with a loud gob into the corner. 'The Turks help other Muslims if they are in trouble in Azerbaijan or in Bosnia, but the Christians of Europe have never shown any feelings for their brothers in the Tur Abdin.'

'The worst hunger was the following year,' continued the old priest, ignoring his son's interruption. 'During the siege no one could grow anything, so supplies were almost exhausted. I remember that second winter we were permanently hungry, and would eat anything: lizards, beetles, even the worms in the ground.

'But the Muslims were also growing hungry, and in 1917 disease – cholera I think – struck their camp. God willed it that we did not get the disease in Ein Wardo; somehow we were spared. The attacks grew less and less and gradually we became brave. At night we began to break out and attack their camp. Once we attacked the Ottoman barracks in Midyat.'

'You can still see the bulletholes,' said Yacoub.

'After three years,' continued Abouna Shabo, swiping at the bluebottles which were trying to settle on his face, 'they despaired of ever conquering us and said that we were being protected by our saints, Mar Gabriel, John the Arab and especially Mar Hadbashabo. Eventually a famous imam, Sheikh Fatullah of Ein Kaf, came to the Muslim army and said he would try to make

121

peace between the two sides. The Muslims asked the Sheikh to say "Give up your guns," but the Sheikh, who was an honourable man, advised us not to surrender all our weapons.

'In the end we handed over three hundred of our guns. The Sheikh gave us his son as a hostage and said we should kill him if the Muslims broke their word. He then went on his donkey to Diyarbakir and took a written order from the Pasha-Commander that the soldiers and the Kurds should leave. I will never forget the sight of the Ottoman army taking down their tents and marching away down the valley towards Midyat.

'We gave the Sheikh back his son, saying we could not bear to kill the son of such a man, even if the Ottomans did break their word. Before the siege there were three Kurdish families living in Ein Wardo. When the fighting began we sent them away, but afterwards we welcomed them back. After that we lived together in peace and had no more trouble from the Muslims.'

'What do you mean, no more trouble?' said Bedros. 'Every day now we have trouble. How many Kurds live in the village now? Today they almost outnumber the Christians in Ein Wardo.'

'After the war, when I was a young man,' said Abouna Shabo, 'we were friends. But then we were in the majority, so they could give us no trouble. Now the Muslims have all the power and it is different. My son is right.'

'They give us very bad trouble,' said Bedros. 'In the last three years ten Christians have been killed in the villages around Ein Wardo. We cannot be friends like this.'

'Could we go and visit Ein Wardo?' I asked.

'It is too late today,' replied Bedros. 'It's not worth it. The Kurdish village guards will give you problems. It's after 3.30 already. Get home. Get behind the monastery walls.'

'These days feel just like those before 1914,' said the old priest, pulling himself slowly out of his chair and making his way, bent-backed, across the room. 'It feels like before a storm. You can see the black clouds, and the first drops are already falling.'

'Do you think there will be another massacre?' I asked.

'How many people are there left to kill?' said Abouna Shabo.

'There will not be a massacre,' said Bedros. 'Just a few killings every year. Priests will be kidnapped. Others will be kicked off their land.'

'All is in vain,' said Abouna Shabo, disappearing through the door. 'The English troops will not come!'

'And even if they did come,' said Bedros, showing us out, 'it would be too late now. We would not be here. How many years are left for us? Three years? Five? Ten?'

'Only God knows,' said the old priest. 'Only God knows.'

After Midyat, driving back through the wooden skeletons of the charred olive groves, Yacoub saw something hanging from a tree.

'Did you see that?' he said suddenly. 'In the branches.'

'What?'

'In the trees back there. I only caught a glimpse. It looked like a body.'

'Shouldn't we go back?'

'No,' said Mas'ud firmly. 'It is very dangerous. We must keep going.'

'Why?'

'If it was a corpse the PKK may still be about. They hang village guards by the roadside as an example to other collaborators. We must not go back.'

Mas'ud pressed his foot on the accelerator and the car lurched forward.

'I have heard of this before,' said Yacoub. 'The PKK stuff the collaborator's mouth with banknotes. It is to show that the village guards are taking Turkish money to betray their own people.'

Back at the monastery, Afrem was waiting for us. We told him what we had seen and he agreed that we were right to have pressed on, saying he would send out a search party in the morning. Then he took me aside.

'Listen, William,' he said. 'I have bad news for you. Soldiers were here all day wanting to speak to you. I told them you had already gone, but they did not believe me and waited for five hours. They left just forty minutes ago. They will come back tomorrow. I think you should leave as early as you can.'

'Don't worry,' I said, smiling. 'I'm going tomorrow.'

'It is for the best,' said Afrem gently.

HOTEL CLIFF, HASSAKE, SYRIA, 26 AUGUST

This morning, by the time I had got up, the monastery search party had already returned. They said that whatever Yacoub had seen the previous night, there was nothing there now. There was no body; the branches were empty. Yacoub, still convinced he had seen a corpse, suggested that the army could have removed it at dawn.

The previous night I had wanted to get out of the Tur Abdin as quickly as I could. But now the absence of a dead body swinging from the tree, and the reassuring clarity of the bright morning light, made me think I had perhaps been exaggerating the dangers, and I decided to try to see Ein Wardo before heading for the Syrian border. Yacoub, however, declined to come, saying the road to Ein Wardo had frequently been mined. It was up to me whether I wanted to risk it, but he was staying in the monastery. Nevertheless Mas'ud agreed to take me there as long as we left straight away. We said our goodbyes, and set off just after eight.

In Midyat, Mas'ud stopped to make enquiries in the bazaar. He had been anxious about landmines, but learned that two tractors had passed down the road from Ein Wardo the day before, and decided it would be safe to risk it. We passed the bullet-marked Ottoman barracks the Ein Wardo defenders had attacked in 1917, and headed off up the track.

As we drove the road climbed, and the narrow green valley grew hilly and arid. In the valley bottoms some narrow strips were still under plough, but the slopes were given over to sheep. At one point we passed a shepherd's stone sheiling and were chased for ten minutes by a huge Anatolian sheepdog with a collar spiked like a medieval instrument of torture. A few minutes after the dog had given up chasing us we rounded a bend in the road, and high above us Ein Wardo came into view.

It was easy to see why the Suriani had chosen it for their last line of defence. The village perched on top of a near-vertical moraine at the end of a valley; its slopes were so steep and the gradient so regular that they resembled a man-made *glacis*. At the top of the slope, a ring of stone houses formed a curtain wall as convincing as that of any Crusader castle. It was a perfect defensive position.

Dominating the village at one end of the slope was the church. At first, from a distance, you could see only the square steeple, topped with an ornamental cupola. But when you climbed the snaking path leading up to the village you were presented with a very different view. The four corners of the church were punctuated by massive thick-walled towers, each bantering upwards to a flat terrace. Each tower was pierced by three circuits of narrow loopholes and arrow-slits. A fortified church, it seemed, was the only kind of defence the Suriani could build in the years before the First World War without provoking the suspicion of the Ottoman authorities. All it lacked were crenellations or battlements at the top of the towers.

Leaving Mas'ud with his car at the entrance to the village, I clambered up the slope over a tumble of ruined houses, many still pitted with bullet or shrapnel holes. Compared with the ruinous look of much of the village, the church was still in a very good state of preservation. A series of outhouses (once perhaps the home of the priest) had collapsed and were now roofless, but the main fortification was still quite intact.

I wandered in, through a series of gatehouses each designed to expose any attacker to the full field of fire from the loopholes and wall-walks above. For an emergency measure, built in secret and disguised as a church, it was really an extremely competent piece of military architecture.

Within, the church was still in use. Lamps and fairy lights were festooned over the chancel arch, and the walls were cluttered with sacred images: icons of Eastern warrior saints; sentimental nineteenth-century oleographs of the Holy Family; brightly coloured textiles showing the Sacred Heart or a selection of weeping Madonnas.

As I sat at the back, a very old hunchbacked woman stumbled in, frantically crossing herself. She walked up to the altar and kissed an icon, then touched a cross painted on the apse wall. Turning back, she saw me and came straight up, chattering excitedly in Turoyo. From her imitation of a Maxim gun, it was clear that she was telling the story of the siege, but without Yacoub to interpret I couldn't understand what she was saying. She seemed unconcerned by my lack of comprehension, and pulling at my sleeve, led me up into the corkscrew staircase of one of the towers, chattering without ceasing as we climbed. From the terrace at the top you could see out over miles and miles of the surrounding hills and valleys, the slopes falling away steeply from the base of the towers.

So overcome was I by the beauty of the view that I did not at first see the bags of mortar and the trowels discreetly hidden in a corner of the roof terrace. It was only then that I noticed what I had missed from below, and what no one in Mar Gabriel had told me. The walls of all the towers had recently been reinforced and strengthened. New mortar had been applied to the walls, and the loopholes had been reconstructed. I felt sure it was more than a renovation. The fortress, the last refuge of the Suriani, was being quietly rebuilt, and was now nearly ready for an emergency.

The Suriani were expecting the worst; and the lessons of 1914 had not been forgotten.

Mas'ud and I drove back to Midyat in high spirits. We had got away with it: we hadn't hit a landmine, hadn't been kidnapped by the PKK, and had avoided being threatened by Kurdish village guards or hauled into a Turkish prison. Now we were finished. I had seen everything I wanted to see. I could get out of the war zone and cross the Syrian border; Mas'ud could return to his family. I had not realised the oppressiveness of the sense of imminent danger until now, when I felt its pall rising from us. It was a wonderful feeling: like coming up for air.

We whooped as we passed the shepherd's sheiling and were again chased by the enormous wolf-dog; we cheered and accelerated away down the bumpy potholed track, throwing up a thick dust-trail into which the slavering beast disappeared. As we crossed a ridge and saw Midyat laid out below us, we talked excitedly about what we would do that night, Mas'ud reeling off the enormous dinner his wife would prepare for him when he returned. He was still detailing the different kinds of Kurdish sweets with which he would end this meal, when an army Land-Rover suddenly pulled out from its hiding place behind a pile of discarded roadbuilding material and blocked the road in front of us. As Mas'ud screeched to a halt, only narrowly avoiding crashing into the Land-Rover's side, three soldiers appeared on top of the gravel and levelled their carbines at us.

We got out with our hands raised. The officer asked for our documents, and taking them from us, read out the details down his walkie-talkie. There was a crackle of static and some instructions. Putting our documents into his top pocket, he told us to get back into our car and follow him. The Land-Rover turned around and the soldiers jumped in, keeping their guns pointed in our direction.

At the crossroads in the town centre, the officer conferred with the plainclothes security police in their dark glasses. Two of them got into a waiting white Fiat and followed behind us. Sandwiched in this way, we were escorted out of town to a barbed-wire enclosure a mile or so on the far side of Midyat. Mas'ud looked accusingly at me, but neither of us spoke. I hid my notebooks under my seat. The officer jumped out and indicated that we should follow him. After a week in the company of the Suriani with their Turkish horror-stories, I half-imagined the Turks within to be preparing their thumbscrews and racks. To my alarm and disgust, I saw that my hands were shaking.

Inside, however, we found to our surprise that the Turkish

army could not have been much more polite had we been visiting dignitaries from Ankara. After a short wait in a corridor, we were escorted to the office of an army Captain. He turned out to be young and educated and bored, and seemed surprised and rather pleased to see us. Speaking in fluent French, he told us to sit down while the officer from the Land-Rover related the circumstances of our arrest and handed over our documents. When he had finished he saluted and left the room. The Captain took out a packet of cigarettes and offered it to us, calling at the same time for tea to be brought. Where was I from, he asked. Scotland? Did I have any Johnnie Walker in the car? He was from Istanbul, he said, and was looking forward to going back home on leave. He had had enough of this barbarous end of the country. He asked whether I had been to Istanbul, and I gabbled away nervously about the beauties of his home city. He briefly asked what I was doing in these parts, and I told him I was writing about Byzantine architecture. After twenty more minutes of general conversation, he dialled a number and spoke briefly to the person who answered. Then he apologised to us for the trouble he had caused us and said we were free to go.

Back in the car, Mas'ud leaned back in his seat and exhaled loudly.

'I don't believe it,' he said.

'If the police have been following us,' I said, 'they certainly didn't tell the army about it.'

'He was so friendly.'

'Let's go,' I said, 'before they change their mind.'

Mas'ud twisted the key in the ignition, turned the car around, and drove forward. He had nearly passed through the gates when from the building behind us there came a series of loud shouts. In the mirror we could see two armed recruits running frantically towards us, shouting for us to stop. I felt a lead weight sink to the pit of my stomach. The soldiers beckoned us back, and Mas'ud slowly reversed the car to the command post. We sat there without getting out, wondering what might be coming. There must have been a call from the secret police: who had I talked to? What had they said? Where were my notes?

Seconds later, the Captain came down the steps and walked over to the car.

'Messieurs,' he said gaily. 'Vous êtes idiots.'

So this was how it was going to be. Our eyes met.

'You've forgotten these,' he said.

In his hand he held my passport and Mas'ud's ID card.

'Bonne chance!' he said, smiling broadly and waving goodbye. 'Visit us again soon! Bon voyage!'

III

THE BARON HOTEL, ALEPPO, SYRIA, 28 AUGUST 1994

The Baron is a legendary place. Everyone from Agatha Christie to Kemal Ataturk has stayed here, while Monsieur T. E. Lawrence's unpaid bill of 8 June 1914 is still displayed in a glass cabinet in the sitting room. Downstairs, the decor, untouched since the 1920s, is so redolent of the Levant between the wars that you can almost hear the swish of flapper-dresses and baggy tropical suits echoing from the now chipped and silent dance-floor.

Despite the chaos of Syria's Ba'athist economy and the decay of many of its towns, the Baron is still, from the outside, rather a magnificent building: a stone-built Ottoman villa with a blind arcade of mock-Mameluke arches giving onto a wide first-floor terrace. At the top of the façade are sculpted the words *Baron's Hotel 1911, Mazloumian Frères*, in French, Armenian and Ottoman Turkish. Inside are high-beamed ceilings and brass chandeliers; a large notice dating from the early years of the French Mandate proclaims that the Baron is 'L'unique hôtel de 1ère classe à Alep: confort parfait, situation unique,' while another of the same period, decorated with a watercolour of Ctesiphon, announces that the Simplon–Orient Express can transport you in 'safety, rapidity and economy' from London to Baghdad in seven days (the original promise of six days, obviously over-optimistic, is crossed out).

Yet for all its charm, it would be dishonest to pretend that the Baron has not seen better days. The rooms – which look as though they haven't been painted since Leonard Woolley stayed here on his way to dig the Ziggurat of Ur in 1922 – are now shabby and unloved, with peeling wallpaper and potholed parquet floors. Moreover the *situation unique* – the shady cypresses, the gardens and bubbling canals which Lawrence writes of in his letters – have long since given way to lines of seedy hard-porn cinemas covered with lurid posters of nearly-naked American girls (this week *The Last Virgin in Las Vegas*) into which crowds of hungry-looking Arab boys pour each evening.

In the streets, jammed bumper-to-bumper, 1940s Pontiacs exhale a thick fog of black exhaust. The pollution wafts into the streetside restaurants and clings to the layers of grease dripping from the grilling doner kebabs. In between the *kebabji* and the blue-movie theatres lie the heavy-engineering shops and garages – *Sarkis Iskenian Caterpillar Parts, A. Sanossian Grinding: Vee Rubber Wambo Superstone* – belonging to the Armenian entrepreneurs who for the last forty years have dominated what is left of the once-vibrant Aleppo economy. If, like Lawrence, you tried to go shooting 'one hundred yards in front of the Baron', today you would be more likely to hit either a Bedu aficionado of the *Emmanuelle* films or some grimy-faced Armenian mechanic than the duck Lawrence was after.

Nevertheless, it is still easy to see why this hotel appealed so much to a former generation of English travellers. At eight this morning I woke up, momentarily confused as to where I was, and looked at the wall beside my bed. There hung an English coaching print and a framed portrait of a black retriever with a pheasant in its mouth emerging from a village stream beside a thatched cottage ('The most useful and adaptable of all the retrievers, with a formidable record of wins at county shows, the black retriever has a strong otter-like tail well suited for swimming'). It was then that the penny dropped. The inexplicably horrible food, the decaying neo-Gothic architecture, the deep baths and the uncomfortable beds: no wonder Lawrence and his contemporaries felt so much at home here – the Baron is the perfect replica of some particularly Spartan English public school, strangely displaced to the deserts of the Middle East.

And yet, despite its best efforts, I feel this place growing on me. I have always loved the fact that in Syria you can still walk on Roman roads that have not been resurfaced since the time of Diocletian, or stand on castle walls that have not been restored since Saladin stormed them. In the same way, perhaps I should be pleased that in the Baron you can sleep in sheets that have not been washed since T. E. Lawrence slept there, and even be bitten by the same colonies of bedbugs that once nibbled the great Ataturk.

As I sit here with a glass of whisky under an endearingly ludicrous picture of two top-hatted English coachmen, the troubles of Mar Gabriel feel a world away. But I must record how I got here from the roadblocks and minefields of the Tur Abdin.

After our arrest in Midyat, Mas'ud and I retraced our footsteps along the heavily guarded main roads to Mardin, and there, within sight of the Byzantine domes and cupolas of the monastery of Deir el-Zaferan, drove steeply downhill into the baking mud-steppe of Mesopotamia. From there we headed east again, along the Syrian border, on the main military road which leads through the plains towards the Iraqi frontier and Baghdad. Twin electrified border fences and a minefield flanked us immediately to the right; beyond stretched the plains of northern Syria. The smooth, wide military road was quite empty but for the occasional Turkish tank rumbling slowly in the opposite direction.

Delayed by our arrest and the interminable gauntlet of army checkpoints, we were in danger of failing to get to the border post before it closed for the day. But Mas'ud drove at breakneck speed, and after less than forty minutes the towers of the border town of Nisibis rose shimmering from the plain ahead. During late antiquity Nisibis passed back and forth between the Byzantines and the Sassanian Persians, finally being surrendered to the Persians in 363 A.D. Yet the town somehow managed to maintain an effervescent intellectual life despite its frontline position and the incessant skirmishes between its Persian garrison and that of the

Byzantine frontier post of Dara, less than forty miles to the west.

For after the Sassanian takeover of the city, Nisibis became the principal centre of Persia's large Nestorian Christian minority. Its university of eight hundred students came to rival that of Edessa. Indeed it was through Nisibis – along with the two other great Nestorian university cities, Jundishapur (near Teheran) and Merv (now in Uzbekistan) – that the Nestorians played an important part in bringing Greek philosophy, science and medicine first to the Persian and thence to the Islamic world. Moreover it was from the Nestorian school of Nisibis – via Moorish Cordoba – that many of the works of Aristotle and Plato eventually reached the new universities of medieval Europe.

As far as the Greeks were concerned, however, the loss of the town remained a continual slight to Byzantine pride; and the fact that it came to shelter a population of Christian heretics only made this worse. As a result the city figures surprisingly prominently in Byzantine letters, and John Moschos tells a story about Nisibis which, for all its piety, gives an intriguingly detailed and convincing picture of bazaar life in a Mesopotamian border town in the sixth century.

The anecdote concerns a Christian woman married to a 'pagan' (presumably Zoroastrian) soldier. The soldier had a small sum of capital which he wanted to invest. But his Christian wife (presumably a Nestorian) persuaded him to give it instead to the poor who waited in front of the five-arched portal of the Nisibis cathedral, promising that the god of the Christians would reward him many times over.

'Three months later, the couple's expenses exceeded their ability to pay. The man said to his wife: "Sister, the god of the Christians has not paid us back, and here we are, in need." In reply, the woman said, "He will repay. Go to where you handed over the money and he will return it right away." So her husband set off to the church at a run. When he came to the spot where he had given the coins to the poor, he went all round the church, expecting to find somebody who would give back to him what was owing. But all he found was the poor, still sitting there. While he was trying to decide which of them to speak to, he saw at his

136

feet on the marble floor one large *miliarision* lying there, one of those which he himself had distributed. Bending down he picked it up and went back to his house. Then he said to his spouse: "Look – I just went to your church, and believe me, woman, I did not see the god of the Christians as you said I would. And he certainly did not give me anything, except this *miliarision* lying where I give fifty away." '

His wife told him to stop complaining and to go off and buy some food with the coin. Later the man reappeared with some bread, a flask of wine and a fresh fish. While his wife was cleaning the fish, she found inside a beautiful stone which she suggested he try to sell.

'He did not know what it was, for he was a simple man. But he took the stone and went to the moneychanger. It was evening, time for the changer to go home, but the soldier said, "Give me what you will," and the other replied, "Take five *miliarisia* for it." Believing that the merchant was making fun of him, the man said, "Would you give that much for it?" But the merchant thought the soldier was being sarcastic, so he said, "Well, take ten *miliarisia* then." Still thinking the merchant was making fun of him, the soldier remained silent, at which the other said, "All right – twenty *miliarisia*." As the soldier again kept silent and made no response, the merchant raised his offer to thirty, then to fifty *miliarisia*. By this time the soldier realised that the stone must be very valuable. Little by little the merchant raised his offer until it reached three hundred large *miliarisia*.'

Almost nothing appears to survive today of late antique Nisibis save the cathedral baptistry, dated by a Greek inscription to 359 A.D. Otherwise, Nisibis's muse has long departed, and as Mas'ud raced through the crowded bazaars, sending barrow-boys and pack-donkeys flying into ditches, there was no sign that the town had ever been more than what it was now: a dusty, flyblown frontier post, crawling with Turkish soldiers and gun-wielding security guards. We reached the crossing point – a tin hut and a coil of barbed wire standing beside a single, enigmatic line of Byzantine pillars – just five minutes before it closed. I embraced Mas'ud, wished him luck, and paid him double the amount we had agreed in Diyarbakir.

The Turkish border guards rifled through my rucksack, sniffing suspiciously at the mosquito repellant but, thankfully, ignoring the notebooks. Finally, at two minutes to three, in the sweltering heat of a Mesopotamian summer afternoon, I crossed the no-man's land into Syria.

Immediately the atmosphere changed. Ten years ago, on my first journey around the Near East, I remember my nervousness at leaving the then peaceable countryside of south-east Turkey for what I conceived to be the sinister terrorist state of Syria. Now the roles are reversed. Syria may still be a one-party police state, but it is a police state that leaves its citizens alone as long as they keep out of politics; certainly it feels like the Garden of Eden compared with the tension on the other side of the border. At the immigration shed, Kurdish and Turoyo were being spoken openly. On the roads there were no checkpoints, no tanks, no armoured personnel carriers and no burned-out car-skeletons. The taxi drivers seemed relaxed and happy to drive at night. No one spoke, in hushed voices, of 'troubles', of emptied villages or relatives who had 'disappeared'.

Indeed, at the Hotel Cliff in Hassake where I spent that first night (the name, disappointingly, turned out to be a reference to the Ottoman Caliph, not an ageing pop star), only the endless ranks of framed portraits of President Asad and his sinister son Basil (recently killed in a high-speed car crash) reminded one that Syria was still a Ba'athist dictatorship with a ubiquitous *mukhabarat* (secret police). The regime's claim to legitimacy still rests on the shaky foundations of a series of East European-style 'elections' that are so openly rigged they have become something of a national joke. I remember a story about them from my last visit. After one particularly dubious poll, a group of Asad's advisers is said to have gone to see the President with the results.

'There is good news, Mr President,' they said. 'You are more popular with the people of Syria than ever before. 99 per cent of the people voted for you. Only 1 per cent abstained. What more could you ask?'

'Just one thing,' Asad is said to have replied. 'Their names and addresses.'

The following morning I wandered around Hassake. Behind a modern gloss of avenues, roundabouts and streetlights lay a warren of mud-walled compounds, a timeless labyrinth that could have been built at virtually any time between the Tower of Babel and Operation Desert Storm.

It was in one of these compounds that I found George Joseph, a cousin of one of the monks at Mar Gabriel. George was a huge man with a thick black beard and an enormous paunch. He was very well educated – had picked up some sort of diploma in London – and now made his money running a taxi service and various dubious-sounding import/export businesses operating over the Iraqi and Turkish borders. When I introduced myself he shouted for tea, and quickly persuaded me to take his taxi to Aleppo. I had been planning to take the bus, at a fraction of the cost, but soon found myself convinced by George that his taxi was the only sensible choice.

While a flunkey went off to fill George's pick-up with petrol, we talked about the history of the old Nestorian university in Nisibis, and I asked whether there were any Nestorians still left in the area.

'There weren't any until the Gulf War,' replied George. 'But in 1991 fifty thousand Nestorian refugees fled here from western Iraq. They saw what had happened to the Kurds, and feared Saddam Hussein would use his poison gas on them next.'

'So where are they now?' I asked.

'Most have got away,' said George. 'Some got visas for the West; others have sneaked across the Turkish border. It is easier to get fake passports and visas in Turkey than here.' He broke into a sly grin. 'Smugglers and fakers are not so active in Syria,' he said. 'You have to be very good – very good indeed – to get away with that sort of business here.'

'And the Nestorians who are left?'

'There are about ten thousand of them, still incarcerated in a refugee camp ten miles from here, towards the Iraqi border. It's a horrible place. They're locked up in a barbed-wire pen with only two thousand devil-worshippers for company.'

'Devil-worshippers?'

'Yezidis,' said George. 'They're an Iraqi sect. Strictly speaking they're actually devil-propitiators, not devil-worshippers. They call Lucifer 'Malik Tawus', the Peacock Angel, and offer sacrifices to keep him happy. They believe Lucifer, the Devil, has been forgiven by God and reinstated as Chief Angel, supervising the day-to-day running of the word's affairs.'

'And how do they get on with the Nestorians?'

'Actually very well,' said George. 'Some people believe that the Yezidis were originally a sort of strange Gnostic offshoot of the Nestorian Church. I don't know whether that is true, but the Yezidi priests and the Christian bishops certainly make a point of visiting each other on their different feast days. '

Either way, I thought, it was a wonderfully exotic idea: respectably robed Nestorian bishops presenting their compliments to the Chief Priest of the devil-worshippers on the occasion of Satan's birthday. As George talked, I could not stop thinking about the extraordinary camp full of Yezidi devil-worshippers and Nestorians, the most ancient heterodox (and, in the eyes of many, heretical) Christian Church still in existence.

The Nestorians had initially disagreed with the Orthodox over the exact nature of Christ's humanity, maintaining that there were two entirely separate persons in the incarnate Christ, one human, the other divine, in opposition to the Orthodox belief that Christ was a single person, at once human *and* divine. Expelled from the Byzantine Empire in the fifth century, the Church had taken root with astonishing speed further to the east. By the seventh century Nestorian archbishops watched over cathedrals as far apart as Bahrain, Kerala, Kashgar, Lhasa and Sigan-Fu in north-west China. By 660 A.D. there were more than twenty Nestorian archbishops east of the Oxus, and Nestorian monasteries in most Chinese cities. Genghis Khan had a Nestorian guardian, and at one point the Mongol Khans very nearly converted to Nestorianism, which might well have made the Church the most powerful religious force in Asia. But instead, by the early years of the twentieth century a series of genocidal reverses had brought the Nestorians to the verge of extinction. This latest sad imprisonment in a wire pen in the desert was only the most recent in a long series of disasters for the Church that had once brought the secret of silk farming to Byzantium, Greek medicine to Islam, and which, most importantly of all, had helped transmit the forgotten philosophy of ancient Athens back to the West.

Separated from the rest of Christendom by their extreme isolation, the Nestorians have preserved many of the traditions of the early Church which have either disappeared altogether elsewhere, or else survived only in the most unrecognisable forms. Their legends – about the Holy Wood of the Tree of Life and the Holy Spices of the Tree of Knowledge – are fragments of fossilised early Christian folklore, while their eucharistic rite, the Anaphora of the Apostles Addai and Mari, is the oldest Christian liturgy still in use anywhere in the world.

Once, browsing in a library in Oxford, I remember stumbling across a rare copy of *The Book of Protection*, a volume of Nestorian charms and spells. It was a strange and wonderful collection of magical formulae which purported to have been handed down from the angels to Adam and thence to King Solomon. The spells the Anathema of the Angel Gabriel for the Evil Eye, the Names on the Ring of King Solomon, the Anathema of Mar Shalita for the Evil Spirit, the Charm for the Cow which is Excited towards her Mistress – gave a vivid picture of an isolated and superstitious mountain people, surrounded by enemies and unknown dangers. They also emphasised the Nestorians' backwardness in the face of the artillery of their enemies – among them was a charm for Binding the Guns and the Engines of War:

> By the Power of the Voice of our Lord which cutteth
> the Flame of the Fire, I bind, expel, anathematise the
> bullets of the engines of war, and the balls of the guns
> of our wicked enemies away from him who beareth this
> charm. By the prayers of the Virgin, the Mother of Fire,
> may the stones which they fling with the machine and

with the guns not be moved, nor heated, nor come
forth from the mouth of our enemies' machines against
the one who beareth these charms, but let our enemy
be as dead as in the midst of the grave . . .

Yet this desperate primitiveness in war was apparently coupled
with an unwise enthusiasm for violent blood feuds with their
neighbours. Alarmed Anglican missionaries who tried to make
contact with the Nestorians in the nineteenth and early twentieth
century reported that they would go into battle against their tribal
enemies led by their bishop, wearing his purple episcopal trousers,
and that their priests would return bearing the severed ears of
their victims. On one occasion a dog-collared Anglican vicar was
invited to lunch by a Nestorian chieftain and had the temerity to
refuse, offering some lame excuses. 'It is my hope that you will
come and stay,' repeated the chieftain. 'If you do I shall be proud
to receive you; if you do not, my honour will make it needful for
me to shoot you.'

I told George how much I wanted to try to get into the camp
and talk to the Nestorian refugees. But even as I was speaking he
shook his head. It was impossible for outsiders to get in or out
of the camp, he said. It was surrounded by barbed wire, and the
only gateway bristled with *mukhabarat*. I would be wasting my
time even to try. The most I would achieve, he said, would be to get
arrested by President Asad's secret police, something he strongly
advised against. 'But you could always try to interview some Nestorians when you get back to England,' he suggested.

'What do you mean?'

'I believe there is a very large Nestorian community in . . . is
there somewhere in London called Ealing?'

'*Ealing?*'

'Yes, I think that's right,' said George. 'It was in Ealing that the
current Nestorian Patriarch was crowned. There should be far
more Nestorians in London than here. Ealing has the largest Nestorian community in Europe.'

Such are the humiliations of the travel writer in the late twentieth century: go to the ends of the earth to search for the most

142

exotic heretics in the world, and you find they have cornered the kebab business at the end of your street in London.

I threw my rucksack into the back of George's pick-up; we drove through the streets of Hassake and out into the cotton fields beyond. It was a bright late-summer day. A strong wind was blowing, and billowing clouds were gusting over the steppe. Unveiled Bedouin women were standing in lines in the fields, picking the white buds with babies strapped to their backs. Their faces were tattooed, and their headdresses were fringed with glinting silver coins. Their dresses were of deep purple velvet, belted at the waist.

We crossed the bridge over the Khabur River, and almost immediately we entered the desert. The road stretched straight ahead, its converging lines bisecting a flat horizon of dry and lifeless sand.

'My father was nearly killed on this road,' said George, breaking the silence.

'How?'

'It's a long story.'

'This is a long drive.'

'Well,' said George, 'in 1929 my father bought sixty thousand acres of desert near Hassake on the Khabur River. Until the Mandate, the area was deserted except for Bedouin. But the French offered land to anyone who would irrigate it and grow crops. My father was a younger son and inherited nothing from his father, so he took on the challenge. It was backbreaking work and he nearly went mad in the heat of the desert. But after five years of hard work, of watering and planting the land, he finally had a very successful harvest and made a big profit: fifty gold pounds. It was more than enough to pay off the money he had borrowed to buy the land. But he had a problem: he did not know how to get the gold from Hassake to Aleppo, as the road used to be famous for its brigands. But he knew it was probably less safe still among the Bedouin in Hassake, so he asked an Armenian driver with an old model-T Ford to take him the next time he went to Aleppo. The day came, and my father put the money under his girdle and set off with the Armenian.

'Halfway along the road, in the early evening, in the middle of the desert, they saw a very old Bedu. He was standing in the road, hitchhiking. My father said, "Poor man, let's pick him up," but the Armenian said he never took in strangers. They drove on, but then they began to feel guilty, for they knew the old man would be stuck in the desert all night. So they went back and picked him up. The Bedu was very grateful; he said, "*Salaam alekum*,' and sat smiling in the back.

'Then ten minutes later the old man pulled out two revolvers. He put one against the neck of my father, the other against the neck of the Armenian, and ordered that they stop the car. My father went mad: he was carrying on him every dinar he had earned for five years. So he begged the Bedu to be honourable and show mercy to two men who had tried to help him. But the Bedu merely sneered and said: "Undress." The Armenian undressed and turned out his pockets, but he had only a small amount of money. So the Bedu pointed a gun at my father and said that now he should undress. My father undressed very, very slowly. The Bedu began to get impatient. He said: "Hurry, hurry." My father took off his jacket, then his shirt, then his vest. "Hurry," said the Bedu. So my father took off his trousers, and as he did so the fifty gold pounds fell out and rolled onto the ground.

'The Bedu could hardly believe his eyes, and he jumped to catch the coins before they rolled off the embankment. As he did so my father kicked him in the face. The Bedu took off – into the hands of the Armenian. The Armenian held him while my father grabbed the guns. There they were in the road in the middle of the desert, two of them in their underpants, all of them scrabbling around trying to kill each other. The Bedu produced a knife, but the Armenian got him into an armlock with one hand and tried to strangle him with the other. All this time my father was punching the Bedu. He had lost all control: he had the strength of a madman. At first it was fear, then it was for revenge.

'After a while the man was overpowered, but not before all three of them were covered with blood. So the Armenian said: "We cannot leave this man here. Tomorrow he will be waiting for us to return, and he'll have forty other tribesmen with him.

144

We must kill him." But before my father had time to answer, the man fell down. He was stone dead.

'The Armenian said, "What did you do?" To which my father replied, "You killed him." "No," said the Armenian. "*You* killed him." They argued for a few minutes, then drove on in silence, leaving the dead Bedu by the road. They were very nervous. Neither of them had ever been in such a situation. After fifteen miles they came to a French patrol. The officer ordered them to stop and asked them what they were doing on the road so late. He could see how nervous they were, and became suspicious. So he ordered them out of the car, and as soon as they got out he saw the blood covering their shirts.

'The Armenian said, "It was his idea. He's just killed a Bedu hitchhiker." My father answered, "No, no – it was him." The Frenchman told both of them to be quiet. He put them in handcuffs and searched them. In the back of the car he found the Bedu's ID. "Was this the man you just killed?" he asked. Both men were silent. Then the policeman said: "Perhaps I should tell you that this is Ali ibn Mohammed, the most wanted brigand in the Near East. There is a reward of one hundred gold pounds for anyone who finds him, dead or alive." "Ali ibn Mohammed?" said my father and the Armenian, both looking at each other. "The most dangerous robber in Syria?" "It was me that killed him," said my father. "He's lying," said the Armenian, "I killed him." "No. I did . . ." '

'What happened?' I asked.

'They split the reward,' said George, smiling. 'In the end. After much argument.'

Towards late afternoon we saw in front of us a trickle of molten mercury: the Euphrates lit up by the sinking sun. It was pale and ghostly and shrouded by a thin halo of mist. To one side rose the hump of a prehistoric tell, and beside it a modern suspension bridge guarded by two sleeping Syrian army guards. We rolled over the bridge and onto the Aleppo highway.

The desert was now flecked with round, white Bedouin tents. Around them were flocks of thin sheep, each one throwing up its own faint slipstream of dust. Occasional villages of mud-brick rose from the sand, their shattered beehive domes clustered like a line of broken eggs in a punnet. Usually these villages seemed to be deserted, but some were still occupied, their ancient curves topped by television aerials and telephone wires.

As we drove on, the Bedouin encampments became more frequent. Then we came to a hillside covered in graves. The shanty towns and slums of Aleppo's outer suburbs opened up before us; and ahead rose the earthen drum of Aleppo's great citadel.

ALEPPO, 2 SEPTEMBER

Yesterday evening I fulfilled a promise I had made in Mar Gabriel.

Just before I arrived there, the Abbot had received from the printers in Istanbul a set of postcards. They reproduced some of the more remarkable illustrations from the medieval Syriac manuscripts in the Mar Gabriel library. The Abbot was very excited by his new pictures, and begged me to deliver a boxful to his Metropolitan in Aleppo.

Getting to see Metropolitan Ibrahim, however, proved more of a struggle than I had expected, if only because I made the mistake of accepting the offer of one of the Baron's own taxi drivers to take me there. The man was an Armenian which, I figured, would make him more likely to know his way around Christian Aleppo than a Muslim driver; but in the event all it actually meant was that he had a healthy thirst for Armenian cognac, a half-drunk bottle of which lay in his glove compartment, and from which he occasionally took a swig when we stopped at traffic lights. Thus fortified, he drove me at high speed around a bewildering variety of cathedrals, belonging in turn to the Chaldeans, Latins, Greek Orthodox and Greek Catholics, before finally admitting that he had no idea where the cathedral of the Syrian Orthodox was situated.

Eventually we pulled in at a rival taxi rank: 'Please,' I said

146

to one of the drivers, 'I am looking for the Syrian Orthodox cathedral.'

TAXI DRIVER: You want cathedral? Which cathedral? We have many cathedral in Aleppo.

W. D.: I'm after the Surianis' cathedral.

TAXI DRIVER: Which Surianis? We have many Surianis in Aleppo. Syrian Catholics, Syrian Protestants, Syrian Orthodox . . .

W. D.: I want the Syrian *Orthodox*. I think I said that to begin with.

TAXI DRIVER: Which Orthodox? In Aleppo . . .

W. D. (*getting irritated*): Syrian Orthodox.

TAXI DRIVER (*surprised*): You want Syrian Orthodox?

W. D.: Yes.

TAXI DRIVER: Not Syrian Catholics?

W. D.: No.

TAXI DRIVER: Not Assyrian Orthodox?

W. D. (*explosive*): I WANT THE SYRIAN ORTHODOX CATHEDRAL.

TAXI DRIVER (*pensive*): Syrian Orthodox cathedral. (*Pause*) That I don't know.

Luckily, someone at the next stand did know, and after he had explained its whereabouts we set off again at terrifying speed, the Armenian driver attempting to mollify me with a display of his party trick, changing gear with his foot.

'Where you from?' he asked, changing down to second with his right foot while his right hand fumbled for the bottle in the glove compartment.

'Scotland.'

'I have been to New York and to L.A.'

'Holiday?'

'Little bit holiday.'

'What do you mean?'

'I went for operation. American hospitals very good. Last year I had car accident. Big problem . . .'

The Syrian Orthodox, it turned out, had cunningly secreted

their cathedral behind a filling station in the Suleymaniye district of the city; we had already passed it several times without noticing it. The Metropolitan's Palace was even more successfully hidden: it lay tucked in behind the back of the cathedral. I was met at the gates of the palace by a raven-robed flunkey and led up, past the long black cathedral Cadillac (emblazoned on its back window with a colour sticker of the Metropolitan's coat of arms) to a first-floor reception room. There I was shown to a gilt armchair beneath a huge photograph of a beaming President Asad, and a fractionally smaller portrait of the Syrian Orthodox Patriarch of Antioch.

After a few minutes the door was flung open and the small, round figure of Gregorios Yohanna Ibrahim walked in, backwards. In his hand he held a portable telephone into which he was talking animatedly, while at the same time waving goodbye to a young couple with his free hand. He turned a pirouette and advanced towards me, his free hand extended. As he did so he finished his telephone call, snapped shut the phone with a flick of his thumb, and popped it into his cassock pocket.

'Mr William?' he said. 'I've been expecting you. I received a letter from Mar Gabriel telling me you were coming. Come, let me show you something which will interest you.'

The Metropolitan took me over to a trestle-table at the side of the room, pausing only to sign a document that a bowing function-ary offered him. On the trestle lay some architect's plans.

'At the moment there are no functioning Syrian Orthodox mon-asteries in Syria,' he said, unrolling the blueprints. 'But now I'm going to rebuild Tel Ada. For many years this has been my dream. It was the monastery that the young St Symeon Stylites joined when he first left home. According to the great fifth-century Bishop Theodoret of Cyrrhus – you know his *History of the Monks of Syria*? I will lend you a copy – there were once 150 monks at Tel Ada, but it has been a ruin for nearly thirteen hundred years. Little is left. We bought the land from the farmer in 1987 and have just had our plans authorised by the authorities in Damascus. Look.' The Metropolitan pointed to a geometric shape at the centre of his blueprints. 'The church is to be based on St Symeon's church at Qala'at Semaan: it will be an open octagon and in the middle will be our stylite's pillar.'

'As a symbol?'

'No, no. It will be the real thing. It will have a stylite on top of it.'

'Are you being serious?'

'Perfectly serious.'

'But how are you going to find a stylite?'

'We have one already. Fr. Ephrem Kerim has volunteered to be our first pillar-dweller. He is in Ireland presently, at Maynooth, finishing his thesis. When he has his doctorate he wishes to mount a pillar.'

'I don't believe it,' I said.

'But it is true.'

'I thought stylites had died out hundreds of years ago.'

'No,' said the Metropolitan, shaking his head. 'According to my researches there were still stylites in Georgia in the eighteenth century. It's a bit of a gap, but hardly unbridgeable.'

'And your friend, Fr. Ephrem, is really prepared to spend the rest of his life perched up on . . .'

'He is determined to become as like St Symeon as he can,' said Mar Gregorios. 'But if he does find it too difficult, I know several keen young novices who will be happy to take it in turns to be stylites with him.'

'A kind of relay stylitism?'

'If you like.'

I frowned: 'But . . .'

'It is good to imitate the saints,' said the Metropolitan, anticipating my objections. 'They are an example to all of us.'

'Isn't it a bit exhibitionist to stand on a pillar?' I said.

'On the contrary,' said Mar Gregorios. 'For the stylites of old the opinion of this world was nothing. The saints became stylites for their own good, for the salvation of their own souls. For them the material world, their own bodies, were of no account. The spirit was all that mattered. To punish their bodies on columns gave emphasis to the world of the spirit.'

'Do you think you will become a stylite,' I asked.

149

'No,' replied the Metropolitan, smiling. 'I am too old.'

I gave him the parcel containing the postcards, and as he opened it he quizzed me about the situation in the Tur Abdin.

'It's very bad,' he said when I described what I had seen. 'The Turks . . . why do they do this? What have we ever done to them?' He shook his head. 'My father was from the Tur Abdin, my mother's family from Diyarbakir. After the massacres they were the only surviving children from both their families. All their brothers and sisters were killed. In 1921 my grandfather managed to get his children across the border to Qamishli; they crossed at night with a small group of friends. The French were here and my parents thought they would protect them. In Turkey there was still terrible insecurity – Kurdish tribesmen were still circling the country killing and enslaving any Christians they found. My mother's parents had crossed the year before and she was born here in Aleppo.

'So you are a refugee on both sides of your family?'

'I was born in Qamishli,' replied the Metropolitan. 'My father had been a landowner in the Tur Abdin, but of course after he came to Syria he had nothing: everything had to be left behind. So he worked the land of a rich Syrian family. Eventually he became their foreman. But despite this we have never thought of ourselves as refugees. Syria was where the Suriani had come from: the ruins and graves of our forefathers lie all around. We have always thought of ourselves as citizens, not refugees.'

'And do you think the Christians are safe in Syria today?'

'Christians are better off in Syria than anywhere else in the Middle East,' said Mar Gregorios emphatically. 'Other than Lebanon, this is the only country in the region where a Christian can really feel the equal of a Muslim – and Lebanon, of course, has many other problems. In Syria there is no enmity between Christian and Muslim. If Syria were not here, we would be finished. Really. It is a place of sanctuary, a haven for all the Christians: for the Nestorians and Chaldeans driven out of Iraq, the Syrian Orthodox and the Armenians driven out of Turkey, even some Palestinian Christians driven out of the Holy Land by the Israelis. Talk to people here: you will find that what I say is true.'

What Mar Gregorios said was indeed what I had been told ever since I had crossed the Syrian border. I heard more of the same at lunch today with Sally Mazloumian. Sally's husband, the great Krikor ('Coco') Mazloumian, owner and manager of the Baron for as long as anyone could remember, had died last year, leaving Sally widowed and shipwrecked in Syria with her family 'spread out across the world like United Nations: Aleppo, Geneva, New York...' Krikor had been succeeded as manager by his pipe-smoking, labrador-patting eldest son, the only member of the next Mazloumian generation to stay on in Syria. He was now known, like his father before him, simply as Baron Mazloumian.

The Mazloumians' house lay immediately beside the hotel, in the same compound. Gathered there, under the framed photographs of a succession of turn-of-the-century Mazloumians, were a dozen Aleppo Armenians, all of whose parents and grandparents had been survivors of the Armenian genocide, who had somehow escaped from the death-marches across the desert and found shelter in the narrow alleys of Aleppo. They had gathered, as they did every Sunday, to see Sally, to toast the memory of her late husband, and to raise their glasses to Armenia.

The elderly people sat back in the faded chintz armchairs and talked about old times. As they did so their stories came spilling out: the usual, familiar litany of indescribable Armenian tragedies: grandmothers raped, uncles beaten to death, aunts dying in the desert from thirst and starvation, all set against the counterpoint of how Syria provided refuge for the few straggling survivors.

'When the Ottoman army surrounded them, the Armenians of Zeitun defended themselves for two months,' said one man. He was old and grey, but his eyes were bright and animated as he told his story. 'Then the Catholicos from Sis came and persuaded them to surrender. He said: "I have promised that you will all give in your guns, and the army has promised you will be safe." My grandfather did not believe the word of Turks, so he and my father stayed in the redoubt. But his wife, who thought the Catholicos should be obeyed, took all my uncles and aunts and went back to their village. That night they were all clubbed to death...'

Everyone competed to tell their tales. 'There's not one Armenian

151

family in Aleppo that hasn't got a better story than *Dr Zhivago*,' said Sally proudly. 'But don't expect any of them to give you a properly ordered account. They get much too excited.'

'My grandfather was saved by a friend,' said a well-dressed businessman with an American accent. 'Khachadurian was a shoe-maker who made special boots for the Ottoman army. He was an Armenian, but he was important to the military so he was spared. They gathered the Armenians into a walled graveyard, but the shoemaker came in and started taking boys out. He said, "This is my son-in-law, this here is my nephew, that is my grandson. I need them all for my business. If you Turks want your boots you must let me have my workers." He saved thirty in all, so many that he could barely feed them all: my father had only one piece of bread each day, and that he had to share with his sister.'

Quite suddenly and unexpectedly the businessman began sob-bing. His transatlantic self-assurance crumpled like a punctured balloon. He bowed his head. Sally said: 'It's all right, Sam. Don't continue. It's all right.'

'When the fighting started, my father fled to the mountains,' said an old widow, filling the silence. 'They had begun collecting Armenians for "deportation". Although he was only twelve, my father guessed what was happening. So he ran off up the hill above his house, barefoot in the snow. He was lucky: 90 per cent of the Armenians in the columns did not make it. There were forty-seven people in my father's family. They all died. Only he was left.'

Sam, the businessman with the American accent, lifted his head. 'I want to finish,' he said, dabbing his cheeks. 'I met Khachadurian in 1962 in Beirut. He was ninety years old, completely blind. My father was with me: he kissed Khachadurian's hand and told me to do the same. He said: "Without that man I would be dead now. And you would never have been born." '

'Both my parents walked to Aleppo,' chipped in another old man, as determined as the others to tell his story. 'My father was naked by the time he got here – his rags got so full of holes they just fell off. The Arabs clothed him. Later my parents found shelter in the Jewish Quarter, the Hayy el-Yehudi. Ten Armenian families put all their resources together and rented one room . . .'

'When my grandfather first came here all the Armenians were still poor,' said a younger woman, a musician, who had just returned from giving a concert in Yerevan. 'They had arrived penniless, but they worked night and day just to make sure that their children were educated.'

The massacres, everyone agreed, had changed the face of Aleppo: before the First World War there were only three hundred Armenian families in the town; by 1943 Armenian numbers had topped 400,000.

But as I had already learned, the Armenians were not alone. Between 1914 and 1924 similar waves of Suriani (and to a smaller extent Greek Orthodox) refugees followed in their wake. The influx turned Aleppo into a Noah's Ark, a place of shelter and safety for all the different Christian communities driven out of Anatolia by the Turks. The officials of the French Mandate welcomed the exiles, partly out of genuine sympathy for their plight, and partly in the hope that the Christian refugees would act as a break on the new Arab nationalism. Moreover, the French felt that the Christians would naturally be more enthusiastic supporters of their rule, and systematically gave them preferment in government jobs.

After Syria's independence in 1946, this inevitably led to a backlash. Although Michel Aflaq, one of the founders of the Ba'ath Party, was a Christian, as was Faris al-Khuri, a leading figure in the Syrian Nationalist movement who later became Prime Minister, anti-Christian feeling was widespread (and, in the post-colonial circumstances, understandable). There were attempts to make Islam the official religion of the country, and at one stage the imam of the Great Mosque in Damascus declared that as far as he was concerned, an Indonesian Muslim was closer to him than al-Khuri, his own (Christian) Prime Minister. The increasingly Islamic tone of the Syrian establishment led to perhaps a quarter of a million Christians leaving Syria throughout the 1960s; from Aleppo alone as many as 125,000 Armenians emigrated to Soviet Armenia. These refugees included the current Armenian President, Levon Ter Petrosyan.

The period of uncertainty for Syria's Christians came to an end with Asad's *coup d'état* in 1970. Asad was an Alawite, a member of a Muslim minority regarded by orthodox Sunni Muslims as heretical and disparagingly referred to as Nusayris (or Little Christians). Asad kept himself in power by forming what was in effect a coalition of Syria's many religious minorities – Shias, Druze, Yezidis, Christians and Alawites – through which he was able to counterbalance the weight of the Sunni majority. In Asad's Syria Christians have always done well: at the moment, apparently, five of Asad's seven closest advisers are Christians, including his principal speechwriter, as are two of the sixteen cabinet ministers. Christians and Alawites together hold all the key positions in the armed forces and the *mukhabarat*. While the official population figures are distrusted by everyone I spoke to, the Christians themselves estimated that they now formed slightly less than 20 per cent of Syria's total population, and between 20 and 30 per cent of the population of Aleppo, giving that city one of the largest Christian populations anywhere in the Middle East.

The confidence of the Christians in Syria is something you can't help noticing the minute you arrive in the country. This is particularly so if, like myself, you cross the border at Nisibis: Qamishli, the town on the Syrian side of the frontier (and the place where Metropolitan Gregorios Yohanna Ibrahim was brought up) is 75 per cent Christian, and icons of Christ and images of his mother fill almost every shop and decorate every other car window – an extraordinary display after the furtive secrecy of Christianity in Turkey. Moreover Turoyo, the modern Aramaic of the Tur Abdin, is the first language of Qamishli. This makes it one of a handful of towns in the world where Jesus could expect to be understood if he came back tomorrow.

The only problem with all of this, as far as the Christians are concerned, is the creeping realisation that they are likely to expect another, perhaps far more savage, backlash when Asad dies or when his regime eventually crumbles. The Christians of Syria have watched with concern the Islamic movements which are gaining strength all over the Middle East, and the richer Christians have all invested in two passports (or so the gossip goes), just in case Syria turns nasty at some stage in the future.

'Fundamentalism is building up among the Muslims,' said a

pessimistic Armenian businessman I met while wandering in the Aleppo bazaars. 'Just look at the girls: now they all wear the *hijab*: only five years ago they were all uncovered. After Asad's death or resignation no one knows what will happen. As long as the bottle is closed with a firm cork all is well. But eventually the cork will come out. And then no one knows what will happen to us.'

In the meantime, while the Christians nervously sing Asad's praises, most of the Sunni majority continue to grumble about his repressive Ba'athist government and the ruthlessness of his secret police, although several Muslims I talked to did admit to a grudging admiration for their dictator's sheer shrewdness and tenacity. In the absence of any legal opposition, disaffected Syrians have taken refuge in a series of jokes at the expense of the Alawite ruling clique. The taxi driver who took me back from the Syrian Orthodox cathedral told me this Asad story as we crawled through the bazaars behind an ambling train of pack-mules:

'My cousin is a taxi driver in Damascus. One day he was waiting by some traffic lights when a limousine with clouded glass windows smashed into his rear. The back of the taxi was completely wrecked. My cousin is a hot-blooded man – we all are in my family – so he jumped out and began to harangue the occupants, calling them sons of unmarried mothers, brothers of incontinent camels, fathers of she-goats and so on. After two minutes of this, the rear window of the limousine lowered half an inch, and a visiting card was thrust through the crack. On it was written a single telephone number. My cousin started shouting, "What is the meaning of this?" but the window was wound up again and the limousine swerved around him and his concertina-ed taxi, leaving him shouting into space.

'My cousin was determined to get some compensation from the rich man who owned the car, so the following day he went to a phone box and rang the number that had been written on the card. He started by softening the man up with a few pleasantries, then went on to demand a new taxi, saying that fifteen people depended on the money he brought home, that his wife was sick and that his daughter was getting married the following year.

155

'There was no response to this, so my cousin began to get angry again, comparing the man to the vomit of an Israeli dog and the worms which wriggle in the belly of a wild pig. He had been speaking like this for five minutes when suddenly a quiet voice on the end of the line said: "Do you have any idea who you are talking to?"

'"No," replied my cousin.

'"You are speaking to Hafez al-Asad," said a sinister voice. "As you may be aware, I am the President of the Syrian Arab Republic."

'"I know who you are," said my cousin without hesitation, "but do you have any idea who *you* are talking to?"

'"No," said the voice, surprised.

'"Thank God for that," said my cousin, slamming down the phone and running back to his car as fast as he could, before the *mukhabarat* could trace the call and treat him to an extended stay at President Asad's pleasure.'

ALEPPO, 4 SEPTEMBER

I sat up last night reading the book lent to me by the Metropolitan, *The History of the Monks of Syria* by Theodoret, Bishop of Cyrrhus. Theodoret turns out to be a near contemporary of John Moschos, and if this book is anything to go by, even more eccentric in his tastes.

If Theodoret is to be believed, the greatest celebrities of his day were not singers or dancers or even charioteers, but saints and ascetics. St Symeon Stylites the Elder, whose pillar lay a few miles west of Aleppo, was a case in point.

'As his fame circulated everywhere,' wrote Theodoret, 'everyone hastened to him, so that with everyone arriving from every side and every road resembling a river, one can behold a sea of men standing together in that place. Not only inhabitants of our part of the world, but also Ismaelites, Persians, Armenians and men even more distant than these: inhabitants of the extreme west, Spaniards and Britons and the Gauls who live between them. Of Italy it is superfluous to speak. It is said that the man became so celebrated in the great city of Rome that at the entrance of all the workshops men have set up small representations of him, to provide thereby some protection and safety for themselves . . .'

Theodoret, as the principal chronicler of the great Byzantine ascetics, was effectively the leading celebrity biographer of his day, and his works were read as far away as Anglo-Saxon Canterbury. But his subjects – suspended in cages, walled up in hermitages, buried in cisterns – presented a rather different set of difficulties to the figures whose peccadilloes and appetites are so minutely examined by hack biographers today. For if Symeon was the most famous of Theodoret's celebrity subjects, he was by no means the most eccentric. There was, for example, Baradatus, who Theodoret congratulates for having devised 'new tests of endurance'. On a ridge above his hermitage he constructed out of wood 'a small chest that did not even match his body and in this he dwelt, obliged to stoop the whole time. It was not even fitted together with planks, but had openings like a lattice; and because of this he was neither safe from the assault of the rains nor free from the flames of the sun, but endured both.'

Eventually Baradatus's bishop persuaded him to come out of his latticed coffin, but far from going into ascetic retirement the hermit merely devised an even more unusual way to follow his calling. Baradatus decided that his new ploy was going to involve standing up all the time. But as this was a fairly common form of asceticism at the time (no less a figure than the youthful St John Chrysostom once pursued this method of self-punishment for two years without a break), Baradatus seems to have come to the conclusion that standing up for the rest of his life was, on its own, not going to be enough. He therefore decided to make things more difficult for himself. He covered his entire body 'with a tunic of skins – only around the nose and mouth did he leave a small opening for breath', so that in addition to having to stand all day he would also be baked alive in the sweltering Syrian midsummer heat: a sort of Byzantine boil-in-the-bag monk.

This was, however, tame stuff compared to one of Theodoret's heroes, Thalelaeus, who constructed a cage, then hung the contraption in the air. 'Sitting or rather suspended in this, he has spent ten years up till now. Since he has a very big body, not even sitting can he straighten his neck, but he always sits bent double with his forehead tightly pressed against his knees.'

When Theodoret went to visit this strange figure, he found him 'reaping the benefit of the divine gospels, gathering benefit therefrom with extreme concentration'. Only at this point does it seem to have occurred to Theodoret that this sort of behaviour was, perhaps, just a little strange. 'I questioned him out of desire to learn the reason for this novel mode of life,' wrote the Bishop. Thalelaeus had his answer ready: life, he said, was to be lived as uncomfortably as possible as an insurance policy against worse discomforts in the life to come: 'Burdened with many sins, and believing in the penalties that are threatened, I have devised this form of life, contriving moderate punishments for the body in order to reduce the mass of those awaited. For the latter are more grievous not only in quantity but also in quality, so if by these slight afflictions I lessen those awaited, great is the profit I shall derive therefrom.'

In most other societies, ascetics like this might perhaps be regarded with a certain amount of suspicion; but in Byzantium it seemed that every village wanted some self-torturing hermit to live among them, to bring them good luck, to cure them of diseases and demons, and to intercede for them both at the wordly palace of Constantinople and the more distant court of Heaven. Hermits were considered especially lucky to have around when they were dying: that way the village could claim the corpse, and add to its stock of sacred relics. If Theodoret is to be believed, hundreds of eager Byzantine peasants seem to have hung around dying saints, waiting to slice up the old men as soon as they dropped off their perches – quite literally in the case of stylites.

Theodoret records one such case, when word got out that a famous hermit named James of Cyrrhestica was reported to be dying. On a previous occasion when James had been seriously ill, Theodoret had had to exert all his episcopal authority to disperse a crowd of sickle-wielding relic-seekers. But a little while later, when James's condition suddenly worsened, Theodoret was away on business to Aleppo, and the people of Cyrrhus were forced to take the law into their own hands.

'As many [peasants] were coming from all sides to seize his body,' wrote Theodoret, 'when they heard what was happening, all the men of the town, both soldiers and civilians, hastened together [to where James lived, on a hilltop four miles to the west], some taking up military equipment, others using whatever weapons lay to hand. Forming up in close order, they fought by shooting arrows and slinging stones – not to wound, but simply to instil fear [in their rustic rivals]. Having thus driven off the local inhabitants, they placed the hermit on a litter while he was quite unconscious of what was happening – he was not even conscious of his hair being plucked out by the peasants [as a relic] – and set off [with the comatose hermit] to the city.'

As a result of a series of such pre-emptive swoops on dying ascetics, Cyrrhus became so clogged with relics that Theodoret lobbied to have it renamed Hagiopolis, the city of saints. On my map, the town's ruins lie forty-five miles to the north of Aleppo. Tomorrow I plan to drive out there, taking the Metropolitan's book with me, and see what is left of Theodoret's bishopric.

ALEPPO, 5 SEPTEMBER

There turned out to be no bus to Cyrrhus, so I decided to hitchhike instead. I woke early and filled a light pack with feta cheese, some flat bread and a bottle of weak Syrian beer. Then, taking a hotel taxi to the edge of town, I began to walk.

It was a beautifully cool and surprisingly cloudy day – a welcome change from the blazing skies and enervating heat that had followed me ever since Athos. Before long I came to a roadside stall run by a solitary Bedu. The stall was made of palm fronds and sold nothing but branches of ripe dates. I bought a sprig and when, half an hour later, I was picked up by a Kurdish truck driver, we ate the dates together, spitting the stones out of the windows.

As we headed north-west, the land grew slowly starker: the rich belt of walnut and pistachio trees that had shaded the roadsides on the northern edge of Aleppo gave way to more arid, mountainous territory. On small patches of arable land, teams of blinkered horses in harness pulled primitive wooden ploughs; peasant women in embroidered dresses and white kerchiefs scraped at the soil with picks while their daughters looked on, buckets in hand. Above them, on the edge of the slopes, you could see the ruins of deserted Byzantine watchtowers looking out over the thin soil that had once supported the rich vineyards whose dark Syrian wine was drunk in the taverns of late antique Antioch.

After many miles, on the slope of a hill opposite the road, I saw the ruins of what looked like a large Romanesque basilica sitting in the middle of a small grove of olive trees. It was roofless and deserted, but otherwise almost miraculously intact. Intrigued, I asked my Kurdish friend to drop me off. The truck drove away in a cloud of black exhaust, and in the sudden silence I set off on foot towards the ruins.

The basilica of Mushabbak sits in perfect isolation amid the olive groves, the last surviving witness to a period when these hills supported what must once have been a fairly dense Christian population. If a new wooden roof were raised over the nave, the floor were swept and the gables slightly repaired, the church would be ready for use tomorrow. But, like so many other churches across the Middle East, this astonishing basilica now acts as nothing more than a convenient sheep-pen: as I walked across the fields and through the olives, I could see a shepherd boy drawing water from a well to one side of the ruin. He poured the water into a trough which, as I drew nearer, I realised was actually the old church font. The boy salaamed, and led me inside.

A pair of ewes and four lambs were tethered in the side-chapel. Nearby stood a saddled donkey and a growling sheepdog. Two arcades of massively-built round arches rolled forward along the austere nave towards a gently curving apse; although totally bare of ornament or decoration, there was great beauty in the perfect harmony of the church's proportions. The building was clearly very early Byzantine, dating from around the late-fifth century, but its similarity to Romanesque work was extraordinary, and in its plan and style it almost exactly prefigured the French ecclesiastical architecture of the early twelfth century. In many ways it would not have looked out of place on an Auvergne hillside; yet for all that, its spirit was somehow very different.

When you think of French Romanesque – of Vézelay, Autun, Anzy-le-Duc or Moissac – you are left with an impression of teeming life: biting beasts entwined around capitals; tympana crowded with the twenty-four Elders of the Apocalypse busily fiddling on their viols; angels blowing the Last Trump; the dead resurrecting, emerging like uncurling crustaceans from their sarcophagi. The sculpture is playful, fantastic, anarchic, like those manuscript marginalia where the world is inverted and rabbits armed with crossbows hunt the hunters or chase the hounds.

But here, in this stone husk of Byzantine Syria, a more restrained and puritanical spirit was at work. A *chrismon* – a small equal-armed cross – was carved in a laurel wreath above the central keystone of the arch. Otherwise there was no decorative sculpture to break the stern purity of the stonework. The capitals were non-figurative, and were carelessly, almost accidentally decorated with palmettes and scroll volutes. There were no mouldings above the windows, and no acanthus-work above the doors or around the apsidal arch. Like the lifestyles embraced by Theodoret's ascetics, the guiding spirit of this church was almost fanatically austere.

This shared severity of outlook was no coincidence. For it was in such remote rural settlements that Theodoret's Syrian ascetics were most popular, most especially revered. In the towns, whose populations were better and more classically educated, opinion was sometimes divided about them: already in the fourth century the pagan orator Libanius thought of the monks as 'that black-robed tribe who eat more than elephants, sweeping across the country like a river in spate ravaging the temples and the great estates'. Libanius was clearly not alone in his feelings: in one of his sermons St John Chrysostom (a former pupil of Libanius who later turned against his pagan master) complained that 'wherever the people [of Antioch] gathered to gossip you could find one man boasting that he was the first to beat up a monk, another that he had been the first to track down his hut, a third that he had spurred the magistrate into action against the Holy Men, a fourth that he had dragged them through the streets and seen them locked up in jail.'

But in the farms and villages it was very different. There it was to the freelance and unordained holy men, and not to Imperial officials or the professional clergy, that the simple Byzantine peasants would turn when they were in trouble. As Theodoret once remarked, the holy men replaced the pagan gods: their shrines replaced the temples, and their feasts superseded the old pagan festivals. Theodoret's friend the cage-dwelling hermit Thalalaeus was an example of this. He moved into a still functioning pagan shrine and defeated all attempts to drive him out ('they were unable to move him since faith fenced him around and grace fought on his behalf'). Then he managed to convert the local people with the aid of some supernatural veterinary work: Theodoret himself interviewed some converts who 'declared that many miracles occur through his prayer, with not only men but also camels, asses and mules enjoying healing'. This healing of the village pack-animals seems to have tipped the balance: Thalalaeus had found his way into the farmers' hearts, and with the assistance of his new converts he 'destroyed the precinct of the demons and erected a great shrine to the triumphant martyrs, opposing to those falsely called gods, the Godly Dead'.

By their ability to endure physical suffering Byzantine holy men like Thalalaeus were believed to be able to wear away the curtain that separated the visible world from the divine; and by reaching through they gained direct access to God, something that was thought to be impossible for the ordinary believer. For by mortifying the flesh, it was believed that the holy men became transformed: 'If you will, you can become all flame,' said Abba Joseph in one of the stories of the desert fathers, holding up his hand to show fingers which had 'become like ten lamps of fire', radiant with the 'uncreated light of divinity', the same form of illumination that is shown surrounding the great saints in icons. In this heightened state the holy men were believed to be able to act as intercessors for their followers at the distant court of Heaven, and like the old gods had the power to give children to barren women, to cure the sick, and to divine the future.

But perhaps the holy men's most important task was to fight demons. The world was believed to be besieged by invisible agents of darkness, and to sin was not merely to err: it was to be overcome by these sinister forces. Demonic activity was a daily irritation, and was believed to intrude on the most ordinary, domestic activities. A recently discovered papyrus fragment tells the story of the break-up of the marriage of a young Byzantine couple, a prosperous baker and the daughter of a merchant: 'We were in time past maintaining a peaceful and seemly married life,' they wrote in their divorce petition, 'but we have suffered from a sinister and wicked demon which attacked us from we know not whence, with a view to our being divorced from one another.' In much the same vein John Moschos tells the story of a nunnery in Lycia which was attacked by a troop of demons; as a result 'five of the virgins conspired to run away from the monastery and find themselves husbands'.

Like the Muslim *djinns* which superseded them, Byzantine demons lurked especially in old temples and remote hillsides such as that around my isolated basilica: the *Life* of an Anatolian holy man named Theodore of Sykeon tells how a group of farmers digging into a mound of earth on a distant hillside inadvertently released a great swarm of demons that took possession not only of them, but of their neighbours and their animals; only a holy man like Theodore was able to drive the evil spirits back into their lair and seal them in. Monks and holy men were thought of as 'prize-fighters' against the Devil's minions, and only with their help – and their amulets, relics and remedies – could demons be fought or defeated. Across the east Mediterranean that tradition still continues: to this day Christian monks are believed to be powerful exorcists, a talent they share with their Islamic counterparts, the Muslim Sufi mystics.

I thought of this as I walked along the empty country road, hoping for a lift to Cyrrhus. It was two hours before I had any luck. My saviour was Monsieur Alouf, an old francophile Arab with an astonishing resemblance to Omar Sharif. No one lived at Cyrrhus any more, he said as we drove off, but he knew the way as there was the shrine of a famous saint, Nebi (prophet) Uri, on the edge of the ruins. He was not busy today, added M. Alouf. If I wanted, for a small price he could drive me all the way there. He named a reasonable figure and I accepted his offer.

We headed north along a narrow hill road. The further we drove, the more olives came to dominate the thin soil. As we crossed a narrow ridge, a great panorama of silver-grey trees unfolded before us, chequering the hills in a regimented gridiron. On some south-facing slopes, a few peasant families were beginning the olive harvest. Rickety wooden ladders were being propped against the gnarled old olive trees while sheets were laid out on the ground; tethered donkeys stood about nearby, their empty saddlebags ready to receive the harvest. Nearby, groups of baggy-trousered harvesters loaded olive sacks onto waiting horsecarts.

We passed a waterfall in which some small children were splashing about, then crossed a pair of beautiful hump-backed Byzantine bridges. One of these, I knew, had been commissioned by Theodoret himself. We were on the edge of our destination.

The sheer remoteness of the place was surprising, but in retrospect this was something I should have expected. In his private letters, Theodoret was always complaining about the provincial character of his bishopric. Brought up in a well-to-do family in metropolitan Antioch, he often found life in distant Cyrrhus frustrating. He begged his correspondents for gossip from Constantinople, and complained that there was not a decent baker anywhere in his bishopric. In one particularly revealing letter, he calls Cyrrhus 'a little city' whose ugliness he claimed to have 'covered over' by lavish spending. In another, addressed to his friend the sophist Isocasius, he writes of his excitement when a skilled woodworker arrived in town. In Antioch no one would have noticed such an unexceptional occurrence, but in Cyrrhus everyone in authority – the Governor, the General, Theodoret himself – wanted to employ him, and Theodoret promises to send the carpenter on to his friend as soon as he has finished with him.

After three miles of increasingly precipitous mountain slopes, the shattered ruins of Cyrrhus rose quite suddenly from the olive groves. A jumble of broken buildings – the arc of a theatre, fragments of arcaded public buildings, a few random columns and pillar bases – littered the ground. Few buildings stood higher than a couple of courses. But dominating everything, crowning the horizon on a precipitous rock in the centre of the ruins, rose the jagged silhouette of the citadel which had been rebuilt and refortified by Justinian as a defence against the Persians.

M. Alouf dropped me off by the honey-coloured skeleton of one of the Byzantine gateways, and I climbed up towards the fort, following the line of the basalt-black town walls. Basking lizards scuttled between the stones. Although it was now midday it was still cool; grey clouds billowed over the citadel and a fresh breeze was blowing. Halfway up the hill I came across a great stumbling tortoise crunching amid the stones as he began, with infinite slowness, to dig in for the winter with a slow-motion breaststroke of legs and ebony claws. The weather was turning: summer was drawing to a close.

Alone of the buildings of the city, the citadel stood intact: the great round corner bastions and the square turrets of the wall-walk that connected them still rose in several places to their original height. I clambered up onto the parapet, sending loose rubble rolling down the hill behind me, and sat there munching my bread and cheese, looking down over the broken remnants of Theodoret's city.

In the middle, a little to the north of the citadel, you could see the outline of Theodoret's cathedral, the great church of Saints Cosmas and Damian, a long apsidal-ended basilica standing out clearly from amid the square foundations of the city's smaller secular buildings. To one side of the cathedral stood what must have been the bishop's palace. It was to this building, I thought, that Theodoret would have returned from one of his interviews, thrilled that some wiry old hermit had let him break down the sealed door of his cell, or that some famously bad-tempered stylite had granted him permission to place a ladder against his pillar and climb up for a chat. On the other side of the cathedral, linked to the south wall of the apse, stood the foundations of a small annexe, probably a shrine. I wondered, as I headed off down the hill, whether it was here that the hermit James had eventually ended up, despite all his efforts to resist Theodoret's attempts to add him to the Cyrrhus relic collection.

Outside the walls, at the opposite end of the town to the cathedral, rose the silhouette of a late antique martyrium. It had a six-sided pyramidal roof and its stone was of a wonderfully rich colour, like the crust on Cornish clotted cream. Sometime in the thirteenth or fourteenth century A.D. this elegant classical building had been walled around and converted into the shrine of a Sufi saint. The shrine was still functioning, and it was there that I had agreed to meet M. Alouf.

I found him sitting cross-legged on a carpet in the prayer hall of the small mosque that had been built beneath the tower. He was talking to the Sheikh who looked after the shrine, a limping old man with a stick, baggy *sharwal* trousers and a thin grey beard; his *keffiyeh* was wound into a turban with its end trailing down the back of his neck. From the ceiling immediately above the Sheikh dangled a bunch of dried yellow flowers. I asked my friend what they were there for.

'The Sheikh says they are to stop anyone ever again putting the evil eye on the mosque,' said Alouf.

'Someone has put it on before?' I asked.

'Sadly yes,' replied the Sheikh. 'Before we put those up, two thieves came and stole all the carpets, the clock, the fan and the loudspeaker from the mosque. Come and see.'

He led us through a door into the vaulted burial chamber of the tomb. Cuckoo-like, the cenotaph of the Muslim saint had been placed immediately above the spot where the original Roman occupant must have been laid.

'This is where the sick people come to spend the night,' said the Sheikh. 'In the morning they are cured, thanks to Nebi Uri. It is a

166

holy place but those thieves dug down here. They thought they would find money, but all they did was to desecrate the grave. Afterwards I said to Nebi Uri, "You must take more care of yourself," and I struck his tomb twice with my stick to show that I meant it.'

'You talk to the saint?' I asked.

'Of course,' said the Sheikh, laughing indulgently, as if I were questioning him about something so obvious that only a foreigner could possibly ask it. 'Every day.'

'How?'

'He comes to me in dreams,' said the Sheikh. 'He gives me advice and instructions: "Don't leave my shrine, look after it, make it nice." '

'What does he look like?'

'He has a round face, a thick black beard . . .'

'And his clothes?'

'I don't know: I see only his face,' said the Sheikh. 'Twenty years I have been Sheikh here. And before me my father, and before him his father.'

'For many generations?'

'Many. I am Abdul Mesin, my father was Maamo, his father Sheikho, Sheikho was the son of Misto, Misto was the son of Maamo, son of Ishan . . . Before that I don't remember. It is far away.'

'Tell me about Nebi Uri,' I said.

'You don't know about Nebi Uri?' asked M. Alouf, surprised. 'But he is revered by Christians also. Many Christians – Armenians, Suriani, Catholics – come here to pay their respects. Nebi Uri is in your Bible as well as our Koran, I think.'

'He is?'

'He was the leader of the Prophet David's army,' said the Sheikh. 'David had him killed so that he could marry Nebi Uri's beautiful wife. Two angels, Mikhail and Jibrael, appeared and asked David why he needed an extra wife when he already had ninety-nine others. You know this story?'

'Yes. I think we Christians know Nebi Uri as Uriah the Hittite.'

It was an unlikely tangle of tales: a medieval Muslim saint buried in a much older Byzantine tomb tower had somehow been confused with the Biblical and Koranic Uriah; perhaps the saint's name *was* Uriah, and over the passage of time his identity had been merged with that of his scriptural namesake. More intriguing still was the fact that in this city, long famed for the shrines of its Christian saints, the Muslim Sufi tradition had directly carried on from where Theodoret's Christian holy men had left off. Just as the Muslim form of prayer, with its bowings and prostrations, appears to derive from the older Syriac Christian tradition that I had seen performed at Mar Gabriel, and just as the architecture of the earliest minarets unmistakably derives from the square late-antique Syrian church towers, so the roots of Islamic mysticism and Sufism lie with the Byzantine holy men and desert fathers who preceded them across the Near East.

Today the West often views Islam as a civilisation very different from and indeed innately hostile to Christianity. Only when you travel in Christianity's Eastern homelands do you realise how closely the two religions are really linked. For the former grew directly out of the latter and still, to this day, embodies many aspects and practices of the early Christian world now lost in Christianity's modern Western incarnation. When the early Byzantines were first confronted by the Prophet's armies, they assumed that Islam was merely a heretical form of Christianity, and in many ways they were not so far wrong: Islam accepts much of the Old and New Testaments, and venerates both Jesus and the ancient Jewish prophets.

Certainly if John Moschos were to come back today it is likely that he would find much more that was familiar in the practices of a modern Muslim Sufi than he would with those of, say, a contemporary American Evangelical. Yet this simple truth has been lost by our tendency to think of Christianity as a Western religion rather than the Oriental faith it actually is. Moreover the modern demonisation of Islam in the West, and the recent growth of Muslim fundamentalism (itself in many ways a reaction to the West's repeated humiliation of the Muslim world), have led to an atmosphere where few are aware of, or indeed wish to be aware of, the profound kinship of Christianity and Islam.

It is this as much as anything else that has made the delicate position of the contemporary Eastern Christians – awkwardly caught between their co-religionists in the West and their strong cultural links with their Muslim compatriots – increasingly untenable in recent years. Hence the vital importance of the syncretism which still exists at shrines like that of Nebi Uri. Such popular syncretism – Christians worshipping at Muslim shrines and vice versa – was once much more general across the Middle East, but now survives only in a few oases of relative religious tolerance. The practice emphasises an important truth about the close affinity of the two great religions easily forgotten as the Eastern Christians – the last surviving bridge between Islam and Western Christianity – emigrate in reaction to the increasing hostility of the Islamic establishment.

'Very many Christians still come here,' continued the Sheikh, breaking into my thoughts. 'Mainly they are sick people who want to come and get healing. We had one Christian girl last week. She was sick for many months – her head was bad – and Nebi Uri appeared to her in a dream. So she came here and spent the night on the tomb. The next day she was healed. Last Friday she returned with a sheep, all covered with flowers and ribbons and with its horns dyed with henna. After prayers they cut its throat. Then they cooked it and everyone ate it.'

'Does this happen often?'

'Every week. I say some prayers over the animal, then afterwards the people slaughter it themselves, just over there by the wall.'

'And it's always sheep?'

'No,' said M. Alouf. 'Usually it is, but sometimes people slaughter a young camel, an ox-calf or a young goat. Whatever it is, it must be a good animal – not a dog – and it must be young and healthy. It must not be ill or pregnant.'

'Afterwards,' said the Sheikh, 'they drag the animal round the grave three times and pour some of the blood over Nebi Uri's grave and onto the doorway leading into the chamber. It is to thank Nebi Uri for fulfilling their wish.'

'Before they come,' explained Alouf, 'they will always have

promised such-and-such an animal to Nebi Uri if he performs some favour for them. So when he does what they want they must fulfil their promise.'

'We believe that if they give a different – or less good – animal or do not come at all, then Nebi Uri will punish them,' said the Sheikh.

'How?'

'The punishment can take many forms,' said M. Alouf. 'He can give an illness or cause a *djinn* to take possession of the person. There are many forms of misfortune he can visit on the man who breaks his vow.'

'Once a man who had died was brought here to be buried. They left him by the well outside to wash him. But some time before he had made a promise to Nebi Uri and not honoured it. So when they brought him here the spring dried up and they could not wash the corpse. Nebi Uri did not want him near him. He had rejected him and the man had to be buried elsewhere. The next day water reappeared in the well.'

'If a saint rejects a dead man it is the worst thing that can happen,' said Alouf. 'We regard that as a very great insult to the honour of a family.'

'But if a man is generous and gives a good sheep to fulfil his vow,' said the Sheikh, 'then we believe that that person will ride that sheep at the Day of Judgement. The sheep will carry him into Paradise.'

'And the Christians believe this too?'

'There is no difference between ourselves and the Christians on this matter,' said the Sheikh, 'except that sometimes the Christians make the sign of Christ over the forehead of the person whom they want Nebi Uri to cure.'

As we were talking the Sheikh had led us up a flight of monolithic stairs onto the vaulted and arcaded terrace on the roof of the Byzantine mausoleum. Each side of the hexagon was broken by a great arch, from which sprung the pyramid above us. Through one of the arches I looked out over the rustling trees of the tomb compound. At the gate of the shrine a tractor was unloading a trailer-full of Kurdish workers. The old men were streaming inside for Friday prayers while the children waited with their mothers by the well-head outside.

The Sheikh stood facing south, raised his hands to his ears and called the *azan*. His soft and gentle voice, undistorted by amplification, drifted out over the ruins of Theodoret's cathedral, over the olive trees and the shattered graves of the myriad saints and martyrs of Hagiopolis, to the lavender-blue hills of the Kurd Dagh beyond.

ALEPPO, 9 SEPTEMBER

This morning, my last in Aleppo, I stumbled by accident upon the most unexpected survival from Byzantium that I have yet come across on this trip. Hidden away in a church in the grimy backstreets of the city, like a rare fossil secreted in some obscure quarry-face, there survives, apparently unpolluted by changes in fashion, an ancient form of plainsong that appears to be the direct ancestor of Gregorian chant. If so, extraordinary as it seems, it may represent one of the principal roots of the entire Western tradition of sacred music.

It was Metropolitan Mar Gregorios who first put me onto the trail. During our meeting he had mentioned in passing that among the different groups that had taken shelter in the winding bazaars of Aleppo were the Urfalees: the descendants of the Syrian Christians of Urfa, ancient Edessa. In what I had read of Urfa's recent history, and from what I had picked up when I visited the town last month, I had understood that the town's Syrian Ortho-dox community had suffered the same fate as its unfortunate Armenians. But apparently this was not the case. Although a great many of the Urfa Suriani were indeed massacred during the First World War, there were still enough left in 1924, when Ataturk retook the town from the French, to make the Turkish leader worried about Urfa's ethnic purity. He therefore ordered the immediate expulsion of all those Christians who had so far failed to succumb to the Ottomans' bayonets.

The Urfalees had left Edessa in a succession of great wagon-caravans, and somewhat to their own surprise, made it safely across the Syrian border. There they were escorted by the French Mandate officials to a field full of tents on the outskirts of Aleppo. They are there still, although as with the refugee camps of the Palestinians constructed twenty-three years later, the tents have given way to a jumble of ragged concrete buildings. Mar Gregorios had told me that one last survivor of the original exodus was still alive, and he arranged a meeting.

I found Malfono Namek's flat up a steep staircase off the narrow, grubby lanes that now make up the Hayy el-Surian, the Quarter of the Syrian Orthodox. Malfono [Teacher] Namek had a thin, ascetic face, a small toothbrush moustache and an alert owl-like expression. He wore a 1930s pinstripe suit, like those worn by bootleggers in Al Capone films. After we had drunk tea, I asked Malfono Namek whether – as he must have been very young at the time – he could remember anything of the Urfa he had left in 1924.

'Anything?' said Malfono Namek. 'I can remember everything! I even remember what we were reading in school the day the order to leave came through from Istanbul. If I went back to Urfa today I would know my quarter, my street, my house! It is still my town, even though I have been in Syria for seventy years now.'

The old man thumped the table: 'I would go back tomorrow,' he said. 'But of course the opportunity has never come.'

'How old were you when you had to move?'

'I was twelve. We were each allowed to take one suit of clothes, a couple of blankets and food for one week. Everything else – churches, convents, lands, schools, possessions, money – it all had to be left behind. I remember well: it was wintertime so I wore *shalwar* and a thick jacket. I remember saying goodbye to our Turkish friends and leaving the house and . . .'

He frowned: 'When I think of this I feel so angry . . . It was the Turkish government's fault. Many of our Turkish neighbours were very sad to see us go. They were very sorry for us. You know I still have one friend left alive in Urfa? We write to each other. It is seventy years since we last saw each other, but still we correspond. It was the Turkish government: they called us *gavour* [infidels] and said we had to go. It was they who hated the Christians, not the people of Urfa.'

I asked if, at the time, he had realised what was happening.

'No, not at all!' said Malfono Namek. To my astonishment he threw back his head and laughed. 'At the time I was far too excited. We left in wagons for Ain al-Arab, where we were to catch a train. I was very happy: I had never seen a train. And when we arrived I was very pleased. I had never even imagined such a big and magnificent town existed anywhere on earth. Aleppo was much bigger than Urfa. It had such splendid buildings, and gas street-lighting at night. I saw carriages for the first time, and automobiles: at that time there were maybe ten or fifteen cars in the streets of Aleppo, while none had ever been seen in Urfa. Instead of streetlights, we had been used to carrying paraffin lamps from house to house. For a boy of twelve it was very exciting.'

The old man shook his head. 'The disillusion came later, when we found there was nothing for us except tents. It was February and very cold and there was nothing to eat. I was unhappy in our tent. There was no money, no light, no water. I could not understand the language. All of a sudden we felt strangers ... It took many years for us to feel at home here. In fact it was only recently that we Urfalees finally got a proper church of our own.'

'You don't pray with the other Suriani?'

'No, no,' said Malfono Namek. 'We have to have our own church as we have our own liturgical practices, and because our chant is very different from – and much older than – the music of the other Suriani.'

When I questioned him further, he said that the people of Urfa had scrupulously preserved the traditional chants of ancient Edessa, and in particular the hymns composed by St Ephrem the Syrian, the greatest of the town's saints. An Italian musicologist was currently in Aleppo, he said, studying the Urfalees' chants; if I accompanied him to vespers in the Urfalees' church, Gianmaria

173

Malacrida would probably be there and I could talk to him afterwards.

The old man put on a Homburg hat and, reaching for his stick, led me slowly down the stairs. Together we walked through the lanes of Aleppo, Malfono Namek chivalrously tipping the brim of his Homburg whenever we passed one of his friends. The streets were narrow and medieval-looking which, when we came to it, made the brash new Urfalee church of St George look more surprising still. It stood out like an office block in a Georgian crescent, all pre-stressed concrete and gleaming modernity, as different from the austere classical chapels of the Tur Abdin as could be imagined. Inside it was worse still: jarring Technicolor icons hung from the brightly-lit walls; at the back of the altar, behind the priest, a barrage of fairy lights winked like a neon advertisement in Piccadilly Circus.

But for all the flash modernity of the setting, the singing was still astounding. A cortège of elderly priests conducted the service, accompanied by a string of echoing laments of almost unearthly beauty, sinuous alleluias which floated with the gentle indecision of falling feathers down arpeggios of dying cadences before losing themselves in a soft black hole of basso profundo. At the elevation, the altar boys rattled *flabellae*, ecclesiastical fans which are often depicted on Pictish and Irish cross-slabs, but which died out in the West before the Norman Conquest, and have survived in use only in the Eastern Churches.

When the service had drawn to a close, the congregation – pious ladies with rigid perms and lacy white veils, old men in light tropical suits – poured outside. On the steps Malfono Namek introduced me to Gianmaria Malacrida. Malfono explained that I had recently been in Urfa, and I said I was interested in the Italian's theory that the Urfalees had managed to preserve the chants of late antique Edessa.

'It's a very difficult subject,' said Gianmaria, offering me a cigarette and lighting up himself. 'I've been working on the music of Urfa for seven years now, and it may take that long again before I manage to prove anything conclusively.'

The three of us walked round the corner to Gianmaria's flat.

It was bare and almost empty of furniture, but its shelves groaned with weighty reference books, stacks of notebooks and lines of neatly catalogued cassette tapes.

'What I don't understand,' I said, 'is how you can ever know that what we heard tonight is unchanged since the Byzantine period.'

'We don't know for sure,' replied Gianmaria. 'Up to now there have been no specialised studies of the Urfalees' music, and before my coming here the music was never written down. But it does appear to be a very early and very conservative tradition. There is no hard evidence, but it is difficult to believe that the form of this music has been substantially changed over the ages: sacred traditions change very, very slowly, if at all, over the centuries. Yesterday I was listening to the tapes I made seven years ago when I first started working on this. Although nothing is written down, since then there has not been one change – not one note has been added or omitted.'

'And if there have been no changes made to this music, what does that mean?'

'In manuscripts of the hymns of St Ephrem of Edessa – some of the very first Christian hymns ever composed – Ephrem writes in about 370 A.D. that he took his melodies and rhythms from Gnostic songs composed by the Edessan heretic Bardaisan. He says that their 'sweet rhythms still beguiled the hearts of men' – in other words that they were still popular and everyone in Edessa knew the tunes. Ephrem merely added new words – and orthodox sentiments – of his own. So if there has been no change to those melodies over the centuries, they should, in principle, be those composed by Bardaisan.'

'In the third century A.D.?'

'Bardaisan died in 220, so they could be earlier still, late second century.'

'And how does this compare with the oldest texts of Western music?'

'There is no agreement on which is the oldest Western text. There are four contenders, all of them very early forms of Gregorian chant. The most likely is Ambrosian, the chant of Milan; but there's also Romano Antiquo, the chant of Rome; Mozarabic, that of Spain; and Gallican, early French plainchant. They all represent very ancient forms of music, almost certainly dating back to the fifth century in the case of Ambrosian, but we have no musical notation written down for any of them before the tenth century A.D.'

'But their melodies could be as old as those of Urfa?'

'In principle,' said Gianmaria. 'But in practice that is extremely unlikely.'

'Why?'

'Because the earliest forms of Western plainchant all have markedly Eastern characteristics.'

'In other words they look like imports?'

'Exactly. And there is firm documentary evidence, in the church of Milan at least, that this new Western chant was deliberately modelled on older Syrian practice: St Ambrose's biographer writes that the hymns and psalms of the church of Milan "should be sung in the Syrian manner" because it was so popular.'

All this fitted in very well with what I knew from my own reading. Certainly there was no doubt that Syrian music was regarded with reverence throughout the Byzantine world. There are references in the sources to bands of Syrian monks bursting into song in Haghia Sophia, astounding the Sunday congregation with their strange litanies to the crucified Christ. Moreover the greatest of all Byzantine composers, St Romanos the Melodist, was a Syrian from Emesa (modern Homs), just to the south of Aleppo. His hymns and antiphons took Justinian's Constantinople by storm, but they have been shown to be heavily indebted to those of St Ephrem of Edessa. Furthermore, St Hilary of Poitiers, who first introduced the hymn to Europe – and likewise drew heavily on St Ephrem's Edessan hymns for his models – seems to have first heard the new form when he was exiled from Gaul to Asia Minor by the Emperor Constantius.

'So is it possible that what we heard tonight may be the most ancient form of Christian music still being sung anywhere in the world?'

'That's what I am investigating. Coptic and Eastern Chaldean chants are also very old. They may have affinities with certain types of very ancient Jewish synagogue chants, particularly those preserved by the Jews of the Yemen. If so, elements in their tradition may predate the Urfalees' music. But from what we know of the sources, the chants of ancient Edessa should be the oldest original chants in the Christian tradition. What we heard tonight shows every sign of being the unadulterated music of late antique Edessa. If that is so – and it's a big if – then you could certainly argue that it may well be the most ancient Christian chant still in existence, yes.'

'And so the ultimate origin of the Western Gregorian tradition, and everything else that followed – the root from which Palestrina, Allegri and Victoria all grew . . . ?'

Gianmaria stubbed out his cigarette. 'That's speculation,' he said. Then he shrugged his shoulders and smiled. 'Wait until my research is published.'

THE CONVENT OF SEIDNAYA, 11 SEPTEMBER

A series of lifts – a truck, a pick-up and finally a tractor – brought me to the ruined Byzantine town of Serjilla in time for lunch. I sat at the brow of the hill munching the sandwiches they had packed for me at the Baron, looking down over the extraordinary expanse of late antique buildings spread out across the valley below.

It was the sort of classical townscape that you normally see only in Roman and Byzantine mosaics. There were houses, a church, an inn, a set of baths, a couple of villas facing onto their own courtyards, and a scattering of farm buildings, with the pitched rooflines of still more pedimented and colonnaded buildings visible over the brow of the hill. Elsewhere such late classical towns are represented only by bald archaeological sites: tidied lines of bleached pillars, crumbling metopes and fallen architraves. But here, through a strange accident of fate, more intact domestic

Byzantine buildings lay clustered at my feet in this obscure valley than survive today in all three of the greatest Byzantine metropolises – Constantinople, Antioch and Alexandria – put together.

The perfection of preservation here is extraordinary. Outside some of the houses you can still see olive presses – round basins with a stone funnel leading into a lower tub for the pressed oil – standing as if ready for this year's olive harvest. The colonnade of the inn still provides shade from the sun; the town meeting house, with its pedimented roof and tabernacled windows, still exudes an air of pompous provincial pride, as if the Byzantine gentlemen farmers who lived here were only out in the fields, overseeing their labourers, and would be back in the evening to discuss some weighty matter of village politics.

The view before me was almost exactly as it would have been when John Moschos passed through these hills on his way to Antioch at the end of the sixth century. Looking inside one villa, peering under the superbly carved entablature of a doorway, I could see in the darkness that the first-floor ceiling was still totally intact: in two thousand years, the earthquakes and upheavals that had levelled Antioch had left not one crack in this structure. Only the total absence of furniture and wooden fittings hinted at what had happened to this fine late antique townhouse; and after the perfection of the view from the top of the hill, I was almost disappointed not to find tables and chairs in the kitchens, nor plates of fruit waiting on the dressers, as they do in the mosaics at Antakya.

On the lower slope of the hillside, behind the town baths, lay an empty Byzantine sarcophagus. Its heavy granite cover was half broken off and there seemed to be no one about, so I hid my heavy rucksack inside it, out of sight under the remaining half of the covering slab, and set off across the low hills towards the neighbouring town of al-Barra.

It was a cool, bright autumn afternoon and thick clouds were racing overhead, casting quick-moving shadows over the massif. The hills were rolling and stony, and on the summits square Byzantine watchtowers rose vertically from the scree. Descending into al-Barra I found myself facing a small, square fifth-century church. It had a triple-arched portal, with each doorway surmounted by a finely carved tympanum. The doorways led into a tiny interior, only three bays long. The capitals were covered with vine-scroll interlace, each leaf raised by drilling away the stone behind it, as with an engraving; between the fronds small equal-armed Greek crosses nested like birds among the grapes and the vine tendrils.

I clambered up onto a wall and from that height saw what was invisible from the ground: that littered throughout the olive groves was another complete Byzantine ghost town, the stone skeletons of towers, vaults, and half-collapsed townhouses rising everywhere from the soft loam. At the edge of the trees, to the east, some of the largest and airiest of the villas were still inhabited. From my vantage point I could see a Syrian woman in a patterned headscarf peeping out of a late Roman window in one of the largest houses. A washing line ran from the final pillar on her colonnade to the handle of a massive Roman sarcophagus to one side; on it, children's clothes were hanging out to dry in the afternoon sun. Nearby, hens were perching on another fallen pillar which had been hollowed out to make a drinking trough. But the villagers clearly disdained to live in the slightly less grand villas that lay on the lower ground, a little deeper into the groves; after all, these houses had only four or five main rooms, which did not leave enough space for the stabling of horses, asses, goats and sheep; nor, as I discovered when I made a closer inspection, did they have any baths with hypocaust systems, so useful for keeping bantams in.

Carrying on through the trees, I began to climb over a small drystone wall that separated the land of two farmers; only when I was halfway over did I notice that the wall was made up of a pile of discarded doorjambs, carved tympana and inscribed lintels, an almost ridiculous richness of fine Byzantine sculpture piled up between the trees. Only in Syria, I thought, could a currency of this richness be so debased in value by the embarrassment of its profusion that it could be used for so humble a purpose as walling.

A little beyond this wall, across the ruins of the town's old marketplace, lay a pyramid. It rested on a squat cube of warm honey-coloured limestone. At the corners of the cube four stumpy pilasters rose to a quadrant of richly curlicued Corinthian capitals. Bands of deeply cut acanthus ran along all four sides of the cube, the swirling leaf-patterns broken by a series of medallions. These turned out to contain the *chi-rho* monogram that Constantine turned into the symbol of his new Christian Empire. The apparently pagan pyramid was in fact a very unusual early-fifth-century Christian monument.

Inside the half-light of the tomb chamber lay five great sarcophagi. Unusually, the lids still sealed the caskets shut; the sleepers slept on undisturbed. In the centre, flanked on either side by two smaller caskets, lay the great sarcophagus of what was clearly the family patriarch: a ton of polished porphyry, unornamented but for a massive *chi-rho* monogram contained within a laurel wreath. The sheer baroque bulk of the sarcophagus somehow suggested a portly landowner, a big-bellied, bucolic figure, dangling grapes into his open mouth as he reclined on his couch.

The pyramid lay in front of the ruins of a magnificent villa, three storeys high. The way the pyramid was located in relation to the house implied that it must have been the dynastic mausoleum of the family who had lived there, not dissimilar to the arrangement – centuries later, in a very different world – at Castle Howard.

Now the villa was deserted except for a single tethered donkey belonging to one of the olive harvesters. But as I wandered around its collapsing and deserted rooms I wondered about the family that had lived here. Who had built this small palace? The provincial governor? A local landowner? A prominent senator, returning to his home town for burial after a life of politicking in the capital? The house and its adjacent tomb indicated the existence of an entire world – that of the provincial Byzantine aristocracy – which is passed over in the written sources. In the tenth century there are the writings of the misanthropist Cecaumenus, a grumpy provincial squire who advised his readers to avoid the court, lock up their daughters and keep their wives far from any visitors; but from the early Byzantine period there is relatively little to illuminate the life of the landowning class in the eastern provinces, except when such a figure forms the background for a saint's miracle story or emerges briefly from obscurity to lead a rebellion or champion some obscure heresy.

The sheer magnificent solidity of the family sarcophagi, the confidence and certainty of the workmanship and the conservative nature of the design seemed to hint at a world far removed from the nervy credulity of Theodoret's monks suspended in their cages and raised on their pillars. They also emphasised the degree of continuity between the late classical and the early Byzantine world, a continuity that is easily forgotten when reading the chroniclers' narratives of interminable palace coups, mutinous Gothic generals and collapsing frontiers.

For this ostensibly Christian monument is only barely converted from paganism, and the thinnest veneer of Christianity rests uneasily on what is unashamedly a pagan classical pyramid. Looking at the great porphyry caskets, I wondered whether the calm certainty of the mausoleum was a sham – a brave attempt to maintain classical values in a world where the surface of ancient life was being betrayed at every turn: in the new-fangled clothes that were being worn, in the beliefs that were held, in the strange chants of the Syrian monks and the prophecies of the stylites. Or did it in fact represent the reality? Did the people in these sarcophagi still lead a version of the old life of the late classical landowner: their youth spent in the law school at Beirut or the School of Libanius at Antioch; a period as a provincial official posted to Hippo or Harran; or perhaps a spell in the army on the Rhine frontier, peering over the cold battlements of Cologne or Trier to catch a glimpse of a Gothic raider padding across the ice into Roman territory; then the return to the home estate and the comforts of the richest and most civilised part of the Empire, with winters of hunting and feasting, the occasional marriage party of a neighbouring landowner or a trip to the theatre at Apamea; of afternoons wallowing in the baths at Serjilla and evenings spent reading Homer by the light of an oil lamp. Wandering through the Byzantine villa, through a succession of cool, high-ceilinged rooms, the stone still fitted perfectly, joint by joint, a classical pediment on every window frame, I felt sure that more of the ancient world had survived for longer in the Byzantine East than any of the surviving sources – including John Moschos – now indicate.

Lost in my Byzantine thoughts, I hadn't noticed that it had turned chilly. A faint yellow-gilt pallor now hung over the olive groves, and the oblique late-afternoon light threw long shadows among the trees. Worried that I had already spent too long in al-Barra, I set off at a brisk pace on the road back to Serjilla to pick up my rucksack before darkness fell. As I walked I wondered what had happened to these strange, deserted Byzantine towns. They certainly had not been burned and destroyed by raiding parties of Persians or Arabs; their marvellous preservation showed that. So what did happen?

No one is sure, but the results of a number of recent digs appear to have convinced archaeologists that the entire Levantine coast underwent some form of major economic and demographic crisis towards the end of the sixth century, a full half century *before* the Arab conquest. Plagues, political upheavals, the Persian wars and the raids of desert nomads were responsible for the gradual erosion of urban life and its replacement by a landscape of small villages and monasteries. Some of the larger secular estates and their estate villages might have survived for a while (including that, perhaps, of the entombed aristocrat of al-Barra), but in most places the ancient Levantine trading towns – places like Palmyra, Bosra and Jerash – disappeared forever, forgotten by the world until the Scottish painter David Roberts popularised their ruins, turning them into neat idylls, perfectly tailored to the tastes of nineteenth-century European romantics. While the ancient classical trading towns were falling into decay, in the countryside the ever-growing cohorts of monks and hermits were gradually settling in and taking over the abandoned forts, forums and pagan temples.

Certainly in the pages of John Moschos the three great metropolises – Antioch, Alexandria and Constantinople – still appear to be thriving: there are, for example, stories about labourers rebuilding public edifices in Antioch. But elsewhere in the eastern

Previous page Qala'at Semaan, the Basilica of St Symeon Stylites, Syria.

Above Deserted Byzantine buildings, Serjilla, Syria.

Left Late antique pyramid tomb, al-Barra, Syria.

The Convent of Seidnaya, Syria.

Drive-in Armageddon, Beirut.

The Monastery of Koshaya, Qadisha Valley, Lebanon.

Sculpture from the Temple of the Sun, Ba'albek.

provinces there are only very occasional glimpses of the old classical civic life, with its theatres, schools, brothels, markets and circuses. We hear, for example, about an actor from Tarsus who cohabits with two concubines and 'performs deeds truly worthy of the demons who urged him on', implying that the Tarsus theatre was still functioning healthily. At the same time we know that the ancient trading city of Apamea still had a functioning hippodrome, for Moschos tells us how a former champion charioteer from the town went on to become a monk in Egypt, where he was later captured and enslaved by desert nomads.

Moreover, *The Spiritual Meadow* contains occasional references to merchants and trade, which implies that international commerce – the prerequisite for true urban life – had not yet completely died. At Ascalon Moschos hears about a merchant whose ship has sunk and so is thrown into prison, while his wife is forced to prostitute herself in order to pay his debts. On another occasion he tells of a gem engraver travelling by sea; he hears from his cabin boy that the crew is about to murder him for his boxes of precious gems, so he throws the entire hoard overboard.

But these stories are exceptions. Far more common are tales set against a background of small villages or remote estates, or else in the distant wilderness where hermits can live alone for years undisturbed by anyone – so much so that their deaths can go unremarked for decades. In one particularly macabre tale, a community of monks see mysterious lights at night at the top of the mountain high above their monastery. When daybreak comes they send up a party to investigate, who find that the source of the strange celestial aura is a small cave. Inside they discover an anchorite in a hair shirt. One of the monks embraces the ascetic, only to realise that he is dead. Although his body is miraculously well preserved, a note written by the dying monk indicates that he had 'departed this life' more than seventeen years previously.

The degree to which monasteries, with their mystical and otherworldly outlook, came to dominate the culture of the region is demonstrated by a set of gospels illuminated in the sixth century at the lost monastery of Beth Zagba, believed by Byzantinists to lie somewhere in the hills around Serjilla. In the illustrations of the Rabula Gospels, the angels are as real as the saints, who in turn are drawn to look like local monks: gaunt rustics caught in mid-argument, hands wildly gesticulating, their expression masked beneath thick growths of beard. In the most famous picture, of the Ascension, Christ hovers in his fiery chariot only just out of reach of the apostles. No dramatic gulf separates his divine world from that of his followers; he is the same size as them, has similar features and wears similar clothes. No barrier separates the natural from the supernatural.

Another illustration, that of Christ Enthroned, takes this immediacy even further. Christ is shown in majesty, on a golden throne studded with huge cabochon jewels. But around him, flanking him on either side, are not the expected crowd of seraphim and cherubim but a crowd of rough-robed Syrian monks. They are hooded and cowled in their sober brown sackcloth, hair grey, eyes staring, gospel books clutched to their chests as if they were clustered around the abbot in the chapter house or refectory. There is none of the chill remoteness of much late Byzantine art; here the superhuman is considered tangible and everyday, the divine imminent and directly accessible.

This sort of mystical abstraction is a world away from the practical late Roman farmers of Serjilla or the pyramid-dynasty of al-Barra. And yet if recent scholarship is correct, it seems increasingly likely that the two worlds – those of the gentrified landed estates and the isolated wild-eyed illuminator monks – coexisted side by side in these hills, and that the transition both from the pagan-classical to the Byzantine-Christian, and then, three centuries later, from the Byzantine-Christian to the medieval-Islamic, was a far more gradual process than the traditional accounts of violent change and invasion would allow.

In the Middle East, the reality of continuity has always been masked by a surface impression of cataclysm.

Returning in the dusk to Serjilla, I narrowly avoided being torn limb from limb by a pack of enormous sheepdogs. I had just rescued my pack from its sarcophagus and was returning up the hill when the beasts came howling out of the shadows, closing in on me with great leaps and bounds. With only seconds to spare, I managed to scramble up the fallen wall of a tumbledown Byzantine farmhouse, and stood there perched on a projecting gable like a stylite on his pillar. Pulling my rucksack up after me, I looked down to see three wolf-dogs growling below me, mouths open, each exhibiting a truly Baskervillian set of fangs. It was little comfort to think that sheepdogs also seem to have been a hazard of the region in Byzantine times: the unattractive anti-Semitic monastic rabble-rouser Barsauma survived an attack by dogs during his youth, which according to his biographer was understood to presage his future sainthood.

Eventually, just when I was beginning to think that I was going to have to spend the night up on my perch, the shepherd – a small fifteen-year-old boy – came up. He scattered the three dogs as easily as if they were poodles with a torrent of abuse and a hail of small pebbles. At my request he escorted me out of the ruins and onto the track before returning to his flock and the night-shelter of the old Serjilla bath house.

Quickening my pace, and mouthing prayers that I would not pass any more shepherds or their dogs, I headed back to the main road, and just managed to catch the last bus of the day before darkness fell. It was heading south.

A two-hour drive brought me to Homs. At the time of John Moschos, Homs was known as Emesa, and was home to figures as diverse as, on the one hand, Romanos the Melodist, and on the other, St Symeon the Fool, who used to defecate in the centre of the marketplace and complained that the girls of Emesa were 'as licentious as any in Syria'. Homs was famous for its taverns, jugglers, mimers, prostitutes, dancing girls and beggars, as well as for the overheated libido of its clergy: Deacon John of Emesa, the Casanova of the Byzantine Church, was notorious for his habit of making love to all the most beautiful married women in his congregation. Homs was also the place where the early Anglo-Saxon pilgrim St Willibald was imprisoned for several months on his way to Jerusalem. It is still one of the principal Christian towns in Syria, but today is famous only for the stupidity of its inhabitants: contemporary Homsis play the same role in Syrian jokes as the Polish do in those of America, the Irish in Britain, and Kerrymen in Ireland. I decided against staying the night in the city and headed on instead to the convent of Seidnaya, the most important of the three Byzantine monasteries still functioning in Syria.

On the rattling country bus I sat beside an old Arab farmer. Discovering where I was going, he regaled me with stories of the exploits of a figure he called Malik Jylan of Rum. It was only later, when I read about the myth of the monastery's foundation by the Emperor Justinian, that I realised that my companion had been telling me a version of the same story: of how the Emperor – Malik Jylan in Arabic – out on a hunting expedition, had chased a stag up a rocky eminence. Just as he was about to draw his bow, the stag changed into the Virgin Mary. The Virgin commanded him to build a convent on the site, which, she said, had previously been hallowed by Noah himself, who planted a vine there soon after the Flood. According to my friend on the bus, if I understood him correctly, the Emperor then installed his own sister as the first abbess. The origin of the legend would appear to be etymological: in Aramaic Seidnaya means both 'our lady' and 'a hunting place'.

The road wound steeply up into the hills, and the bus stopped in village after village. By the time it dropped me off in the dark at the bottom of the hill leading up to the monastery it was after nine o'clock, and I was worried that the abbey gates would have closed for the night. Exhausted, I trudged uphill towards the lights of the convent, which sat, more like a crusader castle than a shrine, on a spur of rock at the very top of the village. In the cold and the darkness I was anxiously aware that the last bus had just departed and that the small village around the foot of the rock contained no hotel or lodging house.

The gateway of the convent was reached up a steep flight of stairs; and at the top, to my relief, I found that the door was open. Walking into an empty courtyard, my feet echoing on the flagstones, I wondered where the nuns had gone. Then I heard the distant sound of Orthodox chant drifting from the church and headed towards it.

Two nuns in black veils were chanting at a lectern, while a priest, hidden behind the iconostasis, echoed their chants in a deep reverberating bass. The church was no older than the early nineteenth century, despite some medieval masonry low down in the walls of the nave. But its atmosphere was as authentically Byzantine as any I had seen on Athos. The only light came from a few flickering lamps attached to steel chandeliers suspended from the ceiling on gold chains. As the candle-light waxed and waned with the draught, the frescoes in the domes and semi-domes flashed momentarily into view then disappeared again into the shadows.

When the travel writer Colin Thubron visited the convent in 1966, he claimed to have witnessed a miracle: to have seen the face of the icon of Notre Dame de Seidnaya stream with tears. In the same church I too witnessed a miracle, or something that today would certainly be regarded as a miracle in almost any other country in the Middle East. For the congregation seemed to consist not of Christians but almost entirely of heavily bearded Muslim men. As the priest circled the altar with his thurible, filling the sanctuary with great clouds of incense, the men bobbed up and down on their prayer mats as if in the middle of Friday prayers in a great mosque. Their women, some dressed in full black *chador*, mouthed prayers from the shadows of the exo-narthex. A few, closely watching the Christian women, went up to the icons hanging from the pillars of the church, kissed them, then lit candles and placed them in the candelabra in front of the images. As I watched from the rear of the church I could see the faces of the women reflected in the illuminated gilt of the icons.

Towards the end of the service, the priest reappeared with a golden stole over his cassock and circled the length of the church with his thurible, gently and almost apologetically stepping over the prostrate Muslims blocking his way, treading as carefully as if they were precious Iznik vases. While I had seen Muslims and Christians praying together on the island of Buyuk Ada, off Istanbul, this was something quite different: a degree of tolerance – in

187

both congregations – unimaginable today almost anywhere else in the Near East. Yet it was, of course, the old way: the Eastern Christians and the Muslims have lived side by side for nearly one and a half millennia, and have only been able to do so due to a degree of mutual tolerance and shared customs unimaginable in the solidly Christian West.

How easy it is today to think of the West as the home of freedom of thought and liberty of worship, and to forget how, as recently as the seventeenth century, Huguenot exiles escaping religious persecution in Europe would write admiringly of the policy of religious tolerance practised across the Ottoman Empire. The same broad tolerance that had given homes to hundreds of thousands of penniless Jews, expelled by bigoted Catholic kings from Spain and Portugal, protected the Eastern Christians in their ancient homelands, despite the Crusades and the continual hostility of the Christian West. Only in the twentieth century has that traditional tolerance been replaced by a new hardening in Islamic attitudes; and only recently has the syncretism of Cyrrhus and Seidnaya become a precious rarity.

As vespers drew to a close the pilgrims began to file quietly out, and I was left alone at the back of the church with my rucksack. As I was standing there I was approached by a young nun in a knitted black balaclava; it was shaped a little like the Sutton Hoo helmet, with a long tailpiece which trailed down the back of her neck. Sister Tecla had intelligent black eyes and a bold, confident gaze; she spoke fluent English with a slight French accent. She asked me where I was from, and after I had told her I remarked on the number of Muslims in the congregation. Was it at all unusual, I asked.

'The Muslims come here because they want babies,' said the nun simply. 'Our Lady has shown her power and healed many of the Muslims. Those people started to talk about her and now more Muslims come here than Christians. If they ask for her she will be there.'

As we were speaking, we were approached by a Muslim couple. The woman was veiled – only her mouth was visible through the black wraps; her husband, a burly man who wore his beard without a moustache, looked remarkably like the wilder sort of Hezbollah commander featured in news bulletins from southern Lebanon. But whatever his politics, he carried in one hand a heavy tin of olive oil and in the other a large plastic basin full of fresh loaves, and he gave both to the nun, bowing his head as shyly as a schoolboy and retreating backwards in obvious embarrassment.

'They come in the evening,' continued the nun. 'They make vows and then the women spend the night. They sleep on a blanket in front of the holy icon of Our Lady painted by St Luke. Sometimes the women eat the wick of a lamp that has burned in front of the image, or maybe drink the holy oil. Then in the morning they drink from the spring in the courtyard. Nine months later they have babies.'

'And it works?'

'I have seen it with my own eyes,' said Sister Tecla. 'One Muslim woman from Jordan had been waiting for a baby for twenty-five years. She was beyond the normal age of childbearing, but someone told her about the Virgin of Seidnaya. She came here and spent two nights in front of the icon. She was so desperate she ate the wicks of nearly twenty lamps.'

'What happened?'

'She came back the following year,' said Sister Tecla, 'with triplets.'

The nun led me up the south aisle of the church, and down a corridor into the chapel which sheltered the icons. At the doorway she removed her shoes and indicated that I should do likewise. I placed them with my rucksack, beside the great mountain of footwear already deposited in the antechamber and Sister Tecla led me into the muffled sanctuary. It was darker even than the church, with no windows to admit the faint light of the moon and stars which had cast a silvery light over the high altar during vespers. Here only the twinkling of a hundred lamps lit the interior, allowing us to avoid tripping over a pair of Muslims prostrated on their prayer carpets near the entrance.

'And you have no objection to so many Muslims coming here and praying in your church?' I whispered.

'We are all children of God,' said Sister Tecla. 'The All Holy One brings us all together.'

She kissed an icon of the warrior saints Sergius and Bacchus, then turned back to face me. 'Sometimes the Muslims promise to christen a child born through the Mother of God's intervention. This happens less frequently than it used to, but of course we like it when it does. Others make their children Muslims, but when they are old enough they bring them here to help us in some way, perhaps with cleaning the church or in the kitchens.'

The shrine of the icon was thick with the low murmur of prayer and chanting; those pilgrims who were talking to each other did so in hushed voices. Behind me a Syrian paratrooper in full khaki fatigues entered the shrine, having first deposited his heavy boots by the entrance. He advanced towards the icons on his knees, crossing himself all the while and murmuring prayers to the Virgin. Here, you felt instinctively, rather than in the church, was the centre of the convent's devotion.

In the lamplight, smoke-blackened icons were everywhere, some of them very fine. There was a Beheading of John the Baptist, from which pious pilgrims had scratched out the face of the executioner; there were several of the Panaghia, including one in which the Madonna was shown with thin, almond-shaped eyes as if she was a Persian princess; there was a fine image of the Dormition, the composition of which, intriguingly enough, seemed to be derived from the Ascension in the Rabula Gospels. But the most famous of the images of Our Lady of Seidnaya, the sacred icon supposed to have been painted by St Luke, was invisible, so cluttered was it with knotted silk ribbons, scribbled petitions and silver plaques representing the parts of the bodies of the pilgrims which had been healed through the Virgin's prayers.

As Sister Tecla led the way from the shrine she said, 'Come: I will take you to the guest rooms. You must eat before you go to bed.' Up to that point neither of us had broached the subject of where I was to spend the night.

In the guest rooms I was shown to a divan, while a servant

took my rucksack to my cell. Sister Tecla poured me a small cup of bitter Arab coffee from a thermos flask, then sent the servant to the kitchens for some food. It arrived a few minutes later, brought by a young novice: a plate of thin soup and some feta cheese accompanied by flat pitta bread. Sister Tecla sat opposite me as I ate, and I asked her about an unexpected photograph which was framed on the wall beside my table.

'These are our Syrian cosmonauts,' she said, pointing to a picture of three men in space suits clutching their helmets under their arms rather as stage ghosts hold their heads. 'They spent a month together on the Soviet space station Mir.'

'But why is the picture here?' I asked.

'It was given to us by the cosmonauts after they returned to Syria.'

'They came here?'

'Of course. All three are Muslims, but they visited Seidnaya before they went, to pray for good luck. As soon as they had returned safely they came here again.'

'To tell the nuns about their adventures?'

'No, no,' said Sister Tecla, looking at me as one might at a rather dim ten-year-old. 'They came to thank the Virgin and give us presents: this picture and a sheep.'

'A sheep?'

'A sheep.'

'As . . . as a pet?'

'No, no,' said Sister Tecla, frowning again. 'The cosmonauts came here to cut the sheep's throat, of course.' She gave me another withering look. 'It was a sacrifice to the Virgin,' she said, 'to thank her for their safe return from outer space.'

IV

HOTEL CAVALIER, BEIRUT, LEBANON, 23 SEPTEMBER
1994

After a fortnight of glorious indolence staying with friends in a diplomatic suburb of Damascus, I was woken this morning by the sound of Bing, their Filipino manservant, blow-drying my now spotlessly clean rucksack.

Slowly the daunting prospect of the day ahead began to take shape: leaving the soft beds, the cool blue swimming pool and my hospitable hosts – all for the uncertainties of the Lebanon, a country which for the last two decades has been virtually a synonym for anarchy.

To an earlier generation, Lebanon brought to mind images of skiing amid the cedars and sunbathing on the lido at Byblos, followed by flighty evenings in the casinos of Jounieh. But for those of us who grew up during the eighties, Beirut is of course associated with a rather different set of images: grainy front-page pictures of the massed Palestinian corpses at Sabra and Chatila; Don McCullin's photographs of the fire-blackened ruins of the lunatic asylum the Israelis bombarded with phosphorus; television pictures of the hostages; the impacting shells of the bloody militia wars – the PLO versus the Phalange, the Phalange versus Amal, Amal versus Hezbollah, Hezbollah versus the PLO. None of these made one in a particular hurry to rush to see the country for oneself.

195

For two weeks this diary has lain unwritten, unread, under a pile of freshly washed and immaculately ironed clothes. Since I last opened it in Seidnaya, the days have been filled neither with writing nor research; instead I have spent an unscheduled fortnight on the carousel of Syria's diplomatic whirl: a *soirée* at the Greek Ambassador's (dancing until 2.30 in the morning); a vast dinner with an Armenian entrepreneur; trips in the Land-Rover to an old ruin or a new restaurant; swimming; lunch in a palace in the old city; drinks with a Damascene aesthete amid his collection of icons. After the tensions of Turkey and the Spartan eccentricities of Seidnaya and the Baron it was a welcome – in fact an almost unbelievably wonderful – change. The only real irritation in the entire period was the incessant noise of building in the apartment above that of my hosts, where a *mukhabarat* general was about to move in and where the builders were busy installing marble floors, mirrored ceilings and pink bathtubs with gilt taps the shape of flying swans – apparently the sort of kitsch accessories that make secret policemen feel at home.

But now I was ready to move on, and the more I heard about Lebanon the more fascinated I became by the prospect of that strange country. Over drinks, people would tell the most bizarre stories about the war and its aftermath: the time the victorious Palestinian militias exhumed the Christian dead from the cemetery at Damour, scattering a couple of hundred cadavers and skeletons around the streets, all of them still dressed in the frock-coats and Sunday suits in which they were buried a century earlier; stories of Beirut's cockerels, that appeared to be suffering from a form of post-traumatic stress syndrome (they start crowing at midnight, only to fall silent at dawn); the renowned Lebanese vineyard of Château Musar, that only lost one vintage during the entire war – in 1984, when the front line between the Christian and Muslim militias ran between the vines and the winery.

Most of all, however, I was becoming fascinated by the Maronites. They sounded very different from any of the other Christian communities I have so far come across on my journey. Although they do not appear in *The Spiritual Meadow*, the Maronites started off as a cult around a Byzantine hermit who was a near-contemporary of John Moschos. Indeed St Maron's ascetic tendencies were so extreme that he earned a place in Theodoret's compendium of eremitical eccentricity, *The History of the Monks of Syria*. In this, their first appearance in history, the Maronites started as they meant to continue: on St Maron's death a 'bitter war' broke out among his followers and their neighbours over the saint's body: 'one of the adjacent [Maronite] villages that was well populated came out in a mass, drove off the others and seized this thrice-desired treasure'.

Later, the Maronites' somewhat eccentric theology came to be deemed heretical by the official Byzantine Church. The details of this are wonderfully Byzantine: Monothelitism, the particular brand of Christology then favoured by the Maronites, had originally been promoted by the Emperor Heraclius as a compromise definition of the person of Christ which would be acceptable to both Orthodox and Monophysites and so unite the divided Empire; inevitably, however, it was rejected by both parties, leaving the unfortunate Maronites, the only community to accept the definition, to be branded as heretics and persecuted accordingly. This was largely due to the influence of John Moschos's travelling companion Sophronius, who in his old age became a rigorously Orthodox Patriarch of Jerusalem, and set himself up as the most bitter opponent of Monothelitism.

To escape further Byzantine harassment, the Maronites were gradually forced to emigrate from their low-lying Syrian heartlands into the impenetrable fastness of Mount Lebanon. There, amid the cliffs and narrow passes, they were able to defend themselves against all their enemies, both Christian and Muslim, until centuries later, at the time of the Crusades, they came into communion with Rome and managed to form an alliance with the Franks. It was an alliance that very loosely, in one form or another, was to continue up to the twentieth century: in 1920, out of the Syrian territories they inherited from the Ottoman Empire at the end of the First World War, the French created a 'State of Greater Lebanon' specifically for the Maronites and at the Maronites' explicit request.

In return the Maronites attempted – and indeed still attempt

– to be more French than the French. The Maronite upper classes speak French as their first language and usually refuse to speak Arabic except to servants and tradesmen. Most of them have French Christian names. They send their children to Paris for as much of their education as they can afford. Moreover they adamantly deny their Syrian roots, and in the course of this century have invented an almost entirely mythical Phoenician (i.e. semi-European) origin for themselves, while visualising Lebanon as a sort of Near Eastern outpost of France, a country which they still refer to as 'the nourishing mother'.

Most commentators have tended to attribute the balance of responsibility for the outbreak of the civil war to the Maronites' intransigence, their unapologetic Christian supremacism, their contempt for their Muslim neighbours, and their point-blank refusal to share Lebanon with the landless Palestinian refugees ejected from their homes at the creation of Israel in 1948.

Under the terms of the 1943 Lebanese National Pact, supreme power – in the form of the Presidency – was placed in the hands of the Maronites as a reflection of the Christians' numerical superiority. But by the 1970s the Maronites were no longer the largest single religious group in Lebanon, being outnumbered by both Sunni and Shia Muslim communities. Despite this, the Maronites adamantly refused to discuss any reform that would share power more equally between the different groupings. Instead, they began to arm themselves and to prepare for war.

When the civil war finally broke out, the Maronites were ready. Modelling themselves on the Crusaders, they went into battle with crosses sewn onto their uniforms and icons of the Virgin glued to their rifle butts. Their militias were given neo-medieval names like the Knights of the Virgin, the Youth of St Maron and the Wood of the Cross. Yet for all these chivalrous titles, the Maronite militias were responsible for more than their fair share of the war's worst atrocities: the notorious massacres at Sabra and Chatila, where at least six hundred (and perhaps as many as two thousand) Palestinian civilians were butchered, was the work of the Maronites' Phalange militia, albeit under Israeli supervision.

The Maronite clergy did little to restrain their flock. Expatriate

Maronite priests such as the parish priest of Our Lady of Mount Lebanon, Beverly Hills, exhorted their congregations to donate money to arm the militias, while the Maronites' enemies accused even the supposedly cloistered Maronite monks of involving themselves in arms dealing. Referring to the large sums said to have been raised by the monks for the war effort, the Druze leader Kemal Jumblatt observed that 'the tonsured heads of Lebanese monks give off a golden halo.'

Certainly, as in Byzantine times, the monks involved themselves closely in politics, tending to support the more extreme ultra-nationalist Maronite militias. Most popular of all in the monasteries were the sinister Guardians of the Cedars, whose symbol was a sword-cum-cross amid flames, and whose particular speciality was cutting the ears off their dead Muslim opponents, then displaying them as trophies. The monastic support given to this group continued, despite the Guardians holding a press conference to applaud the Sabra and Chatila massacres and adopting the macabre slogan 'It is the duty of every Lebanese to kill at least one Palestinian.' The monks were, however, prepared to give their support to other suitably extreme figures: on one occasion Fr. Boulos Naaman, the Superior of the Maronite Order of Monks, went so far as to compare one of the most vicious and bloodthirsty Phalangist leaders, Bashir Gemayel, to 'Christ, with complete understanding of his Christian mission'.

The civil war left between 100,000 and 150,000 dead, and no one came out of it well; but the Maronites certainly emerged with their reputation for ruthlessness, brutality and political incompetence enormously enhanced. They also came out of it fatally weakened. By the final stage of the war, which set Christian against Christian, a third of a million Maronites – over a quarter of the entire Christian community in Lebanon – had fled the Middle East for good, joining the haemorrhage of Christians leaving virtually every country of the region.

After lamenting the demise of a succession of Christian communities in the Middle East which failed adequately to defend themselves, it may seem perverse to criticise the only one that has taken serious action in an attempt to hold its own; but even the other Eastern Christians seem to regard the Maronites as something of an embarrassment in their determination to cling on to their privileges whatever the cost. They certainly sounded very different from the defeated and depressed Armenians and Syriacs I had met in Turkey, or the timid, discreet and low-key Christians of Syria.

If nothing else, I told myself, Lebanon was certainly going to be a change.

By ten o'clock Bing had ironed my jacket and arranged the taxi that was to take me over the mountains to Beirut. I ate a last cooked breakfast (when will I next smell bacon and eggs?) and had just finished packing when the windows shook and, with a noise like a revving chainsaw, the Beirut taxi drove up outside the front gate. It was a souped-up American Thunderbird, the size of small tank, with chrome fenders and a sunshade jutting out above the windscreen. It was driven by a Lebanese spiv in Ray-Bans and a leather jacket. I embraced my anxious hosts, then, with another roar, we were off.

Ten minutes took us out of Damascus, and soon the Thunderbird was burning into the scrub beyond. A further forty minutes and we were heading up into the foothills of Mount Lebanon. A convoy of T-72 tanks crunched down the highway in the opposite direction; President Asad waved goodbye from a hoarding. The road wound steeply upwards, corkscrewing through pine trees and slopes of gorse, and suddenly we were there: the Syrian frontier post – a rambling collection of concrete huts huddled among the pines – lay a little above us at the summit of the mountain.

The border formalities on the Syrian side were surprisingly quick and efficient, easier indeed than it used to be to pass from one European country to another. The guards collected our passports from the car, like waiters in a drive-in McDonald's, then brought them back again a minute later, stamped with their exit visas. We drove on through a no-man's land, past the skeletons of three burnt-out cars — although, rather disappointingly after all I had read about the war, these looked as if they had crashed rather than suffered the strafing of Israeli F-16s. To our right rose a slope of conifers from which wafted the acrid scent of pine resin. We turned a corner and there, amid the trees, recently rebuilt, lay the Lebanese frontier post. Outside it flapped the Lebanese tricolour, overlaid with the Cedar of Lebanon.

Entering Lebanon was rather more problematic than leaving Syria. Six mustachioed beefcakes in camouflage jumpsuits kept us waiting for two hours in the cold while a busload of Libyans begged and pleaded to be let in. The border hut was a grim, seedy bunker, the guards were bored, and none of the Libyans had visas. But eventually, after much twiddling of thumbs, the Libyans gave up and got forlornly back into their bus. Our passports were stamped and the chief official wished us 'Bienvenu au Liban.'

The Thunderbird roared back into life, and at some speed we set off downhill into the green basin of the Bekaa Valley. From above, it seemed as beautiful and bucolic as the Valley of Kashmir: rivers, water meadows, green fields, long lines of poplars and beech avenues all turning yellow in the early autumn cold. It looked the picture of pastoral innocence; nothing about the Bekaa indicated it to be the seedbed of one of the world's largest opium harvests and home to some of the Middle East's most formidable drug barons.

As we twisted down the mountain slope, however, the impression of a gentle pastoral oasis quickly disappeared. Rubbish — cartons, old tyres, cans, crisp packets, binliners — lay like a carpet across the ground, as if there had been no refuse collections for twenty years. Disused carrier bags caught in the barbed wire and furred the hedgerows with white polythene. Wrecked buildings dotted the roadside, neither repaired nor demolished since the end of the war three years earlier. The power lines had everywhere been hijacked by pirate operators, and from every pylon a cat's-cradle of wires tangled their way through a hundred illegal connections to the houses lining the roadside.

One of the root causes of the outbreak of the Lebanese civil war is often said to have been the weakness of the country's central government and its inability to control an overheated economy of unregulated libertarian capitalism: no one paid taxes, therefore there was no government spending, therefore no public services were provided. To all intents and purposes there was no state, and everything, for better or worse, was left to the initiative of the individual. In this respect nothing has changed; indeed it looks as if any semblance of central government control has now broken down completely.

One aspect of this is the role still played in Lebanon by the Syrians. Although we had left Syria ten miles behind us, Syrian troops in clumsy, ill-fitting khaki uniforms – very different from the chic designer camouflage of the Lebanese army – still manned checkpoints at intervals along the road. Syrian *mukhabarat* Range-Rovers, their windows blacked out with friezes of Asad posters, stood parked beside pillboxes painted the colours of the Syrian flag. On the concrete crash-barriers beside these Syrian pockets, the otherwise ubiquitous posters of the Lebanese Prime Minister, Rafiq Hariri – all jowls and double chins like some corpulent Italian waiter – were replaced by the Asad family iconography familiar from Syria: Asad in his paratrooper's fatigues, Asad the general with his peaked cap, Asad the statesman in international pinstripe, Asad's dead son Basil in his trademark reflector shades.

Sometimes the hagiography became more whimsical: on one Syrian pillbox, Asad and Basil were transformed into the idiom of Haight Ashbury flower children, their scowling faces hanging from the stalks of bright, naively-painted sunflowers. At other times the iconography of the different power-brokers in Lebanon was strangely intermingled, so that pin-ups of Asad, Basil, Hariri and a brace of turbaned Iranian mullahs (popular among the Shia of the Bekaa) would all appear together on a single crash-barrier, sometimes in the unlikely company of a leggy Lebanese *chanteuse* or some sequined Egyptian movie starlet.

Perhaps strangest of all were the unlikely lines of hoardings that rose above the forbidding ruins lining the highway: a smiling Claudia Schiffer stretched out leopard-like in Salvatore Ferragamo next to a yellow sandstone French colonial villa so riddled with great round shrapnel-holes it resembled an outsized slice of

Emmental; the Marlboro cowboy with his ten-gallon hat and herd of steers beaming out over an apocalyptic wasteland of shattered tower blocks; a metal tube of Bodymist – *un beau corps sans effort* – set against a carbon-black skeleton of twisted metal that had once been a filling station.

From the bottom of the Bekaa we crawled sluggishly up a narrow ridge, a single lane of traffic moving slowly behind a pair of massive Syrian tank-transporters until, at the top, we found ourselves looking down from an unexpected eminence, through a fug of smog, over the ruins of Beirut to the shattered mirror of the Mediterranean beyond. The Thunderbird's outsized bonnet swung over the hogsback of the ridge, and we were off: down we twisted, through a series of S-bends, under the ruins, past the posters: *Salvatore Ferragamo Pour Hiver 94*; an Ottoman villa pock-marked with small-arms fire; *Valentino: En Exclusivité*; a Bible-black hearse parked outside a church; *Martini: Right Here, Right Now*; two decapitated palm trees; *Calvin by Calvin Klein*; a dead tank; *Cool Budweiser – On Tap*; a bombed-out hospital; *Lucky Strike*; a cluster of skyscrapers so pockmarked with shrapnel they looked like a mouthful of severely rotten teeth; *Versatile by Versace* . . .

It was like a morality tale, spiralling downwards through one of the world's greatest monuments to human frailty, a huge vortex of greed and envy, resentment and intolerance, hatred and materialism, a five mile-long slalom of shellholes and designer labels, heavy artillery and glossy boutiques. Like a modern updating of a Byzantine Apocalypse, it was the confusion that was most hell-like: Ayatollah Khomeini, hands raised in blessing, shared a billboard with a bottle of American after-shave; below, huge American cars – Thunderbirds, Chevrolets, Corvettes – roared past building sites where monstrous machines, thickly carapaced like metal-clad cockroaches, moved earth, demolished ruins, dug holes. Occasionally there was an explosion and a small mushroom-cloud of dust as a doomed tower block crashed to the earth, nudged by one of the grunting metal beetles below.

As we corkscrewed down towards the coastal plain the temperature rose and a thick fug of pollution hovered among the ruined buildings like a pall of gunsmoke. Here and there rose a scattering of kitsch new neo-Baroque villas with red roofs and marble balustrades: the product, presumably, of looting, arms or drug-trade money, for precious few legitimate fortunes have been made in this country during the last two decades. But as we drove deeper and deeper into the shattered city, such signs of prosperity became rarer: we headed on, faster now, on a potholed freeway, hotter and hotter, fuggier and fuggier, more polluted, more wrecked.

Yet for all this destruction, in some places the shrapnel marks were strangely beautiful, like a Kandinsky abstract: a perfect peppering of dots and dashes. It was a tribute to the arms dealers' art: a hail of metal perfectly distributed across a plaster canvas. Even the hideous ruins of the sixties blocks had a strange fascination. Some appeared as if newly built; only the puncture-mark of a massive shellhole through the lateral wall of an apartment indicated what had happened to its interior and its occupants. Others were utterly wrecked: a single wall remained like a grave-stone to mark the whereabouts of an entire tower block; at a distance, an oblique exclamation of concrete and a tangle of metal rods – the building's top storey – would remain where it had landed in the aftermath of the blast or the collapse. Strangest of all were those blocks where the collapsed concrete stories were now folded down on top of each other, like a pile of neatly pressed shirts that had been left hanging off the edge of an ironing board, thick layers of tons of pre-stressed concrete curved over the edge of a hundred-foot drop like soft folds of fine cotton.

Despite the mess, astonishingly, the great majority of the wrecked apartments were still inhabited. In some whose walls were so eroded by shrapnel that they resembled pieces of chronically worm-eaten wood, I would notice washing hanging out to dry or perhaps a shadowy figure taking the air on a half-collapsed bal-cony. As twilight fell over the ruined city, pale and ghostly lights began to come on in one after another of the apparently aban-doned blocks. The ruins, it seemed, were vertical shanty-towns, makeshift billets for impoverished Shia labourers or homeless Palestinians, all rushing to fill the vacuum left by the rehoused rich. Most had patched up their flats with pieces of corrugated iron or slashes of black plastic sheeting; but many others, perhaps the newest arrivals, had not. As we drove past, I found I could look into the illuminated interiors of these people's flats, for they were missing walls or had such huge shellholes that entire suites of rooms were opened up for public inspection like some sort of outsized Advent calender. In one flat I saw a man getting dressed, nonchalantly pulling on his jeans. It was an unremarkable, everyday scene, except that the wall of his apartment had entirely disappeared, so that he was framed by the black concrete superstructure around him, lit up like a cinema screen in a dark auditorium.

As we drove on, past the Green Line which for ten years marked the battlefront between Muslim West Beirut and the Christian East, we left the very worst destruction behind us. But the vision got stranger still. For roughly twenty-five years between 1950 and 1975 – the darkest period in Lebanese architectural history – Beirut's developers laboured to convert an Ottoman jewel of rare beauty into the most hideous high-rise city in the entire Mediterranean. Then for the fifteen years after that, from 1975 to 1990, the Lebanese – with a little help from their friends and neighbours – did their best to tear it all down again, using an impromptu mixture of suction bombs, phosphorus shells, rocket-propelled grenades and Israeli napalm. Yet somehow neither the uncommon ugliness of the post war development nor the spectacular pockmarked legacy of the bloodbath that succeeded it were quite as surprising as the almost surreal lines of glass-fronted and spotlit couture shops that have recently reopened amid the craters, and which now line the bombed-out boulevards of Hamra, their windows full of the latest creations by the fashion houses of Milan and Paris.

The tanks and checkpoints, the shrapnel-marked ruins and collapsing, shell-smashed skyscrapers – all these things, featured in a hundred television documentaries, were expected, and seemed somehow obvious from the first moment of arrival. The real revelations on the final stage of the journey into Beirut – particularly after two months in the rural hinterland of eastern Turkey and northern Syria – were the glitzy American limousines queuing at the lights, and the new ice-cream parlours that have sprung up by the gun emplacements. *This?* I thought, after a twenty-year civil war: *This?* Armageddon I expected; but Armani I did not.

Then, quite suddenly, we were through the city and on the seafront, and everything was all right again, as if the war had never happened and the city had never been besieged and destroyed. The houses on the corniche seemed for some reason relatively untouched by the bombardments, and the silhouettes of the seafront palm trees stood undamaged against the darkening sky. There were girls in shorts and boys in jeans and semi-circles of old men on stools sucking hookahs. Dusk was falling now and many people were promenading, taking the air before it grew dark: chic women with Hermès shoulderbags strutted through the traffic, mobile phones held to their ears; little boys in baseball caps raced their bikes along the pavements; couples strolled hand in hand, or dropped into the seaside cafés.

I told my driver to pull in by a newsstand where copies of European newspapers and magazines were on sale. On the top rack, amid the latest issue of American *Vogue*, the London *Tatler* and a French edition of *Hello!*, a line of *Cosmopolitan*s were on sale, one emblazoned with the banner headline: ARE YOU GETTING ENOUGH?

I got back into the car and we drove to the Hotel Cavalier in Muslim West Beirut. There I checked into a room and spent the next few hours in the bar recovering from the journey with the help of several glasses of cold Stella Artois and one of the most optimistic documents I have ever read. Its title: *Lebanon: The Promised Land of Tourism*.

At nine that night I was still sitting in an alcove of the smoky hotel bar reading *Lebanon: The Promised Land of Tourism*. It really was the most remarkable publication. 'Lebanon is the ideal country,' it maintained, 'for those who desire to enjoy their holiday surrounded by a gay nature, between kind and hospitable people and in the solemn scenery of mountains or on the shores of the blue Mediterranean. It is also an ideal country for those who want to pass their holidays in picturesque cities, staying in touristic localities where feasts and manifestations of all kinds are held.'

It was these manifestations that worried me. What sort of manifestations? Massacres? Gang rape? The mass exhumation of corpses? Undaunted, the anonymous writer of *Lebanon: The Promised Land of Tourism* continued in the same vein: 'Among the countries that are proposed to the choice of the modern tourist, Lebanon, better than any other, allows one to make, apart from the first properly said voyage, a second voyage, equally touching and even richer in spiritual treasures – "a voyage in time". Actually, nobody by visiting Lebanon has the chance of feeling lonely! The hospitality of Lebanon has already become proverbial the world over . . .'

Too right, I thought, as Brian Keenan and John McCarthy had discovered. And after all, who could possibly feel lonely when chained to Terry Waite, with the additional diversion of a truckload of grimly bearded Hezbollah for company?

'For,' continued the brochure, 'when the Lebanese utters the famous phrase "*ahlan wa sahlan*" ("welcome") he squeezes it from his heart and uses his tongue only as a tool for expressing it. No wonder the fame of that worldwide saying that Lebanon is the Home of Goodwill! When you leave this Promised Land you will be carrying a gift that no one shall contest, which no custom officer will dare to charge you for . . .'

What was coming next, I wondered? What was this unique duty-free item that it was possible to smuggle through the Lebanese customs? A crate of raw opium? A trunkful of powdered heroin? A ton of Semtex? None of these, apparently:

'. . . that gift, that will lie in the depth of your heart, is a feeling of all pervading gratitude and majesty, a deep rooted human feeling which only great civilisations can offer to their guests.'

I was still wading through great drifts of this slush when I looked up and to my surprise saw across the bar a friend whom I had met and very much liked on a previous assignment in the West Bank. Juan Carlos Gumucio is a huge, Bolivian-born journalist, formerly with Associated Press and *The Times*, now representing *El Pais*. Juan Carlos (or J.C., as he is known) is a heavily built, densely bearded giant with a great mop of wiry hair and a barrel for a belly. He has enormous hands, a loud laugh, and is utterly fearless: apart from Robert Fisk, he was the only Western journalist who dared to stay in Beirut to cover the dramas of the hostage crisis rather than fleeing before the Hezbollah kidnap-gangs. He has survived, so he believes, partly because no one thinks of the Bolivians as an enemy, partly because no one believes the Bolivian government would be able to afford a ransom, and partly because with his swarthy appearance and thick mat of facial hair he is visually indistinguishable from a Hezbollah commander.

Juan Carlos had flown in from Amman an hour before, and rather than going to his room he had made straight for the bar where he was already demolishing a string of double vodkas and tearing into an outsized *shwarma*. He bought me a drink and after we had exchanged gossip about mutual friends in London and Jerusalem, I showed him *Lebanon: The Promised Land of Tourism*, through which he flicked with a growing smile.

'The Lebanese!' he chuckled through a mouthful of kebab. 'They're worse than the Greeks!'

While he read, I asked him what it was like living on in Beirut when all the other journalists had either fled or been taken hostage. 'Weren't you constantly terrified you would get kidnapped?' I asked, thinking of how shaken I had been by Beirut in peacetime. 'Imagine spending seven years in a basement, chained to a radiator.'

'I've been married three times,' replied J.C. without looking up from the brochure. 'It's not so different.' Suddenly he became animated: 'Willy! Look at this!'

He pointed to the back of the brochure. There, hidden away in the final pages, was a series of great double-spreads advertising nightclubs, 'massage parlours' and escort agencies. Busty Russian blondes wielded whips and fiddled with suspender belts; thick-lipped and slim-waisted Filipinas did their best to reveal charms only partially masked by the skimpiest of bikinis.

'The new Lebanon!' he said. 'There hasn't been anything like this here since 1971! *Habibi*' – he was talking to the barman now – '*Habibi*! Get me a phone this minute!'

While the barman went off to find the mobile, J.C. turned to me. 'How this country has changed!' he said. 'When I first came here twenty years ago all anyone knew about Bolivia was that it was the country of Che Guevara. Now all they know is that it is the only other country in the world that makes quite so much money through narcotics.'

The phone arrived and J.C. dialled the number emblazoned below a picture of five smiling brunettes in matching pink leotards. After only three attempts he got through (quite a stroke of luck in a country whose telephone network was fairly recently so bombed-out that it became totally inoperable).

'Hello?' said J.C. 'Hello? Who is that? OK, *habibi*, listen. This is Juan Carlos speaking. I'm a big oil magnate from Texas and I want to know if you can provide me with – how to put it? – an escort service. No, I'm not coming anywhere: you send her to me. No: I'm not going to wait . . .'

He slammed the phone down. 'Damn it! Fucking "Green-sleeves"! They've put me on hold.'

With the eye of a connoisseur, J.C. flicked through the pages of the brochure, finally settling on a pouting black girl lying back on a tigerskin, one long ebony leg raised in the air, the other placed so that her big toe rested on the tiger's outstretched tongue; below was the caption: 'I'm Pussy Cat and you're my Tiger. Come on big boy: make my day.'

Juan Carlos picked up the phone again. 'Right,' he said. '*That* looks like what we're after.'

After four or five attempts, he again got through.

'Hello? That's the manager? OK, listen here *habibi*. This is Juan Carlos. I'm a big diamond millionaire from Amsterdam. I've just had a long flight and need some . . . attention. Can you provide me with some pretty female company tonight, please? Yes: Pussy Cat would do nicely. HOW MUCH? Is that dollars or Lebanese pounds? You must be joking. Look, *habibi*, inflation isn't that bad: I could fly in my girlfriend for less. I'll be back in touch. Thank you very much.'

He put the phone down and turned to me.

'Unbelievable. I can't believe what's happened while I've been away. And to think I was planning on leaving this country . . .'

It took a while to track down the two men who, I felt, would be best able to make some sense for me of the complexities of Lebanon. Both were the authors of exceptional books on the recent conflict. One was a historian, Kemal Salibi of the American University of Beirut, author of *A House of Many Mansions*, a brilliant debunking of the myths in Lebanese history which had led to and exacerbated the conflict. The other was the great award-winning foreign correspondent Robert Fisk of the *Independent*, author of *Pity the Nation*, much the best account of the 1982 Israeli invasion yet published.

Professor Salibi was easily accessible, but Fisk proved a more difficult man to pin down. He has always tended to keep aloof from his journalistic colleagues, and even Juan Carlos, who appears frequently in *Pity the Nation*, had not seen him for months and did not have an up-to-date number for him. He could give me no better lead than suggesting I try ringing the *Independent* foreign desk. Amazingly, the *Independent* also had no address for him, apparently part of the elaborate security precautions Fisk practises which have so far saved him from assassination or kidnapping. The paper did, however, have the number of a satellite phone in New York which, they said, would somehow beam through to Fisk in Beirut.

So it was that I finally got hold of Fisk – who turned out to be living less than half a mile from my hotel – via tens of thousands of miles of cables to New York then back again to Beirut bounced off some satellite. By this route I offered to take him out to lunch. He accepted, suggesting an Italian place in a Druze area near the seafront.

I had arranged to see Professor Salibi that same morning in his office at the American University, which lay only a short walk away from my hotel, and I walked over there after breakfast.

For an institution whose campus had been under siege for a year, whose main hall had been destroyed by a car bomb, whose acting president and librarian had both been kidnapped by Islamic Jihad, another of whose presidents had been killed and many of whose students had been maimed, murdered and wounded, the American University of Beirut looked remarkably like any other university the world over. The Pizza Hut at the gates was full of undergraduates lounging around, making eyes at each other and spooning mountains of ice-cream into each other's mouths. Noticeboards in the porter's lodge advertised student raves along-side the rather more staid option of a forthcoming piano recital. Undergraduates, late for lectures, ran across lawns that had recently supported batteries of anti-aircraft guns. Lecturers, books in hand, walked along the cinder paths chatting to pretty female students whose fathers and brothers had, only months earlier, no doubt been blazing away at each other in the alleys outside.

Salibi had just finished teaching a small class of history students when I walked into his rooms; a sketch map of the Middle East was still chalked up on the blackboard above his seat. We shook hands and I said how surprised I was to see the university looking so normal after all it had gone through in the war. The Professor smiled. 'Thankfully we are a very forgetful culture,' he said, pulling out a chair and indicating that I should sit. 'Those who committed the worst crimes and atrocities have long been forgiven. Few people in Lebanon can afford to bear grudges for too long. Who remembers Sabra and Chatila? At the time it was terrible: who could ever forgive mass murder like that? But twelve years later even the unfortunate Palestinians have probably forgotten and forgiven.'

I asked the Professor how the war had affected him personally.

'I was driven out of the city altogether,' he replied with a smile.

'By the shelling?'

'No, no. I survived the bombardment. I was driven out by a death threat from the Hezbollah. I had to go to Amman. That's where I put together *A House of Many Mansions*. It was written

211

from memory, without a single reference book. You see, I lost all my books in the bombardment.'

'Your house was destroyed?'

'We suffered twenty-six direct hits. I was in the basement at the time. It was a lovely old Ottoman house, built by my great-grandfather: very beautiful. But by the time it was finished the house was uninhabitable.'

The Professor offered me coffee, and as he fussed around with the kettle he talked quite calmly about the destruction of everything he had owned, as if describing some minor inconvenience: a blown fuse, or a broken lightbulb.

'We heard the shelling start and I said it would be a rough night. So we all began to move into the basement, taking all our things with us. Then the three windows above where the children were playing collapsed inwards: glass flew everywhere, but somehow no one was hurt. We ran downstairs after that, with a bottle of whisky and a candle.

'Whenever a shell fell the candle would be blown out. It was very frightening: so frightening that I thought I couldn't go on. After a while you begin to feel sure that the next shell will get you, that you can't possibly survive. You just hope it won't be too painful. Then oblivion sets in. There's a mechanism in the human mind which obliterates terrible memories. I sometimes wonder now whether it really happened.'

'It can't have left you with very warm feelings towards the Palestinians.'

'It wasn't the Palestinians who shelled us,' said the Professor. 'It was the Maronites, the Phalange. Like many Christians who found themselves on the wrong side of the Green Line, I carried on living in Muslim West Beirut where I always had lived. I was unharmed until Amin Gemayel turned his guns on us and began randomly shelling West Beirut. I never approved of the Phalange. They were intolerable. They considered that Lebanese of Christian origin should have rights which Lebanese of non-Christian origin did not have. In a sense it was a racist doctrine. Luckily their policies ended in the failure they richly deserved.'

'So you think the Christians lost the war?'

'There is a widespread feeling that they did. The Phalange wanted one of two things: either to have political control over the whole of Lebanon, or to retreat to the north and partition the country so that they could at least have control over a Christian enclave. They lost both those battles. They couldn't retain unconditional control over the whole country, nor could they create a canton all to themselves. On the other hand they emerged from the war with their share of power virtually undiminished, and in one way came out unequivocally the winners.'

'What do you mean?'

'Before the war the whole idea of Lebanon was in question. It was adamantly rejected by almost everyone except the Maronites, who were believed to have cooked up the idea in collusion with the French. But the war changed all that. There is now hardly a single person in this country who does not have a strong sense of Lebanese identity. They might be Lebanese with Hezbollah sympathies, or Lebanese who want to cooperate with Syria, or Lebanese who think that to cooperate with Syria is anathema. But they have no doubt of their Lebanese identity. So in a way you could say that the Christians won their point.'

'And yet despite this,' I said, 'the Christians are apparently still emigrating from here *en masse*.'

'True. But the reason they are leaving is no longer because they are threatened, or because their country is going to disappear. It is because – how to put it? – they are weary. There is a feeling of *fin de race* amongst Christians all over the Middle East, a feeling that fourteen centuries of having all the time to be smart, to be ahead of the others, is long enough. The Arab Christians tend to be intelligent, well qualified, highly educated people. Now they just want to go somewhere else, make some money and relax. I can understand it. There is discrimination – sometimes very subtle – against them in almost all Middle Eastern countries. Sometimes when I am with Arab scholars there will be sly digs against Arabs who are not Muslims, doubts about how Arab they are, how patriotic they may be.'

'And do you think it really matters if the Christians do leave?'

'It is a very serious matter,' said Salibi. 'Each time a Christian

213

goes, no other Christian comes to fill his place, and that is a very bad thing for the Arab world. It is the Christian Arabs who keep the Arab world "Arab" rather than "Muslim". It is the Christian Arabs who show that Arabs and Muslims are two different things, that not all Muslims are Arabs and not all Arabs are Muslims. You see, many Muslims regard Arab history as having little meaning by itself, outside the context of Islam. In that sense we are the Arab world's guarantee of secularism.'

Salibi leant forward on his desk. 'Since the nineteenth century the Christian Arabs have played a vital role in defining a secular Arab cultural identity. It is no coincidence that most of the founders of secular Arab nationalism were Christians: Michel Aflaq, who founded the Ba'ath Party; George Antonius, who wrote *The Arab Awakening*. If the Christian Arabs continue to emigrate, the Arabs will be in a much more difficult position to defend the Arab world against Islamism.'

'But isn't that battle already being lost?'

'Everyone is very frightened by the spread of fundamentalism,' said the Professor. 'And of course it is unsettling to read about what is happening in Algeria and Upper Egypt. But this is not the end of history.'

He smiled. 'The battle,' he said, 'is not over yet.'

It was raining heavily when I left the university, and Beirut's streets were suddenly awash. The water sluiced down the steep incline of the roads and the cars slewed through the streets, horns blowing, up to their gunwales in water.

'It's the fault of the Syrians,' explained the taxi driver. 'When they resurfaced the roads after the war they covered over the drains by mistake.'

Now the only drain was the sea, and the water – in some places nearly a foot deep – was flowing fast downhill towards the corniche. Getting from the car to the door of the restaurant was an operation that really required fishing waders.

Fisk was already at his table, an unexpectedly boyish figure with a coif of springy hair swept back over his high forehead; only the odd grey strand betrayed the fact that he was actually in his late forties.

'See out there?' he said by way of introduction. 'During the siege Israeli shells used to land all the way along that stretch of road.'

'So you had to forgo the pleasures of pasta during the siege?'

'No, no,' replied Fisk. 'They kept the place open and I used to come here regularly. Always have. Its got a wonderful view – though of course during the hostage crisis I tended to keep my back to the window so I wouldn't be seen by the kidnappers.'

For all his slightly self-conscious bravado, Fisk proved an unexpectedly kind and avuncular figure. Throughout lunch he freely offered advice and was generous with his contacts, flicking through his address book to pass on the phone numbers of war-lords and archbishops, patriarchs, torturers and mass murderers. Nevertheless no amount of kindness could disguise the fact that Fisk was clearly a chronic war junkie, suffering from all the usual side-effects of an addiction to bombs, kidnapping, loud explosions and unhealthy quantities of adrenalin. This first became obvious when, at the end of the *antipasto*, I asked about the possibility of interviewing one of the Phalangist commanders.

'Well,' he said, puffing at a huge cigar he had just ordered at my expense from the *maître d'*, 'it's not easy. Most are dead: assassinated. The rest are in jail, or in Geagea's case about to go there.'

'Who's Geagea?'

'One of the Phalangist leaders implicated in the massacres at Sabra and Chatila. He's going on trial after Christmas.'

'For the massacres?'

'No, no. For blowing up a church.'

'But I thought the Phalangists were all Christian.'

'They are.'

'So why would they blow up a church?'

'It was Geagea's way of warning the Pope not to visit Lebanon. He thought it would be too dangerous for His Holiness.'

'So there are no senior Maronite militia leaders left for me to talk to?'

'Well, I suppose there's still General Lahad of the SLA.'

'The SLA?'

'The South Lebanon Army: the Israelis' puppet Maronite militia in the zone they've occupied in the south of Lebanon.'

'And you think I could get to see him?'

'Piece of cake,' said Fisk, embarking on a lengthy explanation on how I could make contact with the SLA. This involved going to some obscure scrapyard in the suburbs of Beirut and asking for a man called Haddad.

'Don't talk to anyone else. Leave your name and details. Three days later go back. If Haddad gives you the go-ahead – fine. Have you got a map?'

I nodded and reached in my bag for the map of Lebanon I'd bought in the hotel. It was a simplified tourist chart dotted here and there with optimistic little pictures of the country's principal archaeological monuments.

'Well,' said Fisk, wrinkling his nose as he examined my chart, 'for a start you'll need a better map than this. But this will have to do for the time being. Drive south along this road through the Chouf. Then take a left along this little road here. Leave your car there, at that spot: you see? I'll mark it with an X. Get out – very slowly, no sudden movement, they'll have their snipers trained on you already – and walk the final five hundred yards to the SLA checkpoint with your hands on your head. You'll be all right. As long as your name is on the list, that is.'

'It doesn't sound very safe.'

'I would do it – no problem. I went to the SLA headquarters in Marjayoun last month, as a matter of fact. There are Hezbollah all round, of course. They might take a potshot at you, but they generally don't shoot unmarked cars. At least not normally. It's not as if you'd be travelling in an Israeli army convoy, ha ha.'

'Ha ha.' I shuddered at Fisk's idea of an easy assignment and privately made up my mind to forget interviewing Lahad, and to keep well away from the SLA.

Over coffee (for me) and vintage cognac (for Fisk) I mentioned that I had just been to see Salibi and that we had talked about the problems of the Arab Christians.

'The Arab Christians' principal problem is that the West is Christian,' said Fisk, 'and in one way or another since 1948 the West has humiliated the Muslims of the Middle East over and over again. The Christians simply cannot divorce themselves from the West, however many times they tell their Muslim neighbours that Christianity is really an Eastern religion.'

According to Fisk it was nevertheless a myth that the Lebanese civil war was in essence a clash of civilisations, Christian against Muslim. It was, he said, more a case of the Maronites against everyone else.

'The Maronites brought the war down on their own heads. The first event of the civil war was a massacre of Palestinians by a group of Phalangists trying to win power. The Greek Orthodox always realised that the different communities in Lebanon would have to learn to coexist, but the Maronites never came to terms with this. They are a very immature community politically, very stupid, and always letting themselves be used – first by the French, then by the Israelis, now by the Syrians. The Maronites have always really wanted a francophone Lebanon that they can dominate, totally separated from the Arab world, with the Muslims reduced to some sort of folkloric survival tolerated to please the tourists. Is it any wonder that the Hezbollah headbangers now want to kill them all?'

'But all the same, quite a lot of the war did seem to have a Christian–Muslim clash behind it, didn't it?'

'In the course of the war the Phalange attacked the local Armenians and the Greek Orthodox – who themselves quite often fought with the Druze against the Maronites – as well as the Christian Palestinians and other Maronites. Then, at other points, the fighting was almost entirely Muslim against Muslim: in the Camp Wars from 1985 to 1988 it was Shiites against Sunni Palestinians. It's a ridiculous oversimplification – in fact a total misunderstanding – to see the war as a simple Christian–Muslim struggle.'

It had stopped raining as suddenly as it had started and the sun was now shining brightly. So after I had paid the bill, Fisk offered to take me on a tour of his favourite ruins. This didn't turn out to be the sightseeing trip around the archaeological remains of ancient Beirut that I had been expecting. Instead it was a nostalgia tour through the scenes of Fisk's civil war glory days, carefully avoiding any part of the city which still had a house with its roof intact, a window *in situ*, or whose façade was not thoroughly honeycombed with shrapnel holes.

'Look,' said Fisk, nodding excitedly from the back seat of our taxi at a ruinous building opposite. 'Classic sniper's nest.'

'There?' I asked, pointing to a window on the third floor.

'Never *ever* point in Lebanon,' hissed Fisk. 'You'll get yourself killed *very* quickly if you break basic rules like that.'

'What . . .'

'People will think you're an informer, and shoot you. And me too if I'm with you.'

'I'm so sorry . . .'

'But you had the right window. Look again. What do you see?'

'A pile of old sacks?'

'Sandbags, with a crate in between.' Fisk was in his element now, like an overexcited trainspotter let loose in the sidings at Crewe. 'That crate is where the sniper would have rested his rifle. During the war that line of buildings would have had corridors knocked through the houses so snipers could move from one house to another without venturing onto the street. Of course, all that is over now,' he added, with what seemed a touch of sadness.

We drove on, Fisk pointing out sites of interest: 'See that spot? That's where a mine went off, killing a Lebanese journalist. Friend of mine. Horrible business. Blood everywhere. Couldn't even identify the body afterwards . . . And over there, see? That's where Terry Anderson was kidnapped. He was taken off screaming down that road. Didn't get released for years . . . And there: that was the French Embassy. '

'God. What happened to it?'

'Car bomb, shells and everything else. But it's still there, sort of. Which is more than you can say about the American Embassy. It used to stand there.' Fisk nodded at a huge empty lot. 'It was bombed by Islamic Jihad. They finally pulled down what was left last week.'

We drove on, and soon came to a warren of narrow streets. Garbage lay uncollected all around, and every building was badly peppered with shrapnel. It looked as if pretty well everything had gone off here: small-arms fire, mortars, howitzers, aerial bombardment, suction bombs, rocket-propelled grenades, car bombs, the lot.

'Gives you an idea what Beirut used to be like,' sighed Fisk, 'before they started messing around trying to clean it all up.'

'Why are there so many pin-ups of the Ayatollah Khomeni everywhere?'

'This used to be the Jewish area of Beirut. That was the synagogue. But the Shiites have taken it over now. You don't want to come here on your own.'

'What happened to the Jews?'

'After the creation of Israel they stayed on. But after the 1982 Israeli invasion and the siege of Beirut, Jews came to be seen as legitimate targets, so they had to, er . . . leave.'

From the opposite direction a huge armoured personnel carrier rumbled toward us. It was followed by an army truck full of heavily armed Lebanese troops in their camouflage jumpsuits. We pulled in behind the charred carcass of an old Citroën to let them through.

'These patrols go through to make sure there are no armed militia men around,' said Fisk. 'There are, of course, hundreds of them, but they keep out of sight. In fact there's not a family here without a stash of Kalashnikovs and couple of mortars hidden away in their back yard. But they keep them tucked away and the army don't poke around too much. It's an unspoken agreement.'

Fisk gave instructions to the driver and we headed into a great wide square, desolate and empty but for a bronze statue at its centre.

'This was the Place des Martyrs. It was like Dresden until they pulled it all down. Shame, really. In the old days there was almost total silence in this area. No traffic. No people. Just the gentle *crack, crack* of snipers. Wonderful.'

We got out and walked over to the statue. Like everything else in the vicinity it was thoroughly peppered with shrapnel and small-arms fire.

'They're going to leave the statue as a memorial,' said Fisk, 'but everything else is going to go. They're planning to bulldoze it all into the sea.'

He explained about the plans to redevelop the area: the Downtown Project. It all sounded very Levantine. If I understood correctly, the monopoly to redevelop the entire centre of the city had just been awarded by the Prime Minister to a company called Solidere, in which the Prime Minister happened to be a major shareholder.

We walked over to the corner of the square, where a roofless Maronite church stood looking onto the wasteland.

'Follow me,' said Fisk, 'and don't stand on the piles of rubble. You never know where there might be a landmine or a UXB.'

'UXB?'

'Unexploded bomb. Hundreds of them all over Beirut. And landmines. Scattered like confetti all over the shop.'

Following closely in Fisk's footsteps, I was led up to a platform. From it you could look down into a deep hole, thirty feet below. At the bottom, amid the puddles and the rubbish, lay a jumbled pile of old Roman pillars.

'That,' said Fisk, gesturing at it dismissively, 'is all that's left of five hundred years of classical Beirut.'

'It's not much, is it?' I said.

'No,' said Fisk. 'Mind you, had the war continued much longer, modern Beirut wouldn't have looked so different.'

He pointed to the edge of the square. There stood the wreck of what had once been a neo-classical public building dating from the early years of the French Mandate. All that remained was a line of pillars; even the pediment had been completely blown off. The wreck was indistinguishable from the ruins of a classical temple.

'See what I mean?' said Fisk.

Few ancient cities give off less historical resonance than Beirut. Its post-war high-rise hellscape immediately conjures up some terrible Apocalyptic vision of the future, but the city's past casts few shadows over the shellshocked present. Everything old has been swept away or blown up. There is nothing on which the historical imagination can find purchase. It is difficult enough to imagine the city as the elegant Ottoman port it must have been only eighty years ago; the ancient classical past now seems hopelessly distant, almost impossible to visualise.

Nevertheless, in the early Byzantine period the Metropolis of Berytus was one of the principal cities in the Empire: as an intellectual centre it was the site of the Empire's leading law school, while as a centre of commerce it was one of the most prosperous trading ports in the eastern Mediterranean, a major focus of Byzantine silk manufacture and export. Its harbour would rarely have been empty, and during the sailing season – from April to October – would have been cluttered with galleys from Gaul and barques from as far afield as Alexandria, Athens and Carthage.

In Byzantine times a law degree took five or six years to complete, and was a course of study open only to the children of the very rich. Libanius of Antioch mentions one law student, a certain Heliodorus, who was 'a retailer of fish sauce', but such cases were most uncommon: the law students who congregated in Beirut accompanied by their armies of household slaves and concubines were the children of senators, provincial governors and landowners from across the Empire. They came because a Beirut degree was the quickest way to rapid advancement in the Imperial Civil Service, the Byzantine equivalent of a diploma from Insead or Harvard Business School. Indeed Libanius complains loudly and angrily that modern parents were more interested in the prospects of quick promotion afforded by a Beirut law degree than in the more rounded (and old-fashioned) education in rhetoric he offered at Antioch. It is the same cry professors of Classics can be heard uttering today as their brightest students desert them for vocational degrees in economics or the law.

One of the most curious aspects of the history of the east Mediterranean is the way that the character of its cities often seems to remain strangely constant, despite the long series of cataclysmic invasions, genocides and exchanges of population that make up their history. Jerusalem, for example, has always been a centre of religious fanaticism, whether inhabited by Jews, Byzantines, Arabs or Crusaders. In the same way Beirut has always had a reputation for hedonism, sharpened, then as now, by occasional outbreaks of aggressive fundamentalism.

That it was so in the Byzantine period is demonstrated by the fifth-century *Life* of the Monophysite Bishop Severus of Antioch, written by his friend and companion, Zacharias the Rector. The two friends began their secondary studies in Alexandria, where Zacharias comments with a shudder on the number of professors involved in occult activities: many of the senior members of the faculty were apparently in the habit of secretly visiting a clandestine temple of Menuthis packed full of wooden idols of cats, dogs and monkeys.

At Beirut, where the pair went to finish their legal studies sometime in the 480s, things were little better. Though there appeared to be fewer pagans around than in Alexandria, the rich students indulged in all manner of pleasures repugnant to a puritanical Christian like Zacharias: there was a theatre and a circus, while in the evening there were dice games and drinking with dancing girls and prostitutes. This hedonism caused a reaction among the more pious students, rather in the way the excesses of Beirut's wild and salacious nightlife during the 1960s and seventies provoked, a decade later, the puritanism of Islamic Jihad. In response to the law students' orgiastic behaviour, the more zealous of the Christian activists formed religious brotherhoods, urging Zacharias and Severus to attend church every evening, to avoid the theatre and to follow the famous advice of St Jerome that 'he who has bathed in Christ [i.e. been baptised] does not need a second bath': giving the lead, the head of the brotherhood apparently used to wash only once a year.

As in Alexandria, there were scandals involving the occult. The lodgings of the chief suspect were searched, his grimoires confiscated, his magical books burned and his friends denounced to the bishop. One of the accused, Chrysaorius of Tralles, then tried to escape. He rented a ship, loaded it with his books of spells, his concubine and children; they set sail, but soon sank (as ships carrying magicians have a tendency to do in pious Byzantine literature: there are several similar stories involving wicked pagans and magicians coming to damp ends on the high seas in the pages of *The Spiritual Meadow*).

John Moschos seems to have passed fairly quickly up the coast of what was then Byzantine Phoenicia. Indeed he mentions only three places within the boundaries of modern Lebanon: Tyre, Porphyreon and Ba'albek. Byzantine Beirut he does not refer to at all, perhaps because by the late sixth century the city was in serious decline. This was partly the result of the bankruptcy of the local silk industry, when many of the silk merchants were forced to migrate to Persia in search of work, and partly due to a severe earthquake in 551 the last of a series of ominous tremors throughout the early sixth century – which brought down many of the city's buildings. Indeed the evidence of another contemporary traveller, the Italian pilgrim Antonius Martyr, seems to indicate that in 570 'the school of letters' (presumably the law school) had completely ceased to function, and the only place on the Lebanese coast where Antonius saw any prosperity was Beirut's great rival, Tyre. There he reported that the city's looms were still operating, while its brothels were apparently packed to bursting.

I had asked Professor Salibi about rumours I had heard in Damascus, that the remains of Byzantine Beirut had been turning up during demolition work for the Downtown Project. He in turn had put me in touch with Leila Badr, one of archaeologists at the American University who had been involved in the digging.

Dr Badr confirmed that in the rescue excavations which had taken place during the demolitions, the diggers had indeed struck Byzantine levels and managed to uncover long stretches of the Byzantine, Roman and Phoenician town walls, all of which followed roughly the same course. There was not a great deal to see, but it was an important discovery: previously no one had known the boundaries of the ancient town. Some badly preserved fragments of Byzantine floor mosaics had also been found, but these had been sent away for conservation and I wouldn't be able to see them. But, said Dr Badr, there were some other recently-discovered Byzantine remains that I should definitely try to look at.

Apparently just before the Israeli invasion, in early 1982, workmen digging in the sand dunes on the coast at Jiyyeh, twenty miles to the south of Beirut, had stumbled upon a series of well-preserved Byzantine monastic ruins: churches, hostels, halls and agricultural buildings. Inside was a collection of the most remarkable mosaics, many with dated Greek inscriptions. These identified the site as the Byzantine port of Porphyreon, one of the three Lebanese cities visited by Moschos.

Moschos tells two stories about the port. One concerns the companion of his friend, the hermit Abba Zosimos the Cilician, who was bitten by a snake and 'died immediately with blood flowing from all his members'. The other is the tale of Procopius the lawyer, who is away in Jerusalem when he hears that the plague has broken out in his home town. Terrified for the safety of his children, he goes to see the renowned Byzantine holy man Abba Zachaios, and tells him of his fear.

> When [Abba Zachaios] heard this, he turned towards the east and continued reaching up to heaven for about two hours without saying a word. Then he turned towards me and said: 'Take heart and do not be distraught: your children shall not die in the plague. In fact two days from now, the plague shall abate.' And indeed it came about as the elder foretold.

The recent excavations apparently confirmed Moschos's report that Porphyreon was a major port in the late sixth century. It was probably as large as its rival Beirut, and specialised in olive oil production and textile manufacture, and also, as was indicated by its name, in the making of purple dye. Despite the economic crisis plaguing Antioch and much of the rest of the Levantine coast,

224

Porphyreon was clearly still a very prosperous place, and its monastic buildings had once been magnificent.

Almost all the antiquities discovered in Lebanon during the civil war were exported illegally and sold on the black market in Europe and America. At one point things got so bad that in Tyre militiamen were blowing open sarcophagi with dynamite to get at the grave-goods within. But by good fortune Jiyyeh fell within the sphere of influence of Walid Jumblatt, the Druze leader. Jumblatt was a history scholar before turning politician, and almost alone of Lebanese warlords had a sense of the past and understood the importance of a country's archaeological heritage. Dr Badr told me that Jumblatt had kept the mosaics safe during the war, and had recently brought them out and placed them in his palace at Beit ed-Din in the Chouf. The only problem, she said, was that I would need Jumblatt's permission if I was to get in to see them.

Following Dr Badr's instructions, I duly set off in a taxi to the offices of Jumblatt's Progressive Socialist Party. This organisation was, by all accounts, neither progressive nor socialist; rather it was a sort of glorified feudal support group through which Lebanon's Druze were enabled to pledge their allegiance to their tribal chieftain, W. Jumblatt. The office was a suitably rackety-looking place, riddled with the regulation Beirut bulletholes, but I climbed the dingy stairs and at the top almost ran into Jumblatt and his squad of bodyguards.

Jumblatt had the appearance less of a ruthless warlord than of a left-wing Sorbonne sociology don from the barricades of 1968. He was an unexpectedly tall and commanding figure in his late forties, balding, with a large nose and a droopy Mexican moustache. He wore a black leather jacket and tight black jeans, and he spoke fluent English.

It turned out that I had been very lucky. Jumblatt was leaving for France in less than an hour, but agreed to see me for five minutes before he left. Armed Druze flunkies frisked me then ushered me into a study. After twenty minutes Jumblatt walked in and asked how he could help. I explained what I wanted, and he immediately gave his permission.

'Go ahead. Tell my men at the gate that you are my guest. They will show you the mosaics.' Then he added, 'It's so rare to see English writers in Beirut these days. You know Charles Glass?'

'Very well.'

'How is he? Still alive?'

'Becoming rather a playboy in his old age, by all accounts.'

'The Hezbollah should never have let him escape from his captivity,' he said. 'You know he was kidnapped on his way to see me? What about David Gilmour? The last time I was in London he took me to lunch at the Travellers' Club. What's he doing now?'

'He's just written a book on Lord Curzon.'

'David always was an unreconstructed imperialist,' said Jumblatt. 'But tell me,' he asked politely, 'what are you writing about?'

I explained that I was researching a book about the Middle Eastern Christians, and Jumblatt raised his eyebrows: during the war he had been one of the most formidable enemies of the Christian militias. Despite the fact that the Christian forces were supported by both Israel and the Americans, Jumblatt's forces had managed to drive the Christian militias out of the Druze heartlands in the Chouf, and in the process had gained a reputation for savage tenacity. The Druze, it was well known, seldom took prisoners.

'The Maronites have always been their own worst enemies,' said Jumblatt. 'They have always wanted to dominate Lebanon as if it were an entirely Christian state. They have never been prepared to give the majority their rights, to share power or in any way to bring about democratic reforms.'

'I understand you were no friend of the Phalangists during the war.'

'The Phalange was a fascist organisation founded by Pierre Gemayel after a visit to Nazi Germany in 1936,' he said, with indisputable historical accuracy. 'When they started committing atrocities – slitting the throats of three hundred Muslims at road-blocks on Black Saturday in 1975, or massacring the Palestinians in the camp at Tel el-Za'atar a year later – we had to respond. Coexistence is only possible if the Maronites resist their more extreme right-wing tendencies.'

'So are you pessimistic about the future?'

'Lebanon is an artificial creation,' replied Jumblatt. 'It was created by the French in 1920. Economically and politically speaking it has no future on its own. We need the Arabs. We are the gateway to the Arab world: that is our natural environment. We are not some part of the French dominions, or the Vatican, or whatever it is the Maronites want. If they accept this, then maybe this peace will hold.'

One of Jumblatt's aides came in to say that his car was ready to take him to the airport. Jumblatt pulled himself out of his chair. 'I will miss my plane,' he said. 'I'm sorry. I hope you get to see your mosaics.'

As we walked down the stairs together Jumblatt made some remark about the civil war, and I asked him whether he thought that in retrospect it could have been avoided altogether.

'If the Maronites had been less intransigent,' he said, shrugging his shoulders. 'Then maybe . . . But the ifs of history: if Cleopatra's nose had been one inch longer,' he said, 'would Antony have lost the battle of Actium?'

The road to the Chouf led through the squalid southern suburbs of Beirut. Thirty years ago, this road bordered Ouzayeh Beach. It was once the Ipanema of Beirut, the favourite playground of *le tout Beirut*. Now it is Hezbollah territory, and a vast meandering shanty-slum of tin sheds and breezeblock huts, cheap restaurants and rundown bakeries lines the strip between the road and the now almost invisible beach.

On the central reservation, running between the two lanes of the road, rose a series of giant hoardings depicting the hugely enlarged features of a line of Iranian mullahs. Each cleric stared out blankly through heavy Joe-90 spectacles, under a tightly wrapped and immaculately starched white turban: as strange and surreal a sight as a line of giant Andy Warhol Marilyns raised above a motorway. Interspersed between the mullahs, much smaller and crudely nailed onto a low picket of wooden posts, stretched a line of idealised portraits of smiling, bearded *shaheedin*, the Hezbollah 'martyrs' who had died fighting the Israelis in occupied southern Lebanon. To indicate the heavenly bliss currently being enjoyed by these fighters, their heads were sometimes shown floating on clouds of white cumulus. Other hoardings showed the Dome of the Rock in Jerusalem, inscribed with a series of fearsome invocations to Free Palestine and Crush the Zionist Entity, along with other varieties of the sort of bloodcurdling threats, promises and admonitions which Shia fundamentalists like to read as they drive into town to do their shopping.

It had turned wet and windy, and each time the taxi dived into one of the deep brown puddles that filled the potholes in the road, an explosion of muddy water splashed over the bonnet and windscreen. As we bounced along, past tumbledown garages, scrapyards and tyre shops, I could see thickly bearded Hezbollah men pottering around with spanners under the bonnets of battered, shrapnel-shattered Datsuns or war-weary Volvos; others were holding pots of paint and paintbrushes with which they dabbed on splashes of colour here and there in an attempt to distract attention from the dents and bulletholes that dotted their cars' chassis. I remarked to the taxi driver, Nouri Suleiman, that I had expected somewhat higher-calibre weapons than sprayguns from these men.

'Guns are not so useful now we are at peace,' he replied. 'At the end of the war a new M-16 used to cost $1,000. Now you can buy one for $100. A pistol used to be $500. Now it's down to $150.'

'So a pistol is now more expensive than an M-16?'

'That's because people still like to have small guns,' replied Nouri.

'Why?'

'They're useful. You can't hide an M-16, but it's easy to hide a pistol. Put it in your pocket or a briefcase. No problem.'

From the back of his glove compartment he whipped out a small snub-nosed pistol and showed it to me: 'You see? Easy to hide. No problem.'

We drove on through the uncontrolled ribbon of Beirut's rambling southern suburbs, past the sad, huddled slums belonging to the landless Shias and the barbed wire and collapsing shanties of various miserable-looking Palestinian refugee camps. Half an hour later we arrived at the outskirts of Damour, the Christian town that had suffered most severely in the civil war. First it was attacked and pillaged by the Palestinians in revenge for Maronite atrocities against them in Beirut. Most of the inhabitants escaped by sea, but 350 remained in their homes. When Arafat's gunmen stormed into the town on 20 January 1976, the Fatah guerrillas machine-gunned the men, raped the women and dynamited the houses. It was then that the Palestinians, apparently dissatisfied at having had the chance to wreak revenge on so few living Maronites, hit upon the idea of exhuming their dead and scattering the cadavers around the ruins of the town they had just desecrated. Later on, the town was captured and destroyed a second time, on this occasion by the Israelis, before being resettled on their departure by the Druze. Jumblatt now keeps his principal office in Damour. But there are no Christians living here any more.

We drove quickly through what was left of the town: a few houses, all riddled with bullet and shrapnel holes; the odd ruin of a sixties bungalow, now overgrown with vines and creepers; a scrappy plantation of banana palms; a few old Druze men sitting around on their covered verandahs looking out into the drizzle in their white *keffiyehs* and baggy black *charwal* pantaloons. We then took a left turn and began winding upwards into the steep, thickly-wooded slopes that led into the Chouf.

It was raining hard now, and the gleaming road was slippery with fallen leaves. Cars coming down from Beit ed-Din sluiced past us, windscreen wipers on full. Low cloud obscured the tops of the mountain peaks rising above us; below, the valleys fell away in a steep precipice of abandoned cultivation terraces and balding beech trees, their few remaining leaves turning bright autumnal yellow. For the final twenty minutes of the journey, as on the way into Beirut, we found ourselves crawling uphill behind another pair of the ubiquitous Syrian tank-transporters, each weighed down with its cargo of two Soviet T-72 battle tanks. Looking at the map, I realised that the Israeli Occupation Zone, the current front line between the armies of the Jewish state and the local Hezbollah guerrillas, lay only twelve miles to the south.

At the top of the mountain, in Deir el-Qamar, the driver stopped to fill up with petrol and to let his battered radiator cool down. Deir el-Qamar was a fine medieval town and, uniquely in Lebanon, had been well preserved, thanks to Walid Jumblatt's interest in conservation. It was built of warm honey-coloured sandstone and was full of old Ottoman khans and churches, lovely even in the rain. As I sat in a café, warming my hands around a glass of tea, I caught sight of a Maronite priest in black cloak and biretta hurrying along the road outside, a bent figure scurrying under the shelter of a wide umbrella. I had understood that the Christians of the Chouf, like those of Damour, had been driven out of the area during the fighting. Surprised, I chased after the priest and invited him into the café to join me. Clearly as amazed to see me as I was to see him, Père Abbé Marcel abi-Khalil accepted.

The old priest shook his wet umbrella and folded it up. 'Before the fighting,' he said, 'Deir el-Qamar was half Christian and half Druze. The Chouf was traditionally a Druze area, but the Maronites began to migrate here from the north in the eighteenth century. By 1975, before the fighting, there must have been five thousand Christians living here, maybe twice that number in summer.'

He sipped his tea. 'Then there was the War of the Mountains,' he said, 'and all the Christians left. Today there are no more than one thousand of us living here.'

'So some Christians have returned?'

'Yes. They've started trickling back. Jumblatt is giving them a little money to help them start again. He is a good man. He has suffered himself – his father was assassinated – so he knows what it is to suffer loss. He wants to heal the wounds.'

'I'm surprised to hear a Maronite say that.'

'In 1860 the Druze and the Christians fought each other, but from then until the war we lived happily side by side. In our school we used to have 150 Christians and 350 Druze.'

'Druze? In a Christian school?'

'*Mais oui*,' said Fr. Marcel. 'The fathers taught everyone, whatever their religion.'

'So what went wrong during the war?'

'It was Geagea and his Phalange. Before he came to the Chouf, we had lived together peacefully for generations. But while the Israelis were here in 1982, Geagea's men fought against the Druze in the Chouf and in Sidon. Geagea treated the Druze very badly. He made many murders. The Israelis pretended not to see and let Geagea do what he wanted. As a result, when they withdrew, everyone attacked the Christians. We were besieged and for three months there was nothing to eat: only grass. The Red Cross sent food but the Druze ate it on the way. In the end the Syrians supported Jumblatt and Geagea lost his war. Because of what he did, the Christians were expelled from both here and Sidon. We have a saying: "Where Geagea sets foot, no Christian remains." With a champion like him, we need no other enemies.'

'Did you meet Geagea?'

'*Bien sûr*,' said the priest. 'I hid him in the school for two months. It was in 1983, after he lost his little war. Personally I did not like him. In fact he almost made me embarrassed to be a Christian. When he left – walking over the mountain, by foot, in disguise – I was glad. He created only trouble for us.'

The driver came into the café and said that the car was ready. Fr. Marcel swallowed the last of his tea and we both stood up.

'Now Geagea has gone and the war is over, it is better in the Chouf,' said the priest as we walked outside. He raised his umbrella. 'The Druze have even begun coming to church again.'

'The Druze come to your church?'

'They always have. We have a miraculous picture. When they need babies or are ill or in difficulties they come here. They give oil and incense and are healed.'

He shook my hands warmly. 'In this part of the world,' he said, 'for all our difficulties, religion has not just torn people apart. It has often brought them together. It is important to remember that.'

The great early-nineteenth-century palace of Beit ed-Din lay a short distance away, on the opposite side of the valley. Its double gates were bolted shut, and in front stood three Druze guards, all armed with Kalashnikovs. They were warming their hands around a spluttering brazier, with their guns slung casually from the shoulders of their damp greatcoats. The driver got out and talked to them, saying that I was a friend of Jumblatt. They immediately bowed and pushed open the gates.

Through the gatehouse, in the fading light, the palace felt like a Cambridge college out of term time: echoing, empty courtyards led one into another, damp with fallen leaves and swept by sudden gusts of rain. In the centre of the principal courtyard lay a low black marble monument to Kemal Jumblatt, Walid's assassinated father. The guard led me past it, and turning on his flashlight, conducted me down, through a narrow warren of dark passageways, into the drafty vaulted basements that had once been the palace stables and dungeons.

The guard fumbled for a switch. Suddenly the great arcaded underpass was lit up by racks of powerful spotlights. I had been expecting a modest collection of interesting new finds, but nothing had prepared me for the wonderful quantity of Byzantine artwork Jumblatt had managed to save. There, laid out on the walls and on the floor, in room after vaulted room, unstudied by scholars, unknown to the outside world, lay what is without doubt the most magnificent collection of Byzantine floor mosaics to survive to the present day outside the city of Byzantium itself: more than thirty large, room-sized mosaics dating from the mid-sixth century, and as many smaller fragments. It was a truly extraordinary abundance of fine late antique art, certainly one of the very greatest Byzantine finds to have come to light this century.

The Porphyreon mosaic-makers appear to have been influenced less by Imperial fashions in the capital – where, judging by the floors in the Great Palace, gory hunting and gladiatorial scenes were *de rigueur* – than by work from contemporary monastic sites in Byzantine Palestine. They too used relatively large tesserae and show a preference for geometric subjects over figurative ones. Most of the mosaics are filled with intricate patterns: *trompe l'oeil* based on interlocking cross-shapes, hypnotic swirls of peltas, chevrons, swastikas and key patterns. Some of these interlace patterns resemble similar designs on fragments of floor mosaic from the Byzantine monastery of St Stephen, just outside the Damascus Gate in Jerusalem. Others contain tangles of vine-scroll ornament closely paralleled by a lovely mosaic that decorated the great Armenian monastery which once stood a short distance from St Stephen. One of the mosaics in the basement depicts a mallard and two ducks resting on a lilypond in a style very close to the mosaic of the River Nile at Tabgha on the Sea of Galilee. The link to Palestine is therefore striking, and it seems entirely possible that the same *atelier* of mosaic-makers served both northern Palestine and what is now southern Lebanon.

The somewhat austere choice of subject-matter almost certainly represents a conscious reaction against the sort of voluptuous late Roman pavements discovered outside Antioch and Carthage. On these mosaics plump, disrobed goddesses sport with hoary satyrs, while gods and demi-gods, Hercules and Dionysus, lie befuddled on their couches, overflowing rhytons raised in the air as they engage in riotous drinking contests: hardly the sort of scheme to appeal to ascetic early Christian monks. What is perhaps more unexpected is that the Porphyreon mosaics also represent a striking contrast to the worldly triumphalism of the Imperial panels at Ravenna, where the apse walls of San Vitale are filled with magnificent depictions of Byzantine court ceremonial: long lines of Justinian's world-weary bishops and sycophantic courtiers, flanked by Theodora's urbane and gossipy ladies with their gold and pearls and silks.

Instead there is something decidedly puritanical in the spirit of Porphyreon, a spirit which mirrors the often austere monastic outlook of John Moschos. Indeed they are products of the same world. Several of the mosaics have inscriptions which reveal them to date from exactly the period Moschos was collecting material for *The Spiritual Meadow*. One inscription shows that the mosaic – a series of interlocking lozenges containing bears, storks, stags and a gazelle – was commissioned as a memorial 'for the rest of the soul of Elias' in December 594/595 A.D. In other words it is quite possible that both John Moschos and the men from Porphyreon that he mentions in *The Spiritual Meadow* – Procopius the lawyer and Abba Zosimos the Cilician – could have seen some of these mosaics being made, and may even have walked over their gleaming, newly-laid tesserae.

Yet the feature that is perhaps most interesting about the work at Porphyreon is the mosaic-makers' strong preference for the geometric over the figurative. Of sixty-three mosaics, only three depict the human figure: one shows a female saint holding a cloth; another shows a saint (presumably John the Baptist) standing in water and holding a staff; while the third is a personification of Ktisis ('Creation'), shown holding a spear and surrounded by a group of animals – bulls, bears, leopards and a lion. The sixty other mosaics are all, without exception, aniconic and non-figurative.

This is important, for it emphasises quite how far taste was already moving away from the humanism, gaiety and decadence of the late classical world towards the cold and inward-looking intensity of early medieval Byzantium. This was a spirit which was to lead directly to the violent iconoclasm of the eighth and ninth centuries: only fifty years after the completion of the Elias mosaic, the Byzantine Emperor Leo III ordered the smashing of all icons and figurative *ars sacra* across the Christian Empire.

Nor was Byzantium the only force to be affected by this change of feeling: one of the Porphyreon mosaics, dated 500, was laid at exactly the period that an Arab trader from Mecca was touring the Levant, talking to and disputing with Byzantine monks, and formulating his own – thoroughly disapproving – ideas about the depiction of living creatures. The prohibition on reproducing the human form that Mohammed was later to impose on all Muslims still affects a billion people today, and it is fascinating to see the roots of that unease – a feeling that to depict man, to erect graven images, was somehow pagan and obscene – clearly apparent in these mosaics. Certainly the exuberance and vivacity of late antique and early Christian work – the crowding of living forms, of horsemen and their quarry, leaping lions, fleeing gazelles, the Emperor and his consorts, even the querulous saints and the prophets of the Ravenna baptistries – have already given way to a cold, carpet-like abstraction. The birds in the vine tendrils are still and silent and two-dimensional; a chill has descended, and left the mosaics frozen, arrested. There is no movement, no noise. The Bacchic riot of Antioch and the courtly trumpets of Ravenna have been stilled.

I spent two hours in the dungeons of the palace, closely examining the mosaics, astonished by their stern beauty and their fantastically intricate and abstract detailing. Porphyreon was clearly still a prosperous place at a period when most of the other trading ports of the Levant were already in fast decline, and presumably this prosperity was linked to the olive-oil mills that the archaeologists dug up in their rescue excavations. After all, oil was a very valuable commodity, needed by cities around the Mediterranean for both cooking and lamplight, and its price was clearly marked up considerably in the process. St Augustine, used to the cheap oil of his rural North African childhood, could not believe the cost of lamp oil when he arrived in Rome for the first time, and complained bitterly about the expense it imposed on reading at night. But as the rich spread of mosaic-work around me demonstrated, the merchants of Porphyreon had used their profits well.

Carried away by the thrill of being one of the first ever to see these mosaics, I lost all sense of time. But quite suddenly, I was brought back to reality by the sound of a loud explosion outside. The noise echoed around the vaults for several seconds before finally dying away.

'What was that?' I asked the guard.

'It is nothing,' he replied casually, sucking on his cigarette. 'Just the planes of the Israelis.'

'A sonic boom?'

'They make the noise deliberately,' he said. 'Once, twice a day.'

'Why?'

'Just to remind us,' said the guard. 'Just to remind us that they are still there. Just to remind us what they can still do.'

Everyone I talked to seemed to agree. If I wanted to understand the Maronites there was one place I had to go: Bsharre.

In the cliffs below the town, deep in the Qannubin gorge, the first Maronite hermits had taken shelter when they were driven out of Syria by Byzantine persecution in the sixth century. Fourteen hundred years later, at the end of the nineteenth century, the town produced the Maronites' most famous poet and writer: Kahlil Gibran, author of *The Prophet*. This at any rate was what Maronites told me about Bsharre, and what I read in my trusty *Lebanon: The Promised Land of Tourism*.

Non-Maronites also said that I should go to Bsharre, but for rather different reasons. They seemed to regard the town as a sort of Maronite Heart of Darkness, pointing out that Bsharre was the home of the notorious Samir Geagea, and the place from which he drew his most loyal and bloodthirsty troops. If Geagea was the man who for the final stages of the war led the Phalange militiamen who committed mass murder at Sabra and Chatila (as well as slightly smaller and less notorious massacres at two other Palestinian camps, Tel el-Za'atar and Ein Helweh), and who gunned down two of his principal Maronite rivals in their beds, then many of the men who actually performed these atrocities could no doubt now be found sipping mint tea in Bsharre's cafés and bars.

The unusual proportion of psychotics in Bsharre's population seemed to be emphasised by another story I was told. It concerned what happened when, on his death bed, Kahlil Gibran left Bsharre all the royalties from *The Prophet*, then running at an astonishing $1 million annually. The gift did not have the beneficial effect he presumably hoped for. Instead the two rival Maronite clans that dominate Bsharre, the Kayruz and the Tawq, broke into open warfare over the division of the money. For many months the town was plunged into its own miniature civil war, with bombings, assassinations, murders and exchanges of heavy mortar-fire. According to my informants, it was that battle over the profits of a book of mystic poetry, not the words of gentle counsel offered by Gibran, that represented the true face of this town at the heart of the Maronite world.

One Maronite academic friend of mine, now a don at Oxford, also warned me about the primitive behaviour of the people of Bsharre. A couple of years ago he had been sitting on the verandah of a bar in the town, watching the sun going down and drinking a glass of beer with a colleague. Suddenly, from a balcony immediately behind him, a double-barrelled anti-aircraft gun opened up, firing volley after volley into the air. Assuming some sort of air raid was in progress, my friend took shelter behind a nearby wall. But when, after five minutes, no aircraft appeared and the gun continued firing, he darted along the road, climbed up the stairs and knocked on the door of the flat to try to find out what was going on.

'Are you crazy?' he said when the door was opened. 'What the hell do you think you're doing?'

'I'm sorry,' replied the man with the anti-aircraft gun. 'I've just heard that my daughter in Australia has had a baby boy. It is my first grandson. I am so happy.'

As there appeared to be no functioning public transport in Lebanon, to get to Bsharre I was forced to again hire the services of Nouri Suleiman, the extremely expensive taxi driver who took me to Beit ed-Din. Nouri is a septuagenarian former swimming champion who has been taking people around Lebanon since he won the Lebanese national lottery in the 1950s; he spent the money on a new Mercedes which, he tells me proudly, he is still driving forty years later.

But before I could leave to visit this town which, according to *Lebanon: The Promised Land of Tourism*, 'still rings with the soothing sound of Gibran's peaceful words', I had a morning appointment to keep in Beirut. Fisk had told me that the opposition to the bulldozing of what little remained of historic Beirut – the so-called Downtown Project – was being coordinated by one Yvonne, Lady Cochrane, who had memorably described the President's ambitious plans for Beirut's redevelopment as 'the dream of a retarded adolescent'. Lady Cochrane was apparently the head of a family of old Beirut grandees who had come by her very unLevantine name when she married a former Irish Honorary Consul in Beirut, now long since dead.

I suppose I had guessed that Lady Cochrane was not going to be living in poverty in some poky flat when, on the telephone, she gave her address as Palais Sursock in Rue Sursock. But even so I had not expected the vision that confronted me when Nouri's taxi dropped me in front of Lady Cochrane's gates.

In the middle of the drive-in Apocalypse that is post-war Beirut, surrounded by the usual outcrops of half-collapsed sixties blocks – conical termite heaps of compacted, crumpled concrete – there stood an astonishing vision: a perfect Italian Baroque palace, enclosed within its own walled garden. Everything was beautifully kept, with wide terraced lawns framed by a pair of date palms looking down over the smart Christian district of Ashrafiyeh to the blue wash of the Mediterranean far below. A double marble staircase led up to the front door; only the broken balustrade – which appeared to have received a glancing hit from a mortar or a rocket-propelled grenade – indicated that the war had touched this small oasis at all.

I was let in by a servant and conducted to the library. On the wall hung a fine portrait of a seventeenth-century Greek merchant flanked by a series of superb oils of Ottoman townscapes: domes and caïques and wooden palaces on the Bosphorus. Shelves groaned with old leather-bound books; on one side a seventeenth-century escritoire was covered with the latest magazines from London and Paris.

After maybe ten minutes there came the sound of brisk footsteps and a petite but stylish woman walked in, hand extended. She was strikingly beautiful. In the half-light of the library I took her for about forty; only in the course of her conversation did it become clear that she must have been at least seventy, and possibly a good deal older than that.

'Do forgive me,' she said in an old-fashioned upper-class accent, the 'r's slurred almost into 'w's. 'I've been with the lawyer. We're having the most trying time with the Greek Orthodox Bishop next door. He's behaving like a total gangster. All the institutions in Lebanon have collapsed, and the Church is unfortunately no exception. Last year this bishop helped himself to the funds of the Greek Orthodox hospital donated by my family for the benefit of the poor. Now he is now trying to pinch a strip of my garden. You see, the boundary wall was destroyed in the Syrian bombardment.'

'You were bombarded here?'

'Several times.'

'Who by? I thought this part of Beirut escaped the worst of the war.'

'The first time, in '75, it was by the Palestinians. Then there was a second, more serious bombardment by the Syrians in '76. I was the other side of Beirut when it began again: couldn't get across the Green Line. Eventually I found someone who was prepared to bribe the Syrians, brave the shells and take me across. I arrived to find that the house had been appallingly battered. My son was here giving out water from the well in our garden to queues of people from the street. The Syrians had cut the water supply.'

'But the house was still standing?'

'Just about. This room was blown out by a phosphorus bomb. Came back to find the place looking like a surrealist picture. That entire wall had disappeared, but the bookcase was still standing, upright against the sky.'

Lady Cochrane arched her eyebrows: 'Next door the chandelier was blown apart in the blast, the mirrorwork ceiling was destroyed and my late husband's remarkable collection of fifteenth-century Chinese bowls was smashed.'

She stood up and led the way to the door into the hall. 'I suppose we were very lucky that none of the shells cut the main load-bearing pillars, otherwise the whole thing would have collapsed. But by pure good fortune most of them went straight through: down the passage, into the dining room and out the other side into the garden. Ruined my borders. Holes everywhere.'

'And you carried on living here, despite everything?'

'Oh yes. We lived in the shell for seven years. You can get used to anything. In time.'

'And you didn't rebuild?'

'There didn't seem much point while the shelling was continuing. It was 1985 before we felt it was worth trying to begin restoring the house.'

Lady Cochrane led the way into the main hall, an astonishing piece of mid-nineteenth-century Lebanese architecture enclosed by a quadrant of Saracenic arches. At the far end she pointed to an empty space on the wall; a shadow and a copper picture-hanger indicated where a large canvas had once hung.

'We had to sell the Guercino to the Met,' she said. 'It was painted for one of my ancestors, but the Syrians were shelling and we were left with no money at all. Couldn't even pay the servants. I panicked and sold it for a fraction of its worth.'

'And this?' I asked, pointing to a Venetian canalscape. 'Canaletto?'

'No,' she said. 'It's Guardi. But it's nice, isn't it?'

Outside the door of the sitting room my hostess paused by a small Baroque table with finely carved ball-and-claw feet. On it were displayed a few lumps of twisted metal.

'And these,' I said. 'Giacometti?'

'No, no,' said Lady Cochrane. 'Those are shells. All of that lot landed inside the house. Those ones on the left are mortars: used to come whizzing through the house six at a time. Made a terrible racket. We keep them just to remind us what we went through.'

We sat at a table and Lady Cochrane called for coffee. She then talked about her views on the redevelopment of Beirut: how the town had once been a green Ottoman garden city and should now be trying to return to that ideal rather than aiming at a sort of Middle Eastern version of Hong Kong, all high-rise blocks and plate glass. The brutalist architecture, she believed, was partly responsible for the brutalisation of Lebanon.

'In the past rich and poor had their own green space,' she said. 'A workman had something to look forward to: a peaceful evening sitting with his family round a small fountain surrounded by sweet-smelling herbs. Now he comes back to a concrete box in a slum. His children are screaming, the television is blaring. It's no wonder the Lebanese turned somewhat irritable and aggressive during the 1970s.'

A servant padded in with a tray of coffee. Lady Cochrane poured me a cup. In the background a telephone rang and a minute later the servant reappeared and whispered into his mistress's ear. She smiled a broad smile

'Good, good,' she said. 'That was my lawyer. He's rung to say the Bishop has just received the order to stop building in my garden. But you see, that Bishop is a splendid example. The Lebanese who are even remotely civilised are now reduced to a tiny minority. Before the civil war there was an artistic life: painters, musicians, actors. Now there is a terrible exodus of brains and honest people – the best Lebanese, Christian and Muslim, have all left, or are in the process of leaving. Among the Maronites 300,000 – a third of the total community – fled the Middle East in the course of the war. We're left with the bottom of the barrel.'

'Are you a Maronite?'

'I'm Greek Orthodox,' said Lady Cochrane. 'My family were Byzantines from Constantinople: the name Sursock is a corruption of Kyrie Isaac, Lord Isaac. They left at the fall of the city in 1453 and settled near J'bail.'

I asked how much responsibility she thought the Maronites had to bear for what had happened to Lebanon.

'The Maronites presided over both the birth and the death of Lebanon,' said Lady Cochrane. 'Without them, Lebanon would never have existed. With them behaving as they have a tendency to do, it can't go on. Of course, the war brought out the worst in everyone. The Muslims all turned into terrorists and the Christians into mafiosi: kidnapping and robbing people, protection rackets and so on. At the beginning they were so brave and honourable: we willingly gave them money, and even our own sons. But by the end we refused: it was just people like Geagea. Gangsters.'

'I'm off to Geagea territory – Bsharre – this afternoon.'

'Well, you be careful,' said Lady Cochrane briskly.

'What do you mean?'

'During the war my son Alfred went up there to see some friends. On the road, he was stopped by the Marada militia. They put a gun to his head and tied him to a tree. When Alfred was at Eton he quickly learned how to get out of beatings, and this experience came in very handy on this occasion. They said they were going to execute him. He kept telling them he was great friends with the Franjiehs – the ex-President's family who commanded the militia – and said that he was going to spend the weekend with them. Of course he had no such plans, but the lie eventually did the trick. Most of the militia men did not believe him, but Alfred kept going on about his important Maronite friends and eventually one of them got cold feet. The others were saying, "Let's just shoot him and ask questions afterwards," but the one with cold feet said, "No, we must telephone the Franjiehs and check what he's saying." So they did.

'Luckily they got the former President, Suleiman Franjieh. He was a little surprised to hear that Alfred thought he had been invited for the weekend, but he told the militiamen to release Alfred immediately nonetheless. The next day Robert Franjieh, the President's son, rang up here. He and Alfred had known each other since they were in playpens together: it's a very small world here in Lebanon. Robert said: "I'm so sorry, Alfred. Rotten luck. Won't you come to lunch?"'

'And what was Alfred's reply?'

'He said, "Thanks a lot, Robert, but not today. I'm afraid I'm a little busy."'

Oddly enough, before I left England a journalist friend had given me Robert Franjieh's number. Intrigued by Lady Cochrane's story, before I left Beirut for Bsharre I gave him a ring and received an invitation to lunch later in the week. Unlike Alfred, I accepted.

The main road north from Beirut hugged the coast. The cliffs of the mountains rose steeply to our right while a ribbon of new seafront high-rise blocks towered to the left. We headed past the harbour with its phalanx of bulldozers pushing great piles of rubble and tangles of reinforced concrete into the sea, then crawled slowly through a long traffic jam past the casinos, nightclubs and restaurants of Jounieh. A little to the north we passed along a small stretch of six-lane motorway elaborately decorated with strange road-markings and numbers. As none of Lebanon's roads normally have any markings at all (or, indeed, traffic lights, signposts or lighting for that matter), I was baffled by the complex network of characters and symbols, and asked Nouri what they were.

'They were for the planes, sir.'

'I'm sorry?'

'Aeroplanes, sir. During the war, when Beirut airport was on the front line, the air force moved here. This side was the main runway, while the other lane was where the planes were parked.'

Just after Jebail, once famous across the Mediterranean for its orgiastic worship of Astarte, we turned inland, driving up into a dark and narrow river valley, barren but for a thin covering of thorn and gorse. The gradient became steeper. Soon the valley had grown into a great gash, slicing through the landscape with near-vertical cliffs rising on either side of us; on some small ledges, cowering under the weight of strata, you could see the old rock chapels of the early Maronite hermits, some of which – the more accessible ones – had later been dignified with simple façades. Others, stranded high above the abyss and apparently reachable only by rope, gaped out of the cliff-face like yawning mouths.

It was a strange, tortured geology that played around us: the ancient beds of rock were ripped, twisted and contorted like a body turning on a rack. The further we climbed, the deeper the gorge below us sunk until we found ourselves winding along on a narrow road above a dark drop. There were no crash-barriers. Occasionally a small village with a stone chapel would appear, clinging to the ledges between us and the chasm, but as we rose these became more infrequent and increasingly primitive. It grew chilly, and before long we passed the snowline: at first just a soft dusting of snow caught in the shade of the ridges and the old cultivation terraces, then, as we climbed, a thicker covering burying the pavements and masking the slates on the roofs. Our pace dropped to a crawl.

Then, on a remote turning, several miles from the nearest house, we suddenly came upon a roadblock. It was manned by a picket of cold Syrian paratroopers; to one side stood a pair of plainclothes *mukhabarat*. Nouri wound down his window and answered a long series of questions put to him by the secret policemen. Eventually we were waved through, and I asked him what he had been questioned about.

'They asked who you were. Then they asked me about myself.'

'What did you tell them?'

'I said I am Nouri Suleiman, sportsman and swimming champion. I told them I swam the English Channel twice and said that they could ask anyone in Beirut: everyone there knew what I had done. The Syrian said he was a sportsman too. Then I told him that in 1953 I drove Frank Sinatra and Ava Gardner to Ba'albek.'

'What did he say to that?'

'He said: "Who's Frank Sinatra?"'

We drove on in the fading winter light, still snaking upwards, higher and higher into the Qadisha Valley. At some bends in the road, silhouetted against the snow, we passed shrines to the Virgin, each one topped with a small wire cross. No one was about and a chill wind was blowing, yet candles were burning outside most of these shrines, lit by figures unseen and casting flickering shadows over the statues within.

The snow was lying thickly over everything now and the villages we passed through were strangely silent, with closed shutters and empty streets. They had all been summer resorts for the Beirut rich, said Nouri, but the rich had left the country and no one came up here any more. The towns had been out of season for nearly twenty years.

Bsharre sat at the end of the valley, strung out along the edge of the chasm. After two decades of war there was only one hotel left in what had once been Lebanon's premier skiing resort. It was shuttered and darkened; only after ten minutes of hammering did we manage to rouse the caretaker. He let us in, then disappeared, leaving us in total darkness while he went off with his torch to get the diesel generator going. After the lights had eventually flickered on we were taken upstairs by the disbelieving owner. He said he had not had any visitors for a month, and no foreign guests for four years.

At first the hotel was almost unbearably cold, but within half an hour Mr Ch'baat had built a blazing log fire in the grate downstairs, while his wife prepared some hot soup for Nouri and myself. I went to bed soon afterwards with my diary, two hot-water bottles and half a bottle of whisky. I drank it propped up in bed, fully clothed, under two feet of blankets and eiderdowns.

BSHARRE, 5 OCTOBER

Light streaming in through the curtainless windows woke me early this morning. It had dawned a bright, clear winter's day. Pulling on my jacket, I walked out onto the balcony to take in the view.

Our arrival in the dark had given no hint of Bsharre's astonishing position. It was huddled on a narrow ledge between high snow peaks and the dark abyss of the Qadisha Valley. Stone houses with red roofs stretched out along the edge of the cliff in either direction, broken occasionally by the twin towers of a Maronite church. All the churches and chapels were built in the same French colonial mock-Gothic style; indeed the whole town had an inescapably French feel, like some remote Auvergne spa in the depths of winter. Only the extraordinary drama of the geology placed the scene firmly in Asia rather than Europe.

I drank a cup of thick Turkish coffee by the fire in the dining room. Then, leaving a note for Nouri to come and pick me up at the bottom of the valley later that afternoon, I set off on foot for Qadisha, the sacred valley of the Maronites.

The streets of Bsharre were clogged with the snow that had fallen during the night, and the town's traders were out in force, clearing the pavements outside their shops. I followed the road out of town around the edge of the precipice, past the tail of the gorge. To one side stood an orchard, its trees heavy with hard, cold apples. There I left the road and clambered down a steep track. It corkscrewed sharply downwards along the face of the cliff, curling around the jagged contours of the precipice in a series of dizzy hairpin bends. Halfway down I found three woodcutters smoking cigarettes on a treetrunk by the side of the road; pointing down the valley towards the sea they gave me directions to the old patriarchate. It lay four miles down the gorge, they said. All I had to do was to follow the river along the bottom of the valley; sooner or later it would lead me to my destination.

The bottom of the valley was cold and damp in the way that only places never reached by the sun can be cold and damp. The rock of the cliff-face blossomed with a thick beard of moss and strange grey lichens. An untended herd of long-haired goats were nibbling the grass in a small water-meadow by the river; high above, the fire-blackened caves of early medieval hermits hung like swallows' nests beneath overhangs in the rock.

The track passed between the muddy brown river and the rock-face, with a tangle of snow-covered thorns and creepers, vines and aerial roots hanging between the two and occasionally brushing my face as I passed. Every so often the terracing on the far side of the valley would be broken by the platform of a house, but always these were shuttered up and deserted. After a mile or so I passed the carcass of a small goat. Its front half was perfectly preserved, but its back had been eaten away, perhaps by a dog or a large bird of prey. Blood stained the slush all around it. The valley was dark and damp and eerily quiet. The sheer cliff-faces loomed on either side. I quickened my pace.

Eventually, after a four-mile walk, I came to a makeshift sign on which had been crudely scribbled an arrow and the message: SILENCE! PRIÈRE! I left the track in the direction indicated and followed a small path that led up to the right, through a thicket of firs and poplars. There, just a hundred yards from the track, in the shadow of a large fig tree, stood the old Maronite Patriarchate. It was partly built into the face of the cliff and sur-rounded by a scattering of modest stone buildings: a range of cells, a church, some workshops, a kitchen building and a bell tower. Like everything else in the valley it was shuttered, silent and strangely sinister. The only sign of life was a single outsized lizard which shot into a crack in the wall as I climbed up the steps to the cells.

This then was the cold heart of the Maronite world: an abbey said to have been founded by the fourth-century Byzantine Emperor Theodosius the Great, then for a thousand years the hidden Patriarchate of a persecuted (and in Byzantine eyes heretical) Church. Suitably inaccessible for a church on the defensive, Qanubbin's remoteness came to be an obstacle as the Maronites' power grew throughout the eighteenth century, and in 1820 it lost its primacy to the abbey at Bkerke on the cliffs above Beirut. It was finally deserted in the early years of the twentieth century. It is still a sacred site to the Maronites, yet no one seems to come here now, and its doors are all locked and bolted, perhaps to prevent one of the Maronites' many enemies from desecrating their most holy relics.

Disconsolate at finding everything shut up after so long a walk, I rattled irritably on the various doors around the compound. Just as I was about to give up, I noticed a narrow flight of stairs running up the outside wall of a chapel, and found that from the top step I could reach a window whose shutters had been left open. Pulling myself up, I balanced on the window frame and looked down into the unlit interior.

Inside it was pitch dark, but for the faint illumination of the light admitted by the one window. As my eyes adjusted to the gloom I began to be able to make out a vaulted semi-subterranean chamber, around whose walls were scattered some large objects of ecclesiastical lumber. After the long walk down the cliffs and through the valley I felt I had an obligation to be inquisitive. So, mouthing a prayer, I jumped down into the night-blackness of the crypt.

I fell through the darkness for fifteen feet and landed badly on the mud floor. When I had got my breath back I groped around the walls, but there were no light switches, and the doors turned out to be locked rather than bolted. I could not open them and so remained trapped in the darkness, a darkness which grew still more intense when, with a creak, a gust of wind blew one of the two shutters of my window closed.

Slowly, however, my eyes got used even to this deep gloom, and I felt my way over to an object that turned out to be a large metal candle-stand. It contained a bed of waxy sand where a line of votive candles had guttered. Next to the stand was a broken white cross; and beyond that, in the centre of the room, a low rectangular chest on four squat legs. It was flanked on either side by two brass-topped candle-holders on wooden stands. The chest had a glass top and looked rather like an old-fashioned museum display-case, except that it was much lower. I went over and, wiping away a thin lint of cobwebs, peered through the glass to see if I could make out what was contained within.

Near the far end of the case were laid out some clerical vestments of finely patterned lace, above which had been placed a glinting stole of cloth-of-gold. The lace was slightly crumpled, and bringing my face closer to the glass I noticed what looked like a stick poking out from the bottom. Then I realised it was a leg bone, and it finally dawned on me what I was looking at.

At the top of the glass coffin, through a gauze veil, I found myself staring at the mummified face of a long-dead Maronite Patriarch. He was still crowned with his gilded mitre, and his gaunt face was turned slightly on its side, so that his features caught the light from the window. His skin had the consistency of old leather. It was hard and cracked, pitted with small tears and holes, yet every feature was still perfectly preserved: the high cheekbones, the left ear flat and shrivelled like an old buckle, the lips thin and slightly parted, revealing an unsettling line of grinning white teeth.

Then, distantly, from far away in Bsharre, I heard a peal of bells calling the angelus. The noise woke me from my daze and reminded me how imminent was the coming night. I stumbled over to the wall and found to my relief that the stone was pitted with enough cracks and hand-holds to allow me to climb out of the crypt. Two minutes later I emerged blinking into the open. Already it was late afternoon and I had, I calculated, less than an hour to get up the cliff and out into the valley before darkness fell. Wiping the cobwebs from my hands on my trouser legs, I willed myself not to run, but soon found myself stumbling rapidly down the bank to the track.

At first I jogged back along the path, anxious to get up the cliff and out of the valley before the onset of darkness. But after a quarter of an hour I was exhausted, and decided to take a rest on an old treetrunk beside the road.

As I sat there scribbling what I had just seen into my notebook, I heard a branch break behind me. Turning around with a start I saw a bearded old man in rough, dark robes staring at me from a grove of trees a short distance away. We stood looking at each other in silence for a second before, in a low voice, he said: '*Qui est là?*'

I introduced myself and asked him who he was.

'*Je suis le père eremite,*' he said, adding after a pause, '*Le dernier eremite dans Liban. Peut-être le dernier eremite dans le Prochain Orient.*' A proud smile flashed momentarily across his face as he said this. '*Et vous? Vous êtes Chrétien? Catholique?*'

I nodded, and he beckoned me over. He held my hand and peered closely into my eyes. He was old and frail, with long fingers and very white skin, but he had a tremendously gentle face.

'*Venez,*' he said, and led the way up a narrow path overhung with trees and covered with pine needles and acorns. He pulled aside a rough wicket gate and led me towards his hermitage, a small stone hut built against the rockface and enclosing an old cave chapel. To one side stood a small but carefully tended olive grove.

'My predecessor planted those trees in the time of the Ottomans,' said the hermit.

He opened the door of the chapel and indicated that I should go in. Inside it was very cold, but candles flickered against the sanctuary icons, giving off a little reflected light.

'For thirty-five, forty years there were no hermits at all,' said the old man. 'Now I am the only one.'

'When did you begin?'

'At the end of May 1982, on the day of Pentecost. Before that I was the Superior of the Monastery of St Antony at Koshaya, a little down the valley. But I asked for a dispensation from my duties as Abbot so I could become a hermit.'

'Why?'

'It is a vocation. To be a hermit is the summit of the Christian life. Not everyone can do it. For me it was very difficult to separate from my brothers, to give up meat, to live on my own. Most of all it is difficult to pray the Maronite liturgies for hermits – the ancient hermit liturgies of Antioch – which ordain long prayers to perform every day.'

'Very long?'

'Well over eight hours every day. The hermit should be occupied all day with prayer and spiritual reading. According to the Rule of St Antony he is allowed only small breaks to tend his grapes and olives and vegetables. This life is not for everyone.'

'Does it get easier?'

'Every day is difficult. It is the same for all hermits. As you get closer to God your enemy attacks you more. Those who are content to live in sin do not suffer from the temptations of the Devil so badly as those who try to live with God. For a hermit temptation follows you all your life. But after a while you do feel you are making progress. You do feel you are drawing closer to God.'

I asked why it was necessary to leave a monastery to achieve this, what benefit there was in isolation. In answer, the hermit pointed to a small icon of St Antony hanging on the chapel wall. 'The desert fathers had a saying, that just as it is impossible to see your face in troubled waters, so also the soul: unless it is clear of alien thoughts and distractions it is not possible to pray to God in contemplation. It is like two lovers. If they want to discuss their love they want to be alone. They do not want to sit in the middle of a crowd.'

'Is it a happy life?'

The old man considered for a second before answering. 'Yes. It is happy, but only because it is so difficult. That is why the satisfaction is so great when you succeed. The desert fathers had another saying. They said that being a hermit was like building a fire. At first it smokes and your eyes water, but later you get the desired result: after the smoke disperses, the light and the heat comes. So with hermits. In the beginning there is a struggle and a lot of work for those who wish to come near to God and to light the divine fire within themselves. At first they feel lonely and depressed. But after that there is the indescribable joy of feeling the presence of the Lord.'

He paused and looked at me. Then he said: 'Of course there is smoke in every life: misunderstandings, difficulties. Everyone must carry the cross, not a cross made of wood, but the troubles of every day. Some people pretend they have no difficulties, but it is not true. Everyone has their troubles.'

I thought of the troubles which had resounded all around the valley in which the hermit lived, and I asked him whether the war had impinged on his life at all.

'No,' said the hermit. 'It did not come here. This is the Valley of the Saints. It is protected by God. I was never worried. Even though the Christians made many mistakes, I was not frightened. I knew we were still protected.'

'Do you worry that so many Maronites have emigrated now? That they are now a minority in Lebanon?'

'The others will come back, I hope. But that is politics. It is not my world. Whatever happens I will stay. I am a prisoner of God. I cannot leave this place.'

Worried by the fading light, I said goodbye to the hermit and stumbled down the path to the track at the bottom. I walked along it in the gathering darkness until I saw a pair of headlights coming slowly towards me. It was Nouri, worried that I had got lost. Only after I got in and we were heading back towards Bsharre did I realise that I had never learned the hermit's name.

B SHARRE, 9 O CTOBER

The Qanubbin Gorge was once famous for producing saints. Now it is more remarkable for the number of Christian warlords and mafiosi that spring from its soil.

Bsharre claims Geagea; Zghorta, twenty miles further down the gorge, produced the Franjiehs, one of the most powerful clan of warlords in all Lebanon. Geagea is now awaiting trial, but the Franjiehs still live in great style in their feudal stronghold, where they mourn the memory of the greatest of their clansmen, Suleiman 'the Sphinx' Franjieh, mafia godfather, reputed mass murderer and one-time President of Lebanon.

Tales of Suleiman Franjieh's enormities fill the annals of modern Lebanon. There are references to his boasting of the number of men he had personally killed (seven hundred according to one version), and to his policy of getting one of his toughs ostentatiously to shoot dead a Tripoli Muslim every month just to remind the townsmen who it was that controlled northern Lebanon. His most famous outrage took place as part of a vendetta with a rival Maronite clan, the Douaihys, who in his view were beginning to encroach on his political territory. The climax of this dispute saw Franjieh's gunmen massacring the Douaihy family while they were attending a requiem mass a short distance from Zghorta; witnesses claimed that Suleiman was himself one of the gunmen. Different versions of the story circulate, but all agree that a full-scale shoot-out took place during the funeral, with the gunmen of the rival clans blazing away at each other from behind pillars and inside confessionals; that several priests conducting the service were caught in the crossfire and killed; and that the Douaihy clan came off much the worst with at least twelve (and possibly as many as twenty) dead. Certainly at the end of it, warrants were issued for the arrest of forty-five Franjieh toughs, and Suleiman was forced to flee. He went to Syria, where he was sheltered by friends in the Alawi mountains. Their name was Asad, and Suleiman came to be specially friendly with one of them, a young air force officer named Hafez. Twelve years later, in 1970, long after Suleiman had been granted a pardon and allowed to return to Lebanon, Hafez al-Asad seized power in Damascus in a *coup d'état*.

By chance, the same year saw Suleiman elected to the Presidency of Lebanon. His election was reputedly pulled off only when his gunmen, smuggled into the parliament building with the complicity of a sympathetic policeman, enforced a vote in his favour by producing revolvers and turning them on the Speaker. In characteristic style, Suleiman Franjieh used his appointment to fill the Cabinet with his friends and relatives: the Mayor of Zghorta was suddenly promoted from organising flower shows to being Director of the Ministry of Information; Iskander Ghanem, a close personal friend, became Commander-in-Chief of the Army; while Tony Franjieh, Suleiman's eldest son, became the Minister of Posts and Telecommunications. Later, on the outbreak of war, Tony was put in charge of the Franjiehs' personal Marada Militia, where he behaved with characteristic brutality: on one occasion three hundred Muslims were massacred in one day in the Matn region in revenge for four Maronites found slain. Tony continued in this way until, in typical Maronite fashion, he died as he had lived, dispatched by two rival Maronite leaders, Bashir Gemayel and Samir Geagea, in a night raid on the Franjieh summer palace.

The story of the raid was remarkable, and revealed more clearly than anything the medieval feudal reality behind the civilised twentieth-century veneer of Lebanese politics. Just as Jumblatt's Progressive Socialist Party was really only a mechanism for the Druze to support their feudal lords, the Jumblatts, so the dispute between Gemayel, Geagea and Tony Franjieh, ostensibly a struggle for power between two rival Christian militias – the Gemayel-Geagea Phalange, which wanted to partition Lebanon into sectarian cantons, and the Franjiehs' Marada Militia which wished to keep it whole – in fact had its true roots in something more primitive still: a century-old blood feud between Bsharre, Geagea's home town, and Ehden and Zghorta, the Franjieh strongholds forty miles to the west.

The feud was explained to me by Mr Ch'baat at the hotel this morning when he joined me for breakfast. 'Some time about one hundred years ago,' he said, 'a Geagea woman from Bsharre was breast-feeding her child in a village on the coast. Two horsemen from Ehden stopped by her house, and she gave them water and fed their horses. Rather than saying thank you, they killed her dog and threw it in the well. Then they tore the baby in two and shot the mother. When they heard this in Bsharre the priest began to ring the bells. The people gathered by the church and discussed what they should do. Eventually they hit on a plan.'

'What was that?' I asked.

'They walked down to Ehden. They burned the town. Then they killed lots of people.' Ch'baat nodded his head approvingly. 'Since then the two towns have been enemies. There is a saying in Lebanon: "The enemy of my grandfather can never be my friend."'

When I said I was going to visit Ehden that morning, Ch'baat raised his eyebrows. 'Be careful, then. In Bsharre we shoot you in the face, but in Ehden they shoot you in the back. We have a proverb: "You can eat in Ehden, but make sure you sleep in Bsharre. Sleep in Ehden, and they will shoot you while you are asleep."'

Yet by all accounts, this was exactly what Gemayel and Geagea had done to Tony Franjieh on the night of their commando raid on Ehden. On 13 June 1978 Geagea amassed a thousand of his Phalange troops at Jounieh and drove up into the mountains at night. Another force of around two hundred came down from Bsharre. In all around 1,200 Phalangists were involved, all heavily armed with machine guns, cannons and rockets, moving in two convoys of open-topped jeeps.

The diversionary force from Bsharre attacked first, just before four a.m., ambushing and killing the militia men woken by the first sounds of battle. This drew the defenders away from the centre of Ehden, leaving the Franjiehs' Summer Palace undefended. And it was on the Summer Palace, where Tony Franjieh lay sleeping, that Geagea directed the main Phalangist force. He led it into battle himself.

The attack was over in less than a quarter of an hour. Quickly overcoming the few remaining guards, Geagea's force surrounded the building. There was a brief exchange of fire, during which Franjieh managed to wound Geagea severely in the shoulder, but the matter was quickly settled with a grenade. By the time the raiders withdrew, Tony Franjieh and his entire immediate family had been killed.

I pointed out to Ch'baat that rousing a man from his bed and killing him and his family in their pyjamas hardly seemed to square with Bsharre's honourable tradition of shooting people awake and in the face, but he simply shrugged his shoulders. 'Geagea is a very honourable and very holy man,' he said. 'We are very proud of him in Bsharre.'

I listed some more of the crimes I had heard Geagea accused of: as well as the killing of Tony Franjieh, the equally cowardly night murder of another Christian rival, Dany Chamoun and his wife and two small sons (twenty-seven bullets were pumped into the two children); the bombing of the church in Jounieh (apparently an attempt either to keep the Pope away or to persuade the international community that the Christians of Lebanon were being oppressed and terrorised by wicked Muslim extremists); the mass murder and terrorising of the Druze of the Chouf.

'You must not believe what people say about Samir Geagea,' said Ch'baat.

'But you can hardly call him holy.'

'Certainly yes,' he said, quite serious. 'He went to mass every day and prayed by his bed every night. He had a church built wherever he was, wherever he fought. Every Christmas his troops expected money as a present, but instead he gave them prayer books and rosaries. Of course he went to confession every week. He never went into battle without his cross. In his office, he always had a picture of the Virgin and a cross: never any picture of Che Guevara or anything like that.'

We left Bsharre at ten in the morning and took a winding mountain road down towards the north-west. It was a spectacular drive, snaking through the snowy hills and Alpine meadows towards the coastal plain and the blue haze of the coastline. Only the constant punctuation of Syrian army checkpoints hinted at the area's recent history of conflict.

At Ehden a line of Syrian tanks was drawn up outside the French-built colonial post office with its Moorish arcade. I asked

Nouri to take me to the scene of the attack, and we pulled up behind a middle-aged man at the outer gates of the Summer Palace to ask exact directions. He offered to conduct us himself. It was only when he got in that I noticed what it was that he was carrying: not an umbrella as I had at first thought, but a pump-action shotgun.

'Are you a security guard or something?' I asked, alarmed.

'No,' replied the man. 'I was going out shooting.'

'Shooting what?'

'Cats.'

'Cats?'

'Cats. I hate cats.'

'Why?'

'Because,' said the man, 'I like dogs. I like powerful dogs. I have two dobermans at home.'

He reflected on this for a second.

'Cats,' he added, 'are vermin.'

Driving into the gates of the Franjiehs' Summer Palace, the doberman-lover directed us away from the main palace to a small bungalow that stood in the grounds.

'This is where Tony was sleeping when they attacked,' he said.

'Were you here at the time?' I asked.

'No, I was in London. It was midsummer. Geagea only got away with the murder because everyone was away. There were a thousand of them and no one was here to protect Tony. A couple of guards, nothing more.'

The man spat on the ground and pointed over to the gatehouse of the compound. 'They left their jeeps over there and came the final distance on foot. Geagea and his boss, Bashir Gemayel, were standing over there directing everything. Tony heard something and woke up in time to get to the kitchen and shoot six of them dead – and wound Geagea – before they blew him up with a grenade. Without their grenades they would never have been able to kill him.'

The man fiddled angrily with the safety catch of his shotgun. 'They were cowards. After they killed Tony, they walked into the house and shot his wife, his daughter, the maid, even the dog. I didn't think a human being could do that. The girl was three years old; like an angel. Afterwards they found thirty bullets in her body and head. What kind of person could do that?'

'Wasn't there any resistance?'

'Of course. When they heard the shooting, our people came rushing out of their houses to see what was happening. At the same time some reinforcements arrived from Zghorta. Many of the Phalangists were killed, even though most of our people were just armed with knives and shotguns. When they saw that Geagea was wounded the Phalange just ran away. Like cowards. They left their jeeps and machine guns and just ran. We were still hunting them down in the hills days afterwards.'

The man led me over to the bungalow and pointed out the bulletholes around what he said had been the child's bedroom.

'Most of them must have been taking drugs. Something like this no one can do if they are normal. You can kill someone who is three years old? No. No one can do this. Only an animal. But if you take drugs you can. Maybe. Maybe then.'

After all I had heard of the firepower of the different Christian warlords in the mountains, I carried on down to Zghorta half expecting that my lunch with the Franjiehs would be held in some sort of castellated mafia fortress. I could not have been more wrong.

The surviving Franjiehs turned out to live in an elegant new neo-colonial villa, built sometime in the 1970s and surrounded by a thicket of rich green palms. I was conducted inside by an old retainer and left to wait amid the polychrome Moorish arches of a reception room. The walls were decorated with fans of Ottoman daggers and muskets, mounted fragments of Byzantine mosaic and fine Turkish kilims. Along the side of the room were lines of chairs, enough to sit maybe thirty or forty retainers coming to pay their respect to their feudal lord.

No less surprising, when they finally appeared, were the

Franjiehs themselves. Despite quite recently possessing a sizeable private army, indulging in bloody feuds and running one of the most powerful mafia-type networks in Lebanon, nothing said or done by my hosts indicated that they were anything but good-natured, wealthy provincial landowners of the sort you might be pleased to meet anywhere around the Mediterranean. Tony's younger brother Robert, my host, turned out to be gentle and artistic. I had been told by our mutual friend that he was a very different figure from his late father: a reluctant politician, he had voluntarily handed over control of the family's Marada Militia to his nephew, Tony's surviving son. Nevertheless I had certainly not expected such an intelligent and sympathetic figure. Nor was there anything at all sinister about his mother, the late Suleiman Franjieh's elderly widow. I sat next to her at lunch. She was bubbly and apparently sweet-natured, as were her two middle-aged daughters. As we sat around a huge table and course after course of *mezze* were produced by a stream of bowing servants, Mme Franjieh made polite small talk about her visit to England.

'Oh, Monsieur William,' she said in a strong French accent as she poured me some *arak*, 'when I was a little girl in Alexandria all I wanted to hear was the sound of your Big Ben. So famous, so *célèbre* – le Ding of Big Ben: we schoolgirls talked of little else. Now of course they have mended it, and it is not the same. They tried to arrange it but what could they do? When my late husband was President we went to visit Bristol and le Longleat: so beautiful. We have nothing like this in Liban or in Egypt. And your Royal family. Oh! *La Reine d'Angleterre*: so serene. How can her son write this book and say the bad thing about the *Duc d'Edinbourg*? I used to like the Prince Charles, but now . . .'

The highlight of Mme Franjieh's life – judging by the number of times her conversation returned to the subject – was the time she and her husband attended the Shah of Iran's famous *levée* at Persepolis in 1970, ostensibly to mark the twenty-fifth centenary of the founding of the Persian Empire by Cyrus the Great.

'The Shah! Such a charming man. So handsome! Such manners! So many charming people were there at the Shah's party: la Princesse Anne (what elegance!), Monsieur Tito (so big a man!), Monsieur Bhutto and his beautiful wife, Mrs Asad (*maladroite et très silencieuse*), Mrs Sadat (never stopped talking) ... In those days the politicians were more sophisticated, I think. This Clinton – he is like a performing monkey, *non*? He has not got down from his tree. Of course, as I was brought up in Alexandria so I was used to cosmopolitan society. Oh! In my youth in Alexandria: everyone was there: *les Grecs*! *Les Juifs*! *Les Anglais*! The dances! The beautiful hotels! The Cecil, The Windsor, Le Metropole ... *Une glace au chocolat* at the Groppi! Oh! Of course in those days children respected their parents. We always waited for our parents to finish their ice before we began ours. *Qu'est-ce que tu veux, Maman? Oui Maman! Non Maman!* But these days. The young. Other than my darling Robert, Robert who is martyred by his mother, isn't that right, *mon petit*?'

Afterwards, when Mme Franjieh had stopped talking, the ladies departed for their siesta. I was left alone chatting with Robert.

'I was at university when the war broke out,' he said at one stage, breaking into the small talk. 'I was studying to be an architect. All I wanted to do was to start my life. Then suddenly this strange mentality developed: everything became polarised into Christian versus Muslim. All my life I had never asked anyone whether he was a Christian or not. Then quite suddenly you had to give up half your life: half your friends, half the places you knew. I still have more Muslim friends than Christian ones. When the war broke out, I suddenly could not see them, could not speak to them.

'It was amazing to see how the hysteria evolved. In 1969 you began to see lines of friends from a street in Zghorta being drilled: lines of old butchers and grocers learning how to hold a rifle or fire a mortar. Perhaps one guy from the town had been in the army, and he would be there instructing all the old farmers.'

'It must all seem very distant now.'

'No,' said Robert. 'The war lives on. Everything in my life – everything in Lebanon – has been marked by that boundary: everything is either before or after the war. It has changed and brutalised everything. When I was young, if someone died from cancer or an accident, people would stop talking about it when I came into the room. Now I see friends talking about death in front of their children as if they were talking about bread or wine. During the war most people in this country ceased to make an effort, to work or to study: they knew they could be dead the next day, so they lived for the moment. It is the same today. In fact it may be the only thing people *have* learned from the war.'

He sipped his coffee. 'To be honest with you, I don't like to think about the war. I try to forget it, but you can't, of course, not finally, not unless you're insane. I just thank God every day that we can still appreciate, you know, the simple things: flowers, streams, beautiful weather . . .'

Robert was so obviously intelligent and reasonable that I longed to ask him what he thought about his father's mafia activities, but the subject never arose, and it seemed impossible to think of a way of phrasing the question without causing grave offence. But Robert did eventually touch on the murder of his brother Tony.

'I cannot forgive those who were responsible,' he said. 'The other day I was at a dinner party. There were about one hundred people. Suddenly at the other end of the room I saw Solange Gemayel, Bashir's widow. I tried to avoid her, but she saw me across the party and came running across the room. She said: "It is reconciliation time." Why? She does not represent anything. I do not represent anything. Neither of us are politicians. Why reconcile? It would just hurt more. I don't want to be hurt again.'

'What did you do?'

'Out of respect for the guy who was giving the party I could not make a scandal. I had to shake her hand. But I hope I never see her again. Or any of her family. How can you ever forgive the family who shot your brother and his little daughter in cold blood?'

There was one last thing I hoped to do before I left Lebanon and headed south to the Holy Land. I wanted to talk to some of the Christian Palestinian refugees expelled from their ancestral homes at the creation of Israel in 1948. Lebanon's Christian Palestinians were the group which more than any other must have found itself caught in the crossfire during the civil war. As Christians, one might imagine that the Palestinians would have seen them as potential traitors; as Palestinians, the Lebanese Christians would have regarded them as 'terrorists' and vermin, fit only to be exterminated in the most brutal fashion possible. Corralled into their squalid and indefensible camps, the Palestinians suffered more than any other group in the civil war; and in such a situation the friendless Palestinian Christians must presumably have suffered worst of all. Special refugee camps had apparently been set up in Beirut to house this awkward group, and Nouri said he had some contacts who could get me into one of them.

We drove back to the capital by a different route in order to visit the ancient city of Ba'albek, one of John Moschos's stopping points as he passed up the coast of Byzantine Phoenicia. From Bsharre we headed south-east over the high rocky ridges of Mount Lebanon, then corkscrewed down into soft green fields of the northern Bekaa. Despite the fertility of the soil and the estimated ten thousand tons of hashish it produces every year, quite apart from unspecified amounts of raw opium, the Bekaa looked much poorer than anywhere else in Lebanon. Peasants in rags were selling boxes of battered-looking apples by the roadside, and in the fields the untidy brown hessian tents of nomadic Bedouin flapped in the wind. The houses that dotted the roadside were little more than crude concrete boxes, with sacking for windows. Plastic bags and drifts of uncollected rubbish billowed across the valley, past the Syrian army radar station and out into the unseen opium fields beyond.

The poverty of the Shiite farmers of the Bekaa made them

especially fertile soil for the new fundamentalist ideas of the Iranian Revolution. When the Ayatollah's Revolutionary Guards took up station here – with tacit Syrian approval – at the end of the civil war, they quickly evicted the (overwhelmingly Christian) Lebanese army from their barracks in Ba'albek and raised the flag of the Islamic Republic of Iran over the ruins of the Roman Temple of the Sun at the centre of the town. From that point on, Ba'albek became a centre of Iranian-backed anti-Christian militancy.

The Iranians opened a two-storey propaganda office and strewed the Bekaa with posters denouncing the Israeli and American 'imperialists' and their Maronite 'lackeys', while exhorting all good Lebanese Muslims to find salvation through Islamic martyrdom. The Revolutionary Guards and their Shiite Lebanese allies together staged assaults on the Maronite villages in the northern Bekaa while their mullahs recorded viciously anti-Christian sermons to be broadcast on the Iranian-financed Ba'albek Television, the Shia equivalent of the fundamentalist American gospel channels. It was probably in Ba'albek that the suicide bombings which destroyed the American Embassy and military headquarters in Beirut were planned, and it was certainly to Ba'albek that many of the Western hostages were taken and held. Although the hostage crisis is now officially over, only a month ago a group of Danish diplomats were caught indiscreetly taking pictures of themselves in front of the Ba'albek Hezbollah headquarters. They were detained by the Hezbollah for a tense fortnight before a flurry of frantic diplomatic activity finally gained their release.

Though no one in the Bekaa probably realised it, the Shia mullahs were in many ways repeating history when they chose Ba'albek as the centre of their operations. For in late antiquity Ba'albek was also a centre of anti-Christian activity, this time as a beacon of unreconstructed paganism. At the beginning of the fifth century, St John Chrysostom tried to stamp out the militant idol-worshippers of Lebanon by sending a task force of his monks to destroy the area's temples. According to Theodoret, 'Hearing that some of the inhabitants of Phoenicia were addicted to the worship of demons, John selected some ascetics who were filled with fervent zeal and sent them to destroy the idolatrous temples, inducing some ladies of great opulence to defray the monks' expenses; and [in due course] the temples of the demons were thrown down from their very foundations.'

Not in Ba'albek, however. For 150 years later, in the 550s, the Emperor Justinian was forced to again order the destruction of Ba'albek's great Temple of the Sun, which was clearly functioning as busily as it had in the great days of pagan Rome. Justinian sent orders that all pagans must accept baptism, under penalty of confiscation and exile, and to make sure that the temple was not rebuilt, he ordered that many of its largest pillars be shipped to Constantinople, there to be re-erected at the centre of the Emperor's new basilica of Haghia Sophia.

Even these extreme measures did not mean the end of paganism in Ba'albek. In 578 A.D., the year John Moschos set off on his travels, it was learned that the pagans of the town – still apparently the majority of the population – were again actively persecuting their Christian neighbours. The Emperor Tiberius Constantine duly ordered that five pagan priests were to be burned along with their idolatrous writings, and commanded that the remaining pagans of the town be brutally punished by the army. One source talks of there being no fewer than seven purges of pagans during the course of the sixth century, yet none of these measures seems to have had the slightest effect. Ba'albek was still active as a cult centre at the death of the Emperor Maurice in 602 A.D., and continued to flourish as a pagan centre well into the early Islamic period.

Certainly when Moschos visited Ba'albek sometime in the early years of the seventh century, it still had a reputation as a redoubt of impiety. Moschos includes in *The Spiritual Meadow* a story about a blasphemous (and presumably pagan) actor from the city.

> This actor, Gaianas, used to perform in the theatre an act in which he blasphemed against the Holy Mother of God. The Mother of God appeared before him saying: 'What evil have I done to you that you should revile me before so many people and blaspheme against me?'

He rose up and, far from mending his ways, proceeded to blaspheme against her even more than before. Three times she appeared to him with the same reproach and admonition. As he did not mend his ways in the slightest degree, but rather blasphemed the more, she appeared to him once when he was sleeping at midday and said nothing at all. All she did was to sever his two hands and feet with her finger. When he awoke he found that his hands and feet were so afflicted that he just lay there like a treetrunk.

Gaianas apparently spent the rest of his days being carried on a stretcher from town to town across the length of Byzantine Phoenicia warning others not to fall into the same errors as himself. John Moschos points out with some relish, however, that despite his contrition, the Virgin did not see fit to restore his faculties to him.

As we neared Ba'albek, signs of Iranian influence visibly increased. On the roadsides we began to pass the same hoardings of turbaned Iranian mullahs I had seen in Beirut's southern suburbs. Other tableaux, painted in the gaudy primary colours of Egyptian film posters, showed Kalashnikov-wielding Shi'ite fighters blazing away at Israeli troops in southern Lebanon; some of these posters were topped with small pennants decorated with the insignia of the Hezbollah, the pro-Iranian Party of God. The men trudging along the road began to display bushy, moustacheless Islamic beards while their womenfolk became more and more heavily shrouded in layers of thick black *chador*. At every crossroads we were approached by small boys in white cotton robes shaking collecting tins and soliciting donations for the Hezbollah's war against the Israeli occupying forces in the south of the country.

On the outskirts of the town we passed the Galerie Balkajian, a ritzy new Armenian (Christian) furniture shop. It enthusiastically trumpeted its unlikely loyalty to Shia Islam by filling the entire exterior of its warehouse with the iconography of the Islamic Revolution, centred on a huge mural of the Ayatollah Khomeini glaring down over the Dome of the Rock. Beyond the warehouse, the magnificent ruins of some of the most spectacular Roman buildings ever constructed rose above the dusty rundown houses of the modern town. Nervous of Ba'albek's reputation for violence, Nouri opted to stay in the street guarding his precious Mercedes while I went off alone to look at the ruins of the Temple of the Sun.

Like the decor of modern Maronite drawing rooms, the emphasis in the temple's decoration seemed to be on opulence rather than good taste: as you wandered around, you kept thinking: 'How much did this cost?' The temple was a monument to decorative excess: whole gardens of acanthus tendrils and palmettes voluted over the stonework; imperial lion-masks – unembarrassed lumps of high classical kitsch – roared out over the great baroque orgy of the ruins. The columns, each eight feet thick, were taller than any elsewhere in the classical world; each capital was larger than a fully-grown man, and covered with enough different leaf forms to fill a greenhouse at Kew. It was an exuberant, theatrical monument, designed more for ostentation than religiosity, and it undoubtedly achieved its aim. Flanked on either side by snow peaks, sheltered by a windbreak of cypress, it was a wonderfully flash piece of Roman showmanship, and showed that an unrestrained love of glitz is nothing new in this part of the world.

I knew from my reading that the Byzantines had built a fine basilica in the middle of the temple as part of one their periodic attempts to suppress the town's militant population of pagans. Yet despite the temple's generally excellent state of preservation, I looked in vain for any sign of Byzantine work. I have since learned from archaeologists in Beirut that the reason for this was not so much a pagan wrecking campaign as a piece of French colonial *dirigisme*. Apparently when French archaeologists dug the ruins in the 1930s they removed the Byzantine basilica, assuming, with typically Gallic certainty, that posterity would find their reconstruction of a pagan classical altar more interesting than the Byzantine basilica that succeeded it.

I sat in the small Temple of Jupiter, watching a handful of Lebanese tourists circle the ruins. There was a couple with a pushchair, a few modest Shia women in dark headscarves and a carload of noisy Maronite babes in tight hip-hugging jeans, thick lashings of mascara and great bouffant beehives of back-combed hair. Despite the recent kidnapping of the Danish diplomats and Nouri's nervousness, the visitors seemed relaxed and happy as they clambered around the pillars taking photographs of each other, giggling and smiling, determined to make the most of their day out from Beirut.

Then, quite suddenly, a burst of automatic fire echoed over the ruins. A few seconds later there were two more loud bursts of rapid fire followed by a massive explosion on the hillside above the town. As I watched a great brown mushroom cloud of dust and smoke exploded into the air from a ridge half a mile from the temple. I immediately took shelter behind a capital, but to my embarrassment none of the Lebanese jumped or even looked twice at the menacing plume of the explosion. One businessman filming his family with a camcorder swung briefly around to record the cloud of smoke, then swept back to pan over the pediments of the temple and his smiling wife and baby. He saw me picking myself up, dusting the dirt from my jeans, and smiled. 'It is only the Hezbollah,' he said. 'Probably they are just training. Almost certainly they are just training.'

Nouri was waiting, as arranged, in the lobby of the Cavalier at nine this morning. With him was his friend Abed, another taxi driver who said he had good contacts in the Palestinian camps. Abed said he could take me to some Christian Palestinians and suggested we try the Mar Elias refugee camp, not far from the notorious massacre site of Chatila.

The camp was a very different place to the squalid shanty towns I knew from the West Bank. Rather than rotting behind some high-tension razor-wire fence, it lay instead behind a line of smart boutiques – Valentino, Lagerfeld and Benetton – their exquisitely dressed dummies frozen in strange sartorial contortions behind the spotlit plate glass of the shop fronts. No clear boundaries separated the camp from the surrounding houses. Only the extreme, visible poverty of its residents and the density of shrapnel holes pockmarking the façades of the buildings marked it out from its unexpectedly prosperous surroundings.

Abed parked his battered old Mercedes just outside the camp and led me confidently through the narrow warren of breezeblock houses. Mar Elias, he explained, had been one of the luckiest camps in the war. Sure, it had been intermittently shelled by the Israelis, who had used phosphorus and even cluster bombs on the refugees' shacks, but unlike some neighbouring camps it had never been completely flattened by Israeli carpet bombing or Phalange bulldozers, nor had it ever suffered a major massacre like nearby Chatila, Sabra or Karantina. Its residents were very poor, of course, and suffered the same disabilities that hamstring all Palestinians in Lebanon – banned from all but menial jobs, forbidden from buying property or travelling freely, refused access to state schools – but, relatively speaking, they had been lucky. Moreover they were not in any immediate danger of eviction. Lebanese politicians were currently threatening to tear down the Palestinians' camps elsewhere in Beirut and dump the refugees out of sight somewhere on the front line in southern Lebanon. But Mar Elias was built on Greek Orthodox Church land, and if there was no obvious hope of the Palestinians ever being allowed to go back to their homes and farms in what was now northern Israel, then at least they were not in any immediate danger of being expelled from their makeshift camp in Beirut.

As Abed led me through the fetid lanes of the camp, he bumped into a friend, a burly man in a leather jacket. Abed shook his hand then embraced him, kissing him on either cheek in the Palestinian manner. He asked a question in Arabic and his friend pointed out a nearby three-storey house.

'He says that all the residents of that house are Palestinian Christians,' said Abed after the man had gone. 'Let's see if anyone is at home.'

'Who was that?' I asked as we climbed the stairs.

'Abu Nidal.'

'*The* Abu Nidal? The hijacker and bomber?'

'No, not the man himself,' said Abed casually. 'His representative here. He runs the Mar Elias branch of Abu Nidal's Fatah Revolutionary Council '

We knocked on a door at the top of the stairs, and after a minute it was opened by a Palestinian woman in a knotted kerchief. Abed talked to her, and after sizing us up to see whether she believed what he said, and conferring with someone inside, she opened the door to let us in.

'*Salaam alekum*,' she said. 'Welcome.'

Inside, we found the room full of Palestinian women. Our host was called Sarah Daou, and we had dropped in on the morning she happened to be entertaining her mother, Samira, and her pretty teenage sister Ghada. Her two small daughters, Rana and Rasha, fetched us a pair of plastic chairs, while Sarah went off to the kitchen to make us coffee. It was a bare, simple flat, small and undecorated except for a framed picture of the Virgin and a cheap Japanese wall clock; but it was spotlessly clean.

None of the family spoke English, so Abed acted as interpreter. Soon we were hearing a recital of the depressing, but familiar, Palestinian story of loss and dispossession.

'Since the time of Saladin my family had owned several hundred acres of land in the village of Kafr Bir'im,' said Samira, Sarah's mother. She was a large, cheerful middle-aged woman with a wide smile, but her face was heavily lined and there was a weariness in her voice as she told her story. 'The village was north of Acre, near the border with Lebanon. I was only five when we fled, but I remember that Kafr Bir'im was a very beautiful place.'

She made a sweeping upward gesture with the palm of her hand, as if trying to brush away the vision rising before her.

'My father was working in Haifa at the time of the catastrophe,' she said. 'I was at a Sisters of Charity school. I very well remember when the planes were bombing and a house nearby was destroyed. We were all very frightened. We had no idea what was happening or what to do.

'My father was about twenty-five at that time. He was a butcher and worked for a Jewish company in Haifa. He had a very good relationship with his Jewish employer. The man said, "If you are frightened, send your family to Lebanon. Stay here and work for us. Then when the war is over go and collect them." But my father was too afraid. Everyone knew what had happened to the Palestinians massacred by the Jewish terrorists at Deir Yassin, and he was worried that maybe the border would close and he would be separated from us. Then the Jews began firing their mortars into the Arab areas of Haifa and our building was completely destroyed. Luckily, by some miracle, none of us were in at the time, but it made up my father's mind.

'His employer gave him a month's leave and lent us his van. That was how we left Palestine, with my father driving a Jewish van to exile in southern Lebanon. My father's mother-in-law, my grandmother, was a Maronite from that region, so he drove us straight to her house. By that stage the Israelis controlled much of the road, but they did not bother us because we had a Jewish truck. Sometimes the Israeli planes were flying just above us, but they probably thought we were Jews because of the Hebrew writing on the van and they did not bomb us. We were very lucky, but we made one big mistake: we didn't bring anything with us, because we thought the war would only last two weeks, a month maybe. We left everything behind. The only thing of any value that we had with us was my mother's gold earrings. How were we to know the Israelis would never let any of us return to our homes? Later, when the Israeli planes destroyed Kafr Bir'im – they bombed every house in the village – everything we owned, everything we had worked for, was destroyed. Only the church was left standing. Our land was divided between new Jewish settlements, and given to people from Poland and America.'

At that moment, from outside, there came the unmistakable *clack-clack-clack* of automatic gunfire. After my humiliation the day before in Ba'albek, I stayed rooted to the spot and tried to look as if I regularly sat inside Palestinian refugee camps listening to the ominous sound of approaching machine-gun fire. This time, however, I was clearly not alone in being anxious. Everyone immediately got up from their seats and went over to the windows to see what was happening.

'It's outside the camp,' said Sarah.

'Its probably just the Syrian army firing into the air,' said her mother. 'Probably celebrating someone's birthday.'

'The cars are moving normally on the roads,' said Abed, looking over towards where his car was parked.

'Maybe it's an assassination,' said Ghada, our hostess's sister. 'Maybe someone has killed Arafat and now the people are firing into the air to celebrate.'

'Maybe it's the anniversary of the beginning of the *intifada*.'

'Wrong month.'

'Maybe they are celebrating Mr William's visit,' suggested Abed.

'Is this dangerous?' I asked Abed. 'Should we go?'

'It's safer to stay,' he said. 'At least until we know what the problem is.'

Sarah and Ghada stayed by the window, peering nervously in the direction from which the firing was still coming, but their mother, clearly used to such alarms after a life spent in besieged camps, returned wearily to her seat and continued her narrative.

'We stayed all that year in southern Lebanon in my grandmother's house. It was very primitive, and my father couldn't find work because he was a Palestinian. The Lebanese wouldn't even let him drive the van, and eventually he had to sell it. After the nice school in Haifa I hated the life on the farm. My grandmother's house was very small. My uncle was living there with his family, so there were already eight people in the house even before we arrived. It was unbearable: there was no space, no privacy. All the small children were quarrelling all the time. I remember always being hungry. Often we slept without eating. We suffered a lot.

'After a year, when it became clear we would not be allowed back home for some time, we got a tent in the Baas refugee camp near Sidon. The camp had originally been built for the Armenians when they fled to Lebanon in 1916, but they had since become rich and moved out. I remember it was very cold, and when it rained the tent leaked. At night when we were all in the tent there was no room to move, and my brothers had to sleep with their legs outside the tent because they could not fit them inside.

'After some time, in 1953, my father got a job as a UN bus driver between south Lebanon and Beirut. But he never really recovered from losing everything. He hated the tents and he missed his village and his old life in Palestine. He would have given anything to return, but he knew that all his friends who had tried to sneak across the border to their old villages had been shot dead by the Israelis. They gunned down any Arab they saw crossing the border, calling them terrorists. So he had no choice but to stay in the tent. Sometimes he would just sit there looking at the keys of his house in Kafr Bir'im and the title deeds the British had given his father to prove the ownership of our land. He got ill and very depressed. It was as if something had broken inside him. He died in 1956. He was only thirty-four years old.

'Soon after that the UN transferred all the Christians to the Dbayyeh in East Beirut, leaving Baas to the Muslims. At Baas all the children had been going to a UNRWA [United Nations Relief and Works Agency] school. It was very good and things seemed to be getting better. But with my father's death and the transfer to Beirut, all my brothers and sisters had to leave school and begin work. My brothers got work on building sites; as they were Palestinians they could not get work permits, so they were paid only the lowest day-rates. My sisters and I cleaned houses. When I was a little girl in Kafr Bir'im we used to have three household servants and many workers and tenants. Now we had sunk to begging for the most menial work that was available.'

Outside the rattle of machine guns was getting louder and louder, as more and more guns joined in the shooting. At the window Samira's daughters were still nervously discussing what the cause was. As the traffic was moving freely on the roads they still thought that it must be some sort of celebration rather than fighting or an attack on the camp, but they were unable to think of any event which was due to be celebrated. From the window they shouted out to neighbouring families who were also looking nervously out towards the shooting, exchanging ideas about its possible causes.

'Maybe it is to celebrate the heroes of the October [1973 Arab–Israeli] War?' suggested Sarah, repeating the theory favoured by the family in the apartment immediately above theirs.

'Wrong date,' said Ghada.

'Asad's birthday?'

'That was earlier this month. The sixth is Asad's birthday.'

'What about Basil?'

Inside, Samira shrugged off the din and the chatter of her daughters. She had got into the swing of her story and was anxious to continue.

'So were you still in Dbayyeh camp when the civil war broke out?' I asked.

'Yes,' said Samira. 'We were very nervous. You see, Dbayyeh was in the Christian half of the city, and the Phalange attacked and captured it in January 1976. In some of the other camps they captured – Tel el-Za'atar, Maslakh and Karantina – they shot the inhabitants, even the women and children, and bulldozed the camp. But in Dbayyeh – perhaps because it was Christian – they merely sent in their secret police, and tortured only those they thought were Fatah activists.'

'So the Phalange did not hurt you personally?'

'At first we were unharmed. Then one afternoon in early February they came for my husband.'

'You didn't say when you were married.'

'I was married in 1958, when I was seventeen. My husband was a boy from another big Kafr Bir'im family. We had been married eighteen years and had six children when the Phalange captured the camp. I will never forget the day they came for him. They took him at four o'clock, accusing him of being in the PLO. As soon as they took him I managed to get a message to some Lebanese relations of my grandmother who had contacts in the Phalange. They made calls and within four hours he was back here. But what they had done to him in that time!'

'What do you mean?' I asked.

Samira looked down and began to speak in a low voice. 'They had beaten him with metal bars,' she said. 'They used electricity. They burned cigarette butts into him. They broke both his legs, smashed his kneecaps and snapped one of his arms. Also his chestbone. All in four hours!'

'But he survived?'

'When my relative intervened the Phalange were ready to kill him. My relative told the truth: he said that my husband was also a Maronite. The Phalange did not know there were any Palestinian Maronites. After they released him we had him rushed across the Green Line to the American University Hospital.' She added proudly, 'They sent an ambulance. Because he was an employee.'

'He was a doctor?'

'No,' replied Samira, a little crestfallen. 'In Lebanon a Palestinian could not hold such a job. He was a cleaner at the hospital.'

'How long did he take to recover?'

'For four months he was in emergency,' she said. 'After that I made the decision that we would stay in Muslim West Beirut and not return to the east, the Christian half. Before I left Dbayyeh I said to the guards: "I am a Christian like you. But if you treat us like this I will cross to the other side and be protected by the Musulmen."'

'And did they protect you?'

'Yes. The Muslims treated us very well: much better than the Christians. We stayed the rest of the war in West Beirut, but I never heard anyone mention the fact that we were Christians. The Muslims I know are better Christians than most Christians. Jesus Christ said that we should love and care for each other, but the Phalange were very cruel. What the Phalange did was the work of the Devil.'

'The Phalange made me ashamed to be a Christian,' said Ghada, turning her head away from the window for a second. 'The Muslims were much kinder to us. I hated myself for being a Christian when I saw the kindness they showed us.'

'My father was a Maronite,' said Sarah, 'but still I do not like them. The Maronites have no feelings.'

'When we crossed the Green Line we lost everything for a second time,' continued her mother. 'The Phalange wouldn't let us take anything. Like my mother I had only my jewellery. We left all the contents of our house: the TV, the furniture, our utensils.'

'So you were destitute all over again?'

'Not entirely. The PLO gave us a flat on the seafront in Raoche. It belonged to a Christian family who had fled to West Beirut and was partly furnished. Again we began to rebuild our lives. But in 1982 the Israelis invaded and the Israeli warships began shelling Beirut. As our flat was on the seafront it was very exposed. For fifteen days we were being shelled and bombed from both the land and the sea. It was terrifying. Most of all I was frightened for my children, that somehow I would survive and they would be killed. We stayed all that time in a shelter at the bottom of the apartment block, lying on the floor. There were fifty-five apartments in the building, fifty-five families, maybe 250 people. But the Israelis had invented a special kind of bomb which did not explode until it hit the basement, so even there down under the ground we knew we were not safe.

'One day they used one of these [suction] bombs on the building next to ours. It was completely destroyed. The four hundred families in the basement – maybe a thousand people – were all crushed to death. We had several relations in there, from my father's family. They were from al-Bassa, the next village to Kafr Bir'im. Apparently there was a rumour that Arafat was in the basement of that building. Of course it wasn't true, but what did the Israelis care? At about the same time some other cousins of ours were in a building that was shelled by phosphorus. They were killed too, but with phosphorus it is a very slow death. It burns very slowly from your skin down to your bone.'

I knew a little about the Israelis' phosphorus bombing of civilian areas of Beirut from Robert Fisk's book *Pity the Nation.* In a book filled with horrors, the worst moment of all is Fisk's description of a visit to a maternity hospital shortly after this phosphorus bombardment had taken place. There he met a nurse. After the bombardment had ended she had had to put several burning babies into a big bucket of water in order to put out the flames. When she took them out half an hour later, they were still burning. Even in the freezing cold of the mortuary they smouldered. The following morning the doctor took the tiny corpses out of the mortuary for burial. To her horror, they again burst into flames. I shuddered at the memory of this, but Samira was still continuing with her story.

'After fifteen days,' she said, 'a rocket from one of the Israeli ships hit our building. There was an earsplitting sound and the whole tower moved. It felt worse than an earthquake, but luckily the building did not catch fire. Nevertheless when we ventured out of the shelter we discovered that our apartment had been completely destroyed, and we still had to leave. That night when the bombing had stopped we ran down to Hamra Street, where we were given shelter in another basement belonging to some relations.

'Soon after that the Israelis entered West Beirut and the bombing stopped. I saw them the next day when I went to buy bread. Here were the people who had taken my home, who had farmed my land, who broke my father, murdered my relatives and then bombed my apartment. Yet many of them were just little boys. I looked at them and thought: these are the people I hate?' She paused, then added: 'If you are a Christian you have to learn to forgive your enemies. It is not for me to judge them.'

'But doesn't what has happened to you make you question your faith?' I asked. 'Don't you ever wonder how God could allow the sort of horrors you have witnessed?'

'It's not God's fault,' said Samira. 'Its the fault of people. I thank God that he has protected us.'

'What do you mean? You've had a horrific time.'

'We are still in good shape. I don't want money or luxury. I haven't lost any of my children. That's what matters to me. We are still alive and still together.'

'But you are still in exile.'

'Of course,' she said. 'After all I have suffered from the Israelis and the Lebanese I would like to go home even if it meant I was naked and starving. Even after forty-seven years I still feel a stranger in this country, feel that I don't belong. Even if I had lived a hundred years here I would still like to go back to Palestine, go back to Kafr Bir'im where no one can tell me that I'm a refugee and that I don't belong.'

'And do you think you will?'

Her daughter Ghada cut in from her watch by the window: 'Of course not,' she said. 'We would all like to go home. That goes without saying. But after Arafat's surrender, what hope is left?'

But Samira just shook her head and smiled: 'It is in the hands of God,' she said. 'We shall see.'

V

The Monastery of Mar Saba, Israeli-occupied West Bank, 24 October 1994

Again I inhabit a bare cell with white walls and a blue dado. Again, through the window, I hear the quiet rumour of hushed monkish talk, the occasional peal of bells, the purposeful rustle of habits. On the balcony next to mine a black-robed figure with a short beard, long hair and a tall cylindrical hat – Fr. Gregori, the monastery cook – is watering his pots of basil and tending his orange trees. Nearby a myna bird chatters in a cage. It could be Athos, and indeed an old oleograph of the Holy Mountain is framed on the wall of a corridor outside; but one glance at the bare rock wall of the cliff-face opposite my cell places this monastery firmly in the wilderness of Judaea, far from the cooling waters of the Aegean.

This is the desert where John Moschos took his vows and where he spent most of his monastic life, and tales of the monks of these bare hills fill most of the pages of *The Spiritual Meadow*. Having read so much about these Judaean desert fathers it is strange finally to see the austere landscape that forms the background to their exploits. It is stranger still to find many of their superstitions, fears and prejudices alive in the conversation of the monks who still inhabit this, the last of the ancient monasteries of the Holy Land to survive as a functioning community. But the stories of devils and demons, visions and miracles which sometimes seemed ludicrously outlandish when I first read them under a grey London sky sounded quite plausible last night, when told in the starlight looking out onto a cliff-face honeycombed with the cells of long-dead hermits and holy men.

'Look at it!' said Fr. Theophanes, the monastery's tall, gaunt Guest Master, waving a hand at the dark rocky gorge beneath us. 'There it is: the Valley of Doom. The Valley of Dreadful Judgement.'

Below us the monastic buildings of Mar Saba fell away in a ripple of chapels, cells and oratories, each successive layer hanging like a wasps' nest from a ledge on the rockface. Opposite, the top of the cliff wall had turned an almost unnatural shade of red in the last of the evening light. The rock was pitted with caves, each formerly the cell of a Byzantine monk. All were now deserted.

'It's very beautiful,' I said.

'Beautiful?' said Fr. Theophanes, rustling his robes in horror. 'Beautiful? See down there at the bottom? The river? Nowadays it's just the sewage from Jerusalem. But on Judgement Day that's where the River of Blood is going to flow. It's going to be full of Freemasons, whores and heretics: Protestants, Schismatics, Jews, Catholics . . . More ouzo?'

'Please.'

The monk paused to pour another thimbleful of spirit into a small glass. When I had gulped it down, he continued with his Apocalypse. 'At the head of the damned will be a troop composed of all the Popes of Rome, followed by their deputies, the Vice-Presidents of the Freemasons . . .'

'You're saying the Pope is a Freemason?'

'A Freemason? He is the President of the Freemasons. Everyone knows this. Each morning he worships the Devil in the form of a naked woman with the head of a goat.'

'Actually, I'm a Catholic.'

'Then,' said Theophanes, 'unless you convert to Orthodoxy, you too will follow your Pope down that valley, through the scorching fire. We will watch you from this balcony,' he added, 'but of course it will then be too late to save you.'

I smiled, but Fr. Theophanes was in full swing and clearly in no mood for joking. 'No one can truly know what that day will be like.' He shook his head gravely. 'But some of our Orthodox fathers have had visions. Fire – fire that will never end, terrible, terrible fire – will come from the throne of Christ, just like it does on the icons. The saints – those who are to be saved, in other words the Orthodox Church – will fly in the air to meet Christ. But sinners and all non-Orthodox will be separated from the Elect. The damned will be pushed and prodded by devils down through the fire, down from the Valley of Josephat, past here – in fact exactly the route those Israeli hikers took today – down, down to the Mouth of Hell.'

'Is that nearby?'

'Certainly,' said Theophanes, stroking his beard. 'The Mouth of Hell will open up near the Dead Sea.'

'That is in the Bible?'

'Of course,' said Theophanes. 'Everything I am telling you is true.'

I had arrived at the Great Lavra of Mar Saba earlier that afternoon. From Beirut the distance is less than three hundred miles, but this being the Middle East it took a six-hundred-mile detour via Damascus and Amman three and half days' non-stop travel – to get here. I finally crossed the Jordan into Palestine at noon yesterday.

The West Bank, and with it East Jerusalem, were captured by Israel from the Jordanians following Israel's great victory in the 1967 Six Day War. To create a buffer zone between the Jewish state and its hostile Arab neighbours East Jerusalem was annexed, while the West Bank was placed under Israeli military occupation. In defiance of international law both areas have since been subject to a campaign of colonisation: around 150 exclusively Jewish settlements have been established in the conquered territory, between them containing some 280,000 Israeli settlers (including the 130,000 settlers living in East Jerusalem). The military authorities have also appropriated 80 per cent of the West Bank's water, most of which is now piped south to Israel.

The Palestinian *intifada* made this great tract of land familiar territory, images of which were broadcast nightly into the world's sitting rooms, the backdrop to countless scenes of stone-throwing Palestinians confronting the Israeli army. Despite the stumbling peace process and the handing over of some Arab towns to Yasser Arafat's Palestinian Authority, the area, like Bosnia or Rwanda, still seems inexorably linked to violence, refugee camps and army patrols.

What is therefore so surprising when you first leave the small Jericho oasis and your taxi climbs through this great expanse of rolling hill country, past the Bedouin encampments with their brindling sheep and chickens, is the astonishing, unexpected beauty of the West Bank's dry, stony hills. Many of the valleys appear at first to be empty: dry hills whose pale rocks are scattered like lumps of feta cheese amongst the scrub-gorse. But as you wind your way down the slopes, under the weak light of a winter sky, forms begin to take shape: the stone roof of a steading hidden by a small cypress grove, the domes of an abandoned caravanserai, the minaret of a ruined mosque, the gently rolling slopes topped by newly harvested olive groves. It is a familiar Mediterranean picture; the same carefully polled olive slopes form the background to a hundred Tuscan paintings, and nearly a millennium before that, to the landscape mosaics of the Umayyad Mosque in Damascus.

The ancient Palestinian villages that you pass are built of honey-coloured limestone which changes tone according to the colour of the sky. Shepherd boys lead their flocks out into the valleys; old men in full Arab *jellaba* and *keffiyeh* suck hubble-bubbles in the shade of vine trellising; from cafés you can smell the charcoal scent of cooking kebabs and the hot, sweet odour of Turkish coffee. At first sight, the modern West Bank is still much closer to David Roberts's prints of mid-nineteenth-century Palestine than to the harrowing television images of refugees and razor wire.

Yet beautiful as it is, the signs of conflict are still there. In some valley bottoms where there should be cornfields, there are UN camps, home to those Palestinians expelled from their ancestral homes at the birth of Israel in 1948: huge, shockingly dirty shanty towns surrounded by army watchtowers and floodlights. Above them squat newly built Israeli settlements, modern suburban housing estates made up of ranks of detached whitewashed bungalows, with long lines of solar panels glinting on their roofs. Two different peoples, separated by thick tangles of razor wire and a small matter of legal status: the settlers have guns, vote in elections, enjoy Israeli civil justice and can join the army; the Palestinians under Israeli occupation are forbidden to own weapons of any sort, cannot vote in Israeli elections and are subject to the arbitrary and dismissive verdicts of military courts.

The largest of the Israeli settlements is Ma'ale Adumim, a ring of concrete blockhouses, cranes and half-completed apartment blocks, recently built over the site once occupied by the great Byzantine monastery of St Martyrius. It is currently home to thirty thousand Israelis – mostly new emigrants from Russia, Canada and the United States – yet despite the peace process the Israelis have announced plans to double the town's population over the next decade. Around the settlement's perimeter stretches an electrified razor-wire fence. Above it cluster blocks of identical eggbox houses: Milton Keynes transported into the landscape of a medieval Italian fresco.

Just beyond Ma'ale Adumim the road splits. The main branch heads on to Jerusalem. The smaller branch   potholed and neglected – winds off to the south. We bumped along this track for a few miles before arriving at a ledge overlooking the cliffs of the Valley of Kedron, a deep, arid canyon of wind-eroded chalk-like rock. At the top of the far side of this ravine stood a domed Greek Orthodox church, enclosed by a towering wall. Before I did anything else in Palestine – and certainly before I headed on to Mar Saba for the night – I knew I had first to make a pilgrimage to this shrine.

The driver parked the car in front of the gatehouse and I pulled at the bell rope; there was a distant ringing, but no one appeared. I rang the bell a second time, and soon afterwards the wimpled head of a nun peered suspiciously down over the parapet and asked in Greek what I wanted. I explained why I had come. After a few minutes there was a rattling of bolts and the great black gate swung open.

At the far side of the courtyard stood a gleaming new basilica with an octagonal dome, a bell tower and a red-tiled roof; around its edge ran the arcade of a cloister. The nun led me to a small cupola in the centre of the courtyard, and taking a huge bunch of keys from her pocket, unlocked a door. Then she lifted a storm lantern from a niche, lit it and led me down a flight of ancient stairs. From the dark below seeped a dank smell of musty air tinct with the sweet scent of burning oil-lamps.

As we sank deeper underground, masonry gave way to the living rock of a cave wall, and we entered a wide, echoing underground cavern. A pair of recesses at the far side of the cave were illuminated by the dim, flickering light of a cluster of lamps placed in front of two gilt icons, each depicting a heavily bearded Byzantine saint. Another group of lamps flickered at the bottom of the stairs, under an ancient icon of the Magi. To one side of it stood a huge pile of skulls.

'This was the cave where the three wise men hid from King Herod,' whispered the nun, holding the storm lantern aloft. 'St Theodosius saw the cave in a vision and founded his monastery in this place to honour the Magi.'

'And the skulls?'

'They belong to the monks that were slaughtered by the Persians when they burned the abbey.'

'When did that happen?'

'Not so long ago,' she said. 'Around 614 A.D.'

The nun held the storm lantern above the charnel so that the light picked out the sword-gashes cleaving the crania of the topmost skulls.

'What you have come to see lies over there,' she said, pointing at the lamplit recesses on the far side of the cave.

I walked over towards the lamps. As I drew nearer I could see that they rested on a pair of Byzantine grave-slabs, both of which had been propped up some time in the last century by a pair of small neo-classical pillars. On both the tomb-slabs had been carved in shallow relief an intricate design of equal-armed Byzantine crosses, some set in diamonds, others in circles. Between the crosses were carved inscriptions in clear Byzantine Greek. That on the left read 'Sophronius'; that on the right bore the name of John Moschos.

'St John Moschos died in Constantinople,' said the nun, 'but his dying wish was that he should be brought back here to the Lavra of St Theodosius. He regarded this as his home: this was where he was first tonsured, and where he spent most of his life. But the Holy Land was still occupied by the Persians and it was not until much later that St Sophronius was able to fulfil his promise to bring back John Moschos's body and to rebuild the monastery.'

'And the monks?'

'Before the slaughter there were seven hundred elders here. It was the most celebrated monastery in the Holy Land. There was a hospital for lepers and a rest house for pilgrims; also an inner monastery for those driven insane by the rigours of their asceticism. There were four separate churches. Monks came here from as far away as Cappadocia and Armenia . . . But after the Persians the monastery never recovered. It has never had as many monks ever again.'

'And now? How many of there are you today?'

'What do you mean? There is only me. I am the last. A priest is supposed to come from Jerusalem once a week to celebrate the liturgy, but he is old and sometimes he forgets.'

The nun bent forward and kissed the icon of Moschos. 'I will leave you,' she said. 'If you have come all the way to see the grave of St John Moschos you will want to be alone with him. Bring the lantern with you when you have finished.'

Holding the lamp aloft, I looked around the crypt and paused for a second before the macabre pile of skulls. I had read so much about the monks of St Theodosius in the pages of *The Spiritual Meadow* that I felt I must know some of the men who had been slaughtered by the Persians, men whose anonymous bleached bones now lay piled in front of me. They were characters like Brother George the Cappadocian, 'who was pasturing swine in

Phasaelis when two lions came to seize a pig'; rather than running off 'he seized a staff and chased them as far as holy Jordan'. Then there was Moschos's friend Patrick, 'the native of Sebastea in Armenia, who was of very great age, claiming to be one hundred and thirteen'. He had once been an abbot, but 'being very humble and much given to silence' had relinquished his position and 'placed himself under obedience, saying that it was only for great men to shepherd the spiritual sheep'. What had been the fate, I wondered, of another of Moschos's companions, Brother Christopher the Roman? Every night he deprived himself of sleep, performing a hundred prostrations on each of the steps that led down into the cave-crypt, never stopping until the bell rang for matins. I could certainly guess what happened to Brother Julian the Arab. He had made the pilgrimage to the pillar of St Symeon Stylites the Younger on the Mons Mirabilis outside Antioch, several weeks' journey from Judaea; but being completely blind, of all the brethren he must have been the least likely to have escaped the massacre.

Indeed, of the monks of St Theodosius mentioned by Moschos, only two definitely did avoid the Persians' swords. These were 'two brothers [at the monastery] who had sworn an oath that they would never be separated from each other, either in life or death. While they were in the community, one of the brothers was attacked by a yearning to possess a woman. Unable to withstand this yearning, he said to his brother: "Release me brother, for I am driven by desire and I want to go back into the world." But the brother did not want to release him from his vow, so he went to the city with him. The first brother went into a brothel whilst the other stood outside, throwing dust from the ground onto his own head. When his brother who had gone into the bordello came out, having done the deed, the other said to him, "My brother, what have you gained by this sin? Let us go back to our cloister." But the first replied, "I cannot go back into the wilderness again. You go. I am staying in the world."'

Unable to change his mind, the second brother stayed with him, and the pair found work on a construction site on the outskirts of Jerusalem, where a new monastery was being built. 'The brother who visited the brothel would take both their wages and go off to the city each weekend where he would squander their earnings in riotous living. But the other brother never complained. Instead he would fast all day long, performing his work in profound silence, not speaking to anybody.' The other workmen on the building site soon realised that something odd was going on and eventually told the Abbot, Abba Abraham. The Abbot soon winkled out the whole story.

'"It is because of my brother," said the good monk, "that I put up with all this, in the hope that God will look on my affliction and save my friend." When the godly Abraham heard this, he replied: "The Lord has granted you the soul of your brother too." He dismissed the good brother, and behold! Outside the Abbot's cell, there was his fallen brother, crying: "My brother, take me into the wilderness so I can be saved!" He immediately took him and went to a cave near the holy Jordan where he walled him up. After a little while, the sinful brother, having made great spiritual progress in things that are God's, departed this life. The other brother, still faithful to his oath, remained in the cave, and eventually he too died there.'

I stood before the grave of John Moschos, the man whose writings had brought me on this journey, and in whose footsteps I was travelling. On top of the slab rested a modern icon of the man, shown old and grey with a scroll in one hand and a quill in the other. So, I thought, this was where he started off, and where, after all his travels through the width and breadth of the Byzantine Levant, he ended up.

Prompted by the example of the nun, despite having half dropped the habit, I began to pray there, and the prayers came with surprising ease. I prayed for the people who had helped me on the journey, the monks who had showed me the manuscript on Mount Athos, the frightened Suriani of Mar Gabriel, the Armenians of Aleppo and the Palestinian Christians in the camp at Mar Elias. And then I did what I suppose I had come to do: I sought the blessing of John Moschos for the rest of the trip, and particularly asked for his protection in the badlands of Upper Egypt, the most dangerous part of the journey.

Then I rose, climbed the stairs, and emerged blinking into the bright light of the Judaean midday.

The Monastery of Mar Saba lies ten miles from that of St Theodosius, a little to the north of the Dead Sea. Around St Theodosius the soil is still grudgingly fertile, and the olive trees stand out against the terraces cut into the hard white hillsides. But as you drive east, the cultivation recedes. The soil becomes thinner, the valleys deeper, and the villages poorer. The taxi driver warned me that we were entering Hamas territory, and hung a Palestinian *keffiyeh* over half of the windscreen to make sure we would not be mistaken for Israeli settlers and stoned by the local *shabab*.

Passing the last village, we entered the desert; the *locus horrendae et vastae solitudinis* of the Bible. Below us the barren shale hills fell away towards the lowest point on earth, the Dead Sea, a quivering drop of mercury in the far distance. Straight ahead, in the distance a pair of small rectangular Byzantine watchtowers rose vertically against the lip of a deep *wadi*. In the forty miles of landscape visible from the hilltop, those two towers were the only buildings in sight.

It was only when we passed underneath the machicolation of the nearest tower that we caught our first glimpse of the great monastery that lay hidden in the lee of the sheer cliff-face below. It was the most extraordinary sight. The two towers are linked by a jagged wall which sweeps audaciously down in a near-vertical plunge to enclose the monastery's great spread of turquoise domes and cupolas, balconies and cave-cells, staircases and platforms, all propped up on narrow artificial ledges by great ranks of heavy, stepped buttresses. Despite its massive rocky solidity, the monastery's implausible position on a cliff-face in the midst of the wilderness somehow gives the whole place a fantastic, almost visionary appearance, like one of those castles in children's fairy tales capable of vanishing in the blink of an eye.

At the time of John Moschos, the wastes of Judaea had become so densely filled with monks and monasteries that, according to one chronicler, 'the desert had become a city'. Yet of the 150 monasteries founded during the Byzantine rule, only six are still lived in, and of those only one, Mar Saba, still supports enough monks to really qualify as a living monastery. It has been occupied continuously since its foundation in the late fifth century: since the two-week hiatus following the massacre of the monks by the Persians in 614 A.D. – the same raid that devastated St Theodosius – divine office has been sung in the rock chapel of St Sabas every morning for the last 1,380 years. As in St Theodosius, the skulls of the hundreds of monks killed by the Persians, along with those subsequently murdered by marauding Bedouin, have been carefully kept in the abbey church, stacked in neat rows as nonchalantly as other churches might stack their hymn books.

Mar Saba, I quickly discovered, remains the most austere of monasteries. The monks rise at two in the morning and sing the office for five hours, until dawn begins to break over the iconostasis of the abbey church. The fathers then rest until eleven, when they eat their one meal of the day: bread (baked once a week, palatable enough for three days but increasingly hard and stale thereafter), thin soup, boiled vegetables and strong feta cheese. They do not eat meat, and allow themselves fish and oil (for dressing the vegetables) only on Sundays and feast days. After their meal they retire to their caves and cells for the rest of the day, emerging only to sing vespers and compline at the appointed times.

If Mar Saba is now remarkable mainly for the terrible severity of its asceticism, it was once famous for its scholarship and despite the monastery's extreme isolation it was nevertheless one of the intellectual and philosophical powerhouses of Byzantium. When the Anglo-Saxon pilgrim St Willibald visited it in the early eighth century he remarked on the fact that all the monks were busy copying out manuscripts and composing hymns and poems. The monastery's library, now kept in the Greek Orthodox Patriarchal Palace in Jerusalem, is almost unrivalled amongst medieval collections in the esoteric breadth of its interests and the number of languages represented; it is also evidence of the extraordinary quality of the copying and calligraphy produced in the Mar Saba scriptorium.

Here Cyril of Scythopolis wrote his *History of the Monks of Palestine*, an unusually critical and intelligent work of hagiography. Mar Saba's hymnography, the work among others of Romanos the Melodist, was, according to the great Byzantine scholar Brehier, 'the most original manifestation of the poetic genius of the medieval Greeks'. Moreover it was in a cell in Mar Saba that St John Damascene wrote his great *Fount of Knowledge*, probably the most sophisticated and encyclopedic work of theology produced anywhere in Christendom until the time of Thomas Aquinas; indeed, Aquinas drew heavily on John's theology, and wrote that he read a few pages of John Damascene's work every day of his adult life. But the scope of the monastery's manuscript collection, and the erudition of John Damascene, is perhaps most dramatically demonstrated by one of his more unusual productions, the *Romance of Barlaam and Joasaph*, an Indian tale of the Buddha reworked in Christian form; it was later translated from Greek into Latin and widely circulated in the West. But you would never guess any of this from talking to Mar Saba's current inhabitants.

'So, you're a writer, are you?' asked Fr. Theophanes when he brought me my supper on a tray after vespers that evening. 'I've stopped reading books myself.'

'Oh yes?'

'The Divine Liturgy contains all the writing I need. Once you've read the Word of God everything else becomes very dull.'

'They say books are like food,' pointed out Fr. Evdokimos, the Deputy Archimandrite. 'They feed your brain.'

'But Father,' said Theophanes quietly, 'monks should try to eat as little as possible.'

It was nearly dark. We were sitting out on the terrace, watching the last of the light begin to fade from the sky. As we talked, Theophanes took out a box of matches and began to light a pair of battered old paraffin storm lanterns: there is no electricity in Mar Saba.

'Look at those clouds in the east,' said Fr. Evdokimos. 'There may be rain tomorrow. What do you think, Theophanes?'

'The rains here in Palestine are not like the rains of Greece,' replied the other monk. 'There we get big rains – proper cloud-bursts.' He smiled happily at the memory. 'Ah, the rains of Greece,' he said. 'They are a reminder of the Deluge.'

'What did you do in Greece before you became a monk?' I asked Theophanes.

'I was a policeman, in Athens,' he replied, looking up from the lanterns, whose wicks he was engaged in trimming. 'I came here for the first time on a pilgrimage. As soon as I saw this monastery I recognised it as my true home. I went back to Athens, handed in my resignation and said goodbye to my mother. A week later I was back here. Since then I've never left.'

'Never?'

'I went back only once. For forty days.'

'Was that difficult?'

'My mother cried sometimes. But otherwise, no. Things change very quickly. I hardly recognised my old city. My people had suddenly become rich from your European Community. There were so many new buildings. New buildings and new crimes.'

'And you don't miss anything of your old life?'

'What is there to miss? I have everything here.'

'But this must have been quite a change from your previous work.'

'Not so different,' replied the monk. 'Now I am the policeman of my soul. Demons are very like criminals. Both are very stupid. Both are damned.'

The lanterns were alight now, and the flickering of their flames threw shadows over the terrace and across the face of Fr. Theophanes.

'You believe in demons?' I asked.

'Of course. They are in the Bible.'

'Sometimes, when we are praying, the demons make strange noises,' added Fr. Evdokimos, who had been sitting quietly in the corner, stroking his beard. 'At first I thought it was just the animals of the desert. But then I noticed the noises came most loudly when I was praying. It is the demons trying to distract us.'

'Each demon has its own personality,' said Theophanes. 'They live in the desert and come to the cities to make men into criminals and Roman Catholics.'

'They can work miracles and make false prophecies,' said Evdokimos.

'They are worse than criminals,' said Theophanes. 'But here, within the walls of Mar Saba, we are protected.'

'What do you mean?'

'St Sabas is alive here. He protects his monastery. I have experienced it myself.'

'How?'

'Three years ago on a windy night in winter I was praying in my cave. I had not lit a lamp so my cell was pitch black. As I prayed I heard footsteps coming up the corridor. It was the noise of a monk walking: I could hear the rustling of his habit. The footsteps came closer and closer and then stopped outside my room. I waited for the monk to speak, but nothing happened.

'Suddenly I heard very clearly the noise of many feet tripping down the stairs from the opposite direction. They were like madmen, jumping down the steps very quickly – loud, irregular footsteps: there were maybe nine or ten of them, all running. I thought: the Bedouin have climbed the walls and broken in and now they want to kill us all. I froze behind my door, but nothing happened. Five minutes passed. Still they didn't come in. So very slowly I opened the door and went out.

'It was a full moon that night. I could see clearly that the corridor was empty. There was silence in the monastery. I walked up to the courtyard and at that moment I saw Fr. Evdokimos's light moving from the latrines to his room. So I went up and said: "Father – there are thieves in the monastery." He asked: "You are sure?" I said I was. "All right," he said, "we'll look together." So we both took sticks and for an hour we went all around. We searched in the church, in the towers, inside the deepest caves. Nothing: the door was secure and no one had come in over the wall.'

'It was only later,' said Fr. Evdokimos, 'when we discussed the matter with the Archimandrite, that we understood what had happened. The first set of footsteps were those of St Sabas. The rabble were demons coming to turn Fr. Theophanes into a Freemason. St Sabas knew what they were planning, so he stood in front of Fr. Theophanes's door to guard it. Then he chased the demons away.'

'The Devil will capture everyone if he gets the chance,' said Theophanes gravely. 'But the saints protect us. In this monastery I feel secure, although it is in the middle of the desert, with Bedouin all around us. We are protected.'

It was late, and the monks began to drift off to their cells carrying their lanterns. Theophanes showed me to mine and promised to wake me for matins at two.

All night, it seemed, bells were pealing. At one o'clock a monk began to knock the wooden *simandron* to call the brethren from their beds; he rang it again at one-thirty and at five to two. At two I was treated to a full scale bell-ringing display: the bells in the campanile assisted by a selection of handbells, one rung very loudly at the door of my cell by Fr. Theophanes. But as soon as silence had returned I fell asleep again, and it was nearly four a.m. before I finally pulled myself out of bed. It was pitch dark and very cold. I dressed by the light of the lantern, then picked my way down through the empty stairways and corridors of Mar Saba, towards the deep swell and eddy of monastic chant.

In the church all the lamps were lit, casting a dim glow over the basilica. The monastic *kyries* echoed around the dome. Only the occasional creak of a misericord gave away the position of the singers; the monks themselves were invisible in their black robes as they roosted in the choirstalls. Every so often a breeze would swing one of the chandeliers, rotating it slightly so that shadows raced around the church, the returning flash of candlelight picking out the highlights in the frescoes: the wings of angels and the long white beards of the desert fathers. The chant eddied out across the narrow valley, echoed and amplified by the domes and cupolas. As I sat at the back, I kept thinking that the very same sound would have been heard by John Moschos over fourteen hundred years ago.

Towards six o'clock first light began to filter in, gently illuminating the Christ Pantocrator in the dome. Half an hour later, with the sun now rising over the desert, I began to be able to pick out the monks themselves, black bearded, black robed, hooded and veiled in their stalls. What I had initially taken to be a low table near the lectern turned out to be Fr. Evdokimos, kneeling, bent forward on the ground in a long prostration before the iconostasis.

One by one the monks glided from the church, each stopping to kiss images of the saints on the frescoes and icons as they went. I returned to my bed and slept until noon, when Fr. Theophanes woke me with a tray of food: a lump of strong-smelling feta cheese, some coarse monastic bread and, sitting proudly on its own on a white plate, a small round chocolate.

'It is the feast of St Methodius the Stylite,' said Fr. Theophanes gravely. 'This is for you to celebrate it with.'

I spent the afternoon in my cell reading John Moschos's stories of the monks of the Judaean desert. Together, the stories in *The Spiritual Meadow* form a detailed picture of one of the strangest periods in the region's history. For around two hundred years the deserts of the Holy Land were filled not only with 150 fully functioning monasteries, but also with countless cave-dwelling hermits and great herds of 'grazers', nomadic monks who, according to Moschos, 'wander in the desert as if they were wild animals: like birds they fly about the hills; they forage like goats. Their daily round is inflexible, always predictable, for they feed on roots, the natural products of the earth.'

Today it seems inexplicable that so many people – many of them highly educated – from across the width of the civilised Byzantine world would give up everything and travel for thousands of miles to live a life of extreme hardship in the discomfort of the desert; yet to the Byzantine mind nothing could have been more logical. In one of Moschos's stories, a stranger visits the renowned holy man Abba Olympios in his monastery in the heat and humidity of the Jordan Valley. 'How can you stay in this place with its burning heat and so many insects?' he asks. The holy man gives a simple answer: 'I put up with the insects to escape from what scripture calls "the worm that sleeps not". Likewise, I endure the burning heat for fear of the eternal fire. The one is temporary, but of the other there is no end.'

Yet this was not the whole story. While Moschos never underestimates the hardship involved in the life of the desert fathers, he is also well aware of its joys. Indeed one of the principal themes of his writing is that by living in utter simplicity and holiness, the monks were returning to the conditions of the Garden of Eden, in harmony with both the natural world and its Creator. This is particularly true of the grazers, who like Adam ate without planting and were supposed to have command over the wild animals. 'With Christ,' wrote the early Christian traveller Sulpicius Severus, 'every brute beast is wise, and every savage creature gentle.' The close relationship of beasts and saints was not a new theme in monastic literature: the early Coptic *Life* of St Pachomius, for example, tells how the saint summoned crocodiles to ferry him across the Nile, rather as today one might call a cab from a taxi rank. Moreover *The Paradise of the Fathers*, one of Moschos's principal literary models, contains a number of stories on this theme:

'There was an old man who dwelt by the Jordan practising asceticism. One day he went into a cave to escape from the heat, and there he found a lion. It began to gnash its teeth at him and to roar. So the old man said to it, "Why are you annoyed? There is room here to take me and to take you also. If you do not wish to abide with me, arise and go!" And the lion did not carry him off but instead went out.'

Moschos first introduces this theme in a story told by Abba Agathonicos, the Abbot of Castellium, once the sister monastery to Mar Saba, now a ruin five miles further down the Kedron Valley:

'One day,' Abba Agathonicos tells Moschos, 'I went down to Rouba to visit Abba Poemon the Grazer. When I found him, I told him the thoughts which troubled me. When night fell he left me in a cave. It was winter and that night it got very cold indeed. I was freezing. When the elder came at dawn, he said to me: "What is the matter, child? I did not feel the cold." This amazed me, for he was naked. I asked him of his charity to tell me how he did not feel the cold. He said: "A lion came down and lay beside me; he kept me warm."'

But perhaps the most memorable fable of the Eden-like closeness of monks and beasts in the desert is Moschos's famous tale of St Gerasimos and the lion. Centuries later in the West, the story was mistakenly grafted onto the life of St Jerome, apparently through the ignorance of Latin-speaking pilgrims. In the Eastern Church, however, the tale has remained correctly attributed to St Gerasimos, and is still one of the most popular Orthodox saints' tales. Moreover, it is one of the few of Moschos's tales to have entered the repertoire of Byzantine art, and is occasionally found frescoed on Orthodox monastery walls: in Athos, for example, I saw several scenes from the story painted in the porch of the abbey church of the Monastery of Xenophontos. The story is set in St Gerasimos's monastery, 'about a mile from the Holy Jordan'.

'When [Sophronius and I] were visiting the monastery,' writes Moschos, 'the residents told us that St Gerasimos was walking one day by the banks of the Holy Jordan when he met a lion, roaring mightily because of the pain in its paw. The point of a reed was deeply embedded in it, causing inflammation. When the lion saw the elder, it came to him and showed him the foot, whimpering and begging some healing from him. When the elder saw the lion in such distress, he sat down and, taking the paw, he lanced it. The point was removed and also much pus. He cleansed the wound well, bound it up and dismissed the beast. But the healed lion would not leave the elder. It followed him like a disciple wherever he went. The elder was amazed at the gentle disposition of the beast and, from then on, he began feeding it, throwing it bread and boiled vegetables.

'Now the *lavra* had an ass which was used to fetch water for the needs of the elders, for they drink the water of the Holy Jordan which lies about one mile away from the monastery. The fathers used to hand the ass over to the lion, to pasture it on the banks of the Jordan. One day when the ass was being taken to pasture by the lion, it went away some distance from its keeper. Some camel-drivers on their way from Arabia found the ass and took it away to their country. Having lost the ass, the lion came back to the *lavra* and approached Abba Gerasimos, very downcast and dismayed. The Abba thought the lion had devoured the ass. He said to it: "Where is the ass?" The beast stood silent, very like a man. The elder said to it: "Have you eaten it? From now on [as a punishment] you will perform the same duties the ass performed." From then on, at the elder's command, the lion used to carry the saddlepack containing four earthenware vessels and bring water.

'[Many months later] the camel-driver who had taken the ass came back to the Holy City with the animal loaded up with the grain he hoped to sell there. Having crossed the Holy Jordan, he suddenly found himself face to face with the lion. When he saw the beast, he left his camels and took to his heels. Recognising the ass, the lion ran to it, seized its leading rein in its mouth just as it had been trained to do, and led away not only the ass, but also the three camels. It brought them to the elder, rejoicing and roaring. The elder now realised that the lion had been falsely accused. He named the lion Jordanes and it lived with the elder in the *lavra*, never leaving his side for five years.

'When Abba Gerasimos departed to the Lord and was buried by the fathers, by the providence of God the lion could not be found. A little later the lion returned, searching for the elder, roaring mightily. When Abba Sabbatios and the rest of the fathers saw it, they stroked its mane and said to it: "The elder has gone away to the Lord and left us," yet even saying this did not succeed in silencing its cries and lamentations. Then Abba Sabbatios said to it: "Since you do not believe us, come with me and I will show you where Gerasimos lies." He took the lion and led it to where they had buried the elder, half a mile from the church. Abba Sabbatios said to the lion: "See, this is where our friend is," and he knelt down. When the lion saw how he prostrated himself, it began beating its head against the ground and roaring. Then it promptly [rolled over and] died, there on the elder's grave.'

Over the days that followed I explored many of the caves, cells and chapels which honeycomb the cliffs within the great boundary walls of Mar Saba. Earthquakes and Bedouin raids have led to much rebuilding over the centuries, but if you look hard enough, many fragments of the Byzantine monastery known to John Moschos still survive. The great cave chapel 'Built by God' stands as bare and austere as it would have done in the early Byzantine period. The only obvious additions are some late-medieval icons, a line of eighteenth-century choirstalls and the four hundred stacked skulls of the monks slaughtered in the seventh-century Persian invasion. In another grotto, the Retreat of St Sabas, the floor is still covered with the fragmentary tesserae of a simple geometric mosaic dating from the late sixth century. But the most interesting chapel of all is that built around the tomb and hermitage of St John Damascene.

John Damascene is probably the most important figure ever to have taken the habit at Mar Saba. He was the grandson of the last Byzantine Governor of Damascus, a Syrian Arab Christian named Mansour ibn Sargun. Ibn Sargun was responsible for sur-rendering the city to the Muslim General Khalid ibn Walid in 635, just three years after the death of Mohammed. Despite the change from Christian to Islamic rule, the family remained powerful. John's father, Sergios ibn Mansour, rose to become a senior figure in the financial administration of the early Umayyad Caliphate, whose accounts, significantly enough, continued for many decades to be kept in Greek. Because of this John grew up as a close companion of the future Caliph al-Yazid, and the two youths' drinking bouts in the streets of Damascus were the subject of much horrified gossip in the new Islamic capital. In due course John assumed his father's post in the administration, and he remained throughout his life a favourite of the Caliph. This relationship made him one of the very first Arab Christians capable of acting as a bridge between Christianity and Islam, even if, like so many who attempt to bring together two diverging cultures, he eventually ended up being regarded with suspicion by both: dismissed from his administrative job after Caliph Yazid's death and falsely accused of collusion with the Byzantine Emperor, he was nevertheless regarded with great mistrust in the Byzantine capital, where he was dubbed *Sarakenophron*, or Saracen-Minded.

John was in an excellent position to write the first ever informed treatise on Islam by a Christian, and when he retired to Mar Saba he dedicated his declining years to writing doctrinal homiles and working on his great masterpiece, a refutation of heresies entitled *The Fount of Knowledge*. The book contains an extremely precise and detailed critique of Islam, which, intriguingly, John regards as a form of Christian heresy related to Arianism (after all, like Islam, Arianism denied the divinity of Christ). It never seems to have occurred to John that Islam might be a separate religion, and although he looked on it with considerable suspicion, he nevertheless applauds the way Islam converted the Arabs from idolatry, and writes with admiration of its single-minded emphasis on the unity of God.

If a theologian of the stature of John Damascene was able to regard Islam as a new – if heretical – form of Christianity, it helps to explain how Islam was able to convert so much of the Middle Eastern population in so short a time, even if Christianity remained the majority religion until the time of the Crusades. Islam was as much a product of the intellectual ferment of late antiquity as Gnosticism, Arianism and Monophysitism, and like those heresies it had its greatest success in areas disgruntled with Byzantine rule. Many Syrians expressed opposition to Byzantium and its ruthless attempt to impose its rigid imperial theology by converting *en masse* to the heterodox Christian doctrine of Monophysitism; later they greeted the conquering Arab armies as liberators and many converted again, this time to Islam. No doubt they regarded the Arabs' new creed as a small step from Monophysitism; after all, the two faiths started from a similar position: that God could not become fully human without somehow compromising his divinity.

Whatever the reason for its success, Islam certainly appealed to the former Monophysites, and within a century of the Arab conquest Syria was a mainly Muslim country. By contrast, the inhabitants of Palestine, who had done well out of Byzantine patronage of the Holy Places, never showed much interest in converting either to Monophysitism or to Islam, and Jerusalem remained a predominantly Orthodox Christian city until the Crusaders conquered it in 1099.

In Damascene's own lifetime, however, the most influential part of *The Fount of Knowledge* was not the section on Islam, but his attack on the heresy of Iconoclasm. For at the same time as John was becoming a monk, Byzantium was being engulfed by a wave of image-smashing. All the icons in the Empire were ordered to be destroyed, and their painting was henceforth banned. The reason for this may well have been the rise of Islam and the profound soul-searching which the loss of the Levant provoked in Byzantium. Many came to the conclusion that God was angry with the Byzantines for their idolatry, and thus gave the iconoclastic Muslims success in their wars.

Just as John's public life demonstrates the astonishing political tolerance of the Umayyad Caliphate in its willingness to employ a Christian in a senior administrative role, despite almost continuous hostilities with the rest of the Christian World, so his retirement demonstrates the surprising degree of intellectual freedom it permitted. For under the Umayyads John was able to do what no Byzantine was permitted to attempt: to write and distribute a systematic defence of images, in which he provided the fundamental theological counterblast to iconoclasm. John argued that although no man has seen God at any time, nevertheless, since Christ deigned to take upon himself the human form, it was necessary to worship the human face of God in the sacred icon. Moreover he demonstrated that not only was their cult based on reason, but that it was sanctioned by ancient precedent:

> Paintings are the books of the illiterate. They instruct those who look at them with a silent voice and sanctify life ... Since not everyone knows how to read, or has the leisure for reading, the Fathers of the Church saw fit that the Incarnate Christ be represented by images,

like deeds of prowess, to serve as reminders. Often when we are not thinking of the Lord's passion, we see the image of the crucifixion, and being reminded of that salutary passion, we fall to our knees and revere ... If I have no books I go to church, pricked as by spines by my thoughts; the flower of painting makes me look, charms my eyes as does a flowering meadow and softly distils the glory of God in my soul.

This afternoon, after I had woken from a siesta, Theophanes took me to John Damascene's old cell. We walked along the narrow staircases and winding paths that connect the different platforms of the monastery. Eventually we came to a small chapel backing onto the rock wall. 'This chapel was where St John's body used to lie,' said Theophanes, 'before your Pope's Crusaders came and stole him.'

'Where is he now?'

'In Venice,' said Theophanes. 'One of the world capitals of body-snatching and criminal Freemasonry.'

Inside the chapel hung a line of icons, and over the spot where the tomb used to lie, a fresco showing the death of St John Damascene, an icon clutched firmly to his breast. Below this a narrow wooden staircase led down into a tiny cave, its ceiling cut so low as to make standing virtually impossible.

'St John spent thirty years in that place,' said Theophanes. 'Although he could not stand he hardly ever went out of it. He believed he had become too proud because of his high position in the court in Damascus, so he chose this cave in which to live as a monk. He said it was very humbling – very good for the soul – to live in such a place for many years.'

'After an *hour* in there you must feel like a hunchback,' I said.

'Better hunchbacked than damned,' replied the monk.

While Theophanes stood by the empty tomb, contemplating, no doubt, the damnation of the Papist body-snatchers, I clambered down the wooden stairs into the gloom of the saint's cave. On either side two stone benches had been cut from the rock, while ahead stood a low shelf that had once acted as the saint's writing desk. Beyond was a small shrine: at the far end of the cave stretched a recess, four feet high, six feet deep, which John Damascene had used as a bed. A small Byzantine icon of the Madonna hung from the wall; otherwise the cell was almost impossibly austere.

It seemed strange that a book of such breathtaking sophistication as *The Fount of Knowledge* could be produced in so astonishingly crude and primitive a cave. It was certainly an unlikely setting for the writing of one of the most important tracts ever to be penned in defence of artistic freedom. What Damascene wrote in this cave was largely responsible for saving Byzantium from the ban against sacred art that has always been a part of Islam and Judaism. Without Damascene's work, Byzantine *ars sacra* would never again have been permitted, Greek painters might never have been able to pass on their secrets to Giotto and the Sienese, and the course of the Renaissance, if it had happened at all, would have been very different.

Sometime in the late 1960s, soon after the Israeli conquest of the West Bank, the number of monks at Mar Saba fell for the first time below twenty. At this time the Abbot of the monastery had been persuaded by the Greek Orthodox Patriarch in Jerusalem to cease trying to be self-sufficient. He should sell Mar Saba's ancient lands to the Israeli government, advised the Patriarch; the Orthodox hierarchy would invest the money and in return send to the monastery all the cheese and fish the monks could possibly need. The Abbot acceded to the Patriarch's wishes, and ever since then the monks' food has been brought in by van from Jerusalem once a week. The van was due on the last day of my stay at Mar Saba, and Fr. Theophanes promised to arrange that it should take me back to Jerusalem on its return journey.

There were still many Byzantine remains in the valley below the monastery that I had not seen, and I woke early on my final morning, in the hope of seeing some of the more distant cells and grottoes before I was collected later that afternoon.

I was let out by Fr. Cosmas, the gatekeeper, who slid back the heavy medieval bolts of the gate behind me. Outside I found the old path down the cliff-face into the valley. It led off from the top of the cliff beside the Byzantine tower built by the Empress Eudoxia; it had once been home to a small convent of nuns, but was now abandoned and quite deserted. I picked my way down the hairpin bends, stopping to pluck a sprig of wild rosemary from a bush and squeeze it between my thumb and forefinger. As I was standing there, a dun-coloured desert fox darted from its shelter in an abandoned cell and shot off behind a bend in the *wadi*.

At the bottom of the valley I forded the dark waters of the heavily polluted river. It was a steep climb up the other side of the valley, but the reward was a breathtaking view of the monastery. Indeed it was only from the opposite lip of the chasm that the full strangeness of Mar Saba's position became apparent: the great tumble of lavender domes and egg-shaped cupolas were perched precariously on the narrowest of ledges and overhangs. All this was enclosed by the near-vertical wall built soon after the Persian massacre whose massive strength had, for nearly 1,400 years, successfully protected the monks from human and natural calamities.

Looking down the steep slope on which I was standing, I saw that the rockface was pockmarked by the entrances to monks' cells, all of which were now deserted. Some of these cells were little more than burrows; others, perched on ledges above the gorge, were relatively sophisticated conical beehives, intriguingly similar in design to the cells of the Celtic monks of the same period preserved in the more remote corners of Ireland, such as the coastal island of Skellig Michael. Like their Irish counterparts, these cells were drystone, built without mortar, and rose to steeply pitched gables; like the cells of Skellig Michael they were usually bare and unornamented but for an arched prayer niche on the east wall; like them they had the same low entrance capped with a monolithic lintel.

There were also other quite distinct cell-types. Some were partially-walled-up caves. A few were elaborate multi-storeyed affairs containing cisterns, living quarters and oratories; like the *kelli* of modern Athos, these were clearly designed not for single hermits but for the use of small groups of monks: perhaps a superior and four or five of his disciples, or a party from some distant and distinct ethnic group – say Georgians or Armenians – who wished to keep together. In some of the chapels and oratories attached to these more elaborate cells there were still traces of mosaic floorings and even fragments of simple geometric frescoes on the walls: floral patterns created by overlapping circles, or designs of intermeshing crosses.

Different as they were, all the monks' cells in the valley had two things in common. One was that nearly all had been attacked at some stage by treasure hunters who had dug great holes in their floors, presumably in search of buried coins or precious chalices. The other was the prayer niche, a small arched cut in the eastern wall of the cell indicating the proper direction for prayer. As I passed from cell to cell, I realised that the prayer niche must be another of those features of the early Christian world which has been lost to modern Western Christianity, yet which is still preserved in Islam. No mosque is complete without its *mihrab* pointing in the direction of Mecca; yet how many Western churches today contain prayer niches? Certainly all are still orientated towards the east, but the idea of a niche emphasising this fact is now quite forgotten. Just as St John Damascene's life stressed the close relationship between Christianity and early Islam – a kinship and proximity that is now forgotten by both faiths – so the prayer niches contained in the cells around Damascene's old monastery seemed to emphasise how much Islam inherited from the Byzantine world.

As at Cyrrhus, I was left pondering the probability that if John Moschos came back today, he would be likely to find as much that was familiar in the practices of Islam – with its fasting, prostrations, prayer niches and open prayer halls, as well as its emphasis on the wandering holy man – as in those of modern Western Christendom. In an age when Islam and Christianity are again said to be 'clashing civilisations', supposedly 'irreconcilable and necessarily hostile', it is important to remember Islam's very considerable debt to the early Christian world, and the degree to which it has faithfully preserved elements of our own early Christian heritage long forgotten by ourselves.

Fr. Theophanes brought me my lunch on a tray and announced that the van would soon be ready to carry me to Jerusalem. He stood by as I ate, like a *maître d'hôte* waiting to see a diner's reaction to some especially delicate soufflé. This precipitated something of an etiquette problem.

Lunch at Mar Saba was never a very ritzy affair at the best of times, but towards the end of the week, when the bread baked days earlier had hardened to the texture of pumice, and the feta cheese had begun to smell increasingly like dead goat, eating Fr. Theophanes's offerings became something of a penitential exercise, and sounding sincere in one's appreciation of the monks' culinary abilities was a task that needed advanced acting skills. I looked at the lump of rock-bread and the festering cheese, and tried to think of something nice to say about them. Then I had a flash of inspiration.

'Mmm,' I said, taking a sip from the glass. 'Delicious water, Fr. Theophanes.'

This, oddly enough, went down very well.

'The water here is very sweet.' The monk allowed himself a brief smile.

'Very sweet, Fr. Theophanes.'

'During this summer we had a drought. Our cisterns were beginning to run dry. August went by. Then September. One after another our cisterns gave up. We were like the Children of Israel in the wilderness. But St Sabas takes care of us. We are never without some drinking water. We always have the spring.'

'The spring?'

'The spring of St Sabas. He prayed and it came. You do not know the story?'

'Tell it to me.'

'In the days of St Sabas more and more monks were joining the *lavra* to be with the saint. Eventually the number of brethren grew to seven hundred, and there was not enough water to go around. So St Sabas prayed. For thirty days and thirty nights he prayed on the roof of his cell, refusing to eat in the hope that our Lord would look down with mercy on his people. Finally, at the end of the thirty days and thirty nights, it happened to be a full moon. St Sabas went onto the roof for the last time to beg the Lord for mercy. He began to pray when all of a sudden he heard the beating of a wild ass's hooves in the valley below. He looked out and saw the animal. It was charging down the valley as if sent by the Angel Gabriel himself. Then it stopped, looked around and began digging deep into the gravel. It dug for twenty minutes, then it bent down and began to drink.

'St Sabas spent the night giving thanks to the Lord. The following morning he climbed down the cliff. At the bottom, just as he expected, he found that the ass had revealed a spring of living water. It was a constant supply that never ever fails. Even today. And incidentally it tastes very good in ouzo. This is one of the compensations that St Sabas gives us for our sufferings.'

'What are the others?' I asked.

'There are many,' he said. 'But the most remarkable is this: after we leave our mortal frame, our bodies never grow stiff.'

'I'm sorry?'

'After we are dead we never get stiff. We never suffer from . . . how do you say . . . ?'

'Corruption? Decomposition?'

'That's right: decomposition.' Fr. Theophanes rolled the word around his mouth as if savouring the notion of mortal decay. 'But the monks of this monastery, instead of giving off a foul stench of decay, emit a sweet fragrance. Like the scent of precious myrrh.'

I must have looked sceptical, for Theophanes added: 'It is true. Many scientists have visited the monastery and declared themselves baffled. Anyway,' he said, changing the subject, 'what were you doing in the valley this morning?'

I told him, and remarked on the number of cells which appeared to have been desecrated by treasure hunters.

'It is the Bedouin,' replied Theophanes. 'They are always looking for buried gold. Sometimes they ring the bell of the monastery and ask for incense from the cave of St Sabas to help them find their gold.'

'How does that help?'

'Sometimes they find gold in caves or old ruins, but they dare not take it in case it is guarded by a *djinn*. They go to their sheikhs, but they can do nothing, so the sheikhs tell them to come here. The Muslims believe that if they get incense from here they can burn it and the holy fumes will scare away the *djinn*.'

'Do you give them incense?' I asked.

'No. It would be blasphemous to use a holy substance for such a purpose. But sometimes I wonder . . .'

'What do you mean?'

'Well . . . Once a man from Bethlehem came here. He was a taxi driver, named Mohammed. I knew him a little because he sometimes brought monks or pilgrims to us. Anyway, one day he rang the bell and asked for incense, saying that he had found some gold in a pot: it had been turned up by a plough on the land belonging to his family. He said his family were worried in case it was guarded by an evil *djinn*. I said no, he could not have it. Now he is dead. Sometimes I wonder whether I should have said yes.'

'What do you mean, "Now he is dead"?'

'He left here, went home and broke open the pot. Straight away he went crazy. He got iller and iller, skinnier and skinnier. Before, he was a strong man. But slowly he became like a skeleton. Bones, a little skin, nothing more. Finally, three months ago, he died.' Theophanes shook his head. 'The Muslims think the *djinns* are different from demons, but this is just a trick of the Devil. There is no such thing as *djinns*: just devils in disguise. Now this man's soul will go to Hell.'

Theophanes crossed himself, from right to left in the Orthodox manner: 'He lost the gold and he lost his soul. Now he will burn like a Freemason.'

'Fr. Theophanes,' I asked, my curiosity finally getting the better of me, 'I don't understand why you are so worried by the Freemasons.'

'Because they are the legions of the Anti-Christ. The stormtroopers of the Whore of Babylon.'

'I always thought Freemasons just held coffee mornings and whist drives and that sort of thing.'

'Wheest drives?' said Theophanes, pronouncing the word as if it were some sort of Satanic ritual. 'Probably this wheest drive also. But their main activity is to worship the Devil. There are many steps,' he said, nodding knowingly. 'But the last, the final step, is to meet with the Devil and have homosexual relations with him. After this he makes you Pope or sometimes President of the United States.'

'President of the United States . . . ?'

'Certainly. This has been proved. All the Presidents of the United States have been Freemasons. Except Kennedy. And you know what happened to him . . .'

Theophanes was still raving about the Freemasons, and the way they had masterminded the Ecumenical movement and invented the supermarket barcode, when a young novice knocked on the door to tell us that the Patriarchate van was ready to take me to Jerusalem. Theophanes helped carry my luggage to the gate.

'Be careful,' he said, as we stood by the great blue door. 'These are the Last Days. They are near their goal. They are everywhere now. Always be on your guard.'

'Goodbye, Fr. Theophanes,' I said. 'Thank you for everything.'

'They say this may be the last Pope.'

'Yes?'

'Some Holy Fathers have said this. Then the Arabs will be in Rome and the Whore of Babylon will be in the Vatican.'

'And the Freemasons?'

'These people. Who knows what they will do . . .' Theophanes frowned. 'Anyway,' he said, 'you must visit us again.'

'Thank you.'

'Maybe you will have converted to Orthodoxy by then?'

I smiled.

'I will pray for you. While there is still time. Maybe you can be saved.'

Taking a huge key from a gaoler's ring, the monk undid the bolts of the low gate in the monastery wall. 'Think about it seriously,' he said as he let me out. 'Remember, you will be among the damned if you don't.'

The heavy metal door swung closed behind me. Outside, a dust storm was just beginning.

ARARAT STREET, THE ARMENIAN QUARTER, OLD CITY OF JERUSALEM, 4 NOVEMBER

The Armenian Quarter is the most secretive of the divisions of the Old City of Jerusalem. The Muslim, Christian and Jewish Quarters all look outwards; wandering down their cobbles it is impossible not to get sucked into their flea-markets and junk shops, cafés and restaurants. The Armenian Quarter is very different. It is easy to pass it by without realising its existence. It is a city within a city, entered through its own gate and bounded by its own high, butter-coloured wall.

The gatehouse gives onto a warren of tunnels and passageways. Off one of these I have been given an old groin-vaulted room smelling of dust and old age, with a faint whiff of medieval church. In the streets around my room, hidden behind anxiously twitching lace curtains, lives a displaced population, distinct from their neighbours in language, religion, history and culture.

At the time of John Moschos, Jerusalem contained many such communities: large groups of Georgians and Armenians, Syrians and Galatians, Italians and even some Franks, most of whom had initially come to Jerusalem on pilgrimage and stayed on. Although the city is still full of small church missions, usually staffed by clerics on temporary postings, the Armenian Quarter is the last substantial community of permanent Christian exiles resident in Jerusalem.

The surprise isn't that the others have disappeared. It is that the Armenians have managed to remain. For despite the reference in the psalms to 'the peace of Jerusalem', the Holy City has probably seen more rapine and pillage, more regularly, than any comparable patch of ground on the planet. Here the Israelites battled with the Jebusites, Canaanites, Philistines, Assyrians, Babylonians, Persians, Greeks and Romans; here the Arabs eventually succeeded them only to lose control successively to the Crusaders, the Turks, the British and the Israelis. In Jerusalem every street corner has its own martyr or monument, saint or shrine. Its soil is drenched in blood spilt in the name of religion; its mental hospitals are full of whole hagiarchies of lunatics claiming to be David, Isaiah, Jesus, St Paul or Mohammed.

Yet amid this conflict between competing truths and rival certainties, the Armenian quarter is a startling example of peaceful continuity. In the third century A.D., the Armenians were the first nation to convert to Christianity, and they quickly became enthusiastic pilgrims to the Holy Places. Palestine may have been a dangerous spot to visit, but it was usually paradise compared to the Armenians' anarchic homeland. By the time of John Moschos there were over seventy Armenian churches in the city.

The Jerusalem Armenians became adept at living under foreign rule. In the eighth century, when Jerusalem was ruled by the Arab Abbasid dynasty, the Armenians managed to arrange it so that two of the Caliphs had Armenian mothers; in 1099, when the Crusaders captured the town, the first two queens of Jerusalem were also Armenian. Later, when Saladin reconquered the city for Islam, the Armenians played their cards with such skill that they were the only Christians who avoided being expelled or carried off into slavery.

After 1915, following the genocide of perhaps a million and a half Armenians at the hands of the Young Turks, the Jerusalem Armenian Quarter became a place of refuge for many of the ragged

John Moschos's home monastery, Mar Theodosius, near Bethlehem.

The watchtowers of Mar Saba in the wilderness of Judaea.

Above The Monastery of Mar Saba.

Right Fr. Theophanes, Guest Master of Mar Saba, at the monastery gate.

Above St Paul and St Antony breaking bread. Detail of icon at the Monastery of St Antony, Egypt.

Left The same scene carved on a Pictish symbol-stone, St Vigeans, Dundee.

Left Fr. Dioscorus discusses the latest sighting of St Antony, Monastery of St Antony, Egypt.

Below The desert between Asyut and the Great Kharga Oasis.

survivors. Within a couple of years the number of inhabitants in the quarter doubled, and the descendants of these people still make up about half the population of the quarter today.

Having lived through the rule of tyrants such as the hideous Mameluke Sultan, Baybars of Egypt (an ex-slave so ugly that he was once returned to the market by a horrified buyer), it might be expected that the Jerusalem Armenians might consider the current Israeli dominion over the Old City as a relatively benign period in their history; after all, the Jews and Armenians have much in common, sharing a history of wandering, trade, persecution and suffering. But it is not quite as simple as that.

A short distance from my room, in a cloister overhung with pot plants, vines and flowering shrubs, I found the rooms of Bishop Hagop Sarkissian, a friend from previous visits. Bishop Hagop is a gentle amateur antiquary who has renovated many of the medieval chapels in the quarter. His enthusiasm for Armenian architecture has overflowed into his rooms, which are now cluttered with small wooden models of Armenian churches, painstakingly reconstructed from old prints and daguerreotypes.

Bishop Hagop is a small, quiet figure with a lavender-blue cassock and a grey goatee beard. He is generally a gossipy, high-spirited man, but he has a penchant – understandably common among Armenians – for telling depressing stories about the genocide. Hagop's mother was the only one of fifty family members to survive the 1915 massacre of her people; his father, a renowned botanist and ethnographer, was one of the few Armenian intellectuals to escape the Young Turks' purges, and only did so by walking five hundred miles through Anatolia and the Levant disguised as a Turkish woman in full *chador*. Before he died in Jerusalem from the shock of the experience, he managed to finish writing what is arguably the best eyewitness account of the whole Armenian genocide.

As we sat in his rooms sipping fiery Armenian cognac, the Bishop talked angrily about a decision taken by Israeli television some time previously. A documentary film on the Armenian genocide scheduled for prime-time viewing had been mysteriously cancelled at the last minute. There had been a furious response not only from the Armenians but from many Israeli liberals, yet the television executives refused to alter their position.

'The Israelis are always insisting on the uniqueness of their Holocaust,' said Hagop. 'Now it seems they want our genocide to be forgotten. It is as if they want a monopoly on suffering.' The old man shook his head: 'In a million little ways, the Israelis make life difficult for us. Many of my people believe they want to squeeze us out.'

'That is a pretty strong accusation,' I said. On my previous visits the Bishop seemed far too absorbed in the Armenian past to worry much about contemporary politics. So I was surprised when, after downing another glass of cognac, he began to pour out his worries about the future.

'Many right-wing Israelis now say that Jerusalem should belong to the Jews only,' he said, lifting his glass to his lips again. 'These people say that Jerusalem is their eternal capital, and that we are trespassing in their city.'

The Armenians, he said, had been shaken a couple of years earlier when fundamentalist Jewish settlers of the Ateret Cohanim (Garland of the Temple Priests) had used a succession of Panamanian cover-companies to sub-let and take over the St John's Hospice near the Holy Sepulchre in the very heart of the Christian Quarter. The Armenians were more shaken still when it emerged that the settlers had been given $2 million of government funds to effect their purchase.

Under an Israeli Supreme Court ruling, non-Jews are excluded from the Jewish Quarter, and all Arabs resident there in 1967 were evicted from it. At the same time, on 10 June 1967, the entire Maghariba (Moors') district was demolished to create a plaza around the Wailing Wall. The area dated back to the fourteenth century, and included a mosque and shrine of Sheikh A'id; but despite their antiquity the 135 buildings in the district were bulldozed and the 650 Palestinians who lived there were expelled from their homes. Yet while all the two thousand Jews who had lost property there in 1948 had their land restored, none of the thirty thousand Palestinians evicted from the Christian suburbs of West Jerusalem in 1948 were allowed to return to their old homes, nor was any reverse law promulgated to prevent Jews from settling in the Christian, Armenian and Muslim Quarters of the Old City; indeed, funds from the Israeli Housing Ministry are available to finance such colonisation, on the grounds that Jews have a right to settle anywhere in their Holy City.

By Easter 1990, when the St John's Hospice was seized, more than forty properties in the Muslim Quarter had already been acquired by the Ateret Cohanim and other radical settler groups, but the takeover of the hospice was the first attempt by settlers to move into the Christian Quarter. The move quickly snowballed into a major international controversy.

According to a report in the London *Sunday Telegraph*, a Greek priest who had forced his way inside the hospice to try to stop the looting of the property asked a settler to hand him a picture of the Last Supper. The Israeli broke the frame over his knee and trampled the canvas into the floor.

Following this incident, the octogenarian Orthodox Patriarch, the owner of the hospice, led a Maundy Thursday protest march to the property. During the demonstration one of the Greek monks attempted to remove a Star of David which the settlers had just erected over a cross carved above the hospice doorway. As he reached for the star, the Israeli policemen assigned to guard the settlers pushed the elderly Patriarch onto the ground, hit him, then pepper-gassed both him and his monastic entourage. Television cameras recorded the entire incident, setting off a further chain of international protests.

According to Hagop, the settlers were now stepping up their efforts to buy Armenian land in the Old City. Every month, he said, the Armenian Patriarchate received dozens of enquiries from middlemen acting for settlers willing to pay very high prices for a toehold in the Armenian Quarter. Others applied directly. Ariel Sharon, architect of Israel's invasion of Lebanon, had allegedly offered nearly $3.5 million for an empty parking lot and some houses backing onto it.

'We refused, of course,' said Hagop. 'But these people are fanatics. They will never give up.' The Bishop frowned. 'I am seriously worried for our future. We have been here for 1,600 years, yet we cannot be sure what will happen tomorrow. The Israelis claim that they are champions of religious freedom, but behind that smokescreen they make it impossible for our community to flourish. They have not granted one building permit to us since 1967, and they destroy any building we construct illegally. It took four years for us to get a telephone for our infirmary, while a Shin Bet [Israeli Secret Police] informer I know got one within a week. They neglect our streets. The Jewish Quarter is properly maintained, but the streets in the other quarters are subsiding because the old Ottoman-period drainage system is collapsing. It's worst of all in the Muslim Quarter. The people there believe the Israelis want to make their houses uninhabitable so that they have to leave; then the buildings can be acquired by settlers.'

The Bishop snorted: 'They even use their tax system to put our shopkeepers out of business, charging them totally arbitrary tax demands. In 1967 we had eighty or ninety shops in the Old City, now – what? – maybe ten are left, possibly less. All the rest have been bankrupted by tax officials who refuse to believe their accounts. In several cases shopkeepers got demands for more than the entire value of their businesses.'

I suggested to the Bishop that maybe he was getting just a little paranoid. The old man shook his head. 'In the course of the furore over the St John's Hospice it emerged that the Israeli government had allocated 7.5 million shekels [£2.5 million] to buy more Christian and Muslim buildings in the Old City. That figure is not disputed. It is not my imagination. There is a concerted government policy to Judaise the Old City. We are an obstacle to that policy. Sooner or later they will find a way of getting around the obstacle we represent.'

The Bishop poured another glass of cognac for me. 'In my lifetime I have seen my community wither like a diseased tree. The Armenian community used to contain millionaires. Now the young Armenians in my choir look up to their contemporaries who manage to get jobs as waiters in Israeli restaurants. The most ambitious and talented young people are emigrating, to America mainly. They know there is no future for them here. But it's not just the young. Whole families are going.'

When Bishop Hagop had been a young man, he said, there were over ten thousand Armenians in Palestine. Now fewer than two thousand were left. The whole community structure had shrunk. In the old days there had been five Armenian clubs and a theatre group; there had been plays, concerts, gatherings, dances. Now the quarter was a quiet place; those with energy and ability had left and made new lives for themselves in Boston and New York. A shadow had fallen over the Armenian Quarter; the place seemed to be shrinking in on itself.

On my way back to my rooms later that evening I fell into conversation with some Armenian teenagers. To my surprise they echoed the Bishop's despair.

'There is nothing for us here,' said one girl. 'Nothing. If Armenian boys are lucky they will end up washing dishes, or working on a construction site. For us there is even less choice. No non-Jew can get a decent job.'

Another of the teenagers, Krikor, said that the month before there had been a stabbing incident and the Israeli police had randomly arrested him and five hundred other non-Jewish boys. He had been taken to a police station, beaten up and made to stand all day in the sun without water. During the *intifada* that sort of thing had become almost routine.

The girls agreed. One said how, only a week before, she had been beckoned over to a car belonging to an Orthodox Jew which was parked outside the main gate to the quarter. Thinking the man was lost and needed directions, she had bent down to talk to him. The man spat in her face and drove off. She was tired of all this, she said. She wanted to emigrate to Boston, where she had distant cousins.

'The Israelis rule us, but we are not Israeli citizens,' she said. 'We have no votes. We have no influence.'

'They make us feel like a piece of filth they would like to flush down their lavatories,' added Krikor, 'that we are somehow too dirty to be in this town.'

'All of us want to leave,' said the girl. 'Everyday life is just too difficult in Jerusalem. They make *everything* a struggle for us.'

The Armenians were not alone. In the days that followed, as I walked around the Christian Quarter talking to the Palestinian Christians, I found that the inhabitants of the Old City were overwhelmingly gloomy about the long-term prospects of a Christian presence surviving in Jerusalem. Rightly or wrongly, the Palestinians all seemed to believe that there was a concerted campaign to drive them out, or at any rate to make their life so difficult that the majority would opt to leave of their own volition. In 1922, 52 per cent of the population of the Old City of Jerusalem had been Christian; now they made up just under 2.5 per cent of the population of the municipality. There were now more Jerusalem-born Christians in Sydney than in Jerusalem. The Old City ceased to be dominated by Christians in the 1940s; now everyone agreed that it would probably soon have no permanent Christian presence at all.

All this is part of the most dramatic decline in a Christian population to have taken place anywhere in the modern Middle East, with the single exception of Turkish Anatolia. There the progressive campaign of massacres and deportations, culminating in the 1915 Armenian genocide and the 1922 Greco-Turkish transfer of population, left only a few thousand Christians where at the turn of the century there had been around four million. In Palestine the decline of the Christian population over the course of this century has been more gradual, but no less overwhelming.

In 1922, twenty-six years before the creation of the State of Israel, Christians made up around 10 per cent of the population of British Mandate Palestine. The Christians were wealthier and better educated than their Muslim counterparts, owned almost all the newspapers and filled a disproportionate number of senior jobs in the Mandate Civil Service. While numerically they dominated the Old City of Jerusalem – as indeed they had done almost continuously since the fourth century A.D. – their leaders and merchants had already moved out from the narrow streets around the Holy Sepulchre and the Via Dolorosa to build fine villas for themselves in the West Jerusalem suburbs of Talbieh, Kattamon and Bak'a – now home to the better-off Israeli businessmen and Knesset MPs.

The exodus of the Palestinian Christians began in 1948, during the war which followed the withdrawal of British troops from Palestine. In the fighting some fifty-five thousand Palestinian Christians – around 60 per cent of the total community – fled or were driven from their homes, along with around 650,000 Muslim Palestinians. After the Israeli conquest and occupation of the West Bank during the Six Day War, a second exodus took place: between 1967 and 1992 around 40 per cent of the Christians then in the Occupied Territories – a further nineteen thousand men, women and children – left their homes to look for better lives elsewhere.

The great majority of Palestinian Christians now live abroad, in exile: only 170,000 are left inside Israel and the West Bank, compared with the 400,000 living outside the Holy Land, either in squalid refugee camps in Lebanon or elsewhere. The Christians now make up less than a quarter of 1 per cent of the population of Israel and the West Bank. Moreover their emigration rate remains very high, double that of the Muslim Palestinians, not because the Christians suffer any worse indignities than the Muslims, but because being better educated they find it far easier to emigrate and get jobs abroad. So far, the stumbling peace process has done little to stop this flood of emigrants. A recent survey by Bethlehem University showed that around a fifth of those Palestinian Christians still remaining in their ancestral homeland hope to emigrate in the near future.

All this matters very much. Without the local Christian population, the most important shrines in the Christian world will be left as museum pieces, preserved only for the curiosity of tourists. Christianity will no longer exist in the Holy Land as a living faith; a vast vacuum will exist in the very heart of Christendom. As the Archbishop of Canterbury recently warned, the area, 'once centre of a strong Christian presence', risks becoming 'a theme park' devoid of Christians 'within fifteen years'.

The future looks particularly bleak for Christian Jerusalem as

Jewish settler organisations focus their energies on the Holy City. Rings of Israeli settlements are springing up all around East Jerusalem, while within the Old City radical settler groups continue to try to buy up land within the Muslim, Christian and Armenian Quarters of the Old City. Within ten years of the Israeli conquest of East Jerusalem, 37,065 acres of Arab land had been confiscated and settled; today only 13.5 per cent of East Jerusalem remains in Palestinian hands. Less assertive but equally insistent is the Muslim claim to the place they call Al-Quds (the Holy City), as King Hussein and Yasser Arafat compete for the right to protect the Muslim Holy Places. Between these two competing claims, the Christians' stake in Jerusalem seems increasingly irrelevant.

The various Churches in Jerusalem are more than aware of the seriousness of their situation. Traditionally, the forty-seven Christian denominations represented in the Holy City were famous for their pointless and petty squabbling: year after year newspapers across the globe would celebrate Easter with some light Paschal story about the Greek Orthodox feuding with the Roman Catholics over the cleaning of such-and-such a window sill in the Holy Sepulchre or the Church of the Nativity in Bethlehem. But since 1989 the Patriarchs and Archbishops of the major Churches have come together – possibly for the first time since the First Crusade in 1095 – to issue an annual joint statement 'to make known to the people of the world the conditions of life of our people here in the Holy Land who experience constant deprivation of their fundamental rights ... [and to] express our deep concern and alarm for the growing feeling of insecurity and fear among our people and Churches ... [which constitutes] a serious threat to the future of Christianity and its rights in the Holy Land'.

Yet despite the apparent hopelessness of the Christian position, the leaders of the Eastern Churches remain surprisingly defiant. Yesterday morning, armed with a letter from Fr. Theophanes, I was granted a brief audience with the Greek Orthodox Patriarch of Jerusalem, Diodoros I. A hover of black-robed archbishops and metropolitans conducted me into a tall, vaulted reception room. Portraits of centuries of Orthodox Patriarchs stared down impassively from the walls. In the centre of the room, slumped over a large red velvet throne, sat Diodoros, the present holder of the office once occupied by Sophronius. Now very old, he was still a large, powerfully built man with a white beard tumbling down his Patriarchal robes; as he sat on his great gilt throne he resembled an elderly lion with a long grey mane.

'This land,' he boomed, 'this Holy Land, is watered with the blood of the martyrs. It has never been easy for the Christians who live here, and these present times are no different. During the *intifada* we condemned the suppression of our flock. We intervened to get prisoners released. We took food to our people when they were under curfew. We share the aspirations and agonies suffered by our people. The Holy Land has never been a place for quiet contemplation, somewhere peaceful like Mount Athos. Here we have a mission, a mission we have to try and keep going.'

I asked the Patriarch whether he thought the end of the Christian presence in Jerusalem appeared to be imminent, and whether his mission was not now drawing to a close.

'In Byzantine times when we Greeks ruled the Holy Land, this city was entirely Christian,' said Diodoros. 'Of course you cannot compare the present situation with then: our numbers are now very few. But then you do not judge a light by the size of its container.'

The Patriarch rearranged himself on his throne and clutched a miniature icon in a gold setting, suspended on a chain around his neck. 'Even a small oil lamp,' he said, 'can give light to a big room.'

JERUSALEM, 10 NOVEMBER

The Patriarch was right: for the three hundred years of Byzantine rule in Palestine, Jerusalem had been a Christian city; indeed in many ways it was the capital of Christianity. For the barbarians

319

of Dark Age Europe as for the Byzantines themselves, Jerusalem was thought of as the navel of the world, and well into the late medieval period world maps like the Hereford Mappa Mundi depicted the city in the very centre of the earth.

Bishops across Christendom looked to Jerusalem for instruction on how to conduct their Holy Week services and how to order their liturgical calendars; European pilgrims, such as the Spanish nun Egeria, sent back almost ludicrously detailed accounts of the city's liturgical practices to their correspondents, 'knowing how pleased Your Charity would be to learn what is the ritual observed day by day in the Holy Places'. When Pope Gregory I wished to cement an alliance with the Lombards, he sent their Queen a flask of oil from the shrine of the Holy Cross at Jerusalem. Jerusalem was the Holy City, and the eyes of the Christian world were firmly fixed upon it.

All this was a dramatic departure from the situation at the end of the Pagan Empire. Not only had the Romans looked on Palestine as an obscure province wedged between the far richer and more civilised lands of Egypt and Syria, since its destruction by Titus in 70 A.D., Jerusalem had sunk to little more than an anonymous garrison town. As late as 310 A.D. it was possible for the Roman Governor of Palestine, based in Caesarea Maritima (south of modern Haifa), to express ignorance as to the whereabouts of Jerusalem; interrogating a Christian suspect who said he came from the town, the Governor Formilianus replied by asking, 'Jerusalem? Where is that?'

The accession of the Emperor Constantine and the adoption of Christianity as the official religion of the Roman Empire changed all this for ever; overnight the obscure province became the Holy Land, pampered and patronised by a string of emperors, their wives and courtiers. Within a few years of Constantine's Edict of Milan in 313, announcing the official toleration of Christianity, the Emperor's mother Helena had personally travelled to Jerusalem and conducted a series of excavations to locate the Holy Places – even if, as Sir Steven Runciman laconically noted, her discoveries of such relics as the wood of the Holy Cross, were made 'with miraculous aid seldom now vouchsafed to archaeologists'. On the site pinpointed by his mother as that of the Crucifixion and Resurrection, Constantine ordered the building of 'not only the finest basilica in the world, but one where everything shall be of such quality that all the most beautiful buildings of every city may be surpassed by this'. Constantine also commissioned huge basilicas in Bethlehem, at the site of the Nativity, and on the Mount of Olives.

Others soon followed his lead. The Empress Eudoxia, the head-strong wife of the Emperor Theodosius II (builder of the great Land Walls of Constantinople) lived in Jerusalem for sixteen years and spent one and a half million pieces of gold on building pro-jects, at a time when two gold pieces was enough to keep most people in some style for at least a year. Her donations included the Patriarchal Palace, repairs to the city's fortifications, a new loop of wall enclosing Mount Zion within the city limits, and the church and monastery of St Stephen, the place where Sophronius later said the last liturgy before the Holy City fell to the armies of Islam. Eudoxia also built a leper hospital near Herodion on the West Bank, and a tower in the wilderness of Judaea to protect the monks there from the raids of desert nomads. Meanwhile, in nearby Bethlehem, St Jerome had gathered under his wings a gaggle of wealthy Roman matrons. These included an heiress named Paula who 'gave up all her worldly goods' before her pilgrimage to Palestine, yet who still had enough spare change left over to build two monasteries and a hospice, as well as supporting a multitude of monks and paupers, including of course St Jerome himself.

Even the ascetics, living in poverty in the caves and ravines of Judaea, were often from the smartest Imperial families. The monk Photius, for example, was actually the stepson of Justinian's great-est general, Count Belisarius. According to Procopius, Photius escaped from the Empress Theodora's secret torture chambers, into which he had been thrown when he threatened to divulge details of various sexual shenanigans amongst Theodora's ladies in the court at Constantinople. Eluding Theodora's secret police, Photius managed to flee to Palestine, seeking refuge as a monk in the desert somewhere outside Jerusalem.

The wealth and social standing of many of the pious pilgrims who settled in the town is also hinted at by John Moschos. He records a story originally told to him by Amma Damiana the Solitary, mother of his friend the Bishop of Petra. Amma Damiana was related to the Imperial family, and in the story she tells how she persuaded one of her smart Imperial cousins to accept the charity of a poor woman.

'In the days before I was enclosed [as a nun],' said Amma Damiana, 'I used to go to the Church of Saint Cosmas and Saint Damian [in Jerusalem] and spend the whole night there. Every evening there came an old woman, a native of Phrygian Galatia [modern central Turkey], and she gave two *lepta* [small coins] to everybody who was in the church; she often gave me these alms. One day a kinswoman of mine – and of the most faithful Emperor Maurice – came to pray at the Holy City and remained there a year. Soon after her arrival I went to the Church of Cosmas and Damian, taking her with me. While we were in the oratory, I said to my kinswoman: "Look, my lady; when an old woman comes distributing two coins to each person, please swallow your pride and accept them." With obvious distaste, she said: "Do I have to accept them?" "Yes," I said. "Take them, for the woman is great in the eyes of God. She fasts all week long, and whatever she is able to gain by this discipline she distributes to those who are found in the church. Take the coins and give them to somebody else. Do not refuse the sacrifice of this old woman."

'As we were speaking in this way, the old woman came in and began her almsgiving. In silence and with serenity she came and gave me some coins. Then she gave some to my kinswoman too, saying: "Take these, and eat." When she had gone, we realised that God had revealed to the poor old woman that I had suggested to my relation that she give the money away. My kinswoman therefore sent a servant of hers to get vegetables with the two coins. These she ate, and she affirmed before God that they were as sweet as honey.'

The flow of money into the Holy Land brought by the Empire's richest families caused new trades to flourish. Religious tourism, then as now, must have brought in much business for innkeepers and tour guides; certainly by the sixth century there was already a set tour 'circuit', and guide books (some furnished with maps) were available to help the pilgrims understand what they were seeing. Another flourishing cottage industry was the trade in relics. Palestine had something of a monopoly in Old Testament bones, and a good share of New Testament mementoes as well. The relics of Joseph and Samuel, Zachariah and Habakkuk, Gamaliel and St Stephen were all exported during this period, as were the chains of St Peter, the nails which fastened Christ to the Cross and a painting of the Virgin Mary by St Luke. A local Jewess used to display the robe of the Virgin Mary, while the priests of Bethlehem would, for a fee, show pilgrims the bones of the children slaughtered by King Herod, or at least those they had not already sold to the churches and reliquaries of the capital. Famous relics were very expensive – Theodosius II paid a fortune in gold coin as well as a huge gold cross for the relics of St Stephen – but even the most humble pilgrim would be able to afford second-division relics such as casts of Christ's footprints, oil from the lamps at Golgotha and dust upon which the feet of Christ had trod. For the inventive Byzantine entrepreneur, the relic trade must have been an almost inexhaustible source of income.

The Church had much more power here than anywhere else in the Empire. When the local Samaritan population broke out in revolt in 529 A.D., the Emperor Justinian sent to suppress it not a general but 'a monk of high rank named Photion'. Photion fulfilled his duties with somewhat unmonastic zeal, 'fighting against them and conquering them, putting many of them to torture, driving others into exile, and generally inspiring great fear'. According to some sources, more than a hundred thousand Samaritans lost their lives in Photion's purges.

But Jerusalem, like Palestine as a whole, was not just full of clerics, monks and credulous pilgrims; laymen always outnumbered clerics, a fact that caused the always irascible St Jerome some irritation. Writing to his friend Paulinus of Nola, who was planning a trip to Jerusalem, Jerome warned that he should not expect a city of saints: 'It is a crowded place, with the whole variety of people you find in such centres: prostitutes, actors, soldiers, mimes and buffoons. Such a throng of both sexes that you might wish to avoid in part elsewhere you are forced to suffer here in its entirety.' St Basil's younger brother, the choleric Cappadocian Gregory of Nyssa, was equally unhappy at the moral character of the inhabitants of Jerusalem. He wrote home in a fury that 'if God's grace were more plentiful in the vicinity of Jerusalem than elsewhere, then the people who live there would not make sin so much their custom. But in fact there is no sort of shameful practice in which they do not indulge: cheating, adultery, theft, idolatry, poisoning, quarrels and murder are everyday occurrences . . . What proof is there then, in a place where things like that occur, of the abundance of God's grace?'

Indeed the monks themselves could be pretty unruly. They had to be permanently banned from Gaza when they insisted on disrupting night spectacles at the theatre and various festivals they considered 'pagan'. In Chalcedon, on the Asian shore of the Bosphorus opposite Byzantium, when the monks protested about the staging of Olympic Games, the local bishop reminded the leader of the protesters that he was a monk and should therefore 'go and sit in a cell and keep quiet'; but in Palestine the monks were much more numerous and were clearly made of sterner stuff. On one occasion troops had to be used to restore order after the Palestinian monks rose in revolt against a Bishop of Jerusalem they considered heretical. Things got even more out of control during the reign of the heretical Emperor Valens: when the monks demonstrated violently against a bishop he had installed, the Emperor deported large numbers of them, condemning them to the Imperial mines and quarries in the deserts of Upper Egypt.

Sometimes the monks did get away with it, however. Under an oppressive and bigoted late Roman law, the Jews were forbidden to enter Jerusalem except once a year on the Jewish festival of Sukkoth, when they were permitted to come and weep over the ruins of their Temple. In 438 A.D. these regulations were relaxed by the Empress Eudoxia, an act which electrified the Jewish diaspora but outraged the more fundamentalist monks. As the Jews gathered in unprecedented numbers on Temple Mount, the Syrian monk Barsauma led one of the most horrific anti-Semitic pogroms of the period, attacking and killing many of the Jewish pilgrims. Barsauma protested that he and his followers had not been directly involved and that the Jews had been killed by 'missiles coming, as it were, from Heaven'. But the surviving Jews had evidence that this was not true, for they had managed to seize eighteen of Barsauma's followers, and brought them to the Empress for trial. But even the Empress could do nothing in the face of the monastic mob Barsauma was able to muster: cheerleaders in the crowd threatened to burn her, and set up a chant of 'The Cross has conquered'; 'the voice of the people spread and swelled for a long time, like the roar of a wave of the sea, so that the inhabitants of the city trembled because of the noise of the shouting.' Barsauma was never brought to justice, and indeed was later canonised by the Syrian Orthodox Church.

Yet despite such pogroms, rebellions, and internal turbulence, Palestine underwent a massive increase in population during the Byzantine period. Archaeological surveys of pottery picked up in the fields of Israel and the West Bank have found around four times the density of Byzantine pottery as that of the Israelite period, implying that the population during Byzantine rule must have been quite significantly higher than during the centuries preceding it. Whole areas of the region never settled before (or since) were cultivated in this period: in the depths of the Negev desert, for example, six Byzantine towns have been excavated standing in what was then cultivated land. It is probably only in the twentieth century that the population of the region began to equal or surpass the exceptional high point reached during the sixth century.

The seeds of the destruction of Byzantine Palestine may well have lain in the scale of this sudden expansion. Excavations at Scythopolis (modern Beit Shean) have shown that while the town's brothels were flourishing, bathing was falling out of fashion: the town's five bath houses, all flourishing during the Roman period, fell into disuse under the Byzantines. This may have been partly due to the influence of the monks, who regarded the baths with horror and heaped praise on those who refrained from washing for the longest possible period: one story of the desert fathers admiringly tells how a wandering monk chanced upon a saintly hermit in a cave in the furthest reaches of the desert, 'and believe me, my brothers, I, Pambo, this least one, smelt the good odour of that brother from a mile away'. Basic norms of hygiene were not just ignored by the monks and their admirers: they were deliberately, piously flouted.

But it was not just a question of fashion; there were structural problems too. The old Roman aqueducts were clogging up, while in Scythopolis the neatly paved drains built during the pagan Empire fell into disrepair and were replaced by open sewers. In all the Byzantine sites excavated in Palestine and Jordan only two lavatories have ever been discovered, and one of those was located directly over a monastic kitchen.

The result of all this was a wave of epidemics throughout the sixth century. The pages of John Moschos contain many references to outbreaks of plague, and the evidence of modern archaeologists has shown that leprosy, smallpox and tuberculosis were rife, while lice proliferated to an extent unknown in almost any other period of Middle Eastern history.

Many historians now believe that it is in the devastating infections and plagues of the late sixth century that the root cause of the rapid collapse of the Byzantine Levant should be sought.

Every morning during my stay in Jerusalem I toured the lanes and alleys of the Old City, searching out fragments of the Byzantine period, often in the company of Bishop Hagop. The Bishop had cheered up somewhat since our first meeting, and was always at his liveliest in the ancient vaulted passageways of the different quarters, pointing out both the architectural remains littered around us and some of the Old City's more unusual modern inhabitants.

'See that blind beggar? Yes, the man in the wheelchair in front of that Crusader arch. He's only blind from nine until twelve. Then he takes off his dark glasses and has another job, as a waiter in a kebab restaurant in the Muslim Quarter. Very good kebabs, too. Over there, that's the Church of St John the Baptist. It's got some lovely Byzantine stonework but the Greeks have gone and put horrible new frescoes in the apse: bright yellows and blues.'

The Bishop shuddered. 'The taste of some of these modern Greeks . . . Have you seen the mosaic they've put up in the Holy Sepulchre? It looks like something out of Walt Disney. Now, look down here. See the tall man selling olive-wood figurines? He's called Isa. For years he used to be a cook. Specialised in making sandwiches: nice dainty ones for wedding parties. He was famous for his special liver sandwiches and soon became the most popular caterer in the Old City. Then someone noticed that the cat population near his house kept declining every time there was a wedding: eight to ten cats went missing whenever a reception was held. News spread about this, but people kept begging him for sandwiches. In the end he couldn't supply the demand: the cat population ran too low and he couldn't produce the goods. So he got into olive wood instead. But at least he was quite humane with the cats. There's a Cypriot monk who makes his unfortunate cats fast in Lent. He locks them up and you can hear them yowling into the night. And it's not just Lent. About once every year he has dreams in which he thinks he is given an exclusive premonition of the coming of the Messiah. So for a fortnight afterwards he makes these poor cats scream all night in expectation of the Second Coming. Terrible noise. Now, see that pillar . . .'

Perhaps the biggest surprise of our walks was discovering quite how little of Byzantine Jerusalem has survived. While in northern Syria hundreds of unnamed and unknown late antique towns and villages still exist virtually intact, in Jerusalem, once probably the most magnificent provincial town in the entire Christian Empire, only desultory fragments of floor mosaic and piles of collapsed pillars remain to hint at what has been lost. Following the trail of John Moschos's writings around the city takes one to a variety of dank cellars and obscure crypts, but even here there is little surviving that is of more than antiquarian interest. Ironically, the only great Byzantine building left in the city is a mosque – the Dome of the Rock – decorated by Byzantine craftsmen for the new

Muslim conquerors in the late seventh century, shortly after the fall of the eastern half of the Empire. Runciman has called the Dome 'the supreme example of the rotunda-style of building in Byzantine architecture'.

Of Constantine's original Holy Sepulchre very little survives. Fragments of its walls are visible through a dark hole in the side of the Syriac chapel, but most of the existing structure is Crusader, with a few later additions from the Ottoman period. The Nea, Justinian's magnificent New Church of Mary, Mother of God, where one of Moschos's friends, Abba Leontios the Cilician, worked for forty years, has also effectively vanished. Fragments of it – mere lumps of wall, along with some strange vaulted substructures – lie scattered around various undercrofts in the Jewish Quarter. Archaeologists have excavated what remains, and seem excited by their discoveries, but it is almost impossible for the layman to imagine that these sad piles of brick and stone once surpassed many of Justinian's surviving churches – Haghia Eirene in Istanbul or San Vitale in Ravenna – still less that the Nea could be mentioned in the same breath as Haghia Sophia, the greatest of all Byzantine buildings.

The Cardo – the great central bazaar of Byzantine Jerusalem – is a similar story. It dominates the portrait of the city on the sixth-century mosaic map discovered at Madaba in Transjordan in 1884, and fragments of it have been discovered all over Jerusalem. Near the Holy Sepulchre, deep within the bowels of an echoing Russian Orthodox complex known as the Alexander Hospice, one can see a hundred yards of its arcades and paving, as well as a modest Byzantine stab at a classical Triumphal Arch. The Cardo resurfaces again for two hundred yards in a hole in the ground in the Jewish Quarter, beside a line of new boutiques selling bronze *menorah*, Israeli flags and Hebrew T-shirts for the American tourists. It then disappears into the side of a restaurant, never to be seen again.

One place where you cannot see the slightest hint of Byzantine work is at a busy road interchange just outside the Damascus Gate. I went there with Bishop Hagop one damp winter's afternoon, after lunching at an Armenian restaurant near the Austrian

Hospice. The Bishop stood on the pavement beside a new plastic bus shelter and asked me what I could see.

'Well . . .' I ventured. 'A bus shelter?'

'Anything else?'

'A couple of manholes?'

'Exactly. A bus shelter and a set of manholes. But nothing else.'

'No,' I agreed. 'So what?'

'This manhole is all that marks the site of one of the greatest Armenian monasteries of the Byzantine period. To the north-east, over by that filling station, were the monastic buildings of St Stephen's, the largest Greek monastery in Jerusalem. The foundations of its abbey church still survive under the chapel of the French École Biblique. But its monastic buildings were considered long lost.'

I mentioned how Sophronius had said the last mass before the fall of Jerusalem in St Stephen's, and asked when the monastery had been discovered.

'Both monasteries – the Greek and Armenian complexes – were discovered when the Israelis were building a dual carriageway to link some of the new West Bank settlements to the Old City: the settlers said they needed a new road which did not pass through Arab neighbourhoods because of *intifada* stone-throwing. The Israeli archaeologists excavated the ruins, took our mosaic to West Jerusalem, then backfilled both sites.'

'Didn't you protest?'

'Protest? We *begged* them to preserve it. But they would not listen. They said their road was more important. All they preserved was one of our burial chambers. It's under this manhole here. Originally they promised access for pilgrims, and lighting as well, but it never materialised. In Jerusalem we Christians are now too small a community to have any influence. We don't have a lobby. We don't even have a vote. As a result, in the space of a few months, two of the biggest monasteries ever discovered in the Middle East have been erased from the face of the earth. A visitor passing this spot today would never know any Christian building – let alone a pair of the most important monasteries in Palestine – had ever been here.'

329

'They probably didn't have the funds to preserve them,' I said. 'Ruins get bulldozed all over the world.'

'At exactly the same time as the two monasteries were discovered,' answered Hagop, 'builders located the tomb of a fifteenth-century rabbi in the Palestinian village of Silwan, a mile from here. Archaeologically, the site is of no great importance, but tourists are now taken around the tomb, and the impression is given that Jerusalem has always been a Jewish-dominated city. The truth is quite different: for eighteen hundred years the Jerusalem Jewish community was a small minority here. But with the ultimate political status of the town still undecided, it is vital for the Israelis that that truth is suppressed, or at least disguised. Jerusalem is meant to be their eternal capital. These monasteries are evidence of a Christian-dominated Jerusalem. So they were hidden.'

'I'm sure there must have been a good reason for their being bulldozed,' I said. 'I don't believe in conspiracy theories.'

'They promised us a plaque, some sort of memorial,' replied Hagop, scowling. 'Two years later, can you see anything except this manhole? They've still got our mosaic and the bones from the Armenian burial chamber. They're in the storerooms at the back of the Israel Museum. If we don't shout too loud, and behave ourselves, we might get them back. Otherwise we can probably forget it. As for the monastery, we will probably have to wait another century until this road is taken out of commission and we get the site of our shrine back.'

We wandered over the site of the two vanished monasteries, Hagop pointing out the approximate places where various features had stood: a mosaic here, a hospice there, the abbey church here, monastic buildings over there.

'It was a huge complex,' said Hagop. 'From here right over to where that filling station has been built. It was our first Armenian Quarter, another reminder of the continuous Christian presence in this city.'

We headed towards the garage. A little way beyond it stood the École Biblique, where Hagop had promised to help get me a reader's ticket for the library. As we passed the pumps, Hagop suddenly pointed to a sign in the newly planted garden beside the filling station.

'Look!' he said. 'This is new. It must have just gone up.'

We walked closer and read the notice, which was written in Hebrew and English, but not Arabic:

JERUSALEM MUNICIPALITY/MINISTRY OF TRANSPORT
ROAD NUMBER ONE ARCHAEOLOGICAL GARDEN:
FRAGMENTS OF THE THIRD WALL.

'I don't believe it,' said Bishop Hagop.

'What's the Third Wall?' I asked.

'It is the wall built by Herod Agrippa before the Jewish Revolt of 66 A.D. It's an important discovery. Scholars have been arguing for years about where this wall ran, so it's quite legitimate to preserve it. But to keep this when a whole monastic complex has been obliterated before our eyes, right next door to it – that's just nationalistic bigotry. Nothing is erected to commemorate our ruins. There's no mention of them. Nothing. They might as well never have existed. Then they find ten feet of walling from the period of their King Herod and they build a special archaeological garden to preserve it. Do you still call me paranoid?'

Later, in the cuttings library of the *Jerusalem Post* and the archaeological section of the École Biblique, I checked what Bishop Hagop had said.

Like so many apparently trivial disputes in Jerusalem, it turned out that the question of the monastic complex had mushroomed into something of an international scandal. The Christian Churches in the city had been deeply incensed by the authorities' decision to bury a pair of major Christian shrines. They had also been furious at the lack of protection afforded to the ruins, which allowed vandals – allegedly ultra-Orthodox Jewish *haredim* from nearby Mea She'arim, according to the *Jerusalem Post* – to pour tar over a beautiful sixth-century Byzantine mosaic and pile rocks

331

on top of a Christian funerary crypt. Church leaders had given interviews to the international press making clear their view that while finds of importance to Judaism were treated with care and respect, Christian antiquities were being disregarded as part of Israel's campaign to assert its rights to the city. When these interviews had no effect, the heads of all the leading Christian Churches in the Holy Land issued a formal joint statement of complaint about Israeli cultural policies, singling out what they described as Israel's 'depredation' of the Christian archaeological heritage, and threatening to appeal for international protection for their ruins unless 'appropriate and satisfactory measures are taken to preserve our universal Christian heritage'.

According to the official Israeli archaeological report (entitled, significantly enough, *Excavations at the Third Wall*), there were in fact not two but *four* separate monasteries discovered in the excavations north of the Damascus Gate, as well as two hostelries for pilgrims and a large Christian cemetery. Moreover, shortly afterwards, a fifth Byzantine shrine – a small burial chapel decorated with mosaics and rare frescoes – was discovered near the Jaffa Gate during building for the Mamilla Project, a politically motivated scheme intended to 'integrate' the Old City with the new and make it impossible for the two ever again to be divided as they had been from 1948 to 1967, with the Old City going to the Arabs and the New City to the Israelis – a division the Palestinians wish to reinstate. But despite the unprecedented Christian protests, not one of these sites was preserved for posterity. All were reburied, with the exception of the frescoed chapel outside Jaffa Gate, which was bulldozed to make way for nothing more important than an underground parking lot. 'The whole Mamilla Project depends on it [the carpark],' Gideon Avni of the Israel Antiquities Authority told the *Jerusalem Post* by way of explanation.

There is probably nowhere else on earth where the far distant past is so politicised as in the Holy Land. In its 1948 Proclamation of Independence, Israel referred to 'the re-establishment of the Jewish State', thus firmly basing its historic right to exist on the Biblical precedent of the Israelite Kingdom that had thrived in the same area. Since 1967 the same justification has been advanced for the Israeli colonisation of the West Bank and Golan: many of the new Jewish settlements that were set up, such as Shilo, Givon and Katzrin, were deliberately built on sites identified as having originally been colonised by the ancient Israelites three thousand years earlier.

In a situation like this, where contemporary political claims are based on rival interpretations of ancient history, it is almost impossible for archaeologists to remain neutral or objective. There have long been accusations that Israeli archaeologists have a tendency to excavate not so much to illuminate the general history of the region as to uncover their own history, in some cases allegedly digging through and discarding as irrelevant the intervening Turkish, Arab and Byzantine layers. Indeed, to Israel's great credit, many of the fiercest criticisms of this political bias have come from Israeli liberals incensed at what they regarded as the right-wing nationalistic bias of the country's archaeological establishment. In 1992 the Jerusalem-based archaeologist Shulamit Giva accused Israeli Biblical archaeology of being 'a tool in the hands of the Zionist movement [attempting] to find a connection between the ancient history of the Land of Israel and the historic occurrence of the [modern] State of Israel'. Israeli archaeology, she continued, had 'lost its independence as a scientific discipline and become an executive arm of an ideological movement, a nationalist and political instrument which provided "roots" for the new state'.

The distinguished Israeli writer Amos Elon echoed some of Giva's concerns in a long article on politics and archaeology in the *New York Review of Books*. Elon argued that the worst abuses took place in the early years of the Jewish state: 'In the ethnocentric atmosphere of these early years there was a rush to identify Jewish sites, an overemphasis on digging them up, and a tendency to expose to public view the Jewish strata of a site even where other layers may have been historically or artistically more significant or revealing. The task of archaeology was to prove a point about Jews in the Holy Land and not always as it probably should have been, to explore material remains in order to determine the circumstances of ancient cultures and civilisations in a country where they have been so varied and so many.'

Other liberal Israelis have attacked the way the history of the region is presented to tourists. The former Deputy Mayor of Jerusalem, Meron Benvinisti, himself a respected historian of the Crusader period, has attacked the bias in the Tower of David Museum of the History of Jerusalem, the principal museum of the Old City. 'After the Israelite period,' commented Benvinisti, 'the written text informs us that the city was occupied by foreigners. Describing them as foreigners emphasises the exclusivist character of the museum's perspective – only the Israeli-Jewish claim to the city is granted legitimacy. In fact the Israelite period only lasted six hundred years, but all the periods which followed it are represented as a chain of occupations – Persian, Byzantine, Mameluke, Ottoman and British.' Moreover, Benvinisti pointed out that the word 'Arab' does not appear even once in a vast display covering maybe thirty rooms, while the only Arabic name mentioned in the entire complex is that of the conqueror, the Caliph Omar. 'Distorted history is being presented,' he concludes. 'The victor's version of history.'

The archaeologist I most wanted to meet to discuss all this with was Fr. Michele Piccirillo of the Studium Biblicum Franciscanum. Piccirillo is an Italian Franciscan who has lived in Jerusalem since 1960 and who since then has single-handedly rediscovered much of the monastic world described in *The Spiritual Meadow*. In a series of remarkable excavations, he uncovered many previously unknown Byzantine monasteries, chapels, churches and villas dating mainly from the sixth to the eighth century, and in the process brought to light a breathtaking treasury of late antique floor mosaics, including some of the finest mosaic work ever discovered in the Levant. I had seen some of them as I passed through Jordan on my way to Israel, for the finest set of all lies around Madaba and Mount Nebo, immediately above the Allenby Bridge, the frontier post leading into the West Bank. There is little of the ascetic spirit that is visible in Walid Jumblatt's mosaics from

Porphyreon. Instead Piccirillo's mosaics are animated by a remarkable classical *joie de vivre* that hints at a revival of Hellenistic taste – if not a wholesale classical renaissance – in the period immediately after Justinian: leopards chase stags through swirls of acanthus; personifications of the seasons sit enthroned with crown and sceptre, looking on as shepherds process through scrolls of vine branches; satyrs with flutes lead a Bacchic procession while cupids swoop above the orange trees.

But the importance of these new discoveries goes beyond mere aesthetics and art history. Perhaps their most unexpected aspect is the astonishing degree of continuity they reveal. According to Piccirillo, the Arab conquest of the seventh century is archaeologically invisible: the rulers changed, but life went on exactly as before. Indeed much of the finest 'Byzantine' work he has dug up dates from the period immediately *after* the Arab Conquest, when order was better kept, trade was flourishing and the area was released from the crippling taxes imposed by the Byzantine exchequer. 'The archaeologist who searches for a break between the pre- and post-Muslim conquest searches in vain,' wrote Piccirillo in *The Mosaics of Jordan*, the book which sums up his life's work. 'Archaeology demonstrates an uninterrupted continuity between the two periods.'

There are reasons for this. Just as Angle and Saxon mercenaries were drafted into Western Europe to defend Rome's northern borders before the barbarian invasions that brought down the western half of the Roman Empire, so Christian Arab tribes were drafted in by Byzantine rulers to defend the eastern frontiers several centuries before Mohammed. Justinian, for example, had an alliance with two of the Christian Arab tribes: the Banu Ghassan and the Banu Taghlib, both of whom he settled within the boundaries of the Christian Empire. By the time of the Arab conquests, therefore, Arabs already made up a significant minority within the eastern provinces of the Byzantine Empire.

Piccirillo's work has, however, implied that the Arab infiltration of Palestine must have been even more gradual than had previously been recognised; so slow, in fact, that the conquest seems to have brought little immediate change in the

335

racial composition of the inhabitants of the country. After the conquest, the local population soon adopted the Arabic tongue and over the centuries many converted to Islam, but the conquerors' armies were not large and initially provided little more than a military caste superimposed on the existing population. There was no wholesale exchange of population. The Palestinians we see today – and especially the Palestinian Christians – are therefore likely to be the descendants of roughly the same mix of peoples Moschos saw on his travels through this region in the seventh century: an ethnically diverse blend of the many races that have passed through this area since the earliest periods of prehistory.

Piccirillo's evidence is very important, for official Israeli histories still paint a picture of pillaging nomad conquerors sweeping in from the desert, massacring or wiping out the indigenous peoples and leaving the area a depopulated desert – until the birth of the Zionist movement in the nineteenth century. Despite the fact that no serious historian, in Israel or elsewhere, would even begin to try to defend such a crude distortion of Palestine's medieval history, this version still possesses a curious half-life in government propaganda. *Facts About Israel*, for example, is an information book produced by the Israeli Ministry of Foreign Affairs which is prefaced by a fifteen-page account of 'the history of the Land of Israel'. Here, following an extremely detailed account of the Biblical Israelite kingdoms, fourteen hundred years of the region's Islamic history is written off in a small section entitled 'Arabs in the Land of Israel':

> Arab migration in and out of the country started at the time of the Arab conquest of the Land in the seventh century, fluctuating thereafter with economic growth and decline . . . Towards the end of the nineteenth century, when increased Jewish development stimulated economic and social revival in the Land, many Arabs from surrounding countries were attracted to the area by its employment opportunities, higher wages and better living conditions.

I rang Piccirillo and arranged to come around for tea that afternoon. We sat in his small cell in the Studium Biblicum Franciscanum and talked for a long time about his work.

'All the sites I have excavated,' he said, 'call into serious question the old view that the Arab invasions resulted in the destruction of Christian buildings, that the Arabs persecuted the Christians and prohibited the building of new churches. The sheer number of Christian mosaics dating from the Umayyad period constitutes *very* strong evidence not only for the continuity of the Christian presence but also for the tolerance of the new Islamic rulers.'

I asked him about the accusations I had heard of bias in the Israeli archaeological establishment. He was quite clear in his response. Whatever the situation in the early years of the state, he said, current Israeli archaeological methods were thoroughly professional. In his opinion the historical sites of Israel were excavated impartially, without regard to religion. But he was equally adamant about the serious disparity in the presentation of those finds.

'The conservation of Christian remains is systematically less good than the treatment accorded to Jewish remains,' he said. 'Of course conservation is a problem everywhere. But here, where it so easily becomes a political issue, the Israelis should be doubly careful. The fact is that the Holy Land has many communities. Each has its rights, and if a state wants respect it should respect others.'

'How does this neglect show itself?' I asked.

'Synagogues they look after beautifully,' said Piccirillo. 'They cover them with shelters and stop people standing on the mosaics. But newly excavated churches or monasteries they can quite easily rebury, as they did with those outside the Damascus Gate. They would never dream of doing that to a synagogue, and the religious establishment would never let them. With Christian buildings, if they don't bulldoze them, they leave them just as they find them. In Jordan every single mosaic I have excavated is now under specially built shelters, even in specially built museums. But there are churches with good mosaics open to the air all over Israel.'

'Does that matter?' I asked.

'It matters very much. If these Christian sites are not guarded they can get attacked.'

Only a few days before there had been a report in the *Jerusalem Post* of an assault on an unguarded Byzantine church at Mamshit, near the Israeli nuclear facilities at Dimona. 'The vandals, suspected *haredim*, pulled apart colourful mosaics and shattered columns that held up the church's ceiling,' read the report, which said the incident was one of a series over the previous fortnight which had included the vandalising of another Byzantine church at Sussita on the Golan Heights. The *haredim* who were apparently responsible were said to be against archaeological excavations in general, and so were not setting out specifically to target Christian sites; nevertheless, Christian sites did figure on their hit lists.

'But you see,' continued Piccirillo, 'it's not just a matter of protecting from vandals. A mosaic . . .' He broke off and searched for words: 'A mosaic which is not looked after is like a rosary whose string is cut. Once one or two tesserae have gone, the whole mosaic falls apart. In a short time everything – *everything* – is lost.'

JERUSALEM, 14 NOVEMBER

One of the most depressing aspects of Israel and the West Bank is the degree of separation between the two peoples who share the Holy Land. Israelis employ Palestinian labour to do the jobs too badly paid, too dirty or too boring to attract their own compatriots. Palestinians work on production lines, clean the streets, wash the dishes. But beyond that there is no contact and few friendships. There are no mixed dinner parties; intermarriage is virtually unknown. The few places where Palestinians and Israelis meet side by side on equal terms – such as in prayer at the Tomb of the Patriarchs in Hebron – are famous for their tensions rather than for playing any part in bringing together the two mutually antagonistic peoples. The divide appears to be too deep to be bridged.

All this is in stark contrast to the situation during the early Ottoman period, when Palestine, like everywhere else in the Middle East, saw a degree of religious interaction unimaginable today. In Syria I saw that cooperation still surviving in Cyrrhus and Seidnaya, and I was interested to find out if anything of the sort had survived in the Holy Land, if there was anywhere where shrines were places of interaction between the two communities, rather than battlegrounds.

In the École Biblique I had found a book by J.E. Hanauer published in 1907 entitled *Folklore of the Holy Land: Muslim, Christian and Jewish*. It mentioned a shrine in the village of Beit Jala, beside Bethlehem, which at the time was frequented by all three of Palestine's religious communities. Christians regarded it as the birthplace of St George, Jews as the burial place of the Prophet Elias, Muslims as the home of the legendary saint of fertility known simply as Khidr, Arabic for green. According to Hanauer, in his day the monastery was 'a sort of madhouse. Deranged persons of all the three faiths are taken thither and chained in the court of the chapel, where they are kept for forty days on bread and water, the Greek priest at the head of the establishment now and then reading the Gospel over them, or administering a whipping as the case demands.' In the 1920s, according to Taufiq Canaan's *Mohammedan Saints and Sanctuaries in Palestine*, nothing seemed to have changed, and all three communities were still visiting the shrine and praying together. What, I wondered, happened now?

I asked around in the Christian Quarter in Jerusalem, and discovered that the place was very much alive. With all the greatest shrines in the Christian world to choose from, it seemed that when the local Arab Christians had a problem – an illness, or something more complicated: a husband detained in an Israeli prison camp, for example – they preferred to seek the intercession of St George in his grubby little shrine at Beit Jala rather than praying at the Holy Sepulchre in Jerusalem or the Church of the Nativity in Bethlehem. But what of Muslims and Jews? Did they still attend? Beit Jala lay a short distance from Jerusalem, so I drove over to try to find out. By pure good fortune I happened to arrive at the same time as the shrine's Greek Orthodox custodian.

Fr. Methodius – grey-bearded, blue-robed, with a small black chimneypot hat – slammed the door of his Subaru station wagon and locked it with a click of the remote-control bleeper. Then he looked over to the door of his church, and frowned.

There, waiting patiently by the door of the Church of St George, were two Muslim women in white headscarves. One was holding a fine damask veil, the other a small rectangular prayer mat. To one side stood three unshaven Palestinian labourers, each grasping a lead. On the end of each lead was a small, bow-legged, rather scraggy-looking sheep. Fr. Methodius took the gifts from the women with a peremptory nod, and handed the sheep over to the doorkeeper – an ancient hunchbacked Arab in a dirty *keffiyeh* – who led them away to a shed by the monastery gate.

'I'm afraid I won't have time to sacrifice these sheep until Monday,' said Fr. Methodius to the labourers, a little curtly. 'Come back at four if you want to collect the blood.'

The labourers shuffled off backwards towards the road, bowing gratefully, like schoolboys thankful to be dismissed from the headmaster's study. Methodius signalled to me to follow him into the church, and pointedly closed the door behind us.

'Look at this!' he said, holding the prayer mat at arm's length, as if it might somehow infect him. 'It's got a picture of Mecca embroidered on it! You tell me: what can we do with it? And this veil? What's the price of this? Ten shekels? Never mind. Those sheep: that's something.'

'Do you get many Muslims coming here?' I asked.

'Many? We get hundreds! Almost as many as the Christian pilgrims. Often when I come in here I find Muslims all over the floor, in the aisles, up and down' – he made a rocking gesture with his hand – 'bottoms in the air, prayer mats on the floor: yes – in an Orthodox church!'

He snorted into his beard. 'You see, like us they believe this church marks the site of St George's birthplace. And St George is a great saint for them also.'

'And Jews?' I asked. 'Do they come and pray here too?'

'In the old days the Palestinian Jews would come,' replied Fr. Methodius. 'But modern Israelis would never come to such a shrine.'

He led me up to an icon hanging from a pillar in the nave. Beneath the sepia smudge of smoke stains and the clustering silver-work I could just make out the familiar classical face: the young Byzantine cavalryman with his golden breastplate and spear, mounted high upon a white charger.

'All the Arabs – Christian and Muslim alike – call him "Khidr" – the Green One. The Palestinians think St George can help give women babies or bring good crops to their fields or healthy lambs to their sheep. And if they get what they want, then they all come back again and give me these . . .' he stuttered as he searched for the word: '. . . these . . . these . . . rugs.'

'Or a sheep.'

'Yes; that's better. But of course I get to keep only a very small portion. The rest goes to the poor, while the donor takes the blood and smears it on his doorpost. That's the tradition.'

'It sounds very pagan.'

'It may well be,' said Fr. Methodius, his face puckering into a frown.

It was all very curious: Orthodox priests merrily slaughtering sheep, and doing so in homage to St George. Not the way, perhaps, that the Knights of the Garter might expect their patron saint to be venerated. After all, the English have always liked to believe that they have something of a monopoly on St George. If the Victorians had no qualms about proclaiming that God was an Englishman, then few had any doubts at all about claiming for England the country's own patron saint. What English schoolboy did not know the battlecry 'God for Harry, England, and St George'? Did the saint's body not lie in Windsor Castle? Was not his flag the national banner, the linchpin of the Union Jack?

However, no one can travel for very long around the Middle East, particularly among the Christian Arabs, without quickly realising that the English are not the only people to claim St George as their own. The English may fondly believe that they have got

341

their patron saint safely stashed away in St George's Chapel in Windsor, but this will come as news to the nine monasteries on Mount Athos, the thirty-five other churches in Greece, the twenty-four churches and monasteries on Crete and the Greek islands, the six churches on Cyprus, the fifteen churches in Egypt, the five churches in Israel and the West Bank, the citadel in Aleppo and the two monasteries in northern Iraq which also claim the honour of possessing part or all of the ubiquitous and clearly many-boned St George.

In fact the veneration of St George originated in the Byzantine Levant and did not become popular in England until returning Crusaders brought the saint's cult back with them. In 1348 Edward III made St George the patron of the Knights of the Garter, and it was around this time that George seems to have replaced Edward the Confessor as England's national saint.

Although most scholars now tend to accept that St George probably *was* a historical figure, solid facts about England's patron saint are hard to come by. He appears to have been a Christian legionary from Palestine who was martyred for refusing to worship the old pagan gods, probably during the reign of Diocletian (284– 305 A.D.). He may or may not have been the unnamed martyr mentioned as suffering a particularly horrible death in the eighth book of Eusebius's *Ecclesiastical History*, but what *is* clear is that his cult was a very early one, and that it originated in Lydda, now the Tel Aviv suburb of Lod, the Heathrow of the Holy Land, directly under the flightpath of jets heading into Ben Gurion Airport. Nothing else can be said with certainty; already in the sixth century St George was referred to as 'that Good Man whose deeds are known to God alone'.

But lack of facts never stopped medieval hagiographers from assembling impressively detailed saints' *Lives*, and the cult of St George spread with astonishing speed, gathering odd stories and enveloping pagan legends as it went. By the time of Jacobus da Voragine's *The Golden Legend*, written in Genoa around 1260, St George's life-story had become one of the longest epics in medieval hagiography, revolving around the dragon whose breath could 'poison everyone who came within reach'.

What is intriguing about the cult of St George as it is practised today in Beit Jala is the extraordinary degree to which it still resembles the form the cult took *before* it came to acquire all the late medieval accretions that fill out the pages of *The Golden Legend*. On the one hand, then as now, St George is seen as a fertility symbol, a sort of baptised Green Man; on the other he is the Soldier Saint, the combater of demons and the divine champion against the power of evil.

The myths of St George-Khidr have spread across the width of Asia, and from Persia eastwards their links to Christianity have been long forgotten: outside Delhi I was once taken to a cave where Muslim Sufis would go to fast for forty days in order to summon up Khidr, the Green Sufi. Yet it seems that there is nowhere in the East where it is quite as easy to summon up Khidr as in his birthplace at Beit Jala.

'Ask anyone,' said Fr. Methodius when I questioned him on the matter. 'Stop anyone in the street outside and ask if they have seen St George. They will all have stories. Don't take my word for it: go out and see for yourself.'

We left the church and I did as he suggested. The first person we came across was an elderly Muslim gentleman named Mansour Ali. I asked him whether he had ever seen St George.

'Of course,' he said. 'I live just around the corner, so I see him frequently – he is always coming and going on his horse.'

'You see this in dreams?'

'No, when I am awake, in daylight. Khidr is not dead. Whenever we have problems he comes and helps us.'

'In what way?'

'Well, last year I asked him to find work for my children. Within two weeks both my sons had good jobs.'

'For other people he has worked bigger miracles,' said the old doorkeeper, who had shuffled up and begun eavesdropping on the conversation. 'Last month there was a big man from Ramallah. He was very sick: he'd had a stroke and couldn't speak. Half his body had stopped. Well, he came here and took some of the oil from the lamp which burns in front of the icon of St George. Two weeks later he came back with a pair of sheep, completely cured. In fact he wouldn't stop chattering until we locked him out of the church.'

Later, back in the monastery courtyard, I asked Methodius: 'Do you really believe all this talk of miracles?'

He stroked his beard. 'It is according to your faith,' he said after a while. 'If you don't have faith in St George, nothing will happen. If you really believe, then maybe you will be healed.'

'And do you believe?' I asked.

'Well, I'll tell you the greatest miracle,' said Methodius. 'I live here alone: there are no other monks here, and there are no other Christians in the village round about. That doorkeeper – he's a Muslim. So is my sacristan. There are mosques all around: listen – can you hear? That's the call to evening prayer. '

Methodius pulled out his bleeper and unlocked the car. 'There are plenty of Hamas people in Beit Jala,' he said, opening the door of the Subaru. 'And however well Christians and Muslims used to get on, since the rise of Hamas in the last couple of years things have become a little strained. But I'm quite safe, and so is the whole monastery. I sleep easy at night. Now, there aren't many places you could say that of in Israel or the West Bank these days, are there?'

That night, in my rooms in Jerusalem, I thought back to my first stay on the West Bank in the summer of 1990, when I had heard a story that illustrated as well as any the tensions in the occupied region. The story had been told to me in the village of Biddya, and concerned Abu-Zeid, the corrupt village *mukhtar* (mayor) installed by the Israeli military authorities to rule the village for them.

Seven times the villagers had attempted to rid themselves of the hated collaborator, and the story of his eventual demise had rapidly turned into something of a folk tale across the West Bank. I had been wanting to get to Biddya to try to seek out a relatively trustworthy account of the story ever since I had first started hearing heavily elaborated versions of it in the coffee houses of Ramallah, but it was not easy. The village was nearly always under curfew, most recently as punishment for a Molotov cocktail lobbed at a passing Israeli patrol. But at six one morning I had been rung up by my contact in the village, a Palestinian landowner named Usamah, and told that the curfew had been lifted until noon. He said I should get ready; he would pick me up at seven.

We drove out of Ramallah, past an avenue of Israeli army checkpoints – little birds' nests of Uzis and razor wire – and out into the West Bank countryside: low, dry, rolling slopes; silvery olive groves; villages of old stone houses sheltering under the lee of the steeper hills. Only a mile before Biddya did the scene change. Turning the bend of a dry *wadi*, we saw Settlement Ariel ahead of us: a modern Western town with shopping arcades, sports centres and supermarkets. No Palestinian, either Christian or Muslim, ever needed to bother applying to live in Ariel: its houses were available only to Jewish settlers. When local Palestinian labourers at the settlement were forced to wear large badges reading 'Foreign Worker', some liberal Israeli commentators went as far as drawing comparisons with the race laws of Nazi Germany. The badges were later removed.

'That was my grandfather's land,' said Usamah as we passed beneath the settlement. 'It has belonged to this village since the time of the Canaanites. But the Israelis took it in 1977. We've never received any compensation.'

Ariel, Usamah explained, was now home to eight thousand Israelis, but was projected ultimately to house a hundred thousand – a gloomy prospect for Biddya, which, sited precariously beneath the town, looked certain to have all its remaining land requisitioned for new housing estates from which Palestinians would be banned. This year, said Usamah, a further series of olive groves separating the village from the settlement had been seized and bulldozed to provide room for a thousand new houses being built for Soviet Jews fleeing a resurgent Russian racism. Yet again it was the Palestinians who were being made to pay the price for European anti-Semitism.

'A Russian can come to my land tomorrow and have more

right to it than me, my wife or my children,' said Usamah. 'Now the cultivated land has all been taken, and nearly all the olives cut down. Every year they take a little bit more. They think that if they can take it piece by piece there will be no trouble.'

In the end, however, Biddya had not stood by and waited for the slow extinction that was being imposed on it. On the outbreak of the *intifada* Palestinian flags had been raised on the power lines, demonstrations had been mounted, stones thrown. Faced with this defiance, the Israelis could have placed the village under rigorous curfew. This would have limited the trouble but would have been time-consuming, expensive and have tied up large numbers of troops. Far less effort was the option of controlling the village through a client *mukhtar* who, in return for power over the village, would keep order for his Israeli masters.

For seven years Abu Zeid had ruled Biddya as a tyrant, but since his demise the Israelis had been forced to rule the village directly. Neither method had managed to subdue Biddya, but together they had succeeded in ruining it. Of a total population of 3,300, more than five hundred villagers – most of the younger generation – were currently in prison, and forty families had had their houses destroyed. Moreover, after every incident the army made a point of cutting down an olive grove: so far two thousand trees had gone, and only a few remained. Ninety per cent of the village's income used to come from its olives, and it is now bankrupt.

Usamah's uncle, Tariq, was part of the large Nasbeh clan that had ruled Biddya until the Israeli military authorities deposed them. We found him in the walled garden of the family's ancestral house, tending his old musk roses under a trellis of tumbling vines. Usamah had sent word that we were coming, and his aunt, Um-Mohammed, had prepared breakfast for us. She was a big woman and wore a big blue dress, trussed at the waist. At her command we sat on stools, nibbling from the avalanche of olives, mountains of humus and several low ranges of feta cheese she had spread out for our pleasure.

While we ate, Tariq began. 'Abu-Zeid – God burn his bones! – was a very clever man.' He rearranged his shift and twirled his worry beads around his index finger. 'Ya Allah! No one knew how to extort money like him.'

'How did he do it?' I asked.

'The wild dog!' said Um-Mohammed. 'He tried everything.'

'It's true,' said Tariq. 'My great-great-great-grandfather brought Abu-Zeid's Negro forebears here from the Hijaz to be our house-slaves. This was his way of getting revenge.' Tariq shook his head sadly. 'He did everything he could to ruin this village. He would threaten to build a road through someone's house, then collect bribes to stop it. Once he cut off everyone's water and electricity and demanded 500 dinars [£700] from every family before he would reconnect it.'

'Tchk!' said Um-Mohammed, spitting on the ground. 'That was nothing. It was what he did with our land that made us hate him.'

'My younger brother was in prison for throwing stones,' explained Tariq. 'Abu-Zeid came to our house and offered to get his sentence reduced. He asked my father to put his thumbprint on some papers. It was only later that we discovered that he had tricked my father into signing away 110 dunums of our land west of the village. Ariel has an industrial park there now.'

'Abu-Zeid tricked all of us,' said Um-Mohammed. 'Like a mad dog he bit everyone around him.'

'We got a petition signed by every family in the village and took it to the Military Governor. He was a good man, and I think he would have replaced Abu-Zeid. But the settlers at Ariel blocked it. Abu-Zeid was their man. After our petition failed, Abu-Zeid arranged the killing of the old man who had organised the petition. We knew then that we had to destroy Abu-Zeid before he destroyed the village.'

'We are under military occupation,' said Usamah. 'We have no courts or civil authorities to look after our interests. This is what the occupation has reduced us to.'

'At that time we knew nothing about killing,' said Tariq, 'so we hired a Bedouin to do it for us. The Bedouin collaborate with the Israelis and are allowed to join the army and possess weapons. But they will kill anyone if they are paid. My brother knew this killer from Kafr Qasim. After we hired him, this man waited for

Abu-Zeid and shot him with an Uzi. He took fourteen bullets in the stomach. But he didn't die. The Israelis took him to a new hospital in Jerusalem and gave him a new plastic stomach. After a month he was back. The Bedouin is still in prison.'

Tariq popped an olive into his mouth. 'After the Bedouin failed, we vowed to finish Abu-Zeid ourselves. Our first attempt was very amateur. We tried to run him over. The first time we used a car, but he clung onto the bonnet. When the car crashed against the wall, the driver was killed but Abu-Zeid was unhurt. The next time we used a big lorry. That put Abu-Zeid in hospital – he lost his left leg – but although both his younger sons were killed, Abu-Zeid lived.'

'We didn't give up, though,' said Usamah. 'We sent a boy to buy two grenades on the black market in Tel Aviv. When he got back he experimented with one in a cave. It seemed easy to operate, so the next day he threw the other at Abu-Zeid. It sailed through the window of his car, but it was faulty and didn't blow. After that the Israelis gave Abu-Zeid many more weapons and rebuilt his house so that it was like a fortress.'

'Abu-Zeid went crazy,' said Usamah. 'He destroyed the houses belonging to everyone he thought of as an enemy. Then he bought two huge Rottweilers. He used to hobble around the village on his wooden leg, patrolling with the dogs, his brother and his two remaining sons. They beat anyone they found in the streets after dark.'

'Abu-Zeid promised, "Before the next olive season I will have destroyed this village completely,"' said Tariq. 'People said he had gone insane. He blew up the olive press we had been given by the Jordanians before 1967, then began systematically cutting down the olive trees of those he didn't like. But he didn't run away. He knew we would try again, and wherever he went we would find him and kill him.'

'The fifth attempt was a mass attack,' said Usamah. 'The *intifada* was at its height and the *shabab* [young men] had formed hit squads. On 6 March at eight o'clock the *shabab* attacked his house with molotov cocktails. Their object was to blow him up by igniting the gas canisters he kept in his garage. But they didn't know that the Israelis had given the garage new metal doors. As they tried to break in, Abu-Zeid hobbled up onto his roof and began picking them off with his gun. After he had killed four, the village imam broadcast an appeal for help on the mosque loudspeakers. The whole village rushed into the street and joined in. There must have been seven hundred people out there.'

'But we didn't get anywhere,' said Tariq gloomily. 'While we all went off to evening prayers, one of Abu-Zeid's sons slipped out the back and ran to Ariel. When prayers were over, we managed to get into the garage and blow up his bulletproof car. But before we could do anything more the settlers arrived. They were all armed, and began firing into the crowd. Later, when the army came, they put the village under curfew, arrested a hundred people and demolished . . . I don't know how many houses.'

'Ya Allah!' said Um-Mohammed, who had reappeared with a little bowl of humus. 'There wasn't a woman in the village who wouldn't have gladly strangled Abu-Zeid after that.'

'It's true,' said Tariq, raising his eyebrows and giving his beads a twirl. 'But we thought he would not suspect this. So on the sixth attempt we dressed up one of my nephews as a Palestinian woman and sent him off to Abu-Zeid's house with a basket of fruit on his head. Abu-Zeid was sitting outside with Zeid, his eldest son. My nephew put the basket down, pulled out a pistol from under the figs and fired six shots from twenty metres. He hit both men and killed Zeid, but he only succeeded in taking off Abu-Zeid's left arm and wounding him in one lung. Abu-Zeid was fifteen days in intensive care and they had to give him a new arm and a mechanical lung. By this stage he was more like a robot than a man. But within a month he was back.'

'Some in the village believed that Abu-Zeid was some kind of *djinn*,' said Um-Mohammed. 'We thought he would never die.'

'He escaped us six times. *Six times!* But we got him in the end.'

'I saw it with my own eyes,' said Um-Mohammed, rearranging her white calico *chador*. 'It was a few days before the olive season. I was coming back from my brother's house early in the morning when I noticed Abu-Zeid's car coming along the Ariel road. He turned a corner and saw that there was a roadblock. At the same time two *shabab* leapt out from behind a wall and – *pfoo!* – peppered his car with Uzi guns.'

'The Israelis had given him bulletproof windows,' said Tariq, 'but he had left them open.'

'Abu-Zeid tried to reverse and escape, but he hit a wall and they got him all the same.' Um-Mohammed's face exploded into a broad grin. 'He died in great pain. I was so happy.'

'The village gathered around and one of the old men said that they should pour gasoline over the car and burn it, otherwise the settlers might take him away to Tel Aviv and bring him back to life with one of their machines. After his earlier escapes they were worried he might survive even thirty bullets in the chest.'

'But do you know the strange thing?' said Um-Mohammed, scooping up some humus on a piece of pitta bread and popping it into her mouth. 'Because he was half Negro, the smoke was as black as pitch. The place where he died, nothing grows there now.'

'So you understand now why we were so pleased when we finally got him on the seventh attempt?' asked Tariq.

'After we killed him and made a fire of his body, the *Yahoodi* [Jewish] settlers saw the black smoke and came running again. But they were too late. There was only a burned skull, a leg bone, a fire-blackened lung machine and a great pile of plastic sludge that had been his stomach. All they could do was put it all in a sack and give it to his wife. '

'She threw it onto a rubbish tip,' said Um-Mohammed. 'Abu-Zeid had another woman in Kifl Harith. His wife hated him as much as the rest of us.'

'The army put the village under curfew for two weeks,' said Tariq. 'We couldn't even harvest our trees. But no one minded. Inside every house it was like a holiday. People were singing and dancing.'

'Even in the prisons there was rejoicing,' said Usamah. 'All Abu-Zeid's old enemies – there were about two hundred of them in jail at that time – they had a big party also.'

The curfew was due to resume in less than ten minutes. I got up and said my goodbyes, while Usamah hurried me out to the car. We drove out of the village and past the gates and guntowers of Ariel. Under the razor wire, the settlers' bulldozers were at work clearing Biddya's olive groves.

'It was a great day for the village when we killed Abu-Zeid,' said Usamah. 'But in the long run, what difference does it make?'

He stopped the car by a pile of uprooted olive trees and got out, indicating that I should do the same: 'Such trees are 150 years old – three times the age of the State of Israel,' he said, pulling out a clod of earth from the roots and crumbling it in his hands. 'Generation after generation our people have come three times a year to dress, fertilise and harvest these trees. All our life, all our traditions, are connected to such trees. But now they bring their powerful machines from the USA and destroy our inheritance in fifteen minutes. Like us, these trees have deep roots. Look how strongly these roots bond the trees to the soil! But now they are uprooted, and with or without Abu-Zeid, if the settlers get their way we will be next. Sooner or later they will expel us all. It is only a matter of time.'

'The Americans would never let them,' I said.

'Wouldn't they?' replied Usamah.

'You want Utopia?' said Mayor Ron. 'I got Utopia! Look!'

Ron Nachman, the Mayor of Settlement Ariel, called to his secretary. Seconds later she appeared with the official photograph album.

'Ariel was my idea,' explained Mayor Ron. 'In 1977 nobody lived here. There was nothing. Look: here – nothing except a few old trees. Here's me in the first tent . . . and that's the luxury caravan we moved into a little later. Here are the watertanks and the bulldozers. You see these boulders? That's the supermarket now. And over there? Those stones? That's now a lawn.'

The secretary took the album and Mayor Ron settled down behind his desk. Above his head was a plaque:

For representing the people of Judaea, Samaria and Gaza.
For reclaiming our Biblical roots in Eretz Israel.
For courage and conviction and deep vision.
Presented by Americans for a Safe Israel, April 1990.

'I give people the chance to participate in the greatest adventure,' said the Mayor, 'the building of a new town from scratch – from nothing! Developing a new society for all our tomorrows.'

Mayor Ron clearly knows the reputation he has for public relations. He is still a young man, and exudes energy and dynamism. He talks fast, in flawless American.

'Friend, I'll tell you something. Do you know what the Arabs used to ask me? "Ron," they would say, "why do you come to this bare mountain?" I said, "Wait five years – you'll see what we can do with this land."'

'Do you have problems with your Palestinian neighbours?' I asked.

'The Arabs don't have a problem with Jews,' replied Mayor Ron. 'They have problems with Arabs – with the PLO terrorists. The PLO are enforcing a rule of terror around here – anyone who cooperates with us is as good as dead – even the *mayor* of an Arab village near here was gunned down by PLO terrorists, d'you know that? Friend, let me tell you: these Arabs don't want peace *with* Israel – they want a piece *of* Israel.'

Mayor Ron smiled a winning breakfast-cereal smile. 'But I guess you're asking about me personally. No – I don't have anything against Arabs at all. I'm no racist: I have an Arab cleaning lady.' He leaned forwards on his desk: 'That's right – *an Arab cleaning lady*. She is alone with my babies. I can't say everyone would trust an Arab like that.'

Mayor Ron paused to let the full implications of his liberalism sink in. 'You know, William, I am deeply proud of what we've built here. A nice town, a clean town, full of nice people. We accept everybody. Already we are the fastest-growing town in Israel. The land is there. All we suffer from is lack of housing. If we can overcome that, soon we'll be a town of a hundred thousand, and stretch for eight miles over these hills.'

He pointed to an aerial photograph of the area tacked to the wall beside his desk. 'Go on! Walk around! See it for yourself. This is a free country, a democracy – the *only* democracy in the Middle East!'

Outside, tanned, healthy children were racing around the crazy paving on BMX bikes. Long lines of supermarkets, cafés, shops and jeans stores were spread out across a plaza; Kenny Rogers was piped through the Tannoy. Beyond the swimming pool and the ranks of gleaming station wagons in the parking lot, the bare hills of the West Bank stretched into the distance.

The children seemed less keen on Ariel than their Mayor. 'Boring' was the opinion of most of the teenagers I spoke to, 'no nightlife'; but there was no shortage of enthusiasm among the adults. I ended up talking to Dina Salit, who had emigrated five years earlier from Canada. We sipped cappuccinos and picked at chocolate croissants, and while we sipped and nibbled, Dina enthused.

'My husband and I are very happy here, very happy indeed. I mean, if we had just gone to Tel Aviv, we might as well have stayed in Montreal. But here we are making a truly Zionist statement, doing something, you know, totally different. I mean, how many people get the chance to be in on the building of a new town?' Dina beamed at me. 'Here you feel that your presence really makes a difference. Here you feel . . . valued.'

'Yes?'

'*Deeply* valued. Howard is the director of a security company, so he feels valued too.'

'And what about the Arabs?' I asked.

'Before the *intifada* we made friends with several A-rabs,' Dina said, drawing out the first syllable. 'To me, as a Canadian, that was a miracle. I didn't know it could be done. I mean, you know, *A-rabs*. But all the same we did used to have some of the A-rab construction workers in for coffee. I'm not saying we were best friends, that it was a love affair, but it was OK.'

'Has the *intifada* changed everything?'

'Yes and no. We don't have A-rabs in for coffee any more, but you know, the political scene is seldom a topic of conversation here. We're all much more concerned about gossip, or street cleaning,' Dina giggled. 'That's a *much* greater problem!'

I paid the bill, and Dina walked me over to the Ariel bus stop. As we strolled, I asked: 'So what would you say to those Israelis who would give away your settlement and the rest of the West Bank in return for peace?'

'I've never heard any A-rab say they want Judaea and Samaria only,' she replied. 'For them it's only the first step. They want to drive the Israelis into the sea. Everyone knows that. I won't be taken in by that terrorist Arafat – forget it!'

She paused, and in the silence I could hear the strains of Kenny Rogers still drifting over the shopping arcade.

'Arafat and his terrorists are playing political games – and we're talking people's homes. You know what that means? *People's homes.*'

THE ANGLICAN HOSTEL, NAZARETH, 20 NOVEMBER

Around 570 A.D., after he was first professed as a monk at the Abbey of St Theodosius, John Moschos withdrew into the wilderness and spent ten years in the remote cave monastery at Pharan, to the north of Jerusalem.

Pharan, the modern Ein Fara, is reputedly the oldest abbey in Palestine. It was founded in the early fourth century by the great Byzantine hermit St Chariton, who, it is said, settled here in a cave above a pool of pure spring water. There he gathered a community of like-minded ascetics around him, living a life of silence, self-abnegation and severe fasting, interspersed with long hours of prayer. Two hundred years later, Moschos appears to have been drawn to the site less by its antiquity than by the wisdom of its then *hegumen*, Abba Cosmas the Eunuch. In a crucial passage in *The Spiritual Meadow*, Moschos credits Cosmas with first giving him the idea to collect the sayings of the fathers: 'Whilst he [Abba Cosmas] was speaking to me about the salvation of the soul, we came across an aphorism of St Athanasius, Archbishop of Alexandria. And the elder said to me, "When you come across such a saying, if you have no paper with you, write it on your clothing" – so great was the appetite of Abba Cosmas for the words of our holy fathers and teachers.' It was advice that was eventually to lead Moschos to compiling *The Spiritual Meadow*, and so to preserve the otherwise largely unrecorded history of the monks of Byzantine Palestine.

By a remarkable coincidence, at the beginning of this trip, on Mount Athos, I had met a monk who claimed to have been the last hermit to have lived in the very same cave as Moschos at Ein Fara. Fr. Alexandros was a tall, rubicund figure with a faded serge cassock, a short Orthodox pigtail and a grey beard, matted and tangled like John the Baptist's on some early Byzantine icon. I had stumbled across him on a walk one afternoon, soon after digging out the manuscript of *The Spiritual Meadow* from the library at the Monastery of Iviron. He lived alone in a small wooden hut in a clearing in the forest, high above Karyes. It was an idyllic place, a bright and silent retreat, fringed with lilies and ilex and commanding an astonishing view down over the silver domes of the Russian Skete to the deep, fragmented blue of the Aegean far below. But this, Fr. Alexandros told me, was not his home, nor where he longed to be: he had moved to this Greek hilltop only a decade before, after being driven out of his hermitage in the Holy Land.

For most of his adult life, he explained, he had followed the ways of the desert fathers in the cave at Ein Fara, a millennia and a half after St Chariton first founded the monastery. But Fr. Alexandros had been the last of the line. About ten years after the Israeli conquest and occupation of the West Bank, he had begun to receive death threats which he believed came from a group of Israeli zealots who had established a settlement nearby. Then one day in the winter of 1979 his spiritual father and distant neighbour, a Greek monk named Philloumenos, was hacked to death in his cell at Jacob's Well near Nablus; someone had poisoned his dogs, attacked him with an axe, then incinerated his remains with a grenade. Shortly afterwards, Fr. Alexandros returned from a trip to Jerusalem to find his cave-chapel desecrated and his books and possessions scattered and burned. The pulpit in the chapel had been axed into a hundred pieces. The hermit fled, caught ship to Athens, and had eventually found his way to Athos. The cave and spring had apparently since been wired off and absorbed into a new settlement.

Like many hermits, Fr. Alexandros was a deeply eccentric man, a holy fool who talked to his pet owl, fed the lizards, and claimed to receive occasional visits from angels. He was a man whose statements could not, perhaps, be taken entirely at face value. I was therefore a little surprised to discover, on my visit to the Greek Orthodox Patriarchate in the Old City of Jerusalem, that much of what he had said had indeed been true. A bearded Greek Metropolitan who had known both Philloumenos and Alexandros showed me a file full of reports and correspondence about the desecration of the cave of St Chariton and the violent murder in Jacob's Well. A mentally ill Israeli from Tel Aviv had been charged with the Jacob's Well murder, I learned, as well as with two other killings. I was even directed to the Martyrion at the Orthodox Seminary on Mount Zion where Fr. Philloumenos's shattered skull and axe-cloven bones lay on permanent – if rather grisly – display, dressed in his old habit, awaiting potential canonisation.

'He *is* a saint,' I was assured by Fr. Aristopoulos, the earnest young monk who showed me into the Martyrion. 'Fr. Philloumenos received many telephone calls from the Jewish zealots saying he must leave Jacob's Well, that it was their holy place, not ours. After his dogs were poisoned the Patriarch said that he should come away and live in Jerusalem where it was more safe, but every time Philloumenos refused. He was saying vespers when the killer found him and started to chop at him with the axe.'

'He didn't kill him outright?'

'No,' replied the monk, 'but with many cuts: hands off, then feet, then legs. In pieces. Very nasty. Only at the end he threw the grenade.' Fr. Aristopoulos crossed himself in horror. 'But you know, when they held a small service for him four years after his death, they exhumed his relics and found that his body was uncorrupted.'

'But how could it be uncorrupted,' I asked, 'when he had already been chopped up and incinerated?'

'Well not *totally* uncorrupted,' admitted the monk. 'But it was still a very miraculous preservation. After this there were miracles – including healing of the sick – and many visions of Fr. Philloumenos. Some I have seen myself.'

'You've seen Fr. Philloumenos?'

'In my dreams I have seen him,' said Aristopoulos. 'Also I have smelt him.'

'I don't understand,' I said. 'I thought you said his body hadn't corrupted.'

'No, no,' said Fr. Aristopoulos. 'It was a good smell. During the Gulf War the Greek Consulate ordered all Greeks to go home. The seminary was closed and all the students left. I was here alone. I locked up the chapel and for three months I stayed upstairs in my room with my gasmask because of Saddam's Scud attacks. Then in March, when the war was over, I came and unlocked the door and walked in here for the first time since the New Year. It was as if the church was full of incense: a heavy smell, so nice, so sweet. It was coming from Fr. Philloumenos.'

So this, I thought, was how miracle stories began.

I told Fr. Aristopoulos about my meeting with Fr. Alexandros and his story of the assault on his cave. Aristopoulos replied that attacks on Church property were far from unusual. During the Six Day War, he said, the room in which we were standing had been attacked by a lone Israeli soldier who had fired off several shots at the iconostasis before being wounded – so at any rate claimed Fr. Aristopoulos – by a miraculous ricochet from an icon of the *Theotokos*, the Holy Virgin.

Checking these stories in the more sober *Jerusalem Post* archives and with the different Church authorities in Jerusalem, I found that from the early 1970s to the mid-1980s there had indeed been a wave of attacks on Church property. A Jerusalem church, a

Baptist chapel and a Christian bookshop had all been burned to the ground, allegedly by ultra-Orthodox *haredim*, while students from a nearby *yeshiva* had committed serious vandalism at the Dormition Abbey. There had also been a series of unsuccessful arson attacks on the Anglican church in West Jerusalem (the old wooden doors had had to be changed to steel to thwart repeated attempts at igniting them), as well as on two churches in Acre (a Greek Orthodox church in the Old City and a Protestant chapel in the new Israeli suburbs) and an Anglican church in Ramleh.

In addition to this, the Protestant cemetery on Mount Zion – already damaged between 1948 and 1967 when it stood in the no-man's land between Israel and Jordan – had been further desecrated no fewer than eight times. I visited it afterwards: the tombstones had almost all been shattered, metal crosses lay twisted in their sockets, and some of the sepulchres had been broken open; the one standing mausoleum was riddled with bulletholes. As Canon Naim Ateek of St George's Anglican Cathedral in Jerusalem put it after he had spent half an hour listing all the incidents of desecration he knew about: 'Israel would like to give the impression that it champions religious tolerance, but the whole country was built on the usurpation and confiscation of Christian and Muslim land. To this day the confiscation and desecration of Church land and buildings continues.'

Canon Ateek's views are widely held by the Palestinian Christians I talked to in Jerusalem, but there is another side to the story. The Israeli authorities have always roundly condemned the vandalism of Church property and assisted the churches to recover from any serious damage. While ultra-Orthodox Jewish *haredim* remain the chief suspects for most desecrations – and their presence is further indicated by the nature of the Hebrew graffiti sprayed on several of the desecrated sites – their involvement is rarely proven, while in some cases, such as the desecration of the cave of St Chariton, it is not impossible that the attack could equally well have been carried out by disgruntled Arabs. Moreover, while Christian institutions still tend to suffer from abusive graffiti – when Archbishop Desmond Tutu recently visited Jerusalem, for example, the gates of St George's were daubed with 'Go home dirty black Nazi pig' – the wave of arson and vandalism that took place during the seventies and early eighties now largely seems to have ceased, and there has been only one major arson attack in recent years: the gutting of a church in Tiberias.

Certainly, none of these unconnected incidents in any way proves the Palestinian Christians' contention that there is a concerted campaign to drive them out of their ancestral homes. But what they do undoubtedly reveal is a degree of prejudice and intolerance in Israel reminiscent of several other Middle Eastern countries – notably Turkey – where a religiously homogeneous majority is able to lord it over a relatively powerless minority community. Few Western Christians are aware of the degree of hardship faced by their co-religionists in the Holy Land, and the West's often uncritical support of Israel frankly baffles the Palestinian Christians who feel their position being eroded year by year. As Fr. Aristopoulos at the Martyrion put it: 'Had we been Jews and our churches been synagogues, the desecration we have suffered would have caused an international outcry. But because we are Christians no one seems to care.'

The day after I saw Fr. Philloumenos's axe-cleaved remains, I found a Christian Palestinian driver, Sami Fanous, who agreed to take me to see the cave at Ein Fara. I very much wanted to see the ruins of the *lavra* where Philloumenos used to visit his friend Fr. Alexandros, and where, fourteen hundred years earlier, John Moschos had retired to spend a decade of his life in silent meditation.

Since Alexandros's departure, the new Israeli settlement of Pharan had absorbed the cave, the spring and much of the surrounding countryside, and to get to the ruins we had first to get into the settlement. At its entrance, a massive yellow-painted electric steel gate blocked the road; on either side tangles of razor wire led off across the hills as far as the eye could see. Sami stopped the car and we were questioned by the guard. I showed him the monastery marked on a map, and he went off to a sentrybox with my passport. There he conferred with someone on a telephone. He replaced the receiver and came back to tell us to wait. After twenty minutes, the telephone rang, permission was granted, and we were waved through.

The path to the monastery led off from the bottom of one of the settlement's housing estates. I left Sami with his car and headed off down into the valley on foot. All around, the hillsides were hard and dry: compressed beds of geological strata rolled off in great undulating contortions into the distance; there was no tree, and barely a blade of grass visible in the whole great panorama. As I descended into the *wadi*, however, the path turned a corner, and far below, at the lowest point in the valley, there appeared a small oasis: a patch of the densest woodland made up of ferns, pines and palms. From where I was standing I could not see the spring itself, but I could clearly hear it. The distant sound of the running water filled the silence of the *wadi*, echoed and amplified as it bounced off the walls of the ravine. It was an unseasonably hot day, and I shouldered my pack and stumbled down the path towards the sound.

Arriving at the bottom, I took off my shoes and bathed my feet in the clear, cold water. Despite the heat, the area around the spring was cool, shady and peaceful. As I sat there I thought how easy it was to understand why Moschos had chosen this spot to spend his years as a hermit: in such a place, it seemed to me, it must have been easy to foster the great monastic virtues of gentleness, balance, lack of haste and clarity of spirit. All around the spring, peppering the cliffs of the ravine, were the mouths of the caves that had once been filled with Moschos's fellow hermits, men like Abba Paul, 'a holy man of great humility . . . I don't know whether I ever met his like in all my life'; or Abba Auxanon, 'a man of compassion, continence and solitude who treated himself so harshly that over a period of four days he would eat only a twenty-four *lepta* [ha'penny] loaf of bread; indeed sometimes this was sufficient for him during a whole week.' These caves had also been home to Abba Cosmas the Eunuch, Moschos's spiritual

360

father. Moschos only sketches his Abbot fairly briefly in the *Meadow*, but we learn that he apparently had the power to heal the sick, and that even by Byzantine standards he was famous for his ascetic self-control: 'on the eve of the holy Lord's day, he would stand from vespers to dawn singing and reading, in his cell or in church, never sitting down at all. Once the sun had risen and the appointed service had been sung, he would sit reading the holy Gospel until it was time for the Eucharist.'

Other than the bare hermits' caves, only a little survived of the monastery that Moschos had known. There were some crumbling cell walls, a cistern, a few stretches of Byzantine stonework, the odd staircase and a little sagging terracing where the monks had once, presumably, grown vegetables. A Byzantine mosaic was said to survive in the cave church at the top of the honeycomb of interconnected caverns, but it was impossible now to reach it without a rope or a ladder. After an hour poking around, clambering into some of the more accessible cave-cells, I set off up the hill again.

I was halfway up the path when I was met by Sami, my taxi driver. He was clearly very frightened. In my absence, he explained, he had been interrogated by the settlement's security guards. They had confiscated his ID card, and he was now terrified of being detained or arrested. 'Don't say I'm a taxi driver,' he begged. 'Say I'm your friend.'

We got back to the car and drove to the main gate, where a different guard was now on duty. He called for the head of security on his walkie-talkie, and told us to move the car off the road and to wait.

'There are many Arab terrorists in this area,' he said by way of explanation.

We waited for nearly an hour before the head of security turned up. He was a small, tough-looking man in khaki fatigues. A pistol was tucked into his belt and in his hands he held an assault rifle. He cross-questioned me for thirty minutes, examining my maps, my paperback of *The Spiritual Meadow* and my passport over and over again. What was I doing? Was the driver my friend? Where was this monastery I kept referring to? Was it an Arab monastery?

And who was John Moschos? Was he an Arab too? Did I have other Arab friends? Had my Arab friends asked me to do anything for them in the settlement? He then returned to the sentrybox and read my passport details down the telephone to someone. He made several more phone calls and conferred for a further fifteen minutes on the walkie-talkie. Finally he came over and returned my passport and Sami's ID.

'There has been a misunderstanding,' he said gruffly as the steel gate rolled back. 'You can go now.'

But he didn't apologise.

NAZARETH, 22 NOVEMBER

Before I left Jerusalem I had bought a bus ticket to the Egyptian border. From there I planned to make my way to Alexandria. The bus was due to leave in two days' time, but before I left Israel I had a promise to keep.

On my last day in Beirut I had promised to visit Kafr Bir'im, the village from which the Christian Palestinian family I had met in the Mar Elias refugee camp had fled in 1948. The Daous had felt they would be safer if they temporarily left their homes, and as a result of that decision had spent forty-six years in exile in a succession of squalid refugee camps. I wanted to know what would have happened to them if they had decided to stay. Would their life have been any easier in the new State of Israel?

In a general sense I already knew the answer. Compared to their compatriots who fled or were expelled – or indeed those on the West Bank who had been conquered by the Israelis in 1967 and were still under military rule twenty-seven years later – the Palestinian Christians who had stayed on and become citizens of Israel in 1948 had been very lucky. They had Israeli passports, and could vote in Israeli elections. They had access to Israeli educational facilities, enjoyed Israeli civil justice and could even, if they so wished, join the Israeli army. True, there were complaints about land expropriation and discrimination: the councils of Arab towns were said to receive less than a third of the funds available to those with Jewish populations. Yet compared to the dismal fate of those who still languished in refugee camps, the Israeli Arab Christians had been very fortunate indeed. Unlike their counterparts on the West Bank, relatively few have emigrated, and since the foundation of Israel their numbers have quadrupled, from the thirty-four thousand left in their homeland in 1949 to around 150,000 today.

But what I wanted to compare with what I had heard in Beirut was more specific: the fate of the Daous' neighbours in Kafr Bir'im who had stayed on. Samira Daou had told me that when Israeli planes had bombed Kafr Bir'im, her friends and neighbours had taken shelter in the nearby town of Jish. What had happened to them?

After leaving Ein Fara, I got Sami to drive me through the occupied West Bank, past Biddya and Ariel, to Nazareth in northern Israel. Then this morning, after breakfast, we set off north again towards Jish. The drive led past the Sea of Galilee, with its ancient Byzantine churches clustering around the shore, and up, over stark hillsides of black volcanic stone, on towards the north and the Lebanese border.

The countryside was dotted with Israeli *kibbutzim* energetically scratching a living from the harsh soil. But as we drove, Sami pointed out the sites of some of the 385 Palestinian villages – many of them Christian – which had preceded such Israeli settlements in Galilee, until they were systematically depopulated and destroyed by the Jewish Haganah during the war of 1948. It was the cactus plants that always gave the old villages away: however efficiently the Israelis had bulldozed the buildings and erased the Palestinian communities from the map, the old villages' cactus hedges had deep roots, and kept sprouting again and again to mark the sites of the former garden boundaries and the shadows of former fields.

'That was the village of Faradi,' said Sami at one stage, pointing to a few blocks of stone and some cactus plants by the side of the

363

road at the bottom of a hill. 'Now the Kibbutz of Farud farms that land.'

As we climbed the hill, Sami's battered old Mercedes labouring behind a convoy of slow military trucks, the kibbutz's cowsheds and farm buildings came into view, their solar panels glinting in the morning light. Beyond, the low hills and plains of Galilee spread out before us. Despite the mass immigration of the 1920s and thirties, in 1948 the Jews had still formed less than a quarter of the population of this area, and the displacement of the Arab majority had been achieved only by a process which Yigal Allon, the commander of the Jewish military forces in Galilee (and later Deputy Prime Minister of Israel), himself described as 'cleansing'. 'We saw a need to clean the Inner Galilee,' he wrote in his memoirs, 'and to create a Jewish territorial succession in the entire area of Upper Galilee. We therefore looked for means to cause the tens of thousands of sulky Arabs who remained in Galilee to flee . . . Wide areas were cleansed.'

In the process of this 'cleansing' of the Galilee, the Christian Palestinians had offered less resistance than the Muslims, and consequently were better treated. Moreover, Israel was careful not to offend public opinion in the Christian West by over-zealous 'cleansing' in the more famous Christian towns and villages; indeed, special instructions were issued by Ben Gurion himself not to loot Christian holy places such as Nazareth. As the Brigade Commander who captured the city later wrote: 'The conquest of Nazareth has political importance – the behaviour of the [Israeli] occupation forces in the city could serve as a factor in determining the prestige of the young state abroad.'

In nearby Beit Shean (then known by its Arabic name Beisan) the inhabitants were divided in two: Muslims were bussed across the Jordan into exile, while the Christians were given the option of fleeing to Nazareth. Canon Naim Ateek was eleven when he was expelled from his family home in Beisan. 'When the Israeli army came into the town there was no resistance,' he had told me when I had visited him at St George's. 'Then quite suddenly a fortnight later we were given two hours to pack up and leave: the soldiers came around from house to house and said, "If you don't leave we will kill you." We were allowed to take only what we could carry.' Ten years later, in 1958, when travel restrictions on the Israeli Arabs were lifted, Ateek's father took the family back to see their old house. They knocked on the door, but were sent roughly away by a Polish man armed with a rifle. They never went back again.

An hour's drive beyond Nazareth, the road turned a corner and we found ourselves looking down over thick conifer forests to the tower blocks of Safad. 'Before 1948 it was a mixed town,' said Sami. 'There were Muslims, Jews and Christians. Now it's exclusively Jewish. The Christians and the Muslims were driven out by force and were never allowed back again. My mother had cousins there, but most of her family were killed when the Haganah bombarded the Arab part of the town with mortars. A few made it to Lebanon, but we haven't heard from them since the invasion of '82. We don't know whether they are alive or dead.'

Jish lay a short distance beyond Safad, a little higher into the hills. It was a scrappy-looking place, the few old stone houses surrounded by many more new bungalows, the minaret of a mosque and the spires of two churches. Unsure where to begin my enquiries, I asked an Arab woman in a pinafore the way to the priest's house. I was directed a short distance down the street.

The door was opened by Fr. Bishara Suleiman, the Maronite parish priest. He was a tall man with a short clipped goatee beard, and he spoke excellent English (and French, as I later discovered: he had studied theology at the Sorbonne). Unusually for a Middle Eastern clergyman he was dressed not in formal black robes, but in a T-shirt and slacks. I explained the reason for my visit to the town, and he immediately invited me in. At the same time he called to his nephew, John Suleiman, to go and fetch some of the old men from Kafr Bir'im.

We took seats on a balcony, looking out onto the village's olive groves. Fr. Suleiman's wife produced a thermos of strong Turkish coffee from the kitchen, and while we sipped the scalding liquid I asked the priest if he would tell me the full story of what had happened to Kafr Bir'im after the Daous had left it in 1948. Would they have been better advised to stay?

'Very few of our villagers did flee in '48,' said Fr. Suleiman. 'We had always had good relations with the Jews and the British: so much so that in 1936 [during the Palestinian revolt] we were accused of collaboration and had to beg the British to protect us. They sent some Tommies who set up camp on the edge of the village, and after that we had no trouble. We had always helped the Jews entering Palestine from Lebanon, and we thought that if there was any trouble they would help us. That was why most of the villagers stayed on, despite all the stories we heard about Deir Yassin and other massacres nearer here.'

'Such as?'

'The Haganah massacred seventy Arab prisoners at Ein al-Zaytun near Safad. They tied their hands behind their backs. Then they shot them. But we thought nothing like that would happen here, partly because we were Christians and partly because we had always been friendly towards the Jews.'

At this moment Fr. Suleiman's nephew returned with the old village schoolmaster of Bir'im, Elias Jacob.

Elias was a thin, wizened old man. At seventy-five he was a little uncertain on his legs, but still absolutely clear in his mind. He was, said Fr. Suleiman, the best authority on the history of Kafr Bir'im; and as if to prove it, Elias produced from his pocket a slip of paper on which were written the main dates and facts of the story. He didn't want anyone getting anything wrong, he said. He took a seat, threw back a small cup of Turkish coffee, and at Fr. Suleiman's invitation began to talk.

'The Haganah soldiers arrived in our village on 29 October 1948,' he said, checking the date against his notes. 'Most of us remained in our houses, but the old men and the priest received the troops at the entrance of the village with a white flag. We offered them bread and salt, the symbol of friendship and peace.'

'Were they equally friendly?' I asked.

'They were,' said the old man. 'They were very good, very polite. We gave them food and they occupied some houses. They stayed for fifteen days. Then on 13 November 1948 an order arrived that we all had to leave.'

'Were you surprised?'

'We were amazed. At first we refused to go. But then a new officer arrived and he was very different. He said we had twenty-four hours to get out. Then we were afraid. He gave no reasons. He just said that we had to be five kilometres from the village or we would be shot.'

As Elias was speaking we were joined on the balcony by another old man, Wadeer Ferhat. He was a big, high-spirited man with a huge walrus moustache. When he discovered what we were talking about he began shouting in a series of angry outbursts of guttural Arabic. Sami translated.

'Mr Wadeer says that they threw the people out from their homes into the countryside. They had no tents. Some found shelter in caves. Everyone else just squatted under trees or in the fields. It was November, but much colder than this year. By December there was thick snow. He said several babies died from exposure.'

Wadeer continued shouting, hands flying in the air in a series of graphic gestures.

'He says he was thirty-five at the time, but that both his parents were very old, over seventy. He says that they cried for many days because they had lost their homes and their land.'

'What Wadeer has not said,' pointed out Elias Jacob, calmly consulting his fact sheet, 'was that before we left, each of the 1,050 villagers was given a number, granting them Israeli citizenship. We tidied and cleaned our houses because we thought we would soon be allowed back. After a time the Minister for Minorities, Mr Bichor Shitrit, came here. He saw that we were living under trees and ordered that we be given the houses here in Jish which had been vacated by fleeing Muslims. He said that we should wait for just fifteen days, and after that, when the area was calm, we could go back to Kafr Bir'im. In the meantime he allowed a few old men to stay in the village to guard the houses and the crops.'

'What happened then?' I asked.

'Six months later the old men were ordered out of the village, and it became clear that we were not going to get our houses back. So we decided to take the matter to the Israeli High Court.'

'The people of Bir'im have never resorted to violence,' said

Fr. Suleiman. 'We have always fought by law and by Christian principles.'

'In 1953 we finally won the case,' continued Elias. 'The court ordered that the evictions were unjust and said we should all be allowed back to our homes and to farm our fields.'

'So why aren't you back there now?' I asked.

'Because the next day the Israeli army declared the area a military zone and banned us from entering it. That afternoon they destroyed Kafr Bir'im by aerial bombardment. We had won the case, but they tricked us all the same. There was nothing we could do.'

Wadeer frowned and banged his fist on the table. Again Sami translated: 'He says all the villagers went up onto that hill and watched the bombing of their homes. They call it the Crying Hill now, because everyone from Kafr Bir'im wept that day. Everything they owned was still in those houses.'

'My father told me they didn't know what was going to happen until they heard the planes begin their bombing,' said Fr. Suleiman. 'It was 16 September 1953. They thought it was going to be the day they returned to their homes. But it was the day we lost them – and our fields – for ever.'

'I had built a house with my own hands,' said Elias. 'It had five rooms. But I lived in it only five months. Everything went. My furniture, cupboards, beds, icons. Worst of all, I lost my books.'

'I remember my father telling me what a wonderful village it was,' said Fr. Suleiman. 'The climate was very good. The soil was fertile. The air was fresh . . .'

'There were figs, olives, grapes, apples, springs of fresh water . . .' said Elias.

'And many wells,' added Wadeer in Arabic. 'I can see the whole village very clearly when I close my eyes. I remember every house, every building.'

'But when the Israeli air force began bombing there was nothing we could do,' said the old teacher. 'We could do nothing – nothing but go up to the hill and spend the whole day weeping like children.'

'We were betrayed,' said Wadeer.

'We still feel betrayed,' added Fr. Suleiman.

A silence fell over the balcony.

'So what happened to your land?' I asked eventually.

'In 1949 they gave some of our fields to a new kibbutz, Kibbutz Bar'am,' said the teacher, consulting his precious list of facts and figures. 'The kibbutz was built on 350 dunums of our land. Then in 1963 they established Moshav Dovev, with another two thousand dunums.'

'The site of the village is now a National Park,' said Fr. Suleiman. 'At the entrance to it they have put up a sign saying that "Bar'am Antiquities" date from the Second Temple Period. It's true that there are the ruins of a Roman-period synagogue in the middle of our village, but the sign gives the impression that the remains of our houses are all Roman ruins. The schoolchildren who are taken around it think that our old buildings – our stables and schools and houses – are like the ones you see at Pompeii.'

'We've been edited out of history,' said the old teacher. 'They don't admit to our existence. Or to the existence of our fathers and grandfathers and great-grandfathers.'

'I and my father dug a well,' said Wadeer. 'Now there is a sign there saying that it was built by someone called Yohanan of Bar'am at the time of the Romans.'

'Who is Yohanan of Bar'am?'

'Apparently a leader of the Jewish Revolt in 66 A.D.,' said the teacher. 'Though we in the village had never heard of him until the park was built.'

'They've made it as if my well is part of ancient Jewish history,' said Wadeer. 'But I dug that well with my own labour!'

'Another man, a friend of mine called Farah Laqzaly, made a sculpture of the Madonna,' said Elias. 'I remember seeing him making it. But now they say it is centuries old. They took it to Kibbutz Sasa and put it on display.'

'If the village is now a park, does that mean I could go and visit it?' I asked.

'Of course,' said Fr. Suleiman. 'And we will come too. No one from Bir'im misses a chance to return.'

Everyone rose. Wadeer and Fr. Suleiman's nephew John went in the priest's old station wagon, while Sami and I followed with Elias the schoolteacher. It was a short drive from Jish to Kafr Bir'im, less than ten minutes.

At the entrance to the park new Israeli flags were flying above a neat parking lot. In it sat two enormous tour buses. A large sign next to the ticket office did indeed read BAR'AM ANTIQUITIES, just as Fr. Suleiman had said. In English and Hebrew – though not in Arabic – it told the ancient Jewish history of the site. No mention was made of the medieval and modern Arab history of the ruins, and there was no reference to the bombing of the village in 1953. The brochure available at the ticket office was a little more forthcoming, remarking at the end of a long description of the synagogue that 'until 1948 Bar'am was a Maronite Christian village. During the War of Independence, the villagers were evacuated and the site is now under the auspices of the National Parks Authority.'

Fr. Suleiman shrugged when I showed him the leaflet. 'Of course they do not tell the truth of what really happened to us,' he said, adding proudly and without irony, 'But at least they don't make me pay to get in. It's because I'm a priest, you see.'

Meanwhile the two old men were already halfway across the ruins. Far from being depressed at seeing the flattened remains of their childhood village, they were almost skipping with excitement: 'It always makes us happy to breathe the air of Bir'im,' said Wadeer.

'The Daous' house stood over there,' said Elias, pointing to some foundations sticking out of the carefully manicured grass. 'The family of Ghattas lived beside them in that house, beside the pine trees. After 1948 two of their boys ended up in Brazil, where they became famous footballers. You haven't heard of Rai and Socrates? They played in the World Cup. Now, see over there, where those American tourists are standing? Yes, those two with the baseball caps. Those are the ruins of the old synagogue. And over here: that's our church. It was the one building the Israelis left standing when they flattened our homes.'

'And those gothic arches?' I asked. 'To the side of the church. Are they Crusader?'

'No, no,' said Elias, frowning. 'Those arches are all that remains of my school. This was my classroom.'

Elias stood in the middle of what was now a carefully tended patch of grass. 'For four years I taught in here, from 1944 to 1948. This was the door. The blackboard was here. But that was forty-five years ago now.'

Wadeer began rattling away in Arabic; this time it was Fr. Suleiman who translated.

'He says he was taught in here. In his day it was a Jesuit school. The teacher afterwards became the Maronite Patriarch, Cardinal Kreish. He was very strict. He would beat the children with a canvas shoe and sometimes also with a stick.'

Wadeer walked over to the corner of the plot, making whacking gestures with his wrist.

'He says the stick was kept here. Everyone in the class tasted the stick. No one dared to play tricks.'

Fr. Suleiman had got out his keys and was now opening the door into the churchtower. We all followed him up the winding stairs. Halfway up, Wadeer began to gesture excitedly at the wall of the staircase.

'Look! Look!' he said. 'Yes, here: here is my name. I was fifteen when I wrote that.'

At the top, a grille in the roof looked down into the nave below. Through it you could see two graves.

'That was the grave of the parish priest,' said Fr. Suleiman. 'They let us bury him here in 1956. It was the first time we had been allowed back into the village since the bombing. The military gave us authorisation, as long as we didn't take more than three hours.'

'Between 1948 and 1967 there were soldiers everywhere,' said Elias. 'We were not allowed to come here at all.'

'Once my goats escaped and came here,' said Wadeer. 'I came to get them back and was caught. They took me to the military tribunal in Nazareth. I spent a month in prison and had to pay a large fine.'

'Now it is much better,' said Fr. Suleiman. 'If we pay, we can come as often as we like. And they let us use the church for free on Easter, Christmas, Palm Sunday and Pentecost. Also for burials. They do not charge us for that.'

All six of us were now standing against the parapet looking out over the countryside around us.

'When we come here we are happy,' said Elias. 'All the old memories come back. We remember many things: the streets, the homes, the neighbours. Everything. My house was over there, at the end of the village to the right. But it was completely destroyed.'

'Over there,' said Wadeer, pointing to the horizon, 'that is the hill where we stood when they destroyed the village.'

'See through those trees?' said Fr. Suleiman, pointing into the distance. 'That is Kibbutz Bar'am. And over there, to the north? That's Moshav Dovev. They took two parts of our land, but this, to the south: that is free. Where the forest is now growing, that used to be our fig trees and our vineyards. There are ten thousand *dunums* which are not used. That is all we want.'

'It would be so easy,' said Elias. 'We don't even need ten thousand *dunums*. Five thousand *dunums* would do. We would accept anything.'

We began to file down the stairs. The priest closed and locked the door behind us.

'But, you see, they are worried it would be a precedent,' said Fr. Suleiman as we walked back to the carpark, past the American tourists who were now eating a picnic at a wooden table by the ticket office. 'They say that once you let one Arab back, you admit that the others have rights too. That is why, despite everything, they dare not give us back what is ours. Israel says it is a democracy, and it is true. But it seems that for us Palestinians there is no justice.'

'We've told the government that Kafr Bir'am is like a house of three rooms,' said Elias, looking back at his old village. 'One is now the kibbutz. One is the moshav. One is empty. We don't ask much. But that we must have.'

VI

HOTEL METROPOLE, ALEXANDRIA, EGYPT,
1 DECEMBER 1994

I am sitting writing in the first-floor breakfast room of the Hotel Metropole. At the far side of the room waiters in white jackets and black bow ties hover at the edge of the parquet floor; a classical frieze of naiads and centaurs runs along the dado overhead. Pale warm winter sun streams in through the open shutters; outside you can hear the rattle and clang of the trams and the clip-clop of horse-drawn cabs passing up the Grand Corniche. The sky is clear, the wind is high, and beyond a shivering screen of palms the Mediterranean stretches out into the distance.

After the incessant tensions and hatreds of Israel, the glib self-righteousness of the settlers and the bleak despair of the Palestinians, Alexandria feels refreshingly detached from the troubles of the Middle East; indeed it feels detached from the Middle East altogether. The cafés with their baroque mirrors and gleaming tables have a vaguely French or Viennese air to them, while the façades of the townhouses with their stained tempera and shuttered windows are strikingly Italianate. But, if anything, the city feels Greek. Alexandria was, after all, founded by a Greek and remained a Greek-dominated town until the 1950s, when Nasser expropriated the Greeks' banks and businesses and expelled the families who owned them. The Jews, the French and the English were thrown out at the same time, leaving the city – always something of a European expatriate exiled on the coast of Africa – a cold cadaver, its magnificent art deco buildings still intact but emptied of the men and women who built and owned them, a city 'clinging to the minds of old men like traces of perfume on a sleeve: Alexandria the capital of Memory'.

I first came to Alexandria through the pages of Lawrence Durrell's *Alexandria Quartet*. A bound volume of the four novels has accompanied me all the way through this journey, and has formed a welcome counterpoint to the sometimes grim otherworldiness of the monasteries I have visited on the way. During long monastic mid-afternoons, when the sun beat down on the dust-dry guest rooms and nothing stirred, with no noise to break the slow intake and recoil of the cell's faded curtains, how reassuring it could be to set aside the *Sayings of the Desert Fathers* and sit reading instead of brothels and dancing girls, of corrupt merchants and voluptuous landowners, 'libertines who were prepared to founder in the senses as deeply as any Desert Father in the mind', as Balthazar puts it in *Justine*.

From my table I can see across Saad Zagloul Square to the Hotel Cecil, where Justine first makes her appearance 'amid the dusty palms, dressed in a sheath of silver drops, softly fanning her cheeks with a little reed fan'. The gilded birdcage lift is still there; potted palms still frame the great marble staircase in the lobby. But the cast is impossibly different from the bright thirties figures with whom Durrell peoples his novels. There are no beautiful Jewish women with dark gloves and skimpy cocktail dresses; no pashas or beys arriving for secret assignations in their great silver Rolls-Royces; no Armenian bankers discussing intrigues amid the potted palms. Instead Alexandria is now, for possibly the first time in its history, a truly Egyptian city, looking more towards the deserts of the south than to the wider Mediterranean world.

Deserted by its entrepreneurs – its Greeks and Jews and Armenians – impoverished by nationalisation and decades of corrupt state socialism, Alexandria is now full of Egyptian holidaymakers dressed in their village *gelabiyas* and turbans. *Mukhtars* from the delta – rough-skinned, unshaven – sit cross-legged on the esplanade nibbling nuts or watching through clouds of smoke as the barrow-vendors fry whitebait or grill their corncobs. The old art deco mansions of the seafront have been divided up into decrepit hotels and poky flats. There is laundry hung out to dry on each collapsing balcony, and brickwork showing through the leprous stucco. Below, under the flapping awnings of the cafés, *fellahin* women with tattoos on their faces sit nibbling at sticky pastries.

The shops and hotels may still recall the multinational Levant of the late Ottoman Empire – Épicerie Ghaffour, Cinéma Metro, Hotel Windsor, Maison Paul, Bijoux Youssouffian – and some of the most famous names are still extant: the Trianon, even Pastroudis (where the fictional Nessim would drink coffee with Justine, and where, in reality, Cavafy would sip coffee with E.M. Forster). But, like everywhere else in the old Ottoman world, the multinational has given way to the mono-ethnic, the cosmopolitan to the narrowly national, and all these establishments are now Egyptian-owned and now have a specifically Egyptian – not an international – flavour.

You have to look quite hard to find any last remnants of the old order lurking in the backstreets of the town. At the synagogue, now heavily guarded by paramilitary Egyptian police, Joe Harari, the elderly custodian, opened the great double doors to reveal the echoing emptiness of the vast neo-classical prayer hall.

'Over a thousand people could fit in here,' said Joe. 'And this was just one of fifteen synagogues in Alexandria.'

Each of the one thousand seats had a nameplate on the back, but now only sixty Jews are left in Alexandria, a city that once, in the early centuries A.D., had the largest Jewish population in the world. Moreover, there is no rabbi, and as these last survivors are almost exclusively old women, there are not enough men left to form a *minyan* (quorum). So the synagogue remains unused, except by a family of pigeons roosting above the *bema*.

'Israel took all our young men,' said Joe as we sat drinking coffee in his office afterwards. Above his head, flanking the framed photographs of President Mubarak and the Lubavitch Rebbe, were wooden plaques recording the names of the synagogue's donors:

Mme Esther Hopasha, L.E.5,000; Jacques Riche, L.E.200; Emilio Levi, L.E.50 . . .

'Now there is peace,' said Joe, 'maybe some of them will return.'

'Did you ever consider emigrating?' I asked.

'I was born in Alex,' replied the old man. 'My mother is from Alex. All my life I have lived in Alex. I was married here. I've seen Israel for one week only, when I was taken there by Sadat. Why should I go?' The old man gestured at the streets behind him: 'This is my home,' he said.

'What do you miss most of the old days?' I asked.

'Family,' he replied. 'Sisters, cousins, friends. When they had to leave, everyone cried. My sister had to sell her house in one week. She was alone – her husband was away – so she had to manage by herself, with two small children. Of course she got a very bad price. She left with just two suitcases. Almost everything was left behind. Now one of her sons in the States is Vice President of . . . of . . . something beginning with tri. Trident? Tristar?' Joe beamed proudly.

'Israel was necessary, maybe,' he added. 'But because of it Alexandria can never be as before.'

'You should have seen it,' agreed Olga Rabinovitch, who had just walked into the office and had overheard Joe's last remark. Olga was a thin, elegant old lady with brightly rouged lips. She must once have been very beautiful. This, I thought, was what Justine would look like now if she had stayed on in Alexandria.

'Ahh,' she sighed, sitting down. 'When I was young – sixteen, seventeen, eighteen – the operas came from France. The theatre, the ballet . . .'

'Edith Piaf visited once,' said Joe.

'And the streets!' said Olga. Her right hand caressed the thin string of seed pearls hung around her neck. 'You should have seen the shops. You should have seen Sharif Street in the thirties!'

'The beautiful women . . .'

'The most lovely women in the world.'

'. . . with beautiful dresses and jewellery . . .'

'What luxury there was!'

'There used to be so much work. So much prosperity . . .'

'Of course, it's changed completely.'

'For a`start, in the old days the Egyptians were not much in evidence here.'

'The kind of people you see on the Corniche. They would not have been there.'

'They were living in the suburbs. This area was like a European colony.'

'Now anyone who is not an Egyptian is like a fly in the milk.'

'It's a complete change.'

'All the beautiful old villas with trees and flowers – they've destroyed everything to build these . . . awful, *awful*, ugly buildings.'

'When I go around now, I get lost.'

'To live here now you have to stay at home,' said Joe, toying with his coffee cup. 'Just to look at the streets makes me sad.'

'Some of the Egyptians are very nice,' said Olga. 'But they are the old ones. Brought up with Europeans.'

'And they don't go out much.'

'You know I live in a home for old ladies now?' said Olga. She sounded bewildered by the information, as if she had just woken up there for the first time that morning. 'It is called the Casa di Riposo – run by the Italian sisters. I left my apartment: it was too big and my servant got sick. The home is very nice, very clean. But I have nothing to do.' She crossed her legs: 'I sold everything. Except a portrait of myself when I was young.'

'She was so beautiful,' said Joe. 'You cannot imagine.'

'Everyone looks at it and says, "Oh, how beautiful!" But look at me. You wouldn't know now, would you?'

Olga looked at me. Again she asked, this time almost surprised: 'Would you?'

Five minutes' walk from the synagogue, opposite the Metro Cinema, lies the Élite Café. Its octogenarian owner, Miss Christina – all kaftan and coloured beads – is one of Alexandria's few remaining Greeks.

'Alexandria was a Greek town,' she said, sitting down at a table near the window. 'But few of us are left. Every year, little by little, we get smaller. In twenty years no one will be left.'

Miss Christina gestured to the dance floor at the back of the café: 'See over there?' she said. 'When I was young we used to have a Greek dance-band at the back here. We were dancing until two, three o'clock in the morning. Going out, eating breakfast at the Cecil, then off somewhere else.'

'But no longer.'

'No!' Miss Christina laughed. 'Things are very calm now. The Egyptians don't dance. They are very polite. They like their families. They go to bed early. And the Greeks who are left are not much better.'

'No?'

'No. The Greeks here are not so rich or so interesting. They are neither industrialists nor poets. They're just shopkeepers. None have . . . you know, pictures by Picasso or Cézanne or anything nice like that. All the old families – the Dositsas, the Antoniadis, the Sakalaritas – they've all gone.'

Miss Christina shrugged her shoulders. 'Now books are my greatest friends here. Even if they have given me cataracts from reading by bad light in bed.'

I asked whether the change in Alexandria had happened slowly.

'Phh!' spluttered Miss Christina, raising her eyebrows. 'It happened overnight. After Nasser threw the Europeans out everything ground to a halt: the Italian opera, the French concerts, the theatre. Before that Alexandria was like Paris. It was the most creative town – all these different cultures collaborating and mingling with each other: conferences, lectures, galleries . . . This was the café of the artists. They would all come here. Particularly the writers and the poets.'

'Lawrence Durrell?'

'No, I never met him. But I liked *Justine*. I think it's a good portrait. In fact I have a cat named Justine. But she is very old now.'

'What about Cavafy? Did you know him?'

'Yes, Cavafy I knew very well! Of course, as he died in '33, he was an old man when I was a young girl. But he used to come here every day. We have five of his original manuscripts, including "The God Abandons Antony".'

'So your family knew him very well?'

'His house was just around the corner, in rue Lepsius, and I suppose we did see quite a lot of him. He loved this area. There was a brothel immediately below his rooms – the English used to call it rue Clapsius – the Patriarchal Church was nearby and the Greek Hospital was opposite. He used to say that the area had everything he ever needed in life: "Where could I live better? Below, the brothel caters for the flesh. And there is the church which forgives sin. And there is the hospital where we die."'

Miss Christina smiled. 'That's his portrait,' she said, pointing to a framed photograph at the back of the café. It showed a willowy young man in a three-piece suit with round Aldous Huxley spectacles, a centre parting and a rather anxious expression.

'He was a perfect gentleman: very well dressed,' said Miss Christina. 'But he was very serious. Never smiled. People used to try and talk to him but he always wanted to be alone. Perhaps he was thinking too much.'

Miss Christina sipped her coffee. 'Sometimes he could be very gloomy. He was unhappy whenever he looked in a mirror and saw himself getting older. Every night he would rub cream into his face to try and stop the wrinkles. I think he was afraid of death. But for all that, no one would dispute that he's the best poet in Greek this century.'

'Was he kind to you?'

'To me, yes. When he came here I would always give him a sweet-smelling flower, the *fouli*, a cousin of jasmine. I think he liked that. But in general he did not like women. It was because of his mother.'

'What do you mean?'

'He was the last of eight boys. His mother wanted very much a girl, so she dressed him as one, in little girlie dresses, caressing him very much: "Oh, my sweet boy! My sweet sweet Costakis! Oh, my darling." So he became a homosexual.'

Miss Christina lowered her voice and bent closer to me: 'He

wrote many poems about the bodies of young boys. But he was very careful. He did not expose himself.'

'Expose himself?'

'I mean he never published these homosexual poems,' hissed Miss Christina.

'Why?'

'Because,' said Miss Christina, 'he was absolutely terrified of what his mother might say.'

ALEXANDRIA, 5 DECEMBER

One morning in the first year of the twentieth century a donkey-herder was driving a mule train through the outskirts of Alexandria when the frontmost ass suddenly disappeared into the ground in front of him.

Such events are not uncommon in Alexandria: no other city in the world is given such frequent reminders of the cavernous chambers and unexplored treasures that lie buried just beneath its streets. Only recently a wedding was celebrated in the city centre near the supposed site of the Soma, the lost tomb of Alexander; the pavement opened beneath the bride and she was never seen again.

For centuries Alexandria was not just the capital of Egypt, she was the Queen of the Mediterranean, the greatest port of the classical world. 'She is undoubtedly the first city of the civilised world,' wrote Diodorus of Sicily in the first century B.C., 'certainly far ahead of the rest in elegance and extent and riches and luxury.' Her villas and temples, palaces and monuments, churches and colonnaded avenues extended for many miles beyond the limits of the modern city – and yet not one building of this legendary Alexandria survives today above the ground; everything is hidden beneath the mundane surface of the modern streetscape. Under the city's cheap hotels and bare-shelved shops, its brothels and seedy restaurants, lie many of the greatest buildings of antiquity: the Caesarium, where Cleopatra committed suicide; the Pharos lighthouse (one of the Seven Wonders of the World); the Great Alexandrian library with its seven hundred thousand scrolls; the Mouseion; the Serapium; the tomb of Alexander. All have disappeared, utterly and completely, so that at street level only a handful of fallen pillars and broken capitals remain to mark the site of some of the most magnificent buildings the world has ever seen.

Yet, subtly, the ancient city continues to make its presence felt. Every so often the earth will give way and some unsuspecting Alexandrian will plummet into the cellars of a lost temple or a forgotten palace crypt. Certainly when, in 1900, the donkey disappeared into the ground, the muleteer knew exactly what to do. The authorities were summoned, and they in turn summoned the archaeologists. In a short time work had begun on uncovering one of the most extraordinary complexes of catacombs to survive from the ancient world.

I walked over there this morning from my hotel. Off the backstreets of the town, in a narrow lane blocked by donkey carts and lined with teashops full of old men with hubble bubbles, a low-roofed roundhouse gives onto a circular flight of stairs. The shaft corkscrews downwards for turn after turn, until it leads quite suddenly into a honeycomb of underground chambers. These rock-cut caverns with their flat limestone divans were feasting rooms where bereaved families would meet to toast the memory of dead relatives; though the catacombs were long forgotten, even to legend, the broken fragments of the pots and plates left over from these feasts have given the area its modern Arabic name, Kom el Shogafa, the Mound of Shards.

From the feasting halls, the galleries lead down again, deeper into the ground, darker, further from the light. Down here in the partially flooded depths of the complex lie the burial chambers themselves. What is so odd about this part of the catacomb is less the size or magnificence of the mortuary chambers than the bizarre nature of their decoration. At first sight this decoration appears merely standard Pharaonic: a pair of Egyptian papyrus capitals lead into an inner chamber where the jackal-headed figure of Anubis stands over a recumbent mummy, holding in his hand the bloody heart of the dead man; to one side falcon-headed Horus looks on, impassive.

But the more closely you look, the odder the reliefs become. Flanking the pillars on either side are a pair of medallions sculpted with Greek Gorgon heads, below which rises, in high relief, a pair of very Roman bearded serpents from whose powerfully piled coils emerge the suggestively phallic pinecone sceptre of Dionysus and the serpent wand of Hermes. More confusingly still, on either side of the entrance door stands a single figure. To one side is Anubis again, still with his dog's head, but now dressed up as a Roman legionary with breastplate, short sword, lance and shield; flanking him is an image of the Nile god Sobek, who, despite being a crocodile, has also been squeezed into a legionary's uniform. Whole cultures are colliding here: it seems that the Graeco-Egyptian burial syndicate who commissioned this strange complex would think nothing of being buried in Greek sarcophagi and guarded by Egyptian gods in Roman military uniform.

This subterranean tomb, at first sight merely eerie, is in fact vastly important. A random quirk of fate has left this small upper-middle-class burial chamber as the sole object in the entire city that looks now almost exactly as it would have done to an ancient Alexandrian; it is, therefore, one of the only indicators of the mood of Alexandria at a time when that city was about to become the intellectual capital of Christianity. That mood, as is indicated by the strange syncretic catacomb sculptures, was one of exceptional intellectual tolerance and experimentation: it was a city where, even in death, the inhabitants would attempt to fuse opposites, to reconcile two entirely different artistic traditions and religious pantheons, to mix deities as lightly as Durrell's Alexandrians would mix their cocktails.

This, then, was the heady world into which, in the late first century A.D., Christianity was about to be thrown – and from which the religion would emerge with its theological underpinnings and its artistic iconography altered for ever.

Alexandria was the scholarly capital of the late classical world. Situated at the meeting place of trade routes linking both Asia and Africa with Europe it was quite natural that the city should be a centre of intellectual ferment. Indian *sadhus* wandered its streets, debating with Greek philosophers, Jewish exegetes and Roman architects. It was here that Euclid wrote his treatise on geometry, that Eratosthenes measured the diameter of the world (he was only fifty-four miles out), that Ptolemy produced his astonishing maps and that a great team of seventy-two Hellenistic Jews produced the *Septuagint*, the first Greek translation of the Old Testament.

The same spirit of breezy internationalism that guided the scholars of Alexandria also informed its mystics and its priests. Religions in Alexandria were notoriously porous, ideas and images from one faith trickling imperceptibly into another: the Alexandrian god Serapis, for example, combined elements of the Egyptian cults of both Osiris and Apis, grafted onto that of Greek Zeus.

The arrival of Christianity from Palestine at first merely added to the mix. In the second century, Clement of Alexandria regarded pagan Greek philosophy as divinely inspired, and wrote of Christ driving his chariot across the heavens like the Sun God; indeed many pagans (including the young Tertullian) believed, perhaps correctly, that the Alexandrian Christians actually worshipped the sun, meeting as they did on Sunday, and praying to the east, where the sun rises. Other Alexandrian Christians undoubtedly worshipped Serapis. As late as the early fifth century a pagan philosopher from Alexandria, Synesius, was chosen to be a bishop although he was not even a baptised Christian. He accepted on the condition that though he might 'speak in myths' in church, he should be free to 'think as a philosopher' in private. It was this cross-fertilisation of Christianity with Alexandrian Greek philosophy that drew the developing Christian doctrines away from the strictly Jewish traditions which had given them birth, and which raised the religion – initially a simple series of precepts addressed to the poor and illiterate – to the level of high philosophy.

The evidence of the confusion that resulted from this promiscuous conjunction can be seen most clearly in the Alexandrian Graeco-Roman Museum. Here, in gallery after gallery, there is an easy drift of pagan and Christian motifs, styles, subjects and iconographies. The *ankh*, the Pharaonic symbol of life, appears on early Christian Alexandrian gravestones transformed into an ambiguous looped cross. The image of Isis nursing Horus is reused in the Christian era unchanged, but now depicts the Virgin suckling the Christ child. A sword-wielding Anubis, holding the heart of a corpse, sprouts wings and turns into St Michael weighing the souls of the dead. Apollo raises a lamb over his shoulders and becomes the Good Shepherd. The Romano-Egyptian image of a mounted Horus in Roman military uniform lancing the Seth-crocodile transforms itself into St George on his charger spearing the dragon. Dionysian vine scrolls tangle around scenes of the vintage; the same scrolls, hastily baptised with a cross, tangle on unchanged into the Christian era as a Eucharistic symbol. Nereids and victories swoop down from capitals and turn into angels midflight; pagan deities – Osiris and Aphrodite, Orpheus and Dionysus, Leda and the Zeus-Swan – survive into an afterlife as demons and godlings, removed from the centre of shrines but lurking still unvanquished at the back of Alexandrian churches, as in the dark recesses of Egyptian folk memory, peeping down from architraves or glaring maliciously from the metopes or dadoes.

Amid this fizz of dissolving philosophies, this iconographic metamorphosis, there is a thrilling feeling of being present at the birth of medieval art. On all sides one can hear the soft ripping of gossamer as old pagan images emerge from the Alexandrian chrysalis transformed into the conventional Christian symbols, the same symbols and images that will carry on reappearing in gospel books and altarpieces, stained glass and frescoes, diptychs and triptychs, fixed and immutable for centuries to come.

This afternoon, after a siesta, I returned to the garden of the Graeco-Roman Museum. There I sat in the shade of an orange tree, surrounded by fragments of Byzantine sculpture, reading John Moschos's account of the now buried city from which these sculptures had come.

Moschos and Sophronius spent so much time in Alexandria that in one of his books, Sophronius, a native of Damascus, actually refers to 'us Alexandrians'. The two monks probably paid their first visit to the city in the winter of 578–9, at the very beginning of their travels. They may have had the same weather I am having now: crisp, sunny days growing slowly colder and shorter. Nearly thirty years later the two monks returned, this time by sea, as refugees fleeing the sack of Antioch by the marauding Persian army. On both occasions, Alexandria was their base for an extensive exploration of the monasteries of desert Egypt, reaching, on their second trip, as far south as the Great Oasis.

During this second Alexandrian period, the two monks appear to have based themselves in the city on and off for the seven years between 607 and 614 A D. During this period Sophronius seems to have been suddenly struck down with blindness, then equally suddenly cured during a visit to the Shrine of Saints Cyrus and John at Menuthis (the shrine's own name eventually came to replace Menuthis, so that for the last thousand years the place has been known as Abukir). In gratitude for his miraculous healing, Sophronius wrote a book containing stories of some of the shrine's more remarkable cures, in the process of which he allows us an intriguing peek into what was contained in a Byzantine doctor's bag: if Sophronius is to be believed, a standard prescription was a compote of Bithynian cheese, wax, and roast crocodile.

Following Sophronius's cure, the two monks began to campaign energetically against the Monophysite leanings of the local Egyptians, tendencies that had already begun to lead to a schism between mainstream Orthodoxy (identified with Egypt's Greek-speaking, Alexandrian-based upper class) and the indigenous Coptic-speaking Egyptians (the word Copt simply deriving from the Greek term for a native Egyptian, *Aiguptios*).

Finally, however, in the spring of 614, the Persian army caught up with the two monks. As the Persians breached the walls of the city and put it to the sword, Moschos and Sophronius were again forced to take ship. This time they were accompanied by John the Almsgiver, Alexandria's Orthodox Patriarch, whose biography Sophronius was later to write. In a state of some distress, the party stopped off in Cyprus, where the heartbroken Patriarch died. The boatload of refugees finally reached the safety of the walls of Constantinople some time later, probably towards the end of the year 615.

The burning city they left behind had clearly changed dramatically since the prosperous, free-thinking days of the second and third centuries A.D. This was not just because Alexandria was already full of penniless refugees fleeing the earlier Persian assault on Palestine; the change was more profound. For in Alexandria the triumph of Christianity had been effected by hordes of often fanatical Coptic monks who would periodically sweep down from their desert monasteries, attacking the pagans and their shrines, and burning any temples left undefended; in 392 A.D. they finally succeeded in burning the Serapium, and with it the adjacent Alexandrian library, storehouse of the collected learning of antiquity.

The houses of the city's pagan notables were ransacked in the monks' search for idols; no one was safe. The most notorious outrage was the lynching of Hypatia, a neoplatonic philosopher of the School of Alexandria and a brilliant thinker and mathematician. She was pulled from her palaquin by a lynch-mob of monks, who stripped her, then dragged her naked through the streets of the town before finally killing her in front of the Caesarion and burning her body.

This murder was applauded by the monastic chroniclers. 'Hypatia was devoted to her magic, astrolabes, and instruments of music,' wrote Bishop John of Nikiu. 'She beguiled many people through her satanic wiles. [After her murder] all the people surrounded the Patriarch Cyril [who had instigated the mob] and called him "the new Theophilus" for he had [completed the work of Patriarch Theophilus who had burned the Serapium and] destroyed the last remains of idolatry in the city.' The pagans, understandably, were less enthusiastic: 'Things have happened the like of which haven't been seen through all the ages,' wrote one distraught student to his mother in Upper Egypt. 'Now it's cannibalism, not war.' 'If we are alive,' commented another, 'then life itself is dead.'

Nevertheless, there are hints that the intellectual spirit in the city had not died completely. According to Moschos's near-contemporary, the historian Ammianus Marcellinus, 'even now in that city the various branches of learning make their voices heard; for the teachers of the arts are somehow still alive, the geometer's rod reveals hidden knowledge, the study of music has not yet dried up and some few still keep the fires burning in the study of the movement of the earth and stars. The study of medicine grows greater every day, so that a doctor who wishes to establish his standing in the profession can dispense with the need for any proof, by merely saying that he trained at Alexandria.' This seems to have been true: it was in Alexandria that Caesarius, brother of the theologian Gregory of Nazianzen, obtained the qualifications that won him the post of Byzantine Court Physician.

Certainly Alexandria seems to have brought the scholar in Moschos to the fore, and his account of his time in the city depicts him and Sophronius (who was, after all, a Sophist, a teacher of philosophy and rhetoric) engaged in high-minded intellectual pursuits. In one story the pair are attending lectures at the university by Theodore the Philosopher; in another talking to the calligrapher and book illuminator Zoilus the Reader; on yet another occasion, in a charming picture of bookish Byzantine life, they are visiting a bibliophile named Cosmas the Lawyer.

'This wondrous man greatly benefited us,' wrote Moschos, 'not only by letting us see him and by teaching us, but also because he had more books than anybody else in Alexandria and would willingly supply them to those who wished. Yet he was a man of no possessions. Throughout his house there was nothing to be seen but books, a bed and a table. Any man could go in and ask for what would benefit him – and read it. Each day I would go in to him.'

The most intriguing story of all, however, concerns a visit to another scholar friend. The tale is set one hot summer afternoon sometime in the late 580s, with Moschos and Sophronius sheltering from the midday heat in the shade of the monumental *tetrapylon* at the centre of Alexandria. The monks had set out to visit another bibliophile friend, Stephen the Sophist, but Stephen's maid had shouted out of the top window that her master was fast asleep. So while they waited for the Sophist to finish his siesta, the pair amused themselves by eavesdropping on a conversation between three blind men who were also taking advantage of the *tetrapylon*'s shade. They were passing the time by telling each other how they had lost their sight, and the last of the men told a strange and macabre story which Moschos records.

Before he lost his sight, said the blind man, he had been a grave-robber. One day he saw a richly-decked-out corpse being taken through the streets of Alexandria for burial in the Church of St John, and he had made up his mind to plunder the grave. When the funeral had finished, the man broke into the sepulchre and began to strip the tomb. Suddenly he gave a start: the dead man appeared to sit up before him and stretch out his hands towards the grave-robber's eyes. It was the last thing, said the blind man, that he ever saw.

Later on, Moschos heard a similar story about another grave-robber who had broken into a rich girl's tomb in the depths of the night. Again the corpse seemed to come to life, only this time the girl grabbed the robber: 'You came in here when you wanted to,' she said, 'but you will not go out of here as you will. This tomb will be shared by the two of us.' The corpse refused to let the robber go until he promised to repent and become a monk. In shock, the man agreed.

When I first read these stories I had assumed them to be pious superstition, like many of Moschos's other tales. But this afternoon, reading *The Spiritual Meadow* in the museum garden, I suddenly understood where such tales originated. For from the first century A.D. through to the early Byzantine period, it was the custom in Egypt to bury those who could afford it in mummy cases onto which were bound superb encaustic (hot wax) portraits of the deceased; in some cases – there are two fine examples in the Graeco-Roman Museum – full-length pictures were painted onto the mummy's winding sheet itself.

These mummy portraits throw a reflected beam of light on the lost world of classical portraiture, vanished now but for a few frescoes at Pompeii, and more importantly form a bridge between the painting of antiquity and the panel-painted icons of Byzantium. It can be no coincidence that the oldest icons in existence are to be found in St Catherine's Monastery in the Sinai, and that they are painted in the same encaustic technique as their Alexandrian mummy-portrait predecessors. If, as Otto Demus observed, 'the icon is the root-form of the European picture', then in these Graeco-Egyptian mummy-portraits we see the immediate genesis of the icon.

But it is as works of art that the mummy portraits are most striking. They are so real that you can almost hear the sitters speak – as Moschos's grave-robbers seem to have discovered. Even today, behind glass in a museum, the portraits are so astonishingly lifelike that they can still make you gasp as you find yourself staring eyeball to eyeball with a soldier who could have fought at Actium, or a society lady who may have known Cleopatra. There is something deeply hypnotic about the silent stare of these sad, uncertain Graeco-Roman faces, most of whom appear to have died in their early thirties. Their fleeting expressions are frozen, startled, as if suddenly surprised by death itself; their huge eyes stare out, as if revealing the nakedness of the departed soul. The viewer peers at them, trying to catch some hint of the upheavals they witnessed and the strange sights they must have seen in late antique Egypt. But the smooth neo-classical faces stare us down.

Perhaps the most disconcerting thing about these portraits is that they appear so astonishingly familiar: the colours and technique of some of them resemble Frans Hals, others Cézanne, and two thousand years after they were painted the faces still convey with penetrating immediacy the character of the different sitters: the fop and the courtesan, the anxious mother and the tough man of business, the bored army officer and the fat *nouveau-riche* matron, hung with gold, dripping with make-up. Indeed, so contemporary are the features, so immediately recognisable the emotions that play on the lips, that you have to keep reminding yourself that these sitters are not from our world, that they are masks attached to Graeco-Egyptian mummies, covering the desiccated corpses of people who possibly saw the world through the glass of an initiate in the cult of Isis, who maybe married their brother or sister (as late as the third century Diocletian was still trying to outlaw incest in Egypt) and who perhaps studied in the great Alexandrian library before it was burned to the ground by the howling monks of the Egyptian deserts.

As André Malraux put it, these mummy portraits 'glow with the flame of eternal life'. Certainly it is easy to imagine their effect on John Moschos's nervous grave-robbers breaking into a necropolis at night: no wonder they thought the dead had risen.

This evening, my final one in the city, following Miss Christina's directions I found my way along the tramlines to the gathering place of the last Greeks in Alexandria.

The Greek Club consisted of an empty hall, opening onto a trellised courtyard where twenty or thirty elderly Greek couples sat playing backgammon and poker. From the bar, tinned Greek music wafted out into the night. There I found Nicholas Zoulias, the President of the club and an old friend of Miss Christina. Soon a circle had gathered around our table as the old people began to pour out their memories of pre-war Alexandria. They were the same stories I had already heard in the synagogue and the Élite Café: how Alexandria had once been the Paris of the East, the diamond of the Mediterranean, how lively the place had been, how prosperous and creative; and also how little remained of what once was. But what I had not heard before, nor expected, was how little these old men thought of Greece. They regarded Alexandria, their own personal city state, as the apogee of civilisation, and looked on modern Greece as some sort of ill-mannered *parvenu*.

'Alexandria was always more sophisticated than Athens or Saloniki,' explained Nicholas Zoulias, lighting a cigarette. 'One hundred years ago, when Athens was still a village, Alexandria was a cosmopolitan city.'

'Everything you wanted was here,' agreed Taki Katsimbris.

'We don't like the Greeks,' said Michael Stephanopoulos. 'To be honest, I can't live there more than fourteen days.'

'Athens is just the nightclub of Europe,' said Zoulias, sucking his teeth in contempt. 'Nothing more.'

'The Greeks in Greece are more rough than we are,' said Michael.

'They don't know languages as we do,' said Zoulias. 'French, Arabic, English . . .'

'They are as rough as Turks,' said Michael. 'In Greece, if you ask what time it is, they don't answer.'

'If you ask an address in Greece, they will say they don't know. Here they will show you. They'll take you there.'

'They don't have a tradition of hospitality.'

'We are different from them,' said Zoulias. 'We have different food, different speech, different morals . . .'

'We are more like the Egyptians,' said Taki. 'We have the same mentality as them.'

'Many of our grandmothers would wear the veil.'

'They even used to pray like the Egyptians: with a carpet on the floor.'

'What's the difference between Christianity and Islam? It's the same God.'

'But there is nothing like that in Greece. They are very . . . narrow-minded over there. They think only they know what is right.'

'Greece is part of Europe,' said Zoulias, 'and they now have a very . . . automatic way of living. They have speed. They are always running. Here we have an easy way: *wahde wahde* – step by step.'

All the other old men nodded in agreement.

'Here the automobiles are slow,' said Michael. 'The railway is slow . . .'

'And slowly we are dying out,' added Taki.

No one disagreed with what he had said. I asked: 'How long will your community last?'

'Five, ten years at most,' said Zoulias.

'There are only five hundred of us left.'

'All the young are going to Athens. As soon as they finish school.'

'They say they get bored here. They say there are no jobs for them.'

'When Nasser nationalised our factories he signed our death warrant.'

'Many who were rich became beggars. He took everything we had.'

'But they found it easy to get jobs in Greece. Because of their skills and languages. So everyone went.'

'As Nasser had taken everything, they had no reason to stay.'

'When I was a boy there used to be two hundred thousand Greeks in Egypt. Two hundred thousand! Even ten years ago there were five thousand. Now there's just us.'

'We've got ten years. Maximum.'

'Unless those who left come back.'

'I don't think they will,' said Michael.

The old men shook their heads. Taki took a gulp of *arak*. 'They'll stay in Greece.'

'Leaving Alexandria without any Greeks.'

'After 2,300 years.'

'They won't come back.'

'No.'

'But who can say?' said Zoulias, lighting a cigarette. 'Who can say?'

I knew we were in for trouble the minute I saw the taxi.

It was a sort of prehistoric ancestor of the Peugeot, with a patchwork of repainted bumps and scars that gave it a vaguely scaly appearance, like a large lizard or a small dinosaur. The man who was to drive this beast was even less prepossessing. Ramazan was a Bedu from the Sinai. He wore a faded denim waistcoat over an off-white shift, and around his head he wrapped a red and white *keffiyeh*; his chin was darkened by a wispy stab at a beard.

We loaded my rucksack into the boot, and Ramazan turned the ignition. The Peugeot bucked, coughed and staggered like a disgruntled camel. Ramazan tried the ignition a second time, with equally disappointing results. He then got out and did to the car what Bedu tend to do to disgruntled camels who behave in a similar manner. He beat it on its side, kicked its chassis, then whispered some encouraging words into its bonnet. On the third attempt the car hiccupped grudgingly into life and we juddered drunkenly out of the hotel carpark.

I had arrived in Cairo off the Alexandrian train the day before, and had immediately set about trying to obtain permission to visit Asyut, the province in Upper Egypt where the majority of Egypt's Copts have always lived; it also contains the Great Oasis, modern Kharga, the southernmost point reached by Moschos on his travels.

The area has been closed to foreigners since its resurgent Islamic movement began widening its scope from taking occasional pot-shots at the local Copts – whom they have been shooting on and off since the founding of the Muslim Brotherhood in 1928 – to targeting foreign tourists as well. In the process they came close to destroying Egypt's tourist industry, and as a result foreigners have now been banned from the vicinity of Asyut. But journalists have occasionally been allowed into the area to report on the government's (often heavy-handed) attempts to quell the Islamist uprising. I therefore went straight to the Egyptian Press Centre, presented my credentials and duly made an application, in triplicate. I was told to return in a week. Rather than hang around Cairo, waiting for bureaucrats to shuffle my papers and rearrange their red tape, I decided to take the opportunity to visit two important Byzantine sites that I had always wanted to see.

The first was St Antony's, the birthplace of Christian monasticism and the greatest monastery in Byzantine Egypt. The second was the lost city of Oxyrhynchus, once one of Byzantine Egypt's most important provincial towns and subsequently the site of the discovery of the greatest treasure trove of Byzantine documents ever uncovered. Its ruins lay on the way to St Antony's, and when I looked at the map it seemed as if it would be easy to take it in on the way. What I did not take into account was Ramazan's driving. For five minutes the taxi juddered along at ever lower speed through the empty early-morning streets of Cairo. Then it finally stalled at a set of traffic lights. 'No problem,' said Ramazan, ducking to avoid the outsized pink velvet love-heart dangling from his mirror. 'No problem at all.'

As the cars behind hooted angrily, Ramazan disappeared behind the bonnet with a length of metal tubing. There followed the sound of hammering and a strong reek of diesel. Early attempts at reigniting the engine came to nothing, and Ramazan began to look a little worried. But quite suddenly, without anyone apparently turning the ignition key, the car bucked into life and off we set again.

The incident had taught Ramazan a lesson. Henceforth traffic lights were obstacles we carefully ignored, and we shot through all the others we came to with impressive gusto. At any other time of day Ramazan's tactics would have been suicidal. At 5.30 in the morning they were merely very frightening. Bar a couple of scratches on the boot – souvenirs of a brief clinch with a truck carrying watermelons – we emerged from Cairo remarkably unscathed, and headed off southwards, driving parallel to the Nile through the pretty villages of the fertile valley.

Here and there, groups of early risers were sitting outside under the vine trellising of the tea houses smoking the first hubble-bubble of the day; a few women were washing clothes by the canals. Through this pastoral scene Ramazan passed like a rugby player in a ballet. He clearly believed that the key to avoiding further stalling lay in keeping the car travelling at some speed. With this in mind he raced along, cutting into the opposite lane, swerving around bends, one minute narrowly avoiding killing two farmers chatting in the middle of the road, the next coming within inches of knocking down a fat sheikh in a blue shift ambling along on a donkey. In this manner we headed down the Nile, the world's most peaceful river transformed before my eyes into the setting for a one-man dragster rally.

Ramazan's driving may have been terrifying, but it got us to our destination in record time. After two hours' racing down the narrow strip of cultivation that flanks the banks of the Nile we reached Behnasa, the medieval Arab village which grew up on the edge of Oxyrhynchus's ruins. Passing through the village – in the process of which Ramazan came close to overturning an old horse-drawn brougham full of heavily veiled village women – we juddered out of the cultivation into the desert, searching for the ruins marked on my map. We drove into the dunes, then drove back again. The Western Desert stretched all around us, flat, inhospitable and echoingly empty. There were no temples, no pillars, no colonnaded streets, nothing at all except for a single small, mud-brick tomb belonging to a medieval Sufi sheikh.

It was while walking back from the tomb, baffled by the total absence of any visible remains, that I noticed for the first time what I was standing on. Every time my foot touched the ground, the sand appeared to crunch beneath my weight. Bending down, I looked more closely at the surface. The dunes all around were littered with pot shards: handles of amphorae, small roundels of red Samian-ware dishes, the decorated bases of cups, jugs, mugs and bowls. But it was not just pieces of pottery: fragments of brilliant aquamarine Byzantine glass glinted in the winter sun; beside them lay small lumps of slag and smelting clinker, fragments of jet, amber and garnet, pieces of bone and the shells of mussels and oysters.

I walked and walked for the rest of the morning, but the soft crunch underfoot did not stop: the midden extended for many miles. The town of Oxyrhynchus had clearly disappeared, destroyed – presumably – by generations of Nile floods and the robbing of the villagers of Behnasa; but its middens remained: epic drifts of Pharaonic, Graeco-Roman and Byzantine rubbish, left where it had been dropped by the street cleaners nearly two thousand years ago. I was standing on one of the great rubbish dumps of the ancient world.

Pulling at an amphora handle jutting out of the ground, I broke a Byzantine pot, and its contents, a pile of chaff winnowed, perhaps, while Justinian still ruled the Empire, floated away in the winter breeze.

The rubbish dumps of Oxyrhynchus first came to the attention of the outside world in 1895 when reports reached the British archaeologists Bernard Grenfell and Arthur Hunt that the area had begun to yield an extraordinary number of papyrus fragments. What the two men found when they visited the site, however, surpassed their wildest expectations.

'The papyri were, as a rule, not very far from the surface,' wrote Grenfell in the *Journal of the Egypt Exploration Fund* the following year. 'In one patch of ground, indeed, merely turning up the soil with one's boot would frequently disclose a layer of papyri . . . I proceeded to increase the number of workmen gradually up to 110, and, as we moved northwards over other parts of the site, the flow of papyri soon became a torrent which it was difficult to cope with . . .'

What was written on the papyri was every bit as remarkable as the sheer quantity of texts uncovered. On the second day of the excavations Dr Hunt was examining a crumpled fragment which had just been produced by the workmen. It contained only a few legible lines of text, but one of these contained the very rare Greek word '*karphos*', which means 'a mote'. Immediately Hunt made the connection with the verse in St Matthew's Gospel about the mote in your brother's eye and the beam in your own, but with a thrill he realised that the wording on the fragment differed significantly from that of the Gospel. The fragment turned out to be part of a lost collection of *The Sayings of Jesus*, which predated by hundreds of years any New Testament fragment then extant.

By the end of the first season Grenfell and Hunt had discovered an entire library of lost classics: a forgotten song by Sappho; fragments of lost plays by Aeschylus and Sophocles; the earliest papyrus of St Matthew's Gospel then known; a leaf of a previously unknown book of New Testament Apocrypha, *The Acts of Paul and Thecla*. They also unearthed great quantities of historical documents such as the report of an interview between the Emperor Marcus Aurelius and an Alexandrian magistrate, as well as an entire archive of Byzantine correspondence and administrative documents.

This last discovery was not a great cause of excitement to the Victorian excavators, brought up as they were with Gibbon's magisterial contempt for the late Roman Empire. Nevertheless, a century later, these documents are now usually regarded as the most important of all the finds from the site. For in the administrative flotsam from a provincial Byzantine town on the very edge of the Empire, we come closer to the lives of ordinary Byzantines than from any other surviving contemporary source; it casts a bright beam of light on the private life of the world John Moschos knew as he travelled through the last days of the Eastern Empire.

Before setting off on this journey, I had spent a week in the London Library poring through some of the 142 volumes of the Oxyrhynchus papyri that have so far been edited, translated and published. Taken together they provide a uniquely detailed picture of a late antique city: reading them is like opening a shutter onto a sunlit Byzantine street and eavesdropping on the gossip, the scandals and the secret affairs of the people milling about below.

It is the extraordinary randomness of the fragments that forms much of their fascination: we may have lost every one of the seven hundred thousand scrolls of high philosophy and world history stored in the great library of Alexandria, but in obscure Oxyrhynchus we meet the forgotten vendors in the street, the sleepy nightwatchmen on their shift, the disgruntled school-teachers in their classrooms, even the city's teenage girls creeping back from assignations with their lovers. A shoemaker promises to water the tree that stands outside his house. A husband writes to his wife asking her to come to him and 'bring the old cushion that is in the dining room'. A father writes to his son to complain that he has not kept in touch ('I have been much surprised, my son, at not receiving hitherto a letter from you to tell me how you are. Please answer me with all speed, for I am quite distressed . . .'). An indignant son complains to his father that he has been misrepresenting him ('You wrote to me: "You are staying in Alexandria with your paramour." Tell me then, who *is* my paramour?'). A pained lover in desperation scribbles down a spell or a prayer: 'Make her to be sleepless, to fly through the air, to love me with a most vehement love, hungry, thirsty and without sleep until she comes and melts her body with mine . . .'

Some of the most interesting Oxyrhynchus fragments read like pages of tabloid journalism. In one fragment a respectable matron writes to her husband in horror at the promiscuity of their children: 'If you want to know about the harlotries of your daughters, ask the priests of the church, not me, how they leaped out saying, "We want men" and how Lucra was found with her lover, making a whore of herself.'

In another fragment a wife writes to the Oxyrhynchus magistrate to complain about her husband's mistreatment of her and her family: 'Concerning all the insults uttered by him against me. He shut up his own slaves and mine with my foster daughters for seven days in his cellars, having insulted his slaves and my slave Zoe and half killed them with blows. Then he applied fire to my foster daughters, having stripped them quite naked which is contrary to the laws. He also said to the same foster daughters, "Give up all that is hers" . . . He persisted in vexing my soul about my slave Anilla, saying "Send away this slave." But I refused to send her away, and he kept saying, "A month hence I will take a mistress." God knows this is true . . .'

Walking around the midden mounds, I looked over to the green of the cultivation around Behnasa, under whose houses the city centre of Oxyrhynchus had once stood. Somewhere over there must have been the stall of Aurelius Nilus, the egg seller. In one of the Oxyrhynchus papyri he makes a solemn declaration that he will only sell his eggs in the forum and cease to operate on the black market. Somewhere by those palm trees may have been the mansion of Aurelia Attiaena. She walks into history in a fragmentary piece of papyrus bitterly complaining about the treatment she received from her husband: '. . . A certain Paul, coming from the same city, carried me off by force and compulsion and cohabited with me in marriage . . . a female child by him . . . but when soldiers were billeted in my house he robbed them and fled, and I was left to endure insults and punishments to within an inch of my life . . . Then, once more giving way to recklessness, and having a mistress again installed in his house, he brought with him a crowd of lawless men and carried me off. He then shut me in his house for days. When I became pregnant he again abandoned me, cohabiting with his mistress, and now tells me he will stir up malice against me. Wherefore I appeal to my Lord's staunchness to order him to appear in court that he might be punished for his outrages towards me.'

It was disgust with such violent sensuality and grasping materialism that led St Antony, a semi-literate Egyptian farmer from the nearby town of Beni Suef, to reject the world and set off into the desert. As I followed his route through the Eastern Desert in Ramazan's stuttering car later that afternoon, I thought of the untold consequences for the history of the Christian world that St Antony's actions would have.

St Antony first fled to the site of the present monastery in the late third century A.D. in an effort to escape the attentions of a stream of adoring Graeco-Roman intellectuals from Alexandria. Through no apparent fault of his own, the saint had become the darling of Alexandria's fashionable intelligentsia, who revered him for his earthy asceticism and his reputed power over demons. Like modern London literati falling over themselves to become the biographers of Premiership footballers, these Alexandrian sophisticates had turned up in streams at St Antony's cave, causing the baffled hermit – a painfully shy man who had retreated into the sand dunes with the express purpose of avoiding other human beings – to flee from his admirers further and further into the desert.

When his fan club pursued him to the site of the present monastery, located as it was in the middle of some of the most inhospitable sand-wastes in the entire Middle East, the saint realised that he was never going to shake off his followers. He decided instead to organise them into a loose-knit community of hermits, over which he kept watch from a cave a safe distance further up the mountain.

So was born Christian monasticism; and with incredible speed the idea spread. By the early fifth century some seven hundred monasteries filled the desert between Jerusalem and the southern border of the Byzantine Empire; they flourished to such an extent that travellers reported that the population of the desert now equalled that of the towns: 'The number of monks is past counting,' wrote Rufinus of Aquileia after his visit to Egypt only twenty-one years after the death of Antony. 'There are so many of them that an earthly Emperor could not assemble so large an army. For there is no town or village in Egypt which is not surrounded by hermitages as if by walls; while other monks live in desert caves or in even more remote places.'

The story of St Antony's life, which was written within a year of his death by Athanasius, the Bishop of Alexandria, was soon translated into Latin by Evagrius of Antioch for 'the brethren from overseas'; within twenty years it was being read and copied in distant Gaul. Not long afterwards, St Augustine, sitting in Hippo in North Africa, records that he was profoundly moved by a story he heard that two secret policemen from Trier (now part of Germany), having read *The Life of St Antony*, decided to leave their comfortable posts to become monks in Egypt. A century later monasticism was flourishing all over the West, and had become especially popular in Italy and southern France. By 700 it had reached even the Highlands of Scotland: around that time an image of St Antony under a palm tree was sculpted by Pictish monks on the windswept promontory of Nigg near Inverness, hundreds of miles beyond the Roman Empire's northernmost border.

The Monastery of St Antony – which, unlike most of its medieval Western imitators, is still flourishing – lies in the desert some three hundred miles south-east of Cairo, fifty miles inland from the barren shores of the Red Sea. Even today when the monastery is linked to the outside world by a tarmac road, the drive is a long and dispiriting one, through a desolate wasteland: flat, shimmering with heat during the day, icily cold at night, impossibly inhospitable. Yet until forty years ago St Antony's could only be reached by a three-week journey, and it depended for all its supplies on a monthly camel caravan.

The monastery is so well camouflaged against its khaki backdrop that it is almost invisible until you drive up directly underneath it. Then, less than half a mile from your destination, the whole complex comes slowly into focus: out of the sand rises a loop of camel-coloured walls pierced by a series of pepperpot mud-brick bastions. Above these stand two enormous towers – the gatehouse and the Byzantine keep – beyond which you can see the tops of dusty palm trees shivering in the desert wind.

Inside the walls, the monastery looks more like some African oasis village than it does Tintern, Rievaulx, Fountains or any of the great medieval monasteries of Europe. Streets of unglazed mud-brick cottages with creaking wooden balconies lead up to a scattering of churches and chapels; occasionally a small piazza filled with a sway of date palms breaks the spread of cells. Over everything tower the wall turrets and the great castellated mud-brick keep. It is a deeply suggestive spread of buildings – to the European eye like some nineteenth-century Orientalist's fantasy – but to the Byzantines it must have sent out a very different message.

For the monastery's simple mud-brick buildings were constructed in the fourth century in a manner as crude and earthy as the buildings of Byzantine Alexandria must once have been refined and beautiful. This contrast was not accidental. St Antony and the monks who followed him into the Egyptian desert were consciously rejecting everything that Alexandria stood for: luxury, indulgence, elegance, sophistication. Instead they cultivated a deliberate simplicity – sometimes even a wilful primitiveness – and their way of life is reflected in their art and their architecture.

In contrast to medieval Western monks, the Egyptian desert fathers also tended to reject the concept of learning, the worship of knowledge for its own sake. St Antony was particularly scathing about books, proclaiming that 'in the person whose mind is sound there is no need for letters', and that the only book he needed was 'the nature of God's creation: it is present whenever I wish to read His words'. Many of St Antony's Coptic followers emulated his example, preferring a life of hard manual labour and long hours of prayer to one of study. A millennium of classical literary culture came to be forgotten as the works of Homer and Thucydides went unread for the first time; in the words of a monastic chant to the Virgin, 'the many tongued rhetors have fallen as silent as fishes.' As late as the mid-nineteenth century, this attitude to the classics seems to have lingered in Coptic monasteries: when the British bibliophile the Hon. Robert Curzon visited the Monastery of Deir el-Suriani in the Wadi Natrun, he discovered manuscripts of lost works of Euclid and Plato serving as stoppers in jars of monastic olive oil.

Modern Egyptian monks tend to be literate – in fact the majority are university graduates – but their energy is still consciously channelled away from scholarly study and into prayer and agriculture. The monks rise at three in the morning – just as the Cairo nightclubs and casinos are beginning to empty – and spend the next five hours praying together under frescoes of the desert fathers in the ancient early Byzantine abbey church. There then follows a day of gruelling physical activity as the monks attempt, with a certain degree of success, to get the desert around the monastery to flower.

Indeed they are such enthusiastic students of arid farming techniques that yesterday evening after vespers – the one period of the day when the monks are free to mill around – I saw several groups of fixated novices poring over seed catalogues and the latest issue of some obscure farming magazine – *Irrigation Today* or *Bore Hole Weekly* or some such – as excitedly as a gaggle of teenage schoolboys with their first girlie glossy. Because of this agricultural bent, conversation at mealtimes can turn surprisingly technical. Yesterday, when St Antony's Guest Master, Fr. Dioscuros, brought me my supper, he produced a single boiled egg with as much flourish as a Parisian restaurateur might present some incredibly *recherché* piece of *nouvelle cuisine*. Then he waited while I tasted it.

'Very good,' I said, trying to rise to the occasion. 'It must be the most delicious boiled egg I've ever tasted.'

'That's hardly surprising,' replied Fr. Dioscuros. 'It's an Isa Brown.'

Isa, the Arabic form of the name Jesus, is a common name among Copts, so I asked if the egg were named after some pioneering Coptic hen-breeder.

'No, no,' replied the Guest Master, looking at me as if I were some sort of halfwit. 'Not Isa – I.S.A.: *Institut de Sélection des Animaux* near Paris – the most famous poultry centre in the world. Fr. Abbot visited it two years ago. Now all our animals are from the most modern and superior breeds.'

This obsession with state-of-the-art chicken-farming techniques is one of a number of ways in which the modern world has begun to knock at the gates of St Antony's. The abbey has recently abandoned candles in favour of its own electrical generator, and Fr. Dioscuros turned out to have a portable phone tucked away amid the folds of his habit. More radically, the increase in the number of Coptic pilgrims visiting St Antony's has forced the monks finally to abandon their age-old practice of winching visitors into the abbey by a rope (a practice which began in the sixth century A.D. when Byzantine Egypt first began to be assaulted by Bedouin war bands) in favour of the relatively up-to-date option of a front gate.

Nevertheless, these concessions apart, the monks remain wonderfully Dark Age in their outlook and conversation. Exorcisms, miraculous healings and ghostly apparitions of long-dead saints are to them what doorstep milk deliveries are to suburban Londoners – unremarkable everyday occurrences that would never warrant a passing mention if foreigners did not always seem to be so inexplicably amazed by them.

'See up there?' said Abuna Dioscuros as I was finishing my egg. He pointed to the space between the two towers of the abbey church. 'In June 1987 in the middle of the night our father St Antony appeared there hovering on a cloud of shining light.'

'You saw this?' I asked.

'No,' said Fr. Dioscuros. 'I'm short-sighted.'

He took off his spectacles to show me the thickness of the glass. 'I can barely see the Abbot when I sit beside him at supper,' he said. 'But many other fathers saw the apparition. On one side of St Antony stood St Mark the Hermit and on the other was Abuna Yustus.'

'Abuna Yustus?'

'He is one of our fathers. He used to be the Sacristan.'

'So what was he doing up there?'

'He had just departed this life.'

'Oh,' I said. 'I see.'

'Officially he's not a saint yet, but I'm sure he will be soon. His canonisation is up for discussion at the next Coptic synod. His relics have been the cause of many miracles: blind children have been made to see, the lame have got up from their wheelchairs . . .'

'All the usual sort of stuff.'

'Exactly. But you won't believe this' – here Fr. Dioscuros lowered his voice to a whisper. 'You won't believe this, but we had some visitors from Europe two years ago – Christians, some sort of Protestants – who said they didn't believe in the power of relics!'

The monk stroked his beard, wide-eyed with disbelief. 'No,' he continued. 'I'm not joking. I had to take the Protestants aside and explain that we believe that St Antony and all the fathers have not died, that they live with us, continually protecting us and looking after us. When they are needed – when we go to their graves and pray to their relics – they appear and sort out our problems.'

'Can the monks see them?'

'Who? Protestants?'

Above Fr. Christophoros and his cats, Monastery of Iviron, Mount Athos.

Previous page The Monastery of Simopetra, Mount Athos.

Below Haghia Sophia and Haghia Eirene, Istanbul.

Right The Fishponds
of Abraham, Urfa
(Edessa).

Below Qala'at Semaan,
the Basilica of St
Symeon Stylites, Syria.

Above A flock of sheep in the wilderness of Judaea.

Right The ancient fortress, Monastery of St Antony, Egypt.

Below The necropolis of Bagawat, the Great Kharga Oasis.

'No. These deceased fathers.'

'Abuna Yustus is always appearing,' said Fr. Dioscuros matter-of-factly. 'In fact one of the fathers had a half-hour conversation with him the day before yesterday. And of course St Antony makes fairly regular appearances – although he is very busy these days answering prayers all over the world. But even when we cannot see the departed fathers we can always feel them. And besides, there are many other indications that they are with us.'

'What do you mean?' I asked. 'What sort of indications?'

'Well, take last week for instance. The Bedouin from the desert are always bringing their sick to us for healing. Normally it is something quite simple: we let them kiss a relic, give them an aspirin and send them on their way. But last week they brought in a small girl who was possessed by a devil. We took the girl into the church, and as it was the time for vespers one of the fathers went off to ring the bell for prayers. When he saw this the devil inside the girl began to cry: "Don't ring the bell! Please don't ring the bell!" We asked him why not. "Because," replied the devil, "when you ring the bell it's not just the living monks who come into the church: all the holy souls of the fathers join with you too, as well as great multitudes of angels and archangels. How can I remain in the church when that happens? I'm not staying in a place like that." At that moment the bell began to ring, the girl shrieked and the devil left her!' Fr. Dioscuros clicked his fingers: 'Just like that. So you see,' he said. 'That proves it.'

ST ANTONY'S, 11 DECEMBER

The Guest Master has installed me in an ageless egg-domed mud-brick cell. Although it is only 9 p.m., the monastery generator has just been turned off for the night, and I am writing this on a rickety table by the flickering light of a paraffin lamp.

I spent the day reading a book lent to me by Fr. Dioscuros: *The*

Life of St Antony by Athanasius, the early-fourth-century Bishop of Alexandria. Athanasius's *Life* is probably the most influential work of Christian hagiography ever written, and it was the ultimate model for a thousand subsequent saints' *Lives* written across the Christian world in the centuries which followed: the Venerable Bede, for example, drew heavily on Athanasius's exemplar when writing his *Life of St Cuthbert*. Nevertheless, to the modern reader it is a grim, humourless and rather offputting text, too much concerned with ascetic self-torture and the saint's alarming victories over the demon hordes. At one point Athanasius has Antony's cell overwhelmed by an invasion of devils in animal form, so that it sounds rather like feeding time at London Zoo: 'The demons breaking through the building's four walls were changed into the form of beasts so that the place was filled with the appearance of lions, bears, leopards, bulls and serpents, asps, scorpions and wolves ... and the brothers [who came once a month with provisions for him] heard tumults, and many voices and crashing noises like the sound of weapons; and at night they saw the mountain filled with beasts.'

Although this sort of thing clearly appealed to Athanasius's contemporaries, I found that St Antony's charm and power is communicated far more effectively in the simple aphorisms attributed to him in *The Sayings of the Desert Fathers*. Here he emanates wisdom and good rustic common sense, encouraging his followers to live simply, not to fuss unnecessarily and to ignore the opinions of the world. There are two I particularly like:

'Abba Pambo asked Abba Antony: "What ought I to do?" and the old man said to him: "Do not trust in your own righteousness, do not worry about the past, but control your tongue and your stomach."'

And again:

'When Abba Antony thought about the depth of the judgements of God, he asked, "Lord, how is it that some die when they are young, while others drag on to extreme old age? Why are there those who are poor and those who are rich? Why do wicked men prosper and why are the just in need?" He heard a voice answering him, "Antony, keep your attention on yourself; these things are according to the judgements of God, and it is not to your advantage to know anything about them."'

The Coptic monks who live in St Antony's today manage successfully to combine the severity of their founder's way of life with the calm wisdom that emanates from his *Sayings*. Those I have talked to are kind, gentle men, much more modest and reasonable than the bristling Greek brigands of Mar Saba or their sometimes fanatical brethren on Mount Athos. This evening I had a long conversation with Fr. Dioscuros in the refectory of the guest quarters. As the last light was fading gradually from the sky outside, I asked him about his motives for becoming a monk and why he had left the comforts of Alexandria for the harsh climate of the desert.

'Many people think we come to the desert to punish ourselves, because it is hot and dry and difficult to live in,' said Fr. Dioscuros. 'But it's not true. We come because we love it here.'

'What is there to love about the desert?'

'We love the peace, the silence. When you really want to talk to someone you want to sit together in a quiet place and talk, not to be in the midst of a crowd of other people. How can you talk properly in a crowd? So it is with us. We come here because we want to be alone with our God. As St Antony once said: "Let your heart be silent, then God will speak "'

'But you do seem to want to punish yourselves deliberately: the hot, coarse robes you wear, the long Lenten fasts you all undertake . . .'

'Ah,' said Fr. Dioscuros, 'but you see fasting is not punishment. It is a tool, not an end in itself. It is not easy to communicate with God on a full stomach. When you have had a big meal you cannot concentrate your mind. You want to go to sleep, not to sit in church praying. To pray successfully it is better to be a little hungry.'

'But doing without possessions: isn't that a punishment?'

'No, it's a choice. For myself I have begun to get rid of many of the things which clutter up my cell. Last week I threw out my chair. I don't need it. Now I sit on the floor. Why should I bother with extra food, with spare clothes, with unnecessary furniture?

409

All you need is a piece of bread and enough covering for the body. The less you have, the less you have to distract you from God. Do you understand?'

I smiled, uncertainly.

'Well, just look around this room. When I am in here I think that the chair is in the wrong place, I must move it. Or maybe that the lamp is out of oil, I must fill it. Or . . . or that that shutter is broken and I must get it mended. But in the desert there is just sand. You don't think of anything else; there is nothing to disturb you. It should be the same in a monk's cell. The less there is, the easier it is to talk to God.'

'Do you find it easy?'

'It is never easy, but with practice I find it less difficult,' said Dioscuros. 'The spiritual life is like a ladder. Every day if you are disciplined and make the effort you find you will rise up, understand a little better, find it a little easier to concentrate, find that your mind is wandering less and less. When you pray alone in your cell without distraction you feel as if you are in front of God, as if nothing is coming to you except from God. When you succeed – if you do manage to banish distractions and communicate directly with God – then the compensation outweighs any sufferings or hardships. You feel as if something which was dim is suddenly lighted for you. You feel full of light and pleasure: it is like a blinding charge of electricity.'

'But you don't have to come to the middle of the desert to find an empty room free of distractions. You can find that anywhere: in Cairo, or Alex, or London . . .'

'What you say is true,' said Fr. Dioscuros with a smile. 'You can pray anywhere. After all, God is everywhere, so you can find him everywhere.' He gestured to the darkening sand dunes outside: 'But in the desert, in the pure clean atmosphere, in the silence – there you can find *yourself*. And unless you begin to know yourself, how can you even begin to search for God?'

Unlike the other monasteries I have visited on this journey, St Antony's is bursting with young monks, and there are no worries about its imminent extinction; indeed, it is many centuries since it has been so full and so active. The same is true of many of the Egyptian desert monasteries: since the current Coptic Pope, Shenoudah III, assumed office in 1982, there has been a massive revival of monasticism in Egypt, and many ancient monastery ruins, abandoned for hundreds of years, are being brought back into use. Nevertheless, for all this activity, there are some very dark clouds on the horizon, and after I had spent a few days at St Antony's the monks began, very hesitantly, to talk about their worries for the future.

The Copts have suffered petty discrimination for centuries, but the recent revival of Islamist insurgency in Upper Egypt has made their position more dangerous, and their prospects more uncertain, than they have been for years. In April 1992 fourteen Copts in Asyut province were gunned down by the Islamist guerrillas of the *Gema'a al-Islamiyya* for refusing to pay protection money. There followed a series of crude bombs outside Coptic churches in Alexandria and Cairo. Finally in March 1994 armed militants attacked the ancient Coptic monastery of Deir ul-Muharraq near Asyut; two monks and two lay people were shot dead at the monastery's front gate. After centuries of deliberate isolation the world is suddenly pressing in on the Coptic monks in the most alarming fashion.

Like the Suriani in Turkey, the Copts are very reluctant to talk about their worries; hundreds of years of living as a minority under Muslim rule has taught them to keep their heads down. 'We have some small problems,' was all Abouna Dioscuros would say when I referred to the attack on Deir ul-Muharraq soon after my arrival. Slowly, however, the monks have begun to be a little more forthcoming. This morning I tackled one of the older fathers on the subject. To begin with he just looked down at his shoes.

Then, plucking up his courage, his fears came pouring out.

'Deir ul-Muharraq is only the latest massacre,' he said. 'In the last few years many churches were burned, many of our priests and laymen were killed. Every day there are death threats. Around Asyut the *Irhebin* [terrorists] walk into the houses of the Copts. They take money and belongings and if the Copts resist they shoot them dead. The Government does nothing. The police arrest no one, though they know very well who does this. When the *Gema'a* murdered fourteen Copts in one hour in 1992, the government just said: "This is Upper Egypt. Probably it is only a feud. Probably it is two families squabbling: nothing more." Only now, in the last few months, when the *Gema'a* has begun attacking tourists and government ministers, are they taking this threat seriously. Maybe they have left it too late. If they had tackled the problem when it began, all would have been well. But because it was just the Copts who were suffering they did nothing. Now it is out of hand. The *Irhebin* are everywhere.'

Other monks I talked to muttered about the oppressive Hamayonic Laws, the old Ottoman legislation, still extant in Egyptian law, which requires a special decree from the President himself if a Christian wishes to build or even repair a church: technically, the monks should seek a special decree from President Mubarak himself if they wish to repair even a broken lavatory.

'The government does nothing for us,' said one monk, who begged me not to mention his name. 'In Egypt the authorities are very bad to the Copts. No senior policemen are Copts. No judges are Copts. There is no justice for our people. The *Irhebin* know they can attack the Copts and nothing will happen to them. That is why our people are very frightened. That is why we are all afraid.'

Historically, of course, the monks of Egypt have often had to face violence. In Robert Curzon's classic nineteenth-century travel book *Visits to Monasteries in the Levant*, he remarks that 'all [Egyptian monasteries] are surrounded by a high strong wall, built as a fortification to protect the brethren within, and not without reason, even in the present day ... [Many times] I have been quietly dining in a monastery when shouts have been heard, and shots have been fired against the stout bulwarks of the outer walls, which, thanks to their protection, had but little effect in altering the monotonous cadence in which one of the brotherhood read a homily of St Chrysostom from the pulpit provided for that purpose in the refectory.'

Only on one occasion did the strong walls of St Antony fail to protect the brethren within. Sometime in the first decade of the sixteenth century a tribe of Bedouin besieged, attacked and eventually took the monastery, killing most of the monks, camping in its buildings and turning the fourth-century Church of St Antony into their kitchen. There they lit their fires with ancient scrolls and documents from the monastic library; the smokestains still remain amid the ancient frescoes of the church's roof, a daily reminder of the dangers that lurk outside the monastery walls.

In John Moschos's day St Antony's was also threatened by nomadic raiders. Remote as it was from the protection of Egypt's Byzantine garrison, it presented an inviting target to tribesmen in search of plunder. In *The Spiritual Meadow* Moschos retells a story told to him by a 'pagan Saracen' who was hunting in the vicinity of the monastery when he

> saw a monk on the mountain above St Antony's holding a book and reading. I went up to him intending to rob him; perhaps to slay him also. As I approached him, he stretched out his right hand towards me saying: 'Stay!' And for two days and two nights I was unable to move from that spot. Then I said to him: 'For the love of the God whom you worship, let me go!' He said, 'Go in peace,' and it was only thus, with his blessing, that I was able to leave the spot to which his powers had rooted me.

Other monks were less lucky. Between Moschos's first visit to Egypt in the 580s and his return nearly thirty years later, the entire fabric of the eastern Byzantine Empire had begun to crumble. The four monasteries of the Wadi Natrun had been burned and ravaged by the pagan Mazices and the 3,500 monks who lived there had been scattered around the Levant; Moschos was to meet refugees from the monasteries in both Gaza and Alexandria, and according to another source, the *Ethiopian Synaxarium*, many other homeless Wadi Natrun exiles took refuge behind the ramparts of St Antony's.

The Egyptian section of *The Spiritual Meadow* grimly reflects the anarchy of the period and is full of tales of 'barbarians' burning monasteries and leading great caravans of monks stumbling off to the slave markets of the Hejaz. In one story Moschos tells of a Patriarch of Alexandria whose secretary stole some gold from him; in his flight he was captured by 'barbarians' who carried him off into slavery – until the saintly Patriarch forgave him and agreed to ransom him from captivity. Another tale tells of a friend of Moschos who was taken captive but somehow managed to escape and make his way to the *lavra* of Monidia, where Moschos found him full of wise spiritual advice. A third tale tells of a monk who meets three Saracens travelling with a Byzantine prisoner:

> [The prisoner] was an exceptionally handsome young man, about twenty years old. When he saw me, he began crying to me to take him away from them. So I started begging the Saracens to let him go. One of the Saracens answered me in Greek: 'We are not letting him go.' So I said: 'Take me and let him go, for he cannot endure servitude.' The same Saracen replied, 'We are not letting him go.' Then I said to them for the third time, 'Will you let him go for a ransom? Hand him over to me and I will bring whatever you demand.' The Saracen replied: 'We cannot give him to you because we promised our priest that if we took a good-looking prisoner, we would bring him to the priest to be offered as a sacrifice. Now be off with you, or we will cause your head to roll on the ground.'
>
> Then I prostrated myself before God and said: 'O Lord God, our Saviour, save your servant.' The three Saracens immediately became possessed of demons. They drew their swords and cut each other to pieces. I took the young man to my cave and he no longer wished

to leave me. He renounced the world – and after completing seven years in the monastic life, went to his rest.

Yet then as now, the monks seemed to believe that their sufferings were permitted by God for a reason, and that good would come out of disaster.

'God is most easily discernible in times of trouble,' explained Fr. Dioscuros. 'When your troubles cease, then you leave God. But in difficult times men go to God for help.'

'So are you saying that God allows suffering to remind us that He is still there?'

'No,' replied Fr Dioscuros, 'that is not what I meant. But thanks to God good can come out of evil. Christianity in Egypt – our Coptic Church – grew out of the terrible persecutions of Diocletian. The blood of martyrs nourishes the seed of belief.'

Fr. Dioscuros held up the wickerwork Coptic pectoral crucifix that was suspended by a leather thong around his neck. 'What is Christianity,' he said, 'without the Cross?'

That evening, at Fr. Dioscuros's invitation, I attended vespers with the monks.

Walking into the great abbey church was like entering a tunnel. Outside the monastery compound was all bright glare; inside, past the long lines of monastic sandals left mosque-like at the porch, it was so dark that the sanctuary candles and oil lamps blazed like fireflies in the soupy stygian gloom. The darkness drained the church of colour, the shadows of its rigorously simple lines appearing stern and impressive in the glimmering half-light.

As my eyes adjusted, I took in the number of monks drawn up in ranks at the front of the nave. So far in my stay I could not have seen more than a dozen of the brethren. Although I knew the monastery to be bursting with new recruits, the echoing monastic quiet conspired to make St Antony's feel strangely deserted: after the bustle and noise of Alexandria and Cairo, here one could hear every shutter creak as it was blown in the wind, every snatch of whispered monastic dialogue echoing around the ancient mud walls.

Now, as if from nowhere, at least sixty monks had materialised in the nave and all were chanting loudly in a deep, rumbling bass plainchant quite different from the elusive, bittersweet melodies of Gregorian Chant or the angular, quickfire vespers of the Greeks. Individually the gentlest of men, the Copts at prayer made a massive, dense, booming sound, each stanza sung by the monastic cantor echoed by a thundering barrage of massed male voices. The wall of sound reverberated around the church, bouncing off the squinches of the dome, crashing onto the mud-brick roof then down again like a lead weight into the nave. Yet despite its heaviness, there was nothing harsh or brutal about the Coptic chant, the swelling notes of the refrain resolving to give the whole threnody a tragic, desolate air, as if all the distilled deprivations of generations of monks were being enunciated and offered up, at once an agonised atonement for the sins of mankind and an exorcism forestalling the terrors of the night to come.

The service – like all the liturgies of desert Egypt – was conducted in Coptic, a direct descendant of the ancient tongue of the Pharaohs. The same tongue that had sung the praise of the Christian God in this church for more than one and a half thousand years had been used in the great Pharaonic temples of Thebes to praise Isis and Horus for the three thousand years preceding that: of the sacred tongues of the world, only Sanskrit has a comparable antiquity. It is a strange and exotic language whose elliptical conflation of syllables sounded as though they had been specially designed for the uttering of incantations: 'In the name of the Father and the Son and the Holy Ghost, for ever and ever, Amen,' became '*Khenevran emeviot nem ipshiri nembi ebnevma esoweb enowti enowti ami . . .*'

There was a moment of silence as the monks marched from the middle of the nave, through the swirling incense, to a long lectern near the sanctuary where a line of ancient bound vellum lectionaries lay open. There the brethren split into groups. Quietly at first, those on the north began singing a verse of the psalm of the day, those to the south answering them, the volume gradually rising, the stiff, illuminated pages of the service books all turning together as the chant thundered on into the late evening, accompanied now by an occasional clash of cymbals or an ecstatic ringing of triangles. As the service progressed and the tempo of the singing rose, novices swung their thuribles and the great cumulus clouds of frankincense coagulated into a thick white fog in the body of the nave.

Gradually, as the liturgy stretched on into its third hour, the fog of incense grew so thick that the monastic presence at the front of the nave became dim. From my place at the rear all I could see was the distant image of a line of dark figures standing at the lectern, and a little behind them a gaggle of novices in white *gelabiyas* prostrating themselves on the ground. Around me a group of large, black-clad peasant women from Upper Egypt arranged themselves in a circle, earnestly scribbling prayers and petitions onto scraps of paper. Their children and grandchildren were then dispatched to post them in the letterbox attached to the velvet-covered shrine of St Antony. At the very back of the nave another small group of Coptic pilgrims were now circling the icons, touching the face of a saint then kissing his fingers, or attempting to use saliva to stick piastre coins onto the glass of the icon-frame.

As I watched the pilgrims at work, I found myself increasingly distracted by the various images and icons of St Antony which dotted the church. Although they clearly dated from many different periods, their iconography was fixed and consistent. St Antony was shown as an old man whose white beard stretched down to his knees. He was barefoot and wore only a simple monastic habit, belted at the waist; in some icons the habit appeared to be made of animal pelts. Often the saint was shown in the company of his friend St Paul the Hermit: while St Antony was held by the Copts to be the first monk, St Paul was said to be the first hermit. When the two were shown together they were always accompanied by a raven who, according to St Jerome's version of the legend, diligently brought a loaf of bread every day to their cave. In some icons the two men were also accompanied by a pair of lions, again a reference to St Jerome's *Life of St Paul the First Hermit*, which tells how the lions helped St Antony bury his friend:

> Even as St Antony pondered how he was to bury his friend, two lions came coursing, their manes flying from the inner desert, and made towards him. At the sight of them, he was at first in dread: then turning his mind to God, he waited undismayed, as though he looked on doves. They came straight to the body of the Holy Paul, and halted by it wagging their tails, then couched themselves at his feet, roaring mightily; and Antony knew well they were lamenting him, as best they could. Then, going a little way off, they began to scratch up the ground with their paws, vying with each other to throw up the sand, till they had dug a grave roomy enough for a man . . .

The reason for my particular interest in the icons of St Antony was that during the Dark Ages the saint was also a favourite subject for the Pictish artists of my native Scotland, as well as for those across the sea in Ireland. The Celtic monks of both countries consciously looked on St Antony as their ideal and their prototype, and the proudest boast of Celtic monasticism was that, in the words of the seventh-century Antiphonary of the Irish monastery of Bangor:

> This house full of delight
> Is built on the rock
> And indeed the true vine
> Transplanted out of Egypt.

Moreover, the Egyptian ancestry of the Celtic Church was acknowledged by contemporaries: in a letter to Charlemagne, the English scholar-monk Alcuin described the Celtic Culdees as '*pueri egyptiaci*', the children of the Egyptians. Whether this implied direct contact between Coptic Egypt and Celtic Ireland and Scotland is a matter of scholarly debate. Common sense suggests that it is unlikely, yet a growing body of scholars think that that is exactly what Alcuin may have meant. For there are an extraordinary number of otherwise inexplicable similarities between the Celtic and Coptic Churches which were shared by no other Western Churches. In both, the bishops wore crowns rather than mitres and held T-shaped Tau crosses rather than crooks or croziers. In both the handbell played a very prominent place in ritual, so much so that in early Irish sculpture clerics are distinguished from lay persons by placing a clochette in their hand. The same device performs a similar function on Coptic stelae – yet bells of any sort are quite unknown in the dominant Greek or Latin Churches until the tenth century at the earliest. Stranger still, the Celtic wheel cross, the most common symbol of Celtic Christianity, has recently been shown to have been a Coptic invention, depicted on a Coptic burial pall of the fifth century, three centuries before the design first appears in Scotland and Ireland.

Certainly there is a growing body of evidence to suggest that contact between the Mediterranean and the Celtic fringe was possible. Egyptian pottery – perhaps originally containing wine or olive oil – has been found during excavations at Tintagel Castle in Cornwall, the mythical birthplace of King Arthur. The Irish Litany of Saints remembers 'the seven monks of Egypt [who lived] in Disert Uilaig' on the west coast of Ireland. But the fullest account of direct contact is given by none other than Sophronius himself. In his *Life of John the Almsgiver* (the saintly Patriarch with whom he and Moschos fled Alexandria in 614 A.D.), Sophronius tells the story of an accidental voyage to Britain – more specifically, in all likelihood, to Cornwall – undertaken by a bankrupt young Alexandrian aristocrat to whom the Patriarch has lent money:

> We sailed for twenty days and nights [reported the man on his return] and owing to a violent wind we were unable to tell in what direction we were going either by the stars or by the coast. But the only thing we knew was that the steersman saw [an apparition of] the Patriarch [John the Almsgiver] by his side, holding his tiller and saying to him: 'Fear not! You are sailing quite right.' Then, after the twentieth day, we caught sight of the islands of Britain, and when we had landed we found

a famine raging there. Accordingly, when we told the chief man of the town that we were laden with corn, he said, 'God has brought you at the right moment. Choose as you wish either one "nomisma" for each bushel or a return freight of tin.' And we chose half of each. Then we set sail again and joyfully made once more for Alexandria, putting in on our way at Pentapolis [in modern Libya].

I was still thinking over all these curious links joining the Celts with the Copts when vespers finally drew to a close. There was a last procession of the monks around the nave, then slowly the brethren began to file out of the doors into the fresh air and pale evening light.

As I stood outside the church, Fr. Dioscuros came over and introduced me to the Abbot. As we chatted, I happened to mention how St Antony had once been a highly revered and much sculpted figure in my home country. Surprised, the Abbot questioned me closely about the Pictish images of his patron saint, and I described to him the scene shown on a particularly beautiful seventh-century Pictish stone from St Vigeans (near Dundee) which illustrates the scene in St Jerome's *Life of St Paul the First Hermit* where the two saints meet for the first time. They eat together but cannot agree which of them should break the bread. Each defers to the other, until finally they 'agreed that each should take hold of the loaf and pull towards himself, and let each take what remained in his hands'. In the Pictish version of the scene, the two saints are shown in profile as they sit in high-backed chairs facing each other, with one hand each stretched out to hold a round loaf. It was a very different image, I said, from any I had seen in the monastery, all of which showed St Antony standing full-frontal, staring into the eyes of the onlooker, in the classic Byzantine manner.

'You are wrong,' said the Abbot, smiling enigmatically. 'We have your image as well. Come, I will show you.'

We walked through the darkening monastery, the Abbot leading, staff in hand. As we made our way through the maze of mud-brick buildings, monks would emerge rustling from the shadows to touch the Abbot's feet. Eventually we arrived at a stucco-covered building. The Abbot drew a bunch of keys from his habit, selected one and turned it in the lock. The door was stiff, but he pushed it open and led me inside.

The library was narrow, long and ill-lit. On either side stretched glass cabinets, seven shelves high, stacked with a riot of heavy old liturgical books, leather-bound folios and great rolls of charters and manuscripts. Without hesitation, the Abbot walked straight over to a pillar in the middle of the room. On it was hung a framed picture.

'Here,' said the Abbot.

My heart sank. I had dreamed of stumbling across some ancient but unnoticed Coptic icon, a copy of which might have made its way to Dark Age Scotland, there to inspire the Pictish images of St Antony and St Paul I knew so well. But the picture at which the Abbot was pointing was not only a conventional Byzantine-inspired image of a full-frontal standing figure, it was also clearly very late: perhaps seventeenth or eighteenth century.

'But that's just St Antony,' I said. 'It's not Paul and Antony breaking bread. It's not in profile. It's not even . . .'

'Not the main picture,' replied the Abbot gently. 'Look at the side panel.'

I looked where he was pointing. There, under the outstretched arm of the saint, a much smaller scene had been painted. Two figures, immediately recognisable as Paul and Antony, sat facing each other in a cave under a hill, on top of which grew a palm tree. Both figures had one arm outstretched to grasp a round loaf of bread with a line down its centre. It was exactly the image sculpted by the unknown Pictish artists in seventh-century Scotland.

What was more exciting still, the image showed every sign of being closer to the original iconography of the scene than that sculpted on the Pictish stone. There, the two saints sit facing each other in high-backed chairs, unnaturally close. But in the image in the library, the two saints are correctly shown to be in St Paul's cave, each sitting on a rock ledge. Their close proximity, almost head to head, is due to the narrowness of the cave. The oddness of the Pictish scene results from the sculptor moving the saints from the constriction of their cave but otherwise maintaining the original composition.

The only conceivable explanation of the similarity of the two scenes – one in Scotland, one in Egypt, whole continents apart – is that the icon in the library must be a late copy of a much older Coptic original, an earlier version of which had somehow made its way from Egypt to Dark Age Perthshire, either by trade, pilgrimage or in the hands of wandering Coptic monks. Another piece in the unlikely jigsaw linking the deserts of Coptic Egypt with the bleak snowfields of early medieval Scotland had fallen into place. I beamed at the Abbot, immensely pleased.

It was my last evening in the abbey. On the way back to the guest rooms, prompted by the Abbot, I dropped into the abbey church to pray for St Antony's blessing on the last and probably the most dangerous section of this pilgrimage: the journey through Upper Egypt, past the fundamentalist strongholds of el-Minya and Asyut, then on through the Western Desert to the Great Kharga Oasis. I sat in front of the tomb for twenty minutes before heading back to my cell. There I opened this diary, lit the paraffin lamp and wrote into the night.

HOTEL WINDSOR, CAIRO, 15 DECEMBER

A party of Coptic pilgrims took me as far as a filling station outside Suez. After standing there for half an hour with outstretched hand, I was picked up by a *servis* taxi on its way to Cairo.

My companions were a group of drunken Egyptian construction workers. They begged me to change my itinerary: 'Meester! You go Hurghada! Nice! Too much *arak*! Too many girlses! Too many boyses! Nice! Not expensive!' They passed a bottle of *arak* around the taxi, smoked incessantly and told smutty stories about their time at a beach resort on the Red Sea coast. There was much miming of outsized breasts and suggestive waggling of first fingers, followed by gales of laughter. They sung along to wailing Egyptian disco music ('*Isk Isk Iskanderiyaaa . . .*'), stopping only to urinate into the open desert. For five hours I sat in the back, frowning like an outraged Mother Superior.

The *servis* dropped me at a traffic island in the middle of the smoggy, hooting, ill-tempered Cairo traffic. After five days in the calm and quiet of monastic seclusion, I was horrified by everything I saw. Cairo suddenly seemed to be a nightmare vision of hell on earth, fly-blown and filthy, populated entirely by crooks and vulgarians, pimps and pickpockets, a city of seedy degenerates hustling and haggling their way to the fires of Gehenna.

When I had unpacked my rucksack in the comforting quiet of the Hotel Windsor, I opened at random my copy of *The Sayings of the Desert Fathers*. My eye fell on an aphorism of St Antony: 'Just as fish die if they stay too long out of water, so the monks who loiter outside their cells or pass their time with men of the world lose the intensity of inner peace. So like a fish going towards the sea, we must hurry to reach our cell, for fear that if we delay outside we will lose everything we have gained.'

I made up my mind not to linger in Cairo, and to get away as quickly as possible to the troubled desert monasteries of Upper Egypt. Besides, I reminded myself, I had already spent over a month in Cairo earlier in the year.

I had visited Cairo for the first time in early March when the *Sunday Times* had flown me there to interview President Mubarak. The paper's Washington correspondent had passed on to London a leak he had received from contacts in the CIA. Apparently the Agency was gravely concerned that Mubarak's moderate and secular regime was about to fall. I was dispatched to Cairo with a view to recording the run-up to the expected Islamic revolution.

At the time, the CIA assessment did not seem to be over-alarmist. In the spring of 1992, severe cracks in Mubarak's regime had begun to appear. It was at this time that the *Gema'a al-Islamiyya* first began making the headlines with a series of murderous attacks: in April, the fourteen Coptic Christians massacred for refusing to pay protection money; in June, the same group shot down Dr Farag Foda, a secular writer who had dared to condemn the movement in print. At the same time hit-and-run attacks on foreign tour-groups began in earnest, killing eight and wounding nearly a hundred tourists. The following year, in the summer of 1993, the Islamic militants began a series of assassination attempts against the Prime Minister and two other prominent government ministers, all three of whom were wounded. In November the militants hatched a plot – uncovered in advance by the security forces – to blow up Mubarak himself.

By the beginning of 1994 tens of thousands of Islamic activists had been arrested under emergency regulations, while around 330 people had been killed in the accelerating cycle of violence which had developed between the police and the militants. Cassandras among the foreign press began making comparisons with Iran in the period leading up to the Islamic Revolution, or the crisis in Algeria, where around four thousand people had been killed in the previous two years. Others speculated on an unstoppable Islamic fundamentalist wave gathering force along the shores of the Mediterranean, poised – so they said – to sweep away every secular Arab government from Casablanca to Baghdad.

I spent all of March in Cairo investigating the situation. What I found was very different from what the CIA assessment had led me to expect. In Europe and America analysts may have been fretting over Reuters reports of bombs and death threats, but in Cairo the buses continued to run, the shops were open and spring was in the air. The situation in Egypt appeared far more threatening when viewed from the newsrooms of Fleet Street or the conference halls of the Pentagon than it did from the calm and shady banks of the Nile. The tourist fatality rate was still lower than that in, say, Florida. The militants seemed by all accounts to be poorly trained and lightly armed; moreover, they had only limited popular support.

Mubarak was not personally unpopular – he was certainly not

in the situation of the Shah of Iran in 1979 – and it seemed most unlikely that he was in imminent danger of being overthrown by any sort of revolution, Islamic or otherwise. Commentators in Cairo were genuinely baffled when they read some of the grimmer prophecies then being made in the Western press – as indeed was President Mubarak himself: 'It is a PROPAGANDA!' he boomed during our interview when I mentioned the reports suggesting that his regime was tottering. 'A BIG propaganda! I wonder why, whenever some small, small incident takes place here in Egypt, in the foreign media [I read articles claiming] "there is no stability" or "regime is shaking". Even in your *Sunday Times* they were writing this. I was wondering, where are they getting these informations? I was wondering,' and here he leaned forward conspiratorially, 'maybe they are taking their informations from the fundamentals.' When I told him the source of our information his face darkened, adding that the Americans had never understood the Middle East, and probably never would. (At the request of the horrified Interior Minister, I later removed this quote from the published interview.)

In fact, far from tottering, Mubarak's regime seemed that March to be successfully digging in. Everyone I talked to in Cairo repeated the same thing: that since the government crackdown the previous year, things had become much better. The violence – though still extremely bad – was now mainly limited to a few towns and villages in Upper Egypt. As for the conventional wisdom that Mubarak was alienating large swathes of the population by the heavy-handedness of his measures, that was not the story you heard on the streets. While no one denied that the police were capable of behaving extremely roughly with suspects, people complained less about the abuse of human rights than about the fact that the crackdown had been so long delayed.

'The government always knew who the *Gema'a al-Islamiyya* people were,' I was told by Boutros Gabra, a Coptic goldsmith. 'As long as they just shot up a few Copts, the government was happy to tolerate them. Only when they started attacking foreigners and threatening tourism did the government take the necessary steps.'

Nevertheless, while an Islamic revolution appeared improbable, there did seem to be a considerable likelihood that Mubarak's regime would allow – indeed was already allowing – a slow Islamicisation of the country in an effort to appease the more moderate elements of the religious right wing. The censorship powers of the Sheikhs of Al-Ahzar University, the senior Islamic authority in Egypt, had recently been widened. More and more hardline Islamic preachers were appearing on government television, some openly attacking Christianity on the air. Even the vaguest outlines of Christian religious teaching had been taken off the curriculum in government schools, while in many places Coptic schools had had to raise walls around themselves for protection. According to the government's own statistics, mosque building had accelerated dramatically – some 125,000 unauthorised *masjids* had been erected in the last decade alone – but in the same period the Hamayonic Laws had been used to deny permission for the building of more than a handful of churches.

Off the record, many Copts argued that Mubarak's government deliberately turned a blind eye to a culture of anti-Christian discrimination and intolerance, thus indirectly fostering the climate that encouraged anti-Coptic violence. Certainly, whether by accident or design, in the last two decades Copts appeared to have been weeded out of all positions of influence, as army generals, university professors, police officers and senior Cabinet Ministers: although the Copts made up at least 17 per cent of the Egyptian population, not one of the country's provincial governors was a Copt, and Copts made up less than 1 per cent of MPs in the Egyptian National Assembly. As a result of all this there had been two major Coptic migrations: terrorised Coptic farmers from Upper Egypt were selling up their farms and making for the relative anonymity of the cities, while at the same time the urbanised Coptic middle class was emigrating in search of better opportunities and less discrimination abroad. It was estimated that in the past ten years as many as half a million Coptic professionals had left the country, mainly for Australia, Canada and the US.

More worrying still, an increasing number of ordinary Muslim Egyptians seemed to be convinced that a degree of peaceful

Islamicisation – fewer nightclubs, more veils, less alcohol, more *Sharia* law – would act as a panacea for their many problems. It was probably here – in the gradual fundamentalist annexation of Egyptian public life – and not in terrorism or revolution, that the real danger for Egypt's future lay. As a Sheikh I talked to put it: '*Inshallah* the tide of feeling is so strong that no one can oppose it now. We don't need or want violence. The majority are already calling for a society based on the Holy Koran. Until this latest violence the government was moving in the right direction by itself.'

One interview I had in March left a particularly vivid impression on me. It was with a man who was in the process of getting divorced. The bizarre feature of the case was that the couple concerned – Dr Nasr Abu Zaid and his wife Dr Ibthal Yunis, both elderly academics at Cairo University – were very happily married, but were having divorce proceedings forced on them against their will by hardline Islamists who had never even met them.

When the case was first brought to court, most of middle-class Cairo assumed the charge was a joke. Only later did it become apparent that there was in fact an obscure law allowing a complete stranger to initiate divorce proceedings against a married couple on the grounds of incompatibility. The fundamentalists' case was based on their claim that Dr Nasr Abu Zaid's academic writings, which strongly attack the political manipulation of the Koran, show him to be an atheist, and thus an apostate. His wife was a Muslim; *ergo* the two were incompatible.

Although the fundamentalists lost the first round of the case, the affair showed quite how far their writ now ran, and how successfully they have managed to infiltrate Egyptian institutions. The Sheikh who first attacked Dr Abu Zaid, a heavily-bearded TV preacher named Dr Abdul Shaheen, was not openly a member of the Muslim Brotherhood, but was Chairman of the ruling party's Religious Affairs Committee. The university, far from helping Dr Abu Zaid in his fight against this medieval obscurantism, bowed to fundamentalist pressure and turned down his application for promotion. Neither the Student Union nor the University Staff Club uttered a word in Dr Abu Zaid's support; both institutions, it turned out, had effectively been taken over by the Muslim Brotherhood.

I went to see Dr Abu Zaid at the university. A shy, retiring and rather rotund figure, I found him in a corner room of the old colonial Arts Faculty building, protected by a bodyguard.

'I could have simply stated that I was a good Muslim, made a profession of faith and the case would have been dropped,' said Dr Abu Zaid. 'I *am* a practising Muslim, but I was determined not to back down and allow these people to manipulate Islam for their own ends. This was a battle which had to be fought.'

'Do you ever wish you had backed down?' I asked, looking at his guard.

'No,' replied Dr Abu Zaid. 'After Dr Farag Foda was declared an apostate and shot dead by these terrorists, my wife and I have had to live in fear of our lives. But if I was able to choose again, I would still fight on. What is going on in Egypt is a battle between those Muslims who defend the future and those who want to drag us back into the past. More and more people want to take the easiest solution: to smoke the opium of fundamentalism. Someone has to stand up and have the courage to show that in that direction only disaster lies.'

Dr Abu Zaid talked at length about his fight with the fundamentalists, about their attempts to censor his writing and suppress his work. Before I left I asked: was he hopeful for the future?

'For the immediate future,' he said, 'no: I am not hopeful. I don't fear revolution – that is very unlikely. It is the so-called moderates I worry about. They want to suppress rational thought; they won't let anyone oppose them. In the long term history shows that freedom and truth will prevail. But in the short term I think things will get much worse before they get better.'

We walked together through the corridors of the university, shadowed by the bodyguard. As we walked Dr Abu Zaid pointed out how many of the female students now wore the veil.

'My generation has witnessed many ups and downs,' he said. 'After the dreams and hopes of Nasser's revolution in 1952 there have been so many disappointments: the defeat by Israel in 1967, the assassination of Sadat, the Israeli invasion of Lebanon, the

Iran–Iraq war, Desert Storm, the anarchy in Algeria. All of this is stored in the memories of our people.'

He turned to face me. 'After all that,' he said, 'you tell me: would *you* be optimistic?'

In the Byzantine period, Cairo was a small and relatively unimportant riverside fortress guarding the route from Alexandria to the provincial cities upstream. It was known as Babylon-in-Egypt.

The town receives only a couple of passing mentions in the pages of *The Spiritual Meadow*, both times in reference to a prophecy that Moschos's friend Abba Zosimos the Cilician would one day become its Bishop (he did). Few other sources are much more forthcoming, though *The Chronicle of John, Bishop of Nikiu* does describe its surrender to the Muslim General Amr in 641 A.D., when the defenders, deserted by their generals, handed over the fortress – and all the weapons and munitions contained within it – in return for their lives.

It was the Muslims who turned this previously obscure fortress into the first city of Egypt, and the Christians were never as dominant an element in the population of Cairo as they had been in Alexandria; indeed it was only in the eleventh century that the Coptic Patriarch deigned to move his cathedral from Alexandria (by then reduced to little more than a fishing village). Today Cairo has a large Coptic population, possibly numbering as many as three million out of the total of fifteen million, but the Copts lie scattered about the poorer suburbs – where, as fate would have it, the more aggressive fundamentalist factions can also be found.

This afternoon I set out to visit two Coptic churches which had been damaged in the course of the accelerating conflict between the local Copts and their Islamist neighbours. In one case a bomb had been let off outside the church porch; the other had been attacked when a Muslim mob, whipped up by a fundamentalist demagogue, spilled out of a mosque calling for infidel blood. Neither was a major incident, but I only realised quite how frightened the Copts were when, at both churches, those in charge initially denied that there had been any trouble at all, and only admitted the truth when I produced press cuttings outlining what had happened.

Menas, the Coptic taxi driver at the Hotel Windsor, drove me up to the district of Shubra. The streets were wide and the houses were high and brown. Overnight the weather had turned wet, and the air came cold through the open window. The sky was grey and there was mud on the road. Men zigzagged between puddles, their woollen winter *gelabiyas* hitched up to their shins, revealing woolly longjohns beneath. They all had scarves wrapped around their heads.

An armed guard stood outside the Church of el-Adra (the Virgin). He directed me to the office of the priest. Fr. Mark Bishara had a grey beard and wore a domed Coptic hat. As soon as I asked him about the bomb which had gone off outside his church, he rose and began nervously ushering me out of the room.

'This bomb is forgotten,' he said.

'But was it a big bomb? Was anyone killed?'

'It was nothing,' said the priest, by now propelling me towards the door. 'Only two or three were injured. I can't remember the details. No, please, I do not want to talk about it. The matter is finished.'

'Was anyone arrested?'

'The man responsible was captured. I think so.'

'So the government is helping you?'

'Let me not answer, please,' said the priest, half closing the door and looking out through the crack. 'It would not be suitable to write about this matter. It is not good for us. We have no problem. We are very friendly with the Muslims. The government is very well equipped to deal with everything. I have much work, I am sorry . . .'

And with that the door slammed shut. I walked around the church compound, amazed by the priest's behaviour. What was

430

he so afraid of? As I wandered about I heard children chanting, and following the sound I came to a modern building behind the church. It held a line of classrooms, and inside several lay people were teaching small children Bible stories and Coptic hymns. One of the classes was just finishing, and when the children had dispersed I approached the teacher to ask if he could tell me anything more about the blast. Like the priest, he looked very uncomfortable, but did say that the bomb had been hung on the church gate during a service, and that it went off as the congregation trooped out. Luckily it had been a very crude device, and no one was killed, though there had been many injuries. I asked the man if he was worried that the church might be bombed again.

'Only God knows,' he replied.

'Have these attacks made many Copts want to leave Egypt?'

'Yes,' he said. 'Five or six of my own friends have emigrated, not just because of the terrorists, but to find work. In Egypt it is more difficult for Christians to get good jobs than it is for Muslims. For this reason many, many Christians – the clever ones – are going to Canada and Australia. They think it is better for their children.'

'Will you go too?'

'No,' replied the man firmly. 'It is important to remain. We should stay and do our best to defend our religion.'

As I was leaving the church compound, Fr. Bishara hurried out of the door of his office and called after me.

'I'm sorry,' he said gently, reaching for my hand. 'I am a priest. If you want to learn to pray, I can help. If you want to go to Heaven, I can help. But if you want to talk about politics . . .'

He shrugged his shoulders. 'I think you have not spent long in Egypt,' he said. 'When you have been here longer, you will understand.'

From Shubra, Menas drove me to the distant suburb of Ein Shams, now one of Cairo's main Islamist strongholds. As we drove, the houses got poorer and the people more bedraggled-looking. Brick tenements hung with laundry gave way to a shanty-town sprawl. Rubbish was piled on the hard shoulder of the road. It began to drizzle, and the vendors lining the roadside began to strap umbrellas to their fruit barrows. Others – beggars, sweet-sellers and newsboys – cowered in the doorways of cafés, looking out onto the muddy streets. In one doorway I saw an old man emptying out the water from a leaky shoe. Nearby, ragged street children were playing football, using puddles as goalposts.

The drizzle turned to rain and the rain to a downpour. The badly drained streets filled with water as puddles grew into ponds. At one flooded junction, two donkey-carts were ferrying pedestrians across a small newly formed lake.

After much hunting down narrow lanes, we eventually found the Church of St Michael and the Virgin. The priest was not in, and instead I was shown in to meet his wife, who politely offered me tea. But like everyone else that day, she looked suddenly panic-stricken when I tried to turn the conversation towards the attack on the church.

'There is no problem,' she said. 'It is very nice here. Very nice Muslims.' She giggled nervously.

'But didn't a mob of Muslims attack the church only recently?'

'Yes,' replied the woman. 'But do not write this.'

'What happened?' I asked.

'Nothing. The Muslims came to the church. But the police were stronger.'

'Was there firing?'

'No.'

'But I read in the newspapers that several people were killed.'

'A little firing. Maybe. But in the street. Not in the church.'

I felt brutal forcing the woman to say what she wanted to keep hidden, but I really needed to know what had happened. 'How many people attacked the church?' I asked.

'Not many.'

'Roughly?'

'Four hundred. Five hundred. My husband telephoned the government and the police came.'

'They wanted to burn the church,' said a voice from the door. It was the old man who had shown me into the priest's house. He was about seventy, with a greying toothbrush moustache. He had been listening to the woman floundering, and decided to speak up. 'It was a Friday, after Muslim prayers. They came from the Adam Mosque in Ibrahim Abdel Ghazi Street. After prayers had finished, an *Irhebi* in the congregation took the microphone from the imam. He told the people to go to the church and burn it, and to kill policemen. Some good Muslims in the mosque came and told us what was happening, so we had time to lock the gates.'

'Were they armed?'

'They had guns. Many kinds of gun. And some of the *Irhebin* had bombs.'

'Home-made?'

'Yes. Not professional bombs. They threw them over the fence. They didn't make a big fire, just broke one or two windows. Many children were here having lessons. They were afraid and were crying. The teachers took them into the church and made them sing hymns, but still they could hear the chanting outside.'

'What were they chanting?'

'"*Islamaya Islamaya la Mesihaya wa la Yahoudaya . . .*" It means "Islam Islam, no Christians, no Jews." Over and over again they were shouting it. Also "Kill the Christians, Kill the Christians."'

'When we heard this we were all praying,' said the priest's wife. 'But we had confidence that God would help us. My husband was calling the police and Pope Shenoudah. We were not frightened.'

'And the police came quickly?'

'Yes,' said the old man. 'In two big trucks. When the Muslims saw them they ran away. For a month afterwards there were policemen standing every metre along the road.'

'Do you think it could happen again?'

'We hope it will not,' said the woman. 'Afterwards many Muslims telephoned us to say how sorry they were.'

'But none visited us,' said the man. 'Like us, the Muslims are afraid of the *Irhebin*.'

As we drove back to the hotel in the rain, I asked Menas

why the Copts had been so unwilling to talk openly about their troubles.

'They are afraid,' he said. 'They know the government says there is no problem, so they say that too.'

'But isn't that counterproductive?'

'We don't like to create problems with the Muslims. At the moment our life is not too bad. To shout out our complaints will do us no good. The Christians in Europe will not help. Nor will the Americans. There is no one to help us. So we keep quiet. We have no option but to get on as best we can.'

He frowned: 'To be honest,' he said, 'the people are afraid. The Father in the church was afraid. If the government does not like what we are saying, it can be very cruel with us, in many ways: with work, with business, with our families, with our children in schools. They can make our life hell. For this reason the people are not telling you the clear situation.'

He slowed the car to drive through a deep puddle covering the entire width of the road. When we had safely reached the far side he said: 'This is not your problem. It is our problem. You make a book then you go home. But we have to stay here. I know you are trying to help. But you must be very careful. If you are not, you could do us great harm.'

That evening, for the third time since my return from St Antony's, I visited the Press Centre to find out whether my application to visit Upper Egypt had yet been approved.

Predictably, I was informed that no decision had so far been reached. As no decision seemed likely in the near future, I decided to play my trump card. Opening my bag, I presented the bureaucrats with a transcript of my March interview with President Mubarak. Highlighted on the last page was the following exchange:

W.D.: What would you tell people who want to visit Egypt? Is it safe for them to return?

MUBARAK: It is VERY safe. We have so many tourists already.

W.D.: So I could go to Asyut?

MUBARAK: Of course. You can go tomorrow! Some of the people in Asyut are criminals and fundamentals. But the majority of the people in Asyut are very good peoples. VERY GOOD PEOPLES. You can go anywhere. No problem. Do not worry about these so-called terrorists.

At first the transcript caused suspicion, then bewilderment, followed shortly afterwards by a fluster of manic activity. When it was verified that I had actually seen the President and that he had given me his personal permission to visit Asyut, my hotel telephone number was taken and I was told that I would have an answer first thing in the morning.

That call has just come through. A government car will come to pick me up at the hotel early tomorrow morning. There was no problem, said the official; I could go anywhere I liked.

My initial jubilation was, however, tempered by the knowledge that this time tomorrow I will be heading towards Asyut – and into the waiting arms of the *Gema'a al-Islamiyya*. But beyond Asyut, *inshallah*, lies the Great Kharga Oasis, the Alcatraz of Byzantium, and still one of the most isolated spots in Egypt. It was the ultimate destination of John Moschos's travels, and will be mine too.

HOTEL CASABLANCA, ASYUT, 18 DECEMBER

The journey to Asyut started promisingly. At six in the morning a black government Mercedes drew up outside my hotel; inside were a chauffeur and an interpreter (or rather minder) named Mahmoud. The chauffeur loaded my grubby rucksack into the beautifully hoovered boot. The Mercedes purred into life and we set off through the early-morning traffic in rather different style to my last trip in Ramazan's battered Peugeot.

For the first hundred miles there was not the slightest indication of trouble. It was a perfect cold, sharp winter's morning. We followed the same road through the peaceful mud-brick villages of the Nile Valley, with their hookah-smoking farmers and trellised tea houses, the edges of the villages punctuated by mud-brick pepperpot pigeon towers. The road was raised on a brick embankment with bright green paddy fields stretching off on either side. In a few areas the winter crop had already been harvested, and as we passed we could see white egrets standing out against the black alluvial mud.

Village labourers were trooping into the fields, silhouetted as they filed along irrigation dykes, hoes balanced over their shoulders. There were no other cars, though as we neared the larger towns, the roads would clog up with an armada of donkey-carts, or occasionally an old village bus rattling over the railway crossings. Sometimes the Mercedes would have to edge its way through a herd of leathery water buffaloes or a nuzzle of sheep being led into market by long-robed peasants, heavily swathed against the morning chill. Kingfishers hovered above the irrigation runnels. Scenes of Biblical calm surrounded us on all sides. It was impossible to imagine that we were heading into a civil war.

Only after we passed the market town of el-Minya did the atmosphere begin to change. We began to pass police checkpoints – at first every five miles or so, but then more frequently. At the same time the big black Mercedes began to attract more and more attention. People stared at us as we passed; few of them were smiling.

By the time we got to the town of Mallawi the police were everywhere. Sandbag emplacements dotted the rooftops; haphazard brick fortifications guarded the police stations and banks. Not only the police were armed: perhaps one in ten of the local population carried assault rifles as they inspected their fields or drove into town to go shopping, the barrels of the Kalashnikovs poking out of the car windows. Mahmoud, who had started the journey full of soothing words about the Western press exaggerating the problems in the region, began for the first time to look nervous.

To distract myself, I concentrated my attention on the region's history. Every ten miles or so we would pass the ruins of some major Byzantine city or monastery: Hermopolis, the Monastery of the Pulley, Antinoe, Deir al Barsha, Bawit. I pulled out my copy of *The Spiritual Meadow*, finding it some comfort that Moschos had had the same problems when he passed through here in the first decade of the seventh century.

Then as now, Upper Egypt was lawless bandit country, where the traveller proceeded at his own risk. Although subject to frequent armed incursions from Nubia and the deserts to the south, the region seems only to have been defended by a half-hearted regiment of part-time *limitanei* (border troops), who did not apparently take their military duties very seriously. Among the papyri from Oxyrhynchus were discovered the family papers of one Flavius Patermuthis, who describes himself with engaging frankness as a 'soldier of the regiment of the Elephantine, by profession a boatman'. In a similar vein, John Moschos met a pious soldier who used every day to sit weaving baskets and praying from dawn until the ninth hour (3 p.m.), then put on his uniform and went on parade. This carried on for eight years, during which time his commander seems to have been quite unsurprised by his behaviour.

Slack discipline among the *limitanei* exacerbated the region's security problems. When he came to Antinoe, Moschos visited Phoebamon the Sophist, who told him the following story:

> In the district around Hermopolis there was a brigand chief whose name was David. He had rendered many people destitute, murdered many others and committed every kind of evil deed. One day while he was engaged in brigandage on the mountain [behind Hermopolis], together with a band of more than thirty robbers, he came to his senses. Conscience-stricken by his evil deeds, he left those who were with him and went to a monastery.
>
> He knocked at the monastery gate [and in due course] the porter emerged and asked what he wanted. The robber chief replied that he wanted to become a monk,

so the porter went inside and told the Abbot. The Abbot came out and when he saw that the man was advanced in age, he said to him: 'You cannot stay here, for the brethren labour very hard. They practise great austerity. Your temperament is different and you could not tolerate the rule of the monastery.' The brigand said he could put up with these things, but the Abbot was persistent in his conviction that the man would not be able to. Then the brigand said to him: 'Know, then, that I am David the robber chief; and the reason I came here was that I might weep for my sins. If you do not accept me, I swear to you and before Him who dwells in Heaven, that I will return to my former way of life. I will bring those who were with me, kill you all and even destroy your monastery.' When the Abbot heard this, he received him into the monastery, tonsured him and gave him the holy habit. Thus he began spiritual combat [against the demons and devils of temptation] and he exceeded all the other members of the monastery in self-control, obedience and humility.

'There were about seventy persons in that monastery,' adds Moschos, 'and David benefited them all, providing them with an example.'

I was still reading about Moschos's journey through the bad-lands of Upper Egypt when the car was brought to a halt at a heavily guarded checkpoint some fifty miles north of Asyut. From slits in the brick turret surmounting the police bunker, the barrels of three machine guns covered the three approaches to the road junction. An officer barked into his walkie-talkie; a pair of conscripts paced nervously around the bunker, fidgeting with the safety catches of their ancient Enfield rifles. One of them looked no older than sixteen. His boots were old and scuffed, and one of them had no laces. He was clearly very frightened.

Mahmoud got out and talked to the two boys, offering them imported American cigarettes. By the time he returned to the car he had discovered why we had been held up.

'They say that it is too dangerous to go on without a guard,' he said. 'The police killed seven militants last weekend. Then yesterday the militants ambushed and killed three policemen not far from here. The militants need to get another four before they get even. Until then the whole district is on alert. They say we'll have to wait here until someone is free to escort us on.'

'How bad do they say the situation is around here?' I asked.

'They say it is very bad,' replied Mahmoud, shaking his head gravely. 'Very bad indeed.'

Our escort drove up less than fifteen minutes later. I had expected a single conscript with an old gun; what we got, rather alarmingly, were six heavily armed paramilitary policemen in a souped-up Japanese pick-up. We had to struggle to keep up. Every time we neared a village, the pick-up driver increased his speed, while one of the guards would flick off his safety catch, balance on the back-flap and search the rooftops for snipers. Before long we turned off the main Upper Egypt road and headed into the town of Sanabu. This was the place that the *Gema'a al-Islamiyya* had attacked two years before, initiating the current campaign. Two convoys of armed activists had swooped down early in the morning. By the time they withdrew, seven Coptic farmers had been hunted down and murdered in their fields; seven others were shot dead in the streets. I had read brief agency reports on the massacre, but wanted to know more. What had precipitated the attack? Had it been completely unexpected?

We drove fast through the narrow streets of the old town, our escort frantically scouring the rooftops and windows for guerrillas, their rifles raised and their fingers on the triggers. It occurred to me, not for the first time, that there could not be a better way of attracting the attention of the *Gema'a al-Islamiyya* than to travel in a black government limousine with an escort of trigger-happy paramilitaries. If it hadn't been for the difficulty of getting through the police roadblocks, it would surely have been safer to have come anonymously in Ramazan's beaten-up old Peugeot, and perhaps to have pulled on one of his dirty old *gelabiyas* while I was about it. As it was, any self-respecting *Gema'a* active service unit must now have been alerted to the fact that a foreigner was

439

in the area, charging around Sanabu in a ludicrously opulent government Mercedes.

Eventually we came to a halt at a makeshift roadblock in a small square at the centre of the town. The roadblock was made up of a pair of logs balanced on two battered old oildrums. Behind it stood a line of tall men in *gelabiyas* and white turbans, each holding a gun. Behind the men rose the façade of a Coptic church.

'These are village guards,' explained Mahmoud. 'Come on. If you want to do an interview, make it quick.'

I jumped out of the car and was ushered hurriedly into the priest's house beside the church. The paramilitaries stayed outside with their guns levelled, but the leader of the village guards came into the presbytery with Mahmoud and me. With his scarf and dark glasses removed I saw that he was a surprisingly old man, at least sixty. He kissed the priest's hand and sat down beside him. When the two men had introduced themselves, using Mahmoud as an interpreter, I asked them about the events which had led up to the massacre. Slowly the story emerged. It was a tale of almost Sicilian viciousness.

It had all begun several years before, when a Copt decided to sell his house. One of the leading Muslim families in the village, who also happened to be local commanders of the *Gema'a*, had wished to buy it. But they had offered an insultingly low price, and were outbid by a relatively wealthy Copt named Munir who owned the local garage. Gemal Haridi, the head of the Muslim family, made it clear that if he was magnanimous enough to let the sale go ahead between the two Copts, his family would at least expect a considerable cut of the purchase price. Munir refused to pay. Two weeks later, Munir's son, an engineer aged twenty-five, was shot dead as he bent under the bonnet of a car in his father's garage. In the same attack Munir was shot in the foot. He had to have the foot amputated. But he still refused to pay.

Haridi then got some *Gema'a al-Islamiyya* hitmen to murder another relative of Munir who worked in Asyut. The assassins ambushed him as he was walking to work at the Asyut Medical Centre. They were armed with long sickles and killed him by holding him down and cutting off his head. Then they cut his body to pieces. Still Munir remained intransigent: he would not pay a piastre to men who had killed his son and his cousin. The Copts of Sanabu were proud of his resistance, and many others also stopped paying Haridi protection money. Haridi beat up several Copts as a warning. There was no change. Slowly the tension rose. Haridi encouraged the local Muslims to spit at the Copts when they passed them in the street; the Copts sneered back. Haridi decided that the Copts were getting above themselves. They needed to be taught a proper lesson.

Early in the morning of 24 April 1992, Gemal Haridi gathered together a small task force of his extended family and a group of *Gema'a* henchmen from Asyut. He equipped them all with automatic weapons and they hijacked several cars on the main Asyut–Cairo highway. Then they split up. One convoy attacked the fields near the Coptic hamlet of Manshit Nasser, where all the Coptic villagers were engaged in the harvest. The Muslims hunted the harvesters through the stooks and haystacks. Seven Copts were killed, all members of a single family whose fields happened to lie nearest the road. The second convoy, led by Haridi, drove into the town centre of Sanabu. At point-blank range, they shot the Coptic doctor as he opened up his surgery. They killed the Coptic headmaster, hunting him through the school before gunning him down in front of his pupils, riddling his body with more than eighty bullets. Then they killed five Coptic shopkeepers in their shops, before jumping back in their cars and heading on to Asyut. It all took less than an hour.

'I heard the shots as I was getting dressed,' said Amba Dawood, the priest. 'We had been expecting violence, so I was not surprised. From all over the town you could hear the sound of screaming.'

'Every family who had lost one of their members was crying,' said Abdil Mesiyah Tosi, the head of the village guards.

'What about the police?'

'They came, but it was too late,' said Tosi. 'They knew Haridi had already killed three people and was demanding money, but before this they had not intervened at all or offered us protection. By the time they came everything was over.'

'Had you done anything to protect yourselves? Bought guns or anything?'

'No,' said the priest. 'We have always believed that God will retaliate for us.'

'And does He?'

'Of course. Gemal Haridi is in jail now. The other big *amir* of the terrorists in this area, Arafa Mahmoud, was killed by the police one year ago. They ambushed him as he was coming out of a mosque. When they tried to arrest him he resisted, so they shot him dead.'

'So are your relations with the local Muslims improved at all?'

'The majority of Muslim families here are fanatics,' said Tosi. 'After the massacre they did not even come to see what had happened to us.'

'But it is a little better now,' said the priest. 'Since Arafa was killed and Haridi put in jail they have become a little more friendly. These two men were scaring the Muslims and telling them not to deal with the Copts.'

'And the government?' I said. 'Is it helping?'

'Now the government is doing everything possible to crush the *Gema'a*,' said the priest. 'The only trouble we have is when we request to repair our church. I applied to make improvements to it three years ago and still the government has not given us permission. No acknowledgement. Nothing. When the sheikhs ask for something for their mosques the government gives them whatever they want. They are trying to appease the Muslims. But with the Copts they don't even respond.'

'But do you think the worst is over?'

The two men hesitated.

'No,' said Tosi. 'In this village it is a little better, but beyond here it is still very bad. We are still very scared to go to Deir ul-Muharraq, for instance. Many fanatics are living there.'

'It has become a feud between the local Muslims and the police,' explained Amba Dawood. 'If they have the chance, any of the people in that area will try to kill a policeman. In that area there are still shootings every day.'

'So are the Copts leaving?' I asked.

'A few have gone to Cairo,' said the priest. 'But the rest of us are staying.'

'This incident has increased our resolve to stay and fight,' said Tosi. 'This is our country. We will stay here for ever.'

Back on the main road, our escort drove into a lay-by and stopped. The leader, a young major, spoke earnestly into his walkie-talkie. Mahmoud got out and asked what was happening. They explained that as we wanted to go to Deir ul-Muharraq, they needed more guards. Mahmoud returned looking anxious.

'I don't understand what has happened,' he said. 'I last came here three years ago with a party of twenty foreign journalists. Then we went anywhere we liked without an escort. Now they are worried that six guards are insufficient.'

I felt more exposed than ever sitting up on the embankment in our black government limousine. Mahmoud clearly felt the same, and after a couple of minutes he remarked: 'The terrorists hide in canebrakes like these and shoot at passing police convoys. I don't like it.'

To pass the time until our second escort arrived, I went up to the Major and talked to him. He was from Alexandria, he said, and didn't like it in Upper Egypt. The people were very primitive, without any manners or education. I asked him about the *Gema'a*. Thankfully, he said, they had no heavy weapons: no grenades or mortars. Nor were they good fighters. When confronted they always ran away. The problem was that they were invisible. Some were educated, some were small landowners, others were just simple farmers. A few had beards but many had shaved them off. They were always young; otherwise they were indistinguishable from any other locals.

'You never know when something will happen,' he said. 'It can be just like now, very quiet, and suddenly two of your men will be dead. Yesterday afternoon, three of the local policemen were killed on this road just half a mile up there. Earlier in the month one of my boys was gunned down a mile to the south. There is no warning, just a shot and then the peace returns. The worst of it is that you never know when it will happen.'

I went back and waited inside the car. After what felt like an age, but in reality was probably no more than twenty minutes, our new escort arrived and we headed on, now sandwiched between two pick-ups bristling with armed men. A little way along the highway we turned off down a narrow mud track, towards a great plantation of palm trees. Before long the fortified walls of the Coptic Abbey of Deir ul-Muharraq, the Burned Monastery, reared up out of the palms.

The monastery is supposed to mark one of the resting places of the Holy Family on their flight into Egypt, but six months before our visit it had become famous for a less uplifting event.

'This was where Amba Benjamin was standing when the *Gema'a* opened fire,' said Amba Beiman, the monk who met us at the monastery gate. He pointed to a patch of dust at his feet. 'And over here, this was where Amba Agabios fell.'

The old monk bristled through his thick black beard as he pointed out the lines of bulletholes in the plaster of the monastery wall. 'We had a tip-off from one of our tenants that something of the sort was being planned,' he said. 'He had heard his nephew discussing plans to attack the monastery and he came here one night to warn us. Three times we begged the police to give us a guard, but they didn't take any action. Now the terrorists have won martyrs' crowns for Amba Benjamin and Amba Agabios.'

Mahmoud, who had been scanning the surrounding palm trees, hurried us into the monastery and porters closed the great iron-clad gates behind us.

'We monks don't search for martyrdom,' said Amba Beiman. 'But we welcome it if it comes.'

He led us into the monastery. Like a Crusader castle, it was defended by not one but three rings of walls.

'It was Lent, and none of the fathers would normally have left the monastery gates,' said Amba Beiman. 'But Amba Benjamin had come out to talk to a layman who wanted to get married here. Amba Agabios had followed him to tell him that the Abbot

444

had asked him to lead prayers the next day. The gunmen were waiting in a car in the shadows when they opened fire. The layman was shot too, as was a thirteen-year-old boy. He just happened to be passing at the wrong moment.'

The monk shook his head. 'We gave them all nice funerals,' he said.

At this point Mahmoud spoke up: 'Forgive me for asking, Father,' he said. 'I have never been in a monastery before. Do monks weep when one of you dies?'

'Of course,' said Amba Beiman. 'We are human beings. But we live in contemplation. Our senses are especially delicate. Anything can hurt us. Something like this is terrible for us.'

'Aren't you afraid that the Gema'a might come back?' I asked.

'We lost two good fathers in the attack,' said Amba Beiman. 'But we trust in God.'

'And do none of the monks want to move to a safer area, if only for the time being?'

'No,' replied Amba Beiman. 'This is a holy place for us. There have been Christians here ever since the Holy Family took shelter here from King Herod. In dreams some of the fathers still see the Holy Family wandering around here. As monks we should overcome evil, not let evil overcome us. This is a place of visions: we cannot ever leave it.'

By now the sun was sinking low in the sky. Mahmoud urged me to hurry up: he didn't want to be on the roads after dark. But before we left, Amba Beiman insisted on taking us into the innermost courtyard to show us the high castellated keep that the Byzantine Emperor Zeno had built to defend the monks from Bedouin attacks in the fifth century A.D.

'We Copts have always been attacked for our faith,' said Amba Beiman. 'Compared to some of those attacks, this trouble is nothing.'

'What sort of attacks are you thinking of?' I asked, alarmed.

'Oh, the massacres of the Emperor Diocletian, for instance,' replied Amba Beiman. 'Now there was a *real* persecution.'

445

The twilight was giving way to darkness by the time we drove into Asyut, sandwiched between our two escorts. Armed soldiers, heavily swathed against the cold, stood at every junction. Paramilitary police sat in open pick-ups scanning the passers-by. Plainclothes security men stood around with walkie-talkies, clutching machine guns and signalling to police snipers on the rooftops. The town felt like an armed camp.

The police had already arranged a hotel for us. Our escort fanned out and Mahmoud and I bolted from the car into the hotel. That night we slept with three armed men guarding the lobby. The journey and the tension had exhausted me, but I slept calm in the knowledge that the difficult part of the journey was nearly over. Only one last stretch of road remained.

HOTEL OASIS, KHARGA, 20 DECEMBER

Asyut was known in Byzantine times as Lycopolis. The Byzantines regarded it as the back of beyond, the Siberia of the Empire. As such it was a suitable place of exile for those who fell foul of the Emperor or his consort. John of Cappadocia, Justinian's rapacious Praetorian Prefect (known as 'The Scissors' in reference to his tax-collecting methods), was exiled here after incurring Theodora's displeasure; more humble offenders would be dispatched to spend the rest of their lives in forced labour in the Eastern Desert, mining porphyry and granite at the quarry of Mons Porphyrites.

But it was not quite the end of the known world. Beyond Lycopolis lay one last outpost of Byzantine rule, the most distant and inaccessible spot in the entire Empire. To this place the most dangerous criminals and subversives were dispatched. In Byzantium, no crime was taken more seriously than advocating heresy, and it was thus to the Great Oasis, modern Kharga, that Nestorius, one of the most reviled heretics in Byzantine history, was banished after his disgrace at the Council of Ephesus in 431 A.D. John Moschos knew this and includes a story about Nestorius's exile in *The Spiritual Meadow*. Possibly it was his notoriety that attracted Moschos to Lycopolis. Possibly the monk in Moschos was drawn to this place of ultimate spiritual exile, the very last outpost of Christendom. Whatever the motivation, despite the extreme danger inherent in such a journey, Moschos and Sophronius chose to travel to this most isolated oasis settlement, deep in the desert that formed the southern boundary of the Empire.

It was to be the last trip that the friends would make of their own volition. For me too this was to be the end of my journey. At 5.30 a.m. I packed my bags, paid the bill and set out for the last time in Moschos's footsteps.

Our convoy left Asyut at dawn. Mist from the Nile swirled through the riverside streets, deserted except for a scattering of heavily muffled sentries warming their hands at makeshift bonfires. It was still dark and still exceptionally cold. Toad-like armoured personnel carriers and light tanks had been deployed at most of the town's principal road junctions. I had not seen such armour since leaving eastern Turkey, and the sight of it brought back memories of Diyarbakir and the Tur Abdin three months previously.

Despite a similar feeling of political disintegration and, for the local Christians, a sense of siege, the two situations were in fact very different. Indeed the problems faced by the Christians right across the Middle East had proved surprisingly diverse. When I began this journey I had expected that Islamic fundamentalism would prove to be the Christians' main enemy in every country I visited. But it had turned out to be more complicated than that.

In south-east Turkey the Syrian Christians were caught in the crossfire of a civil war, a distinct ethnic group trodden underfoot in the scrummage between two rival nationalisms, one Kurdish, the other Turkish. Here it was their ethnicity as much as their religion which counted against the Christians: they were not Kurds and not Turks, therefore they did not fit in. In Lebanon, the Maronites had reaped a bitter harvest of their own sowing: their failure to compromise with the country's Muslim majority had led to a destructive civil war that ended in a mass emigration of Christians and a proportional diminution in Maronite power. The dilemma of the Palestinian Christians was quite different again. Their problem was that, like their Muslim compatriots, they were Arabs in a Jewish state, and as such suffered as second-class citizens in their own country, regarded with a mixture of suspicion and contempt by their Israeli masters. However, unlike most of the Muslims, they were educated professionals and found it relatively easy to emigrate, which they did, *en masse*. Very few were now left. Only in Egypt was the Christian population unambiguously threatened by a straightforward resurgence of Islamic fundamentalism, and even there such violent fundamentalism was strictly limited to specific Cairo suburbs and a number of towns and villages in Upper Egypt, even if some degree of discrimination was evident across the country.

But if the pattern of Christian suffering was more complex than I could possibly have guessed at the beginning of this journey, it was also more desperate. In Turkey and Palestine, the extinction of the descendants of John Moschos's Byzantine Christians seemed imminent; at current emigration rates, it was unlikely that either community would still be in existence in twenty years. In Lebanon and Egypt the sheer number of Christians ensured a longer presence, albeit with ever-decreasing influence. Only in Syria had I seen the Christian population looking happy and confident, and even their future looked decidedly uncertain, with most expecting a major backlash as soon as Asad's repressive minority regime began to crumble.

Outside Asyut, we passed through a thin strip of arable land: the farmers were rising now, old men on donkeys disappearing down lanes, women carrying panniers of dung on their heads as they walked in pairs down avenues of palm trees. Soon after that we crossed an invisible boundary and left the cultivation for the desert. There our escort turned back, and we pulled in to say goodbye.

'From here it should be safe,' said the Major. 'As long as you reach Kharga by nightfall.'

Ahead of us stretched an apparent infinity of empty desert. The dunes were made not of sand but of a white powder so fine, so light, so easily blown into the atmosphere by the slightest breeze, that the desert seemed to steam like a white swamp. From that swirling surface the powder rose, fugging the atmosphere, obscuring the sun, blowing onto the road and dusting the car bonnet and windscreen.

The desert played tricks with our senses. In such a place it was impossible to verify the size of any object that might break this white madness. Outcrops of rock might be pebbles, boulders or small mountains. At one point, shortly after leaving our escort, we came across a group of workers who were labouring to mend a stretch of road badly damaged by a freak storm that had hit Asyut a month earlier. From a distance the men appeared like giants; as we got nearer they shrunk to dwarves. Only as we passed alongside them were we able to judge their true height with any certainty.

In the entire journey only one geological feature broke the formless hallucination through which we passed. This was the massive faultline which ran straight through the middle of the wasteland. For hundreds of miles the desert extended onwards, completely flat. Then it hit the faultline – a near-vertical cliff-face a thousand feet high – before continuing at the new lower level, as resolutely horizontal as before. It was an extraordinary sight and must have been even more dramatic for travellers like Moschos and Sophronius who passed this way on foot, striding wearily over the sand dunes, the hoods of their habits wrapped over their mouths to keep out the choking white dust.

The face of the cliff was pitted with caves, and I wondered whether any contained a spring that might have allowed monks to live there. It was certainly the sort of remote, suggestively apocalyptic location which would have appealed to the imaginations of the Coptic monks. It made me think of a gruesome story told by the hermit Paphnutius:

> I thought one day that I would go into the inner desert
> to see whether there were any monks beyond me. So I

walked on for four days and four nights, and did not eat bread or drink water. On the last day I came to a cave, and when I reached it, I knocked on the door for about half the day. No one answered me, so I imagined that there was no one there. I looked inside and I saw a brother sitting down, silent. So, I grasped his arm and his arm came away in my hands and was like this earthly dust. I touched his whole body and found that he was dead, and indeed had been dead for many years. And I looked and saw a sleeveless tunic hanging up, and when I touched this, it too fell apart and turned to dust. And I stood and prayed and I took off my cloak, and I wrapped him up. I dug with my hands in the sand and buried him, and I came away from that place . . . [That evening I was still walking when] the sun was beginning to set. I looked up and saw a herd of antelope coming from a distance, and in their midst was a monk. And when he approached me he was unclothed, and his hair concealed his nether parts, serving for clothing around him. And when he reached me he was very afraid, thinking I was a spirit, for many spirits had tried him . . .

After winding our way down the face of the cliff, nothing else broke the relentless white emptiness of the desert until, in the middle of the afternoon, we saw the first hint of green on the horizon. We were held up for a quarter of an hour at an army checkpoint, and shortly afterwards entered the date palm plantations that today, as in Byzantine times, mark the edge of the Great Oasis.

Kharga still feels like the end of the earth. In the 1950s Nasser attempted to move some of the population of the Nile valley to this place, and for ten years much energy was expended in trying to make Kharga into a prosperous and innovative new town. It came to nothing. The city was too isolated and too remote. Since the Second World War it has rained only once in Kharga, for ten minutes, in the winter of 1959. The population, lured there by the promise of grants and tax breaks, slowly drifted back to their homes by the Nile. After Nasser's death the political urge vanished too, the tax breaks dried up and Kharga was left a bleak, empty monument to the clumsiness of central planning, a maze of silent roundabouts, derelict factories and empty apartment blocks.

The vast 1950s Kharga Oasis Hotel is a witness both to Nasser's hopes and, in its terrible emptiness, to their spectacular disappointment. After we had checked in, Mahmoud and I went to eat lunch in the dining hall. There we sat next to the only other guests staying in the hotel. They were engineers refurbishing the huge Kharga prison which, they whispered, was Egypt's principal depository for political prisoners. As in Byzantine times, the Oasis had proved to have only one real use: hermetically sealed by the wastes surrounding it on every side, its isolation and bleakness still made it an ideal place to hide the embarrassing and banish the unwanted. Only the cast has changed, with communists and militant Islamists now filling the cells once occupied by Nestorian heretics.

After lunch, I gave Mahmoud the slip and walked out alone to the place where I wanted to end my pilgrimage, alone. Two miles outside the town, amid the date palms on the edge of desert, there stood the ruins of an ancient Pharaonic temple to the god Amun. In Byzantine times the old Pharaonic priests had been expelled and the site taken over by monks. They erased some of the more erotic of the Pharaonic sculptures and erected in their place a series of pious Greek inscriptions, punctuated here and there with crosses. These were intended to keep away the families of demons the monks believed to have inhabited the temple under its previous management. The ruined temple is almost certainly the site of the Lavra of the Great Oasis which Moschos mentions as having been sacked in a nomad raid immediately before his visit:

> When the Mazices came and overran all that region, they came to the Great Oasis and slew many monks, while many others were taken prisoner. Among those taken captive at the Lavra of the Great Oasis were Abba John, formerly lector at the Great Church of Constanti-

nople, Abba Eustathios the Roman and Abba Theodore, all of whom were sick. When they had been captured, Abba John said to the barbarians: 'Take me to the city and I will have the Bishop give you twenty-four pieces of gold.' So one of the barbarians led him off and brought him near to the city. Abba John went to the Bishop and began to implore him to give the barbarian the twenty-four pieces of gold, but the Bishop could only find eight. He gave these to Abba John, but the barbarian would not accept them. The men of the fortress had no choice but to hand over Abba John, who wept and groaned as he was carried off to the barbarians' tents.

Abba Leo [an old friend of Moschos] happened to be in the [oasis's] fortress at that time. Three days later, he took the eight pieces of gold and went out to the barbarians. He pleaded with them in these words: 'Take me and these eight pieces of gold, and let those three monks go. They are sick and cannot work for you so you will have to kill them. But I am in good health and I can work for you.' So the barbarians took both him and the eight pieces of gold, letting the other monks go free. Abba Leo was carried off by the barbarians and when he was exhausted and could go no further, they beheaded him. Thus did Abba Leo fulfil the scripture: *Greater love hath no man than to lay down his life for his friends.*

Overlooking the monastery ruins, on top of a low hill a short distance out into the desert, lay the Coptic necropolis of Bagawat. I walked over there in the bright red evening sun. The necropolis was like a Byzantine village sitting amid the dunes: long streets of simple *café-au-lait* mud-brick tomb-houses and chapels: some flat-topped, others with domes, a few decorated with blind arcading or naïve frescoes, many severely plain. Some of the tombs had clearly held the bodies of saints or holy men, for their walls were marked with pious Byzantine graffiti: 'Pray for the soul of Zoe',

'Blessings on Theophilus', 'Remember Menas'. But the tombs had decayed in the winds of 1,500 winters, so that the brick was cracked and brittle, and many of the buildings were left like skeletons, without a roof or a back wall. Many had been attacked by tomb-robbers, and deep pits had been dug to reveal the hidden burial chambers. Others had collapsed altogether. The whole complex was windswept and eerie, and a gathering breeze wailed through the broken doorways.

These tombs, I realised, must have been the last thing that John Moschos saw before he left the Great Oasis on the Alexandria road, *en route* to his final exile in Constantinople. Sitting there, looking out over the temple-monastery where his friend Abba Leo had lived before being carried off into slavery, Moschos must have known that his whole world was crumbling. But I wondered whether even he realised the extent to which he was witnessing the last days of the golden age of the Christian Middle East.

Soon after his return to Alexandria, the city was to fall to the Persians. Briefly recovered by the Byzantines, it fell again in 641 A.D., this time to the Muslims. Islam has held it – and most of the rest of the Middle East – ever since. The Christian population that Moschos knew and wrote about – the monks and the stylites, the merchants and the soldiers, the prostitutes and the robber chiefs – all the strange and eccentric characters who wander in and out of the pages of *The Spiritual Meadow*, were conquered and subjugated, their numbers gradually whittled down by emigration, intermarriage and mass apostasy. With occasional intervals of stasis, such as the early Ottoman period, that process has persisted ever since, greatly accelerating in this century. It is a historical continuum that began during the journeys of Moschos and the final chapter of which I have been witnessing on my own travels some fourteen hundred years later. Christianity is an Eastern religion which grew firmly rooted in the intellectual ferment of the Middle East. John Moschos saw that plant begin to wither in the hot winds of change that scoured the Levant of his day. On my journey in his footsteps I have seen the very last stalks in the process of being uprooted. It has been a continuous process, lasting nearly one and a half millennia. Moschos saw its beginnings. I have seen the beginning of its end.

So, as the sun sank down behind the date palms of the oasis, I thought of Moschos standing on this hillside amid these tombs at the end of the world, fretting about the heretics and brigands on the road ahead, checking in his bag to make sure his roll of notes and jottings was safe, then turning his back on this last crumbling outpost of the Christian Empire, and tramping on over the dunes to catch up with the tall, ascetic figure of Sophronius.

I left them there, and wandered back down the hill alone. As I walked, I realised I had now been on the road for more than five months. I had left Scotland in midsummer. Next week would be Christmas. On the front of my diary was a damp-ring left by a glass of ouzo I drank on the Holy Mountain. Inside were stains from a glass of tea knocked over in Istanbul. Some sugar grains from the restaurant in the Baron Hotel have stuck to the pages on which are scribbled my notes from Aleppo. Around these marks, this book is filled with a series of names, places and conversations, some of which even now seem strangely odd and distant.

As I was standing there a flight of brilliant white ibises passed overhead, circling down to roost at the pool beside the old temple. I pulled up the collar of my jacket and headed back out of the desert into the oasis, ready now for the journey home. Darkness was drawing in, and behind me at the top of the hill a chill wind was howling through the tombs.

GLOSSARY

LIST OF BIBLIOGRAPHICAL
SOURCES

INDEX

GLOSSARY

Agah: Kurdish chieftain or commander. A term of respect. (Pronounced Aah)

Amir: (lit. 'rich') Muslim nobleman or commander.

Apophthegmata: (or Apophthegmata Patrum), a collection of sayings of the desert fathers.

Archimandrite: Abbot of an Orthodox monastery or the superior of a group of monasteries.

Arianism: An early Christian heresy, named after Arius of Alexandria (c. 250–336 A.D.), which denied the true divinity of Christ. Arianism became popular in parts of the early medieval West, notably in Visigothic Spain. When Islam first erupted from Arabia, many early Byzantine theologians, including St John of Damascus, believed that the new faith was merely an exotic strain of Arianism.

Assyrian Christians: Name given to members of the East Syrian or Nestorian Church (q.v.). The name derives from the mistaken belief of early Anglican missionaries that the Nestorians were descendants of the ancient Assyrians.

azan: The Muslim call to prayer.

Ba'ath Party: Arab nationalist party, founded by the Michel Aflaq, a Syrian Christian. Different (and mutually hostile) incarnations of the Ba'ath Party are currently in power in both Syria and Iraq.

bema: The elevated platform at the front of a synagogue; also the sanctuary of an Eastern Christian church.

burka: Muslim women's body covering. Generally refers to something more substantial and voluminous than a simple headscarf.

chador: (lit. 'sheet') Muslim women's veil. Can involve anything from a headscarf to a fully-fledged tent. Similar to *hijab* (q.v.) and *burka* (q.v.).

chi-rho: The monogram of Christ, made up of the two Greek letters *chi* and *rho*. Probably introduced by Constantine the Great after his vision before the battle of the Milvian Bridge (312 A.D.).

chrysobul: An Imperial Byzantine letter or diploma granting privileges.

Named after the golden seal of the Emperor with which such an ordinance was impressed.

coenobitic: The centralised form of Byzantine monasticism, involving a communal life for the monks under the rule of an Abbot, as opposed to the decentralised, idiorrhythmic system, where a group of hermits would live largely independent lives, subject only to the vague strictures of a committee (the *epitropeia*), and meeting only once a week for the Divine Liturgy on Sundays. While a form of idiorrhythmic monasticism was the norm among Celtic monks, it was the coenobitic model that really took off in the West, and almost all modern Western monasteries are coenobitic.

Copt: A native Egyptian Christian. The Coptic Church broke off from the Orthodox mainstream after rejecting the theological decisions of the Council of Chalcedon (451 A.D.). Its Orthodox enemies accused it of indulging in the Monophysite heresy (q.v.), something modern Copts deny.

diamonitirion: The monastic passport necessary to enter and stay upon Mount Athos.

djinn: According to Islamic tradition, a djinn is an invisible spirit, composed of flame, often (though not necessarily always) mischievous.

dormition: In Eastern Christian Churches, the Falling Asleep (*dormitio*) of the Blessed Virgin. Corresponds to the Assumption in the West.

dunum: Traditional Palestinian unit of land measurement. One dunum = 919 square metres, 1/11 of a hectare or 0.23 acres.

exo-narthex: The outer narthex or porch of an Orthodox church.

fellahin: Egyptian peasant farmers. Plural of *fellah*.

flabella: Ceremonial liturgical fan. Now usually a stave topped with a metal disk decorated with images of angels. In some cases small bells can be attached to the disk, in which case the flabella is shaken during the most solemn parts of the liturgy to symbolise the participation of the angels. Flabellae were common in Anglo-Saxon England and Celtic Ireland, but died out in the West before the Norman Conquest. Their use has continued only in the Eastern Churches.

gavour: Infidel.

gelabiya: Long Arab gown. Alternative rendering of *jellaba* (q.v.).

Gema'a al-Islamiyya: (lit. 'The Islamic Party' in Arabic) Fundamentalist Muslim guerrilla organisation fighting to turn Egypt into an Islamic Republic. Operates mainly in Upper Egypt and the poorer Cairo suburbs.

Gnostics: Late antique heretics claiming knowledge of hidden spiritual mysteries. Christian gnosticism had its roots in trends of thought already present in esoteric pagan religious circles. Gnosticism took many different forms, but the most popular Gnostic sects were those that followed the teachings of Valentius, Bardaisan and Marcion.

grimoire: A book of spells.

Haganah: (lit. 'defence' in Hebrew) Left-wing Jewish paramilitary organisation operating illegally in British Mandate Palestine from 1920 onwards. Came out into the open in 1948 as the principal Zionist army fighting for the creation of Israel. As well as winning a remarkable victory against the different Arab armies which invaded Palestine on the British departure, the Haganah was responsible for formulating and carrying out 'Plan Dalet', which led to the expulsion of most of the Palestinian population from their ancestral homes and villages.

Haredim: Ultra-Orthodox Jews.

Hegumenos: Archimandrite (q.v.) or Abbot of a coenobitic (q.v.) Orthodox monastery.

Hezbollah: (lit. 'The Party of God') Militant Islamist organisation. Most notorious as the Iranian-backed terrorist outfit responsible for kidnapping the Western hostages and masterminding the hit-and-run guerrilla operations against the Israeli occupation forces in the south of Lebanon. But it is also now a registered democratic party representing the Shia community in the Lebanese parliament, and runs widespread humanitarian and educational projects alongside its paramilitary activities.

hijab: Muslim women's veil or body covering. Same as *chador* (q.v.).

hypocaust: Roman (and Byzantine) under-floor heating system.

iconoclasm: The period of Byzantine history, from 725 to 842 A.D., when the veneration of icons was outlawed and all sacred images were ordered to be destroyed.

iconoclast: One who destroys images and icons. An opponent of iconodules (q.v.).

iconodule: Worshipper of images. An opponent of iconoclasts (q.v.).

iconostasis: The screen separating the chancel from the main area of a Byzantine church. Corresponds to the English rood-screen, except that the Byzantine version is almost always decorated with a number of icons.

inshallah: God willing (in Arabic).

intifada: The popular Palestinian uprising against the Israeli occupation of the West Bank and Gaza Strip.

irhebi: Terrorist (in Arabic).

jellaba: Long Arab gown. Alternative rendering of *gelabiya* (q.v.).

459

katholikon: The principal church of an Orthodox monastery.

keffiyeh: Checkered Arab headscarf. Particularly associated with the Palestinians.

khatchkar: An intricately carved Armenian cross-slab.

kibbutz: An Israeli collective, usually (though now not always) agriculturally based.

Kyrie: (lit. 'Lord' in Greek) The petition ('Lord have mercy') at the beginning of the Divine Liturgy in the Eastern and Roman Churches.

lavra: (sometimes also spelled *laura*) Today *lavra* is a title that can be given to any large Orthodox monastery, but originally it referred specifically to those organised on the idiorrhythmic method: a collection of detached monks' cells clustered around a monastic church. The monks would generally meet only once a week when they would celebrate the Sunday liturgy together; otherwise they lived as semi-independent hermits.

limitanei: Byzantine border troops.

loukoumi: A sticky rosewater confection beloved of Orthodox monks. The Greek version of Turkish Delight.

Magister Militum: Byzantine provincial military governor.

Malfono: Teacher (in Turoyo).

Maronite: An Eastern Christian Church, originally based in Syria, though for many centuries located mainly in Lebanon. The Maronites look to an obscure fourth-century Syrian hermit, St Maron, as their founder. Although it seems certain that the Maronites once subscribed the Monothelite heresy (q.v.), they have been in full communion with Rome since the Crusader period, and today their Patriarch has the rank of Cardinal; but they still use the ancient Antiochene rites.

masjid: Mosque.

medresse: An Islamic college.

mihrab: Prayer niche in mosques, indicating the direction of Mecca.

minyan: The minimum quorum of adult males without which Jews may not celebrate the more solemn prayers and rituals in a synagogue.

misericord: Projecting ledge on the hinged seat of a Western choirstall serving as a support to a standing singer. They are often beautifully carved and decorated.

Monophysite: (lit. 'one nature') The belief that there is only one divine nature in the person of Christ, as opposed to the Orthodox position that Christ has a double nature, at once human and divine. Monophysitism was declared heretical at the Council of Chalcedon (451 A.D.), after which the Coptic, Syrian and Armenian Churches all separated from the rest of the Christian community. Today all these Churches regard the term Monophysite as pejorative, and claim it represents a misunderstanding of their theology.

Monothelite: A compromise definition of the nature of Christ suggested by the Emperor Heraclius in 638 A.D., in an attempt to end the split between Orthodox and Monophysites which was then threatening to break apart the Empire. The definition maintains that Christ has one divine energy and one will. Rejected out of hand by all the parties it was trying to reconcile, the only sect to subscribe to the doctrine were the unfortunate Maronites, who thus came to be regarded as heretics by both the Monophysites and the Orthodox. Persecuted accordingly, the Maronites fled to the heights of Mount Lebanon, where they still remain.

moshav: A small collective farm in Israel.

muezzin: Muslim prayer leader. In the old days used to chant the *azan* (q.v.) from the minaret five times a day, but a bit of an endangered species since the advent of the cassette recorder.

Mukhabarat: Secret police (in Arab countries).

Mukhtar: (lit. 'the man chosen' in Arabic) Village headman.

narthex: Railed-off western portico or antechamber to the main body of an Orthodox church, for the use of women, penitents and catechumens.

Nestorian: An adherent to the doctrines of Nestorius, Patriarch of Constantinople in 428 A.D., who asserted that Christ had two quite distinct divine and human persons, as opposed to the Orthodox position that the incarnate Christ was a single person, at once God and man. Nestorianism was characterised by the rejection of the term *Theotokos* (q.v.). Nestorius was expelled from the Orthodox Church at the Council of Ephesus (431 A.D.) and his followers declared heretics. Modern Nestorians revere the memory of Nestorius but deny that their Church was founded by him, claiming instead that their traditions go back to the apostle Addai who led a mission to Edessa and the Persian Empire soon after Christ's death. They therefore prefer to be known as the Church of the East, the Assyrian Church or the East Syrian Church. Once a major religious force in Asia, with churches dotting the Silk Route from Eastern Turkey to China, the Nestorian Church is now small and internally divided. It is based mainly in Iraq, where its adherents suffer from persecution, although refugees have spread the faith to Syria, India, England, Australia and the US.

nomisma: A Byzantine unit of currency, roughly equivalent to ten pence.

Panaghia: (lit. 'the All-Holy' in Greek) Orthodox honorific for the Virgin Mary.

Pantocrator: (lit. 'All Mighty' in Greek) The image or icon of Jesus ruling as Christ the King, generally placed in the apse or dome of an Orthodox church.

Sassanian: (or Sassanid) The dynasty which ruled the Persian Empire from 211 to 651 A.D. In the early seventh century the Sassanians invaded and occupied most of the Byzantine Levant, sacking Antioch, Jerusalem and Alexandria, until being driven back and defeated by the Byzantine Emperor Heraclius in 651 A.D.

servis: A shared taxi in Arab countries.

shabab: (lit. 'young men' in Arabic) Now generally used in the English-language press to refer to the young stone-throwers of the Palestinian *intifada* (q.v.).

shalwar: Baggy 'Turkish' trousers (or 'Allah catchers').

simandron: The wooden stick 'rung' in Eastern Christian monasteries to summon the faithful to prayer. Introduced after the advent of Islam, when Christians were forbidden from ringing bells.

skete: A minor monastery or large hermitage.

stylite: Byzantine monk or hermit who, following the example of St Symeon Stylites, chose to live on top of a pillar. St Symeon originally mounted his pillar to stop pilgrims attempting to pluck hairs from his cloak or person, but subsequent stylites chose to live up pillars as a specific form of rigorous asceticism which symbolised their attempt to come as close to God as was humanly possible. Stylitism spread as far north as Georgia and as far west as Trier, but it remained most popular in the vicinity of Antioch where, in the fifth and sixth centuries A.D., pillars dotted most of the highest hilltops.

Suriani: The name given to the Syrian Orthodox (q.v.) community in Turkey and Syria.

Syrian Orthodox: At the Council of Chalcedon in 451 A.D., the Church of Antioch was condemned for Monophysitism (q.v.). It broke from the orthodox mainstream and set up a new hierarchy of its own. Surviving persecution first by the Byzantine Emperors, then by a succession of Muslim rulers, the remnants of the Church still survive in eastern Turkey, Syria and parts of southern India. It is also known as the Jacobite Church, while in Turkey and Syria its members are referred to as the Suriani (q.v.).

Tau cross: T-shaped bishop's staff used in Eastern (and Celtic) Churches.

tell: (Arabic) A mound or tumulus covering an archaeological site.

tetrapylon: A ceremonial arch with openings on all four sides.

Theotokos: (lit. 'The Mother of God' in Greek) A title of the Virgin Mary adopted at the Councils of Ephesus and Chalcedon (431 and 451 A.D. respectively) as an assertion of the doctrine of the divinity of Our Lord's person.

wadi: Arabic for valley. A riverbed or gorge, usually dry except in the wet season.

wahde: Arabic for 'gently'.

Yezidis: A rare and esoteric religion, perhaps originally an offshoot of some Gnostic Christian or heretical Muslim sect. Yezidis believe that Lucifer, having extinguished the flames of hell with the tears of his penitence, has been forgiven by God and reinstated as the Chief Angel. Now known as Malik Tawus, the Peacock Angel, he superintends the daily running of the world. Abused as devil-worshippers by their enemies, the Yezidis get on surprisingly well with the Syrian Orthodox, in whose villages many of the Turkish Yezidis live, and whose saints the Yezidis also venerate. The Yezidis can also be found in Georgia, Armenia and Iraq.

BIBLIOGRAPHY OF PRINCIPAL
SOURCES

GENERAL

A.J. Arberry, *Religion in the Middle East* (Cambridge, Cambridge University Press, 1969)

Aziz S. Atiya, *A History of Eastern Christianity* (London, Methuen, 1968)

Norman H. Baynes, 'The "Pratum Spirituale" ', in *Orientalia Christiana Periodica* xiii (1947), pp. 404–14, reprinted in Baynes, *Byzantine Studies* (1955), pp. 261–70

Robert B. Betts, *Christians in the Arab East* (London, SPCK, 1979)

Peter Brown, *The World of Late Antiquity* (London, Thames & Hudson, 1971)

Peter Brown, 'A Dark Age Crisis: Aspects of the Iconoclast Controversy', in *English Historical Review* cccxlvi (January 1973), pp. 1–34

Peter Brown, *The Making of Late Antiquity* (Cambridge, Mass., Harvard University Press, 1978)

Peter Brown, 'Late Antiquity', in Paul Veyne (trans. Arthur Goldhammer), *A History of Private Life: From Pagan Rome to Byzantium* (Cambridge, The Belknap Press of Harvard University Press, 1987)

Peter Brown, *Power and Persuasion in Late Antiquity: Towards a Christian Empire* (Wisconsin, Wisconsin University Press, 1992)

Averil Cameron, *The Mediterranean World in Late Antiquity, A.D 395–600* (London, Routledge, 1993)

Henry Chadwick, 'John Moschos and his Friend Sophronius the Sophist', in *Journal of Theological Studies* xxv, pt 1 (April 1974)

Kenneth Cragg, *The Arab Christian: A History in the Middle East* (London, Mowbray, 1992)

E. Follieri, 'Dove e quando mori Giovanni Mosco?', in *Rivista di Studi Bizantini e Neoellenici* 25 (1988), pp. 3–39

David Fromkin, *A Peace to End All Peace: The Fall of the Ottoman Empire and the Creation of the Modern Middle East* (New York, Avon Books, 1989)

J.F. Haldon, *Byzantium in the Seventh Century: The Transformation of a Culture* (Cambridge, Cambridge University Press, 1990)

Judith Herrin, *The Formation of Christendom* (Oxford, Blackwell, 1987)

Albert Hourani, *Minorities in the Arab World* (Oxford, Oxford University Press, 1946)

Albert Hourani, *A History of the Arab Peoples* (London, Faber & Faber, 1991)

Irmgard Hutter, *Early Christian and Byzantine* (London, Herbert Press, 1988)

A.M.H. Jones, *The Later Roman Empire* (Oxford, Blackwell, 1964, 2 vols)

Walter E. Kaegi, *Byzantium and the Early Islamic Conquests* (Cambridge, Cambridge University Press, 1992)

Ernst Kitzinger, 'The Cult of Images in the Age Before Iconoclasm', in *Dumbarton Oaks Papers* 8 (1954)

Ernst Kitzinger, 'Byzantine Art in the Period Between Justinian and Iconoclasm', in *Berichte Zum XI Internationalen Byzantinisten Kongress* (1960)

Ernst Kitzinger, *Byzantine Art in the Making* (London, Faber & Faber, 1977)

Jules Leroy, *Monks and Monasteries of the Middle East* (London, Harrap, 1963)

Cyril Mango, *Byzantium: The Empire of the New Rome* (London, Weidenfeld & Nicolson, 1980)

Cyril Mango, *The Art of the Byzantine Empire 312–1453* (Toronto, Toronto University Press, 1986)

Cyril Mango, *Byzantine Architecture* (London, Faber & Faber, 1986)

Peter Mansfield, *A History of the Middle East* (London, Viking, 1991)

John Moschos (trans. John Wortley), *The Spiritual Meadow* (Kalamazoo, Cistercian Publications, 1992)

John Julius Norwich, *Byzantium: The Early Centuries* (London, Viking, 1988)

Philip Pattendon, 'The Text of the *Pratum Spirituale*', in *Journal of Theological Studies* 26 (1975)

David Talbot Rice, *Art of the Byzantine Era* (London, Thames & Hudson, 1963)

Lyn Rodley, *Byzantine Art and Architecture: An Introduction* (Cambridge, Cambridge University Press, 1994)

Steven Runciman, *Byzantine Civilisation* (London, Edward Arnold, 1933)

Christoph von Schörnborn, *Sophrone de Jerusalem: Vie monastique et confession dogmatique* (Paris, 1972)

Jean-Pierre Valonges, *Vie et mort des Chrétiens D'Orient* (Paris, Fayard, 1994)

Kallistos Ware, *The Orthodox Way* (Oxford, Mowbray, 1979)

Timothy Ware, *The Orthodox Church* (London, Pelican, 1963)

Bat Ye'or, *The Dhimmi: Jews and Christians Under Islam* (Cranbury, Farleigh Dickinson/Associated University Presses, 1985)

Bat Ye'or, *The Decline of Eastern Christianity: From Jihad to Dhimmitude* (Cranbury, Farleigh Dickinson/Associated University Presses, 1996)

CHAPTER 1

Robert Byron, *The Station, Athos: Treasures and Men* (London, Duckworth, 1928)

Robert Curzon, *Visits to Monasteries in the Levant* (London, John Murray, 1849)

John Julius Norwich and Reresby Sitwell, *Mount Athos* (London, Hutchinson, 1966)

Virginia Surtees, *Coutts Lindsay* (Norwich, Michael Russell, 1993)

CHAPTER II

Alexis Alexandris, *The Greek Minority of Istanbul and Greek–Turkish Relations 1918–1974* (Athens, Centre for Asia Minor Studies, 1992)

Percy George Badger, *The Nestorians and their Rituals* (Reprint: London, Darf Publishers, 1987)

Gertrude Bell, *The Churches and Monasteries of the Tur Abdin* (Reprint: London, Pindar Press, 1982)

Sebastian Brock (trans.), *The Syriac Fathers on Prayer and the Spiritual Life* (Kalamazoo, Cistercian Press, 1987)

Peter Brown, 'The Rise and Function of the Holy Man in Late Antiquity', in *Journal of Roman Studies* lxi (1971)

Robert Browning, *Justinian and Theodora* (London, Thames & Hudson, 1971)

Vahakhn N. Dardarian, *The History of the Armenian Genocide* (Oxford, Berghahn Books, 1995)

Leslie A. Davis, *The Slaughterhouse Province* (New York, Aristide D. Caratzas, 1989)

Glanville Downey, *Constantinople in the Age of Justinian* (New York, Dorset Press, 1960)

Glanville Downey, *A History of Antioch in Syria* (Princeton, Princeton University Press, 1961)

Egeria (trans. George E. Gingras), *Diary of a Pilgrimage* (New York, Newman Press, 1970)

Eusebius, *The History of the Church* (London, Penguin, 1965)

Clive Foss, 'The Persians in Asia Minor and the End of Antiquity', in *English Historical Review* 90 (1975), pp. 721–47

John Joseph, *Muslim–Christian Relations and Inter-Christian Rivalries in the Middle East: The Case of the Jacobites in an Age of Transition* (New York, State University of New York Press, 1983)

J.N.D. Kelly, *Golden Mouth: The Story of John Chrysostom – Ascetic, Preacher, Bishop* (London, Duckworth, 1995)

Michael Lapidge (ed.), *Archbishop Theodore* (Cambridge, Cambridge University Press, 1995)

Samuel N.C. Lieu, *Manichaeism* (Manchester, Manchester University Press, 1985)

H.F.B. Lynch, *Armenia: Travels and Studies* (Reprint: Beirut, Khayats, 1990)

H.J. Magoulias, 'The Lives of Byzantine Saints as a Source for the History of Magic: Sorcery, Relics and Icons', in *Byzantion* 37 (1967), pp. 228–69

Marlia Mundell Mango, 'The Continuity of the Classical Tradition in the Art and Architecture of Northern Mesopotamia', in Nina G. Garsoian, Thomas F. Matthews and Robert W. Thomson (eds), *East of Byzantium: Syria and Armenia in the Formative Period*, Dumbarton Oaks Symposium 1980 (Washington, Dumbarton Oaks, 1982)

Philip Mansel, *Constantinople: City of the World's Desire, 1453–1924* (London, John Murray, 1995)

John Moorhead, 'The Monophysite Response to the Arab Invasions', in *Byzantion* 51 (1981)

J. Naayem, *Les Assyro-Chaldéens et les Armeniens massacrés par les Turcs* (Paris, Bloud & Gay, 1920)

Carl Nordenfalk, 'An Illustrated Diatessaron', in *Art Bulletin* 50 (1968)

Carl Nordenfalk, 'The Diatessaron Once More', in *Art Bulletin* 55 (1973)

Andrew Palmer, *Monk and Mason on the Tigris Frontier: The Early History of the Tur 'Abdin* (Cambridge, Cambridge University Press, 1990)

Oswald H. Parry, *Six Months in a Syrian Monastery* (London, Horace Cox, 1895)

John A. Petropulos, 'The Compulsory Exchange of Populations: Greek–Turkish Peacemaking, 1922–1930', in *Byzantine and Modern Greek Studies* 2 (1976)

Procopius (trans. G.A. Williamson), *The Secret History* (London, Penguin, 1966)

Kurt Rudolph (trans. Robert McLachlan Wilson), *Gnosis* (Edinburgh, T&T Clark, 1983)

Steven Runciman, *The Medieval Manichee* (Cambridge, Cambridge University Press, 1947)

J.B. Segal, 'Mesopotamian Communities from Julian to the Rise of Islam', in *Proceedings of the British Academy* 41 (1955), pp. 109–39

J.B. Segal, *Edessa: The Blessed City* (Oxford, Oxford University Press, 1970)

T.A. Sinclair, *Eastern Turkey: An Architectural and Archaeological Survey* (London, Pindar Press, 1990, 4 vols)

R.S. Stafford, *The Tragedy of the Assyrians* (London, George Allen & Unwin, 1935)

J.M. Thierry and Patrick Donabedian, *Les Arts Armeniens* (Paris, Mazenod, 1988)

Pierre Vidal-Naquet, *A Crime of Silence: The Armenian Genocide* (London, Zed Books, 1985)

Gary Vikan, 'Art, Medicine and Magic in Early Byzantium', in *Dumbarton Oaks Papers* 38 (1984)

Christopher J. Walker, *Armenia: The Survival of a Nation* (London, Croom Helm, 1980)

W.A. Wigram, *A History of the Assyrian Church 100–640 A.D.* (London, SPCK, 1910)

W.A. Wigram, *The Cradle of Mankind: Life in Eastern Kurdistan* (London, A&C Black, 1914)

W.A. Wigram, *The Assyrians and their Neighbours* (London, G. Bell & Sons, 1929)

CHAPTER III

Willi Apel, *Gregorian Chant* (London, Burns & Oates, 1958)

Sebastian Brock, 'Early Syrian Asceticism', in Brock, *Syriac Perspectives on Late Antiquity* (London, Variorum Reprints, 1984)

Peter Brown, 'Sorcery, Demons and the Rise of Christianity', in *Witch-*

craft, *Confessions and Accusations*, pp. 17–45 (Cambridge, Cambridge University Press, 1970)

Peter Brown, 'The Saint as an Exemplar in Late Antiquity', in *Representations* 1 (1983), pp. 1–25

E.A. Wallis Budge, *The Monks of Kublai Khan* (London, Religious Tracts Society, 1928)

Ross Burns, *Monuments of Syria* (London, I.B. Tauris, 1992)

Robert Doran (trans.), *The Lives of Simeon Stylites* (Kalamazoo, Cistercian Press, 1992)

Han J.W. Drijvers, 'The Persistence of Pagan Cults and Practices in Christian Syria', in Drijvers, *East of Antioch: Studies in Early Syriac Christianity* (London, Variorum Reprints, 1984)

W.H.C. Frend, 'The Monks and the Survival of the East Roman Empire in the Fifth Century', in *Past and Present* 54 (1972), pp. 3–24

Nicholas Gendle, 'The Role of the Byzantine Saint in the Development of the Icon Cult', in *The Byzantine Saint*, ed. S. Hackel, pp. 181–6, supplementary to *Sobornost* 5 (1981)

Hermann Gollancz (ed. and trans.), *The Book of Protection, Being a Collection of Charms* (London, Henry Frowde, 1912)

Henry Hill, 'The Assyrians: The Church of the East', in Hill (ed.), *Light From the East: A Symposium* (Toronto, Anglican Diocese of Toronto, 1988)

Dom. Anselm Hughes (ed.), *Early Mediaeval Music up to 1300* (Oxford, Oxford University Press, 1949)

Huneberc of Heidenheim (trans. Talbot), 'The *Hodoeporicon* of St. Willibald', in Talbot, *Anglo-Saxon Missionaries* (1954), pp. 151–77

Hugh Kennedy, 'The Last Century of Byzantine Syria: A Reinterpretation', in *Byzantinische Forschungen* 10 (1985), pp. 141–83

Hugh Kennedy, 'Antioch and the Villages of Northern Syria', in *Nottingham Mediaeval Studies* 32 (1988), pp. 65–90

Patrick Seale, *Asad: The Struggle for the Middle East* (London, I.B. Tauris, 1988)

Georges Tate, 'La Syrie a l'Époque Byzantine', in *Syrie: Memoire et civilisation* (Paris, Flammarion, 1994)

Theodoret of Cyrrhus (trans. R.M. Price), *A History of the Monks of Syria* (Kalamazoo, Cistercian Press, 1985)

Colin Thubron, *Mirror to Damascus* (London, Heinemann, 1967)

J. Spencer Trimingham, *Christianity Among the Arabs in Pre-Islamic Times* (Beirut, Librairie de Liban, 1979)

A. Voobus, *A History of Asceticism in the Syrian Orient* (Louvain, 1960)

Egon Wellesz, *Eastern Elements in Western Chant* (Oxford, Oxford University Press, 1947)

Egon Wellesz, *A History of Byzantine Music and Hymnography* (Oxford, Oxford University Press, 1949)

CHAPTER IV

Robert Fisk, *Pity the Nation: Lebanon at War* (London, André Deutsch, 1990)

David Gilmour, *Lebanon: The Fractured Country* (London, Martin Robertson, 1983)

Charles Glass, *Tribes with Flags: A Journey Curtailed* (London, Secker & Warburg, 1990)

Charles Glass, *Money For Old Rope* (London, Picador, 1992)

Elinor A. Moore, 'Severus of Antioch and the Law School of Beirut', in Moore, *The Early Church in the Middle East* (Beirut, Aleph, 1946)

Matti Moosa, *The Maronites in History* (New York, Syracuse University Press, 1986)

Jonathan Randal, *The Tragedy of Lebanon* (London, Chatto & Windus, 1983)

Kamal Salibi, *The Modern History of Lebanon* (London, Weidenfeld & Nicolson, 1965)

Kamal Salibi, *A House of Many Mansions: The History of Lebanon Reconsidered* (London, I.B. Tauris, 1988)

Anthony Sampson, *The Arms Bazaar* (London, Hodder & Stoughton, 1977)

Ze'ev Schiff and Ehud Ya'ari (trans. Ina Friedman), *Israel's Lebanon War* (London, George Allen & Unwin, 1985)

Colin Thubron, *The Hills of Adonis: A Journey in Lebanon* (London, Heinemann, 1968)

CHAPTER V

Said K. Aburish, *The Forgotten Faithful: The Christians of the Holy Land* (London, Quartet, 1993)

Karen Armstrong, *A History of Jerusalem: One City, Three Faiths* (London, HarperCollins, 1996)

Naim Stifan Ateek, *Justice and Only Justice: A Palestinian Theology of Liberation* (New York, Orbis, 1989)

Dan Bahat, *The Illustrated Atlas of Jerusalem* (Jerusalem, Carta, 1989)

E.A. Wallis Budge, *St George of Lydda* (Oxford, Oxford University Press, 1930)

David Burrell and Yehezekel Landau, *Voices from Jerusalem: Jews and Christians Reflect on the Holy Land* (New Jersey, Paulist Press, 1992)

Taufik Canaan, *Mohammedan Saints and Sanctuaries in Palestine* (London, Luzac & Co., 1927)

Derwas J. Chitty, *The Desert a City* (Oxford, Blackwell, 1966)

Saul P. Colbi, *Christianity in the Holy Land* (Tel Aviv, Am Hassefer, 1969)

Frederick C. Conybeare (trans.), 'Antiochus Strategos' Account of the Sack of Jerusalem in 614 A.D', in *English Historical Review* 25 (1910), pp. 502–17

Cyril of Scythopolis (trans. R.M. Price), *The Lives of the Monks of Palestine* (Kalamazoo, Cistercian Publications, 1991)

Norman G. Finklestein, *Image and Reality of the Israel–Palestine Conflict* (London, Verso, 1995)

David Gilmour, *Dispossessed: The Ordeal of the Palestinians* (London, Sidgwick & Jackson, 1980)

David Grossman, *The Yellow Wind* (London, Jonathan Cape, 1988)

David Grossman, *Sleeping on a Wire* (London, Jonathan Cape, 1993)

J.E. Hanauer, *Folklore of the Holy Land* (London, Duckworth, 1907)

Yizhar Hirschfeld, *The Judaean Desert Monasteries in the Byzantine Period* (New Haven, Yale University Press, 1992)

David Howell, 'Saint George as Intercessor', in *Byzantion* xxxix (1969), pp. 121–36

Walid Khalidi (ed.), *All That Remains: The Palestinian Villages Occupied and Depopulated by Israel in 1948* (Washington, Institute of Palestine Studies, 1992)

Benny Morris, *The Birth of the Palestinian Refugee Problem, 1947–1949* (Cambridge, Cambridge University Press, 1987)

Jerome Murphy-O'Connor, *The Holy Land* (Oxford, Oxford University Press, 1980)

F.E. Peters, *Jerusalem* (Princeton, Princeton University Press, 1985)

Michele Piccirillo, *The Mosaics of Jordan* (Amman, American Centre of Oriental Research, 1993)

Michele Piccirillo, 'The Christians in Palestine during a Time of Transition: 7th–9th Centuries', in Anthony O'Mahony (ed.), *The Christian Heritage in the Holy Land* (London, Scorpion Cavendish, 1995)

471

Michael Prior and William Taylor, *Christians in the Holy Land* (London, World of Islam Festival Trust, 1994)

John H. Melkon Rose, *The Armenians of Jerusalem* (London, Radcliffe Press, 1993)

Edward Said, *The Question of Palestine* (London, Vintage, 1992)

Edward Said, *The Politics of Dispossession: The Struggle for Palestinian Self-Determination 1969–1994* (London, Chatto & Windus, 1994)

Colin Thubron, *Jerusalem* (London, Heinemann, 1969)

Yoram Tsafrir (ed.), *Ancient Churches Revealed* (Jerusalem, Israel Exploration Society, 1993)

Peter Walker, 'Jerusalem and the Holy Land in the Fourth Century', in Anthony O'Mahony (ed.), *The Christian Heritage in the Holy Land* (London, Scorpion Cavendish, 1995)

Keith Whitelam, *The Invention of Ancient Israel: The Silencing of Palestinian History* (London, Routledge, 1996)

John Wilkinson, *Jerusalem Pilgrims Before the Crusades* (Jerusalem, Ariel, 1977)

CHAPTER VI

Nils Aberg, *Occident and Orient in the Art of the Seventh Century* (Stockholm, Wahlstron & Widstrand, 1943–7, 3 vols)

Athanasius, *The Life of Antony* (New York, Paulist Press, 1980)

Alexander Badawy, *Coptic Art and Archaeology: The Art of the Christian Egyptians from the Late Antique to the Middle Ages* (Cambridge, Mass., MIT Press, 1978)

Roger S. Bagnall, *Egypt in Late Antiquity* (Princeton, Princeton University Press, 1993)

Alan K. Bowman, *Egypt After the Pharaohs, 332 B.C.–A.D. 642* (London, British Museum Publications, 1986)

A.J. Butler, *Ancient Coptic Churches of Egypt* (London, Henry Fowden, 1884, 2 vols)

A.J. Butler, *The Arab Conquest of Egypt* (Oxford, Oxford University Press, 1902)

Luciano Canfora, *The Vanished Library* (London, Hutchinson, 1989)

B.L. Carter, *The Copts in Egyptian Politics* (London, Croom Helm, 1986)

Euphrosyne Doxiadis, *The Mysterious Fayum Portraits: Faces from Ancient Egypt* (London, Thames & Hudson, 1995)

472

P.M. du Bourguet (trans. Caryll Hay-Shaw), *Coptic Art* (London, Methuen, 1971)

E.M. Forster, *Alexandria: A History and Guide* (London, Michael Haag, 1982)

G. Fowden, 'Bishops and Temples in the Eastern Roman Empire, A.D. 320–435', in *Journal of Theological Studies* xxix, pt 1 (April 1978)

Michael Gough, *The Origins of Christian Art* (London, Thames & Hudson, 1973)

Bernard P. Grenfell, 'Oxyrhynchus and its Papyri', in *Egypt Exploration Fund Journal* (1896–7)

Wilfred Griggs, *Early Egyptian Christianity* (Leiden, E.J. Brill, 1990)

Michael Haag, *Discovery Guide to Egypt* (London, Michael Haag, 1990)

H. Hondelink, *Coptic Art and Culture* (Cairo, Shoudy Publishing House, 1990)

Walter Horn, 'On the Origin of the Celtic Cross', in Horn, Jenny White Marshall and Grellan D. Rourke (eds), *The Forgotten Hermitage of Skellig Michael* (Berkeley, University of California Press, 1991)

John of Nikiu (trans. R.H. Charles), *The Chronicle of John of Nikiu* (London, Text and Translation Society, 1916)

Jill Kamil, *Coptic Egypt* (Cairo, The American University of Cairo Press, 1987)

J.W. McPherson, *The Moulids of Egypt* (Cairo, NM Press, 1941)

Otto Meinardus, *Monks and Monasteries of the Egyptian Deserts* (Cairo, The American University of Cairo Press, 1961)

Otto Meinardus, *Christian Egypt. Ancient and Modern* (Cairo, French Institute of Oriental Archaeology, 1965)

Otto Meinardus, *Christian Egypt: Faith and Life* (Cairo, French Institute of Oriental Archaeology, 1970)

G.R. Monks, 'The Church of Alexandria and the City's Economic Life in the Sixth Century', in *Speculum* 28, pp. 349–62

Cecil Mowbray, 'Eastern Influence on Carvings at St Andrews and Nigg, Scotland', in *Antiquity* x (1936), pp. 428–40

Elaine Pagels, *The Gnostic Gospels* (New York, Random House, 1979)

Robert K. Ritner, 'Egyptians in Ireland: A Question of Coptic Peregrinations', in *Rice University Studies* 62 (1976), pp. 65–87

Erwin Rosenthal, 'Some Observations on Coptic Influence in Western Early Medieval Manuscripts', in *Homage to a Bookman: Essays on Manuscripts, Books and Printing Written for P. Kraus on his Sixtieth Birthday* (Berlin, 1967)

473

Norman Russell (trans.), *The Lives of the Desert Fathers: The Historia Monarchorum in Aegypto* (Oxford, Mowbray, 1981)

George Scott-Moncrieff, *Paganism and Christianity in Egypt* (Cambridge, Cambridge University Press, 1913)

Sophronius the Sophist, 'The Life of St John the Almsgiver', in Elizabeth Dawes and Norman H. Baynes (trans. and ed.), *Three Byzantine Saints* (Oxford, Blackwell, 1948)

Helen Waddell, *The Desert Fathers* (London, Constable, 1936)

Edward Wakin, *A Lonely Minority: The Modern Story of Egypt's Copts* (New York, William Morrow, 1963)

Benedicta Ward (trans.), *The Sayings of the Desert Fathers* (Oxford, Mowbray, 1975)

Barbara Watterson, *Coptic Egypt* (Edinburgh, Scottish Academic Press, 1988)

Klaus Wessel, *Coptic Art* (London, Thames & Hudson, 1965)

INDEX

Abdul Mesin, Sheikh, 166–71
Abed (taxi driver), 266–70
Abgar, King, 77
abi-Khalil, Père Abbé Marcel, 230–1
Abraham, 74–5
Abraham, Abba, 287
Abraham, Abouna, 95
Abu Nidal, 267–8
Abu Zaid, Dr Nasr, 427–9
Abu-Zeid, 344, 346–51
Abukir, 387
Acre, 358
Acts of Paul and Thecla, The, 399
Adamnan, Abbot, 110
Adolas, 15
Aeschylus, 399
Aflaq, Michel, 153, 214
Agabios, Amba, 444
Agathonicos, Abba, 295
Aghtamar island, 84
A'id, Sheikh, 312
Alawites, 153, 155
Alcuin, 418
Aleppo, 146–60, 171–7; Armenian
    population, 150–3, 287; Baron Hotel,
    171, 5, 146, 177, 196, 454; Christian
    population, 153–4; St George church,
    174, 339–40
Alexander the Great, 52, 380–3
Alexandria, 375–94; Christian
    population, 385–9, 411; Church of
    St John, 390; Élite Café, 379, 392; fall
    to Sassanian Persians (614), 388, 453;
    Graeco-Roman Museum, 386, 387, 391;
    Grand Corniche, 375, 379; Greek Club,
    392–2; Greek population, 259, 379–82,
    392–4; Hotel Cecil, 376; Hotel
    Metropole, 375; Jewish population, 259,
    377–9; library, 388, 392, 399; Moschos's
    stay, 11, 16, 183, 387–91, 419, 453;
    Mound of Shards, 383; Pastroudis, 377;
    occult history, 222–3; Pharos
    lighthouse, 383; Serapium, 383, 388, 389
Alexandros, Fr., 355–7

Allon, Yigal, 364
Alouf, Monsieur, 164–70
Amal, 195
Ambrose, St, 176
Ammianus Marcellinus, 389
Amr, General, 429
Anastasius, Emperor, 100
Anatolia, 27, 51, 80, 316–17
Anderson, Terry, 218
Ankara, 28, 50, 51
Anne, Princess, 258
Anthemius of Tralles, 27
Antinoe, 437
Antioch (Antakya), 53–7, 58–61; Buyuk
    Antakya Oteli, 53, 63–4; Christian
    community, 58–60; economic history,
    13, 224; Kurdish conflict, 52; liturgies,
    91, 250; mosaics, 233, 235; Moschos's
    visit, 57–62, 183; School of, 57, 106, 181
Antonius, George, 214
Antonius Martyr, 223
Antony, St, 401–4, 406–9, 417–18, 420–2
Apamea, 181, 183
Apollonius of Tyana, 66
Aquinas, St Thomas, 290
Arafat, Yasser, 229, 274, 275, 282, 318, 354
Arculph, 110
Arianism, 299
Ariel, Settlement, 345, 347, 351–4, 363
Aristopoulos, Fr., 356–7, 359
Aristotle, 136
Armenian Secret Army for the Liberation
    of Armenia (ASALA), 86
Armenians: in Aleppo, 150–4, 287; in
    Antioch, 60; in Diyarbakir, 80–2; in
    Istanbul, 28, 33–47; in Jerusalem,
    309–16; in Urfa, 77–8; in Turkey, 82–8
Arnas, 120
Asad, Basil, 138, 202, 272
Asad, President Hafiz al: jokes about, 138,
    154–6; portraits, 138, 148, 200; regime,
    142, 154–5, 252, 272, 448
Asad, Mrs, 259
Ascalon, 182

Asterius of Amasia, 39
Asyut: ancient, 446; Copts, 411–12, 440–1;
  departure from, 447; *Gema'a al-
  Islamiyya*, 440–1; Islamic
  fundamentalists, 422; permission to
  visit, 395–6, 435
Ataturk, Mustafa Kemal, 29, 48, 91, 133,
  171
Ateek, Canon Naim, 358–9
Ateret Cohanim, 312, 313
Athanasius of Alexandria, St, 107, 355,
  402, 408
Athos, Mount, 3–11, 20–1; cells, 304;
  monks, 5–6, 20, 287, 409; paintings, 20,
  296
Attargatis, 75–6
Augustine of Hippo, St, 68, 235, 402
Aurelia Attiaena, 401
Aurelius, Marcus, 399
Aurelius Nilus, 401
Auxanon, Abba, 360
Avars, 13
Avni, Gideon, 332
Al-Azhar University, 426

Ba'albek, 261–6; architecture, 94;
  Moschos's visit, 223, 261; Temple of
  Jupiter, 265; Temple of the Sun, 262,
  263, 266
Baas camp, 270–1
Badger, Rev. George Percy, 76–7
Badr, Leila, 223–5
Bagawat, 452
Bangor Monastery, 418
Banu Ghassan, 335
Banu Taghlib, 335
Baradatus 157
Bar'am, Kibbutz, 369, 372
Bardaisan of Edessa, 63, 175
al-Barra, 178–82, 184
Barsauma, 185, 324
Bartholomaios, Patriarch, 32
Basil, St, 324
al-Bassa, 274
Bawit, 437
Baybars, Sultan, 311
Bebek, 47
Bede, Venerable, 110, 408
Bedros (in Midyat), 118–23
Behnasa, 397–8, 401
Beiman, Amba, 444–5
Beirut, 195–6, 203–27, 237–42; American
  University, 211, 219; bombing of, 274;
  Downtown Project, 223; economic

history, 13; Hotel Cavalier, 206–7, 266;
  Place des Martyrs, 196, 219–20
Beit ed-Din, 225, 231–2, 237
Beit Jala, 339–44
Beit Shean, 325, 364
Bekaa Valley, 201–3, 261–2
Belisarius, Count, 321
Ben Gurion, David, 364
Benedict, St, 12
Benjamin, Amba, 444
Benvinisti, Meron, 334
Beth Zagba, 183
Bethlehem, 318, 321, 339
Bhutto, Zulfikar Ali, 259
Biddya, 344–51, 363
Bishara, Fr. Mark, 430–1
Bkerke, 247
Book of Durrow, 109, 110
Book of Protection, The, 141–2
Boulos Naaman, Fr., 199
Brehier, Louis, 290
British Library, 10
Bsharre, 236–7, 241, 245–55; Hotel
  Ch'baat, 244–5, 253
Budak, Afrem, 70, 100, 112–14,
  123–4
Buddhism, 66
Buyuk Ada, 44, 45–7, 187

Caesarius, Court Physician, 389
Cairo, 395, 423–35; Church of al-Adra,
  430; Church of St Damiana, 21; Church
  of St Michael and the Virgin, 432;
  Copts, 21, 411, 429–34; Ein Shams, 431;
  Hotel Windsor, 423
Canaan, Taufiq, 339
Carpocratians, 67
Castellium Monastery, 295
Cathars, 73
Cavafy, Constantine P., 377, 380–2
Cecaumenus, 12, 180
Celtic Christianity, 106, 109–10, 303,
  418–20
Chalcedon, 26, 322; Council of (451), 91
Chamoun, Dany, 255
Ch'ang-an, 26
Chariton, St, 354, 355, 356
Charlemagne, 418
Charles, Prince, 258
Chatila, massacre, 195, 198–9, 211, 215,
  236, 266–7
Ch'baat, Mr (hotelier), 245, 253–5
Chouf, 225–6, 227, 229–31, 255
Christie, Agatha, 133

476

Christina, Miss (in Alexandria), 379–82, 392
Christopher the Roman, Brother, 286
Christophoros, Fr., 6–10, 29–30
Chryaorius of Tralles, 223
Chrysostom, St John: anti-idolatry campaign, 262–3; asceticism, 157; in Antioch, 54, 55, 162; in Constantinople, 29, 36, 55; influence, 68, 413
CIA, 423–4
Cilicia, 86
Cilician Gates, 56
Clement of Alexandria, 385
Cleopatra, 227, 383, 391
Clinton, Bill, 259
Cochrane, Alfred, 242
Cochrane, Yvonne, Lady, 238–42
Codex Sinaiaticus, 9
Constantine, Emperor, 16, 56, 180, 320–1, 328
Constantine XI Palaeologus, Emperor, 108
Constantinople, see Istanbul
Constantius, Emperor, 176
Coptic language, 416
Copts: discrimination against, 20, 411, 424, 425–6; in Alexandria, 388; in Asyut, 395; in Cairo, 21, 429–34; St Antony's followers, 404; St Antony's Monastery, 411–22; violence against, 411–12, 424, 425, 429–34, 444–5
Cosmas, Fr., 303
Cosmas the Eunuch, Abba, 354–5, 360–1
Cosmas the Lawyer, 389
Council of Chalcedon (451), 91
Council of Ephesus (431), 447
Council of Florence (1439), 5, 108
Crusades: Cathars, 73; capture of Jerusalem, 310; Cilician history, 86; cult of St George, 342; Fourth, 9; Islam's relationship with Christianity, 187–8, 299; Maronites, 197; theft of relics, 301
Ctesiphon, 14, 133
Culdees, 106, 418
Curzon, Hon. Robert, 9, 404, 412
Curzon, Lord, 226
Cyril, Patriarch, 388–9
Cyril of Scythopolis, 290
Cyrrhus, 159, 164–71, 188, 304, 339
Cyrus the Great, 258

Damascene, St John, 37, 39, 290, 298–302
Damascus: Great Mosque, 153; siege, 17; Umayyad Mosque, 282

Damiana the Solitary, Amma, 322
Damour, 196, 229
Daou, Samira, 268–75, 363
Daou, Sarah, 268
Daou family, 268–75, 362–3, 370
Daphne, 5
Dara, 136
David (robber chief), 437–8
Dawood, Amba, 441–43
Dbayyeh camp, 271, 272–3
Dead Sea, 288
Deir al Barsha, 437
Deir el-Qamar, 230
Deir el-Suriani, 404
Deir el-Zaferan, 90–8, 109, 116, 135
Deir ul-Muharraq, 411–12, 442, 443–4
Deir Yassin, 269, 366
Demus, Otto, 391
Dereici, 96
Diatessaron, 108–11
Dimitrios, Fr., 30–3, 45, 46, 50
Diocletian, Emperor, 135, 342, 392, 413, 445
Diodoros I, Patriarch, 318–19
Diodoros of Sicily, 382
Dioscuros, Fr., 405–7, 408–10, 411, 415, 420
Diyarbakir, 79–81; bazaar, 77; Christian population, 150; Hotel Karavansaray, 79–80; Kurdish conflict, 47, 49, 447; Mar Gabriel, 47, 102
Domenico, Fr., 62–3
Dorotheus, 56
Douaihy family, 252
Drina, River, 28
Druze, 217, 221–6, 225–32, 253, 255
Durrell, Lawrence, 376, 380, 384

Echmiadzin, 108
Edessa, 64–78, 171–2, 174–7
Edinburgh, Duke of, 258
Edward III, King of England, 341
Egeria, 76
Ehden, 253–4, 255–7
Ein al-Zaytun, 366
Ein Fara, 354–5, 359
Ein Helweh, massacre, 236
Ein Wardo, 114, 116, 119–2, 124–6
Elchasaios, 66
Elchasiates, 66
Elizabeth II, Queen, 259
Elon, Amos, 333
Emesa, 185–6
Ephrem Kerim, Fr., 149
Ephrem of Edessa, St, 176–7

Eratosthenes, 385
Ethiopian Synaxarium, 414
Euclid, 385, 404
Eudoxia, Empress, 299, 321, 324
Euphrates, 145
European Parliament, 86
Eusebius, 342
Eustathios the Roman, Abba, 452
Euthymius of Salonica, St, 4–5
Evagrius of Antioch, 402
Evdokimos, Fr., 290–4

Fanous, Sami, 359–62, 363–5, 367–8, 370
Faradi, 363
Farud, Kibbutz, 364
Fatah, 229, 268
Fatullah, Sheikh, 121–2
Ferhat, Wadeer, 367–72
Fesih (in Diyarbakir), 81–2
Fisk, Robert, 208, 210, 215–20, 237, 274
Florence, Laurentian Library, 109
Foda, Dr Farag, 424, 428
Formilianus, Governor, 320
Forster, E.M., 377
Franjieh, Mme, 258–9
Franjieh, Robert, 242, 258–60
Franjieh, Suleiman, 238, 252–3, 258
Franjieh, Tony, 253–5, 258, 260
Franjieh family, 242, 252–5, 257–60
Freemasons, 280, 301, 308
Fuad, King of Egypt, 18

Gabra, Boutros, 425
Gaianas, 263–4
Gandhi, Mahatma, 29
Gardner, Ava, 244
Geagea, Samir, 215, 231, 232, 241, 252, 253–4
Gema'a al-Islamiyya, 411, 424, 425, 435, 439–45
Gemayel, Amin, 212
Gemayel, Bashir, 199, 253, 254, 260
Gemayel, Pierre, 226
Gemayel, Solange, 260
Genghis Khan, 140
George, St, 45, 47, 339–44, 386
George II, King of the Hellenes, 18
George the Cappadocian, Brother, 285–6
Gerasimos, St, 296–7
Ghada (in Mar Elias), 266–75
Ghanem, Iskander, 253
Ghatta family, 370
Gibbon, Edward, 399

Gibran, Kahlil, 236–7
Gilmour, David, 226
Giotto, 302
Giva, Shulamit, 333
Glass, Charles, 226
Gnostics, 16, 66, 68, 73, 175, 299
Gospel of Barnabas, 62–3
Gospel of Philip, 68
Gospels of St Willibrord, 109, 110
Goths, 13
Great Kharga Oasis, 4, 387, 395, 422, 435, 447, 450–4
Green Line, 205, 212, 239, 273
Gregori, Fr., 279
Gregory I (the Great), Pope, 55, 320
Gregory of Nazianzen, 389
Gregory of Nyssa, 39, 324
Grenfell, Bernard, 398–9
Gulf War, 101, 139, 357
Gumucio, Juan Carlos, 207–10
Güngören, 48, 116

Haganah, 363, 365, 366
Hagiopolis, 159, 171
Haifa, 268–9
Hakkari, 99, 112
Hamas, 288, 344
Hamayonic Laws, 412, 426
Hanauer, J.E., 339
Haran, 75
Harari, Joe, 377–9
Haridi, Gemal, 440–2
Hariri, Rafiq, 202
Hassake, 138–43; Hotel Cliff, 138
Hassana, 113–14
Hebron, Tomb of the Patriarchs, 338
Hejaz, 414
Helena, Empress, 35, 320
Heliodorus, 221
Henry IV, King of England, 108
Heraclius, Emperor, 42, 197
Hermopolis, 437
Herod Agrippa, 331
Hezbollah: in Lebanon, 189, 195, 207–8, 211, 216, 227–8, 264, 266; in Turkey, 96, 103
Hilary of Poitiers, St, 176
Hindus, 66
Hintlian, George, 88
Homer, 47, 181, 404
Homs, 185–6
Hunt, Arthur, 398–9
Hussein, King of Jordan, 318
Hussein, Saddam, 139

Hyderpasha, 51
Hypatia, 388

Ibn Mansour, Sergios, 298
Ibn Sargun, Mansour, 298
Ibn Walid, General Khalid, 298
Ibrahim, Metropolitan Gregorios
  Yohanna, 146, 148–51, 154, 171
intifada, 282, 346, 353
Irish Litany of Saints, 107, 419
Isa (in Jerusalem), 327
Isidore of Miletus, 27
Islam: Arab history, 214, 299–300;
  Nusairi, 73; prayer positions, 105,
  304–5; relationship with Christianity,
  168–71, 187–91, 304–5, 339–40, 426–7;
  Shiite, 153, 217, 219, 228–9, 261–2, 264,
  266; Sunni, 73, 154, 155, 217; tradition of
  tolerance, 19, 187–8
Islamic fundamentalism: growth of, 168,
  214; in Egypt, 20, 214, 411, 424–5,
  429–30, 433, 448; in Syria, 154; in
  Turkey, 31–2; relationship with
  Christianity, 447–8
Islamic Jihad, 219
Ismail (driver), 57, 61
Isocasius, 164
Israel Antiquities Authority, 332
Issus, 52
Istanbul (Constantinople): Armenian
  population, 30–4; Christianity, 19,
  27–31; fall of Constantinople (1453),
  108; Fourth Crusade, 9; Golden Horn,
  26, 29; Great Palace, 26, 41–3; Greek
  population, 27–8, 43, 45–7; Gulhane
  Gardens, 43; Haghia Eirene, 43, 328;
  Haghia Sophia, 27, 39–40, 41;
  Hippodrome, 39; Land Walls, 321;
  Mosaic Museum, 42–3; Moschos's stay
  in Constantinople, 14, 21, 27, 34–5, 41,
  182; Pera Palas Hotel, 28; Phanar, 29–33,
  34, 50; politics, 29; Prinkipo, 44, 45–7;
  Topkapi Palace, 18, 43
Iviron, Monastery of, 3–4, 5–11, 21, 355
Izlo Mountains, 98, 112

Jacob, Elias, 366–72
Jacob's Well, 356
James of Cyrrhestica, 158, 166
J'bail, 241, 243
Jerome, St: advice on bathing, 11, 222;
  advice on Jerusalem, 323; *Life of St Paul
  the First Hermit*, 417–18, 420; lion
  story, 296; patrons, 321

Jerusalem: Alexander Hospice, 328;
  Anglican church, 358; Armenian library,
  83; Armenian Museum, 88; Armenian
  population, 309–15; Armenian Quarter,
  309–12, 315, 318, 330; Cardo, 328;
  Christian population, 316–26; Christian
  Quarter, 316, 317, 339; Church of
  St Cosmas and St Damian, 322; Church
  of St John the Baptist, 327; Damascus
  Gate, 328, 332, 337; Dome of the Rock,
  228, 265, 327; Dormition Abbey, 358;
  fall to Sassanian Persians (614), 14, 42;
  fall to Islam (638), 17, 321; Greek
  Orthodox Patriarchal Palace, 289, 321,
  356; Holy Sepulchre, 318, 328, 339; Jaffa
  Gate, 332; Jewish Quarter, 312–13, 328;
  Magharina, 312; Mamilla Project, 332;
  Muslim Quarter, 313, 318; Nea, the (New
  Church of Mary), 328; Orthodox
  Christianity, 300, 302; Protestant
  cemetery, 358; St George's Anglican
  Cathedral, 358, 364; St John's Hospice,
  312–13; St Stephen's Monastery, 233,
  321, 329; Third Wall, 331–2
Jerusalem Post, 331–2, 338, 357
Jews: archaeology, 332–4; at Beit Jala, 339;
  Barsauma's massacre, 324–5; Byzantine
  stories, 55; European, 19, 344;
  fundamentalist, 312, 315, 331, 338, 358; in
  Alexandria, 375, 377–9; in Beirut, 219;
  Moschos on, 16, 34; Orthodox attitude
  to, 280; Ottoman Empire, 28;
  settlement in Israel, 313, 345, 363;
  synagogue chants, 177
Jish, 363, 367, 370
Jiyyeh, 224
John, Abba, 451–2
John of Cappadocia, 446
John of Emesa, Deacon, 185
John of Nikiu, Bishop, 388, 429
John the Almsgiver, 388, 419
John the Arab, St, 102, 121
John the Baptist, 73
John Tzimiskes, Emperor, 8
Joseph, Abba, 162
Joseph, George, 139–40, 142–6
Jounieh, 255
Julian the Apostate, Emperor, 53, 79
Julian the Arab, Brother, 286
Jumblatt, Kemal, 199, 232
Jumblatt, Walid, 225–7, 229, 230–1, 253,
  334
Justinian, Emperor: Christian-Arab
  alliance, 335; empire, 13, 26–7, 41, 165,

Justinian, Emperor – *cont'd*.
263, 335, 398, 446; Haghia Sophia, 39, 263; legislation, 36; portrait, 14; Procopius's *Secret History*, 37; Ravenna mosaics, 14, 233; Samaritan revolt, 323; Seidnaya story, 186

Kafr Bir'im, 268, 269, 271, 274–5, 362, 365–72
Kafr Qasim, 347
Karantina, massacre, 267, 272
Karyes, 5, 355
Katsimbris, Taki, 393–4
Keban Dam, 85
Kedron, Valley of, 283
Keenan, Brian, 207
Kennedy, John F., 308
Khabur River, 143
Kharga, 395, 447, 449–54; Kharga Oasis Hotel, 451
Khitzkonk, 87
Khomeini, Ayatollah, 203, 219, 262, 264
al-Khuri, Faris, 153
Koshaya, 249
Kreish, Cardinal, 371
Krikor (in Jerusalem), 315
Kurd Dagh, 171
Kurdish war, 31, 47, 50–3, 79, 447, *see also* PKK
Kyriacos, Abouna, 105

la Motraye, M. de, 28
Lahad, General, 216
Laqzaly, Farah, 369
Lausanne, Treaty of (1923), 30
Lawrence, T.E., 54, 133, 134, 135
Lebanese National Pact (1943), 198
Lebanon, Mount, 197
Leo, Abba, 452, 453
Leo III, Emperor, 234
Leontios the Cilician, Abba, 328
Leptis Magna, 94
Libanius, 56, 161, 181, 221
Lindsay, Coutts, 5
Lombards, 13
London Library, 399
Lucian of Samosata, 75–6
Lucine (in Diyarbakir), 81
Lycopolis, 446–7

McCarthy, John, 207
McCullin, Don, 195
Ma'ale Adumim, 283

Madaba, 334
Mahmoud, Arafa, 442
Mahmoud (driver), 435–6, 438–40, 443–6
Malacrida, Gianmaria, 174–7
Mallawi, 436
Malraux, André, 392
Mamshit, 338
Mandeans, 73
Manicheans, 16, 68
Manshit Nasser, 441
Manuel II Palaeologus, Emperor, 107
Mar Bobo, 96
Mar Elias camp, 266–75, 287, 362
Mar Gabriel, 47, 64, 72, 97, 98–115, 168, 287
Mar Hadbashabo, 119, 121
Mar Saba, 279–81, 283–309, 409
Marada Militia, 242, 253
Marcionites, 67–8
Mardin, 97, 135
Mark the Hermit, St, 406
Marmara, Sea of, 26
Maron, St, 197
Maronites: churches, 220; history, 196–9, 243; in Bsharre, 236–7, 242; in Turkey, 63; Lebanese civil war, 20, 198–200, 212–13, 217, 226–7, 241, 251, 273, 448; Phalange, 198, 212–13, 226–7, 236, 273
Martyrion, Mount Zion, 356, 359
Maslakh, 272
Mas'ud (driver), 88–90, 92–100, 115–18, 123, 124–9, 135, 137
Maurice, Emperor, 263, 322
Maydanlar, 83
Mazices, 413, 451
Mazloumian, Krikor ('Coco'), 151
Mazloumian, Sally, 151–2
Mehmed Sokollu Pasha, Grand Vizier, 27
Menas (driver), 430, 431, 433–4
Menuthis, Shrine of Saints Cyrus and John, 387
Messalians, 67
Methodius, Fr., 340–44
Methodius the Stylite, St, 292
Mettin (hotel receptionist), 49–50
Midyat, 64, 72, 98, 115–23, 135
el-Minya, 422, 436
Mohammed, 17, 234
Monidia, 414
Monophysites, 16, 91, 197, 299–300, 387–8
Monothelitism, 197

Mons Mirabilis, 57, 59–60, 286
Mons Porphyrites, 27, 446
Montfort, Simon de, 73
Moschos, John: at Great Oasis, 451–2,
    454; death, 14, 17, 285; grave, 18, 285–7;
    in Alexandria, 11, 16, 387–9, 419, 453;
    in Antioch, 54–9; in Ba'albek, 223, 257,
    259–60; in Constantinople, 14, 21, 27,
    34–5, 41, 182; in Jerusalem, 322; in
    Porphyreon, 223, 224, 233; journey,
    11–14, 19–21, 395, 413–14, 435, 437–8,
    447, 449–50; monastic life, 279, 354–5,
    359–62; on Apamea, 183; on demons,
    163; on Nisibis, 136; on plagues, 326;
    Spiritual Meadow, 4, 12–16, 18–19, 21,
    58–9, 105, 183, 223, 233, 279, 294–7, 334,
    355, 361–2, 390–1, 413–14, 429, 437, 447,
    453
Moshav Dovev, 369, 372
Mubarak, President Hosni, 20, 377, 412,
    423–6, 434–5
Munir family, 440–1
Mushabbak, basilica of, 160–1
Muslim Brotherhood, 395, 427

Nachman, Ron, 351–3
Namek, Malfono, 172–4
Nasbeh clan, 346
Nasser, Gamal Abdel, 375, 380, 394, 428,
    500–1
Nazareth, 363, 364–5, 371
Nebo, Mount, 334
Negev, 325
Nestorian Church, 66, 136, 139–42, 451
Nestorius, 447
New York Review of Books, 111
Nimrod the Hunter, 74
Nisibis, 72, 135–7, 139, 154
Nordenfalk, Carl, 109–11
Nusairi Muslims, 73

Olympios, Abba, 191–3
Omar, Caliph, 17, 334
Osk Vank, 87
Ottoman Empire, 27–28, 48, 188, 197, 339,
    377
Ouranopolis, 4
Ouzayeh Beach, 227
Oxyrhynchus, 396–8; papyri, 399–401,
    437

Pachomius, St, 295
Palestinian Authority, 282
Palestinian Christians: emigration, 20,

213, 316–18; history, 19, 300; in Israel,
    300, 316–26, 362–3; in refugee camps,
    261, 266–75, 287, 317, 363
Palutians, 68
Pambo, Abba, 408
Paphnutius, 449
Paradise of the Fathers, The, 295
Parthenius, Bishop of Lampsacus, 20
Patermuthis, Flavius, 437
Patrick (of Sebastea), 286
Paul, Abba, 360
Paul, St, 59
Paul III Farnese, Pope, 108
Paul the Hermit, St, 417–18, 420–1
Paula, 321
Paulinus of Nola, 323
Persians: attacks on Byzantine empire, 13,
    95, 388; capture of Alexandria, 453;
    capture of Diyarbakir (502), 79;
    capture of Jerusalem (614), 13–14, 42;
    capture of Nisibis (363), 135; massacre
    at Mar Saba (614), 289, 299; massacre at
    St Theodosius Monastery (614), 13,
    284–4, 289
Peter, St, 59
Petrosyan, Levon Ter, 153
Phalange militia: attacks on Christians,
    215–17, 253, 272–3; civil war, 195, 211–13,
    226–5; massacres, 198, 215, 226; origins,
    226
Pharan, 354–5, 359
Philloumenos, 355–7, 359
Phoebamon the Sophist, 437
Photion, 323
Photius, 321
Piat, Edith, 378
Piccirillo, Fr. Michele, 335–8
Pictish Christianity, 421–2
PKK: effects of struggle, 101; government
    response to, 99, 112, 113; Hezbollah
    relationship, 96–7; Midyat raid, 64, 71,
    origins of struggle, 48; roadblocks, 49,
    89–90; treatment of captives, 49–50
Plato, 136, 403
PLO, 195, 272, 273, 352
Poemon the Grazer, Abba, 295–6
Polo, Marco, 82
Pope, Hugh, 47–9
Porphyreon, 223, 224–5, 232–5, 335
Potuoglu, Hilda Hulya, 86
Prinkipo, 44, 45–7
Procopius, 37–9, 40, 321
Procopius the lawyer, 224, 233
Ptolemy, 385

Qadisha Valley, 244, 245
Qala'at Semaan, 149
Qamishli, 150, 154
Qanubbin Gorge, 247, 251

Rabinovitch, Olga, 378–9
Rabula Gospels, 184, 190
Ramallah, 343–4
Ramazan (driver), 395–7, 435, 439
Ramleh, 358
Ravenna, 14, 27, 233, 234–5, 328
Refah party, 29, 28, 44
Rehman (in Diyarbakir), 81–2
Roberts, David, 182, 282
Romanos the Melodist, St, 176, 185, 290
Rosemarkie Stone, 110
Rouba, 295
Rufinus of Aquileia, 402
Runciman, Sir Steven, 18–21, 320, 328

Sabas, St, 292–3, 305
Sabbatios, Abba, 297
Sabra, massacre, 195, 198–9, 211, 215, 236, 267
Sadat, Anwar, 37, 428
Sadat, Mrs Anwar, 259
Safad, 365
St Antony Monastery, Koshaya, 249–50
St Antony's Monastery, Egypt, 396, 403–22
St Azozoyel, Monastery of, 95
St Catherine's Monastery, Sinai, 9, 391
St Damiana, Church of, Cairo, 21
St Jacob, Monastery of, 95
St John's Hospice, Jerusalem, 312
St Joseph, Monastery of, 95
St Martyrius, Monastery of, 283
St Mary of the Waterfall, Monastery of, 95
St Polyeuctes, Istanbul, 44
St Stephen, Monastery of, Jerusalem, 233, 321, 329
St Theodosius, Monastery of, 11, 13, 18, 354
St Vigeans, 420
Saladin, 135, 268, 310
Salibi, Kemal, 210, 211–14, 217, 223
Salit, Dina, 353–4
Samaritans, 323
San Vitale, Ravenna, 233, 328
Sanabu, 439–41
Sappho, 399
Sarkissian, Bishop Hagop, 311, 326, 328–31

Sasa, Kibbutz, 369
Sassanian Persians, 13, 135, 289, 303, 388
Schiffer, Claudia, 202
Scythopolis, 325
Seidnaya, 186–91, 196, 339
Seleucia ad Pieria, 13, 54
Serjilla, 177, 181, 184, 185
Severus, Bishop of Antioch, 222
Shabo, Abouna, 118–23
Shah of Iran, 258, 425
Shaheen, Dr Abdul, 427
Shenoudah III, Pope, 411
Shitrit, Bichor, 367
Sidon, 13
Sienese art, 302
Silk Route, 26, 65, 79
Silpius, Mount, 56
Silwan, 330
Simocatta, Theophylact, 35
Sinatra, Frank, 244
Sisinnios, Bishop, 37
Sivas, 82–3
Skellig Michael, 303
Slavs, 13
Socrates (*Ecclesiastical History*), 40
Somers, Virginia, 5
Sophocles, 399
Sophronius the Sophist: at Great Oasis, 447; death, 18; in Alexandria, 387–90, 419; journey with Moschos, 11, 19–20, 296, 454; *Life of St John the Almsgiver*, 419; Moschos's body, 18, 285; Patriarch of Jerusalem, 18, 197, 318; surrender of Jerusalem, 18, 321, 329
South Lebanon Army (SLA), 216
Stephanopoulos, Michael, 393–4
Stephanos, Catholicos of Armenia, 107–8
Stephen, St, 323
Stephen the Sophist, 35, 390
Studium Biblicum Franciscanum, 334, 337
Sufism, 164, 166, 168, 343, 397
Suleiman, Fr. Bishara, 365–6, 368–72
Suleiman, John, 365, 370
Suleiman, Nouri, 228–9, 237–8, 243–5, 251, 261, 265, 266
Sulpicius Severus, 295
Sunday Telegraph, 313
Sunday Times, 423, 425
Sussita, 338
Symeon, Abouna, 92–8
Symeon Stylites the Elder, St, 59–60, 148, 156
Symeon Stylites the Younger, St, 58–62, 286

Symeon the Fool, St, 185
Synesius, 385
Syrian Orthodox Church (Suriani):
  establishment, 91; in Aleppo, 147–50; in
  Turkey, 19–20, 47–9, 91, 114, 125–6,
  150, 447–8; Urfalees, 171–7; see also Deir
  el-Zaferan, Mar Gabriel

Tamurlane, 95
Tariq (in Biddya), 346–50
Tarsus, 183
Tatian, 108
Tecla, Sister, 188–91
Tel Ada, 148–9
Tel el-Za'atar, massacre, 226, 236, 272
Tertullian, 385
Thalelaeus, 158, 162
Theodora, Empress, 14, 37–9, 233, 321,
  446
Theodore, Abba, 452
Theodore of Mopsuestia, 54
Theodore of Sykeon, 163
Theodore of Tarsus, 54, 106
Theodore the Philosopher, 389
Theodoret of Cyrrhus, Bishop: bishopric,
  159, 164–6; History of the Monks of Syria,
  148, 156–9, 161, 181, 197, 262–3
Theodosios, St, 284–6, 289
Theodosius I, Emperor, 39, 41
Theodosius II, Emperor, 35, 321, 323
Theophanes, Fr., 280–1, 290–4, 301, 302,
  305–9, 318
Theophilus, Patriarch, 389
Thessaloniki, 15
Thierry, J.M., 85, 87
Thubron, Colin, 187
Thucydides, 404
Tiberias, 359
Tiberius Constantine, Emperor, 263
Tigris, River, 26, 73, 79, 88–90
Tintagel Castle, 419
Tischendorff, Herman, 9
Tito, Marshal, 259
Titus, Emperor, 320
Tomas Bektas, Fr., 112–14
Tosi, Abdil Mesiyah, 441–2
Tur Abdin: art, 107, 111; journey to, 64,
  107, 447; Syrian Orthodox Church, 91,
  150; Turoyo language, 154

Turkish Daily News, 64, 71
Turoyo, 112, 118, 154
Tutu, Archbishop Desmond, 358
Tyre, 13, 223

Umayyad Caliphate, 298–300, 337
Um-Mohammed, 346–50
Urfa, 64–79; Fishponds of Abraham,
  73–7; Hotel Turban, 64–5; sculpture
  garden, 69–71; Ulu Jami, 71, 77;
  Urfalees, 171–7
Urfalees, 171–7
Uri, Nebi, 164, 167–70
Usamah (in Biddya), 345–51

Valens, Emperor, 41, 324
Vandals, 26
Vikings, 26
Voragine, Jacobus da, 342

Wadi Natrun, 404, 413–14
Waite, Terry, 207
West Bank, 281–3, 302, 317, 338–51, 363
Wigram, Rev. W.A., 80
Willibald, St, 186, 289
Woolley, Leonard, 134

Xenophontos, Monastery of, 296

Yacoub, Brother, 100–4, 116–19, 123, 126
Yacovos, Fr., 6–7, 10
al-Yazid, Caliph, 298–9
Yerevan, 153
Yezidis, 140, 154
Yohanan of Bar'am, 369
Yunis, Dr Ibthal, 427
Yustus, Abuna, 406–7

Zachaios, Abba, 114
Zacharias, Rector, 222
Zeitun, 151
Zeno, Emperor, 37, 445
Zenobia, 70
Zghorta, 252, 253, 257–60
Zion, Mount, 27, 321, 356, 358, 359
Zoilus the Reader, 389
Zoroastrians, 16, 68, 79
Zosimos the Cilician, Abba, 224, 234, 429
Zoulias, Nicholas, 392–4